Contemporary American
Society and Culture

当代美国社会与文化

主编 林玲
编者 林玲 孙麟 忻华 张新彬

北京大学出版社
PEKING UNIVERSITY PRESS

图书在版编目（CIP）数据

当代美国社会与文化 / 林玲主编 . —北京：北京大学出版社，2023.9
ISBN 978-7-301-34478-1

Ⅰ . ① 当… Ⅱ . ① 林… Ⅲ . ① 英语 – 高等学校 – 教材 ② 美国 – 概况 – 高等学校 – 教材 Ⅳ . ① H319.39

中国国家版本馆 CIP 数据核字 (2023) 第 180752 号

书　　　名	当代美国社会与文化 DANGDAI MEIGUO SHEHUI YU WENHUA
著作责任者	林　玲　主编
责 任 编 辑	李　娜
标 准 书 号	ISBN 978-7-301-34478-1
出 版 发 行	北京大学出版社
地　　　址	北京市海淀区成府路 205 号　100871
网　　　址	http://www.pup.cn　新浪微博：@ 北京大学出版社
电 子 邮 箱	编辑部 pupwaiwen@pup.cn　　总编室 zpup@pup.cn
电　　　话	邮购部 010-62752015　发行部 010-62750672　编辑部 010-62754144
印 刷 者	天津中印联印务有限公司
经 销 者	新华书店
	720 毫米 ×1020 毫米　16 开本　26.25 印张　658 千字 2023 年 9 月第 1 版　2023 年 9 月第 1 次印刷
定　　　价	88.00 元

未经许可，不得以任何方式复制或抄袭本书之部分或全部内容。
版权所有，侵权必究
举报电话：010-62752024　电子邮箱：fd@pup.cn
图书如有印装质量问题，请与出版部联系，电话：010-62756370

前 言

2018年教育部高等学校教学指导委员会制定的《外国语言文学类教学质量国家标准》中指出："外语类专业学生应掌握外国语言知识、外国文学知识、国别与区域知识，熟悉中国语言文化知识，了解相关专业知识以及人文社会科学与自然科学基础知识，形成跨学科知识结构，体现专业特色。"同时，《高等学校外语类专业本科教学质量国家标准》也明确指出："外语类专业是全国高等学校人文社会科学学科的重要组成部分，学科基础包括外国语言学、外国文学、翻译学、国别与区域研究、比较文化与跨文化研究，具有跨学科特点。"相关国家标准的出台，确立了国别与区域研究作为外语学科五大研究领域之一的地位，拓展了外语学科的内涵。作为英语学科区域与国别研究的重点领域，美国研究对于新时代英语学科的内涵建设具有重要意义，构成了培养"会语言、通国别、精领域"的高端英语人才的必要途径。近年来，随着国别与区域研究的发展热潮，全国各大外语院校以及部分综合类高校的英语专业在本科阶段都相继开设了"美国社会与文化""美国历史"等美国研究课程，并设有相应的英语学科硕、博士美国研究专业方向，对于配套的美国研究专业英文教材的需求也随之日益增长。正是在这一背景下，《当代美国社会与文化》编写团队基于多年来在"美国概况""美国社会与文化""美国历史"等英语专业本科课程以及"美国社会与文化专题研究""美国历史专题研究"等研究生课程教学过程中积累的教学素材与课堂实践经验，编写了本教材。本书在编写思路上注重把握学生的兴趣点与学习需求，在系统梳理美国文化概貌的基础上，注重对美国社会发展的历史脉络与变化规律的解读，注重历史文化渊源、发展与当今美国社会热点问题、社会发展趋向之间的关联性分析，培养学生深入分析美国社会文化现象与跨文化思辨能力，旨在顺应时代需求，对接新时代背景下跨文化外语人才与区域国别人才的培养目标。

当代美国社会与文化
Contemporary American Society and Culture

《当代美国社会与文化》在编写内容上体现了较为鲜明的时代特色。本书在人文地理、政治、经济概况、族裔、教育、宗教、家庭生活等传统美国文化教材所包涵的核心主题内容板块之外，还包含了"美国的技术、产业""美国的金融体系"，涵盖控枪、女性堕胎权、平权法案、移民政策的"当代美国社会热点问题"以及"美国环境与环保问题""美国流行文化"等主题章节。教材编写团队教学实践表明，以上主题内容是在当今美国社会发展变化与国际政治新形势下学生迫切需要了解和掌握的重要知识点，对于完备学生专业知识结构、对接新时代跨文化外语人才与区域国别人才培养目标具有重要现实意义。与此同时，本书注重分析美国历史文化传统与当今美国社会热点问题、社会发展趋向之间的关联，注重历史与现实维度的结合，这一侧重点不仅体现于教材主题内容板块的特色，也贯穿于所有章节的编写思路。此外，本书针对每章重点内容提供了若干思考题，有助于学习者梳理章节核心内容，并引导其做深入思考探究。

本书共包含15个主题章节，其中第1、3、4、9、10章由本人编写；第2、8、11、12、13章由孙麟编写；第5、6、7章由忻华编写；第14、15章由张新彬编写。本书可作为"美国社会与文化""美国历史"等英语专业本科高年级美国文化课程的教材与主要教学参考书，并可作为英语专业本科基础阶段必修课"英美概况"的主要进阶参考书以及"英语报刊阅读""政务英语翻译"等课程的背景阅读参考书，也适用于美国研究专业方向、区域国别研究以及国际关系专业研究生教学参考。本书的出版得到了上海外国语大学"一流本科专业建设"优质教材出版项目的资助，同时感谢北京大学出版社李娜编辑认真细致的编辑与出版工作。本书编写语言以自然、流畅、优美为宗旨，在梳理当代美国社会文化概貌与发展特征的同时，力求能为学习者提供一个专业外语学习参考模板，以促进人文知识与外语技能的互融与提升。为此，笔者殷切希望广大教师与同人在使用本教材的过程中不吝指正，并通过我们共同的努力，令其日臻完善。

林 玲
上海外国语大学英语学院
美国研究中心
2023年4月6日

Contents

Unit 1	Land and Cultural Regions	1
Unit 2	The People: Racial and Ethnic Diversity	18
Unit 3	Political System and Government Mechanism	55
Unit 4	Political Parties and Electoral Politics	75
Unit 5	Technology and Industry	90
Unit 6	Trade and Investment	110
Unit 7	The Finance	137
Unit 8	Education	165
Unit 9	Religion in American Culture and Politics	203
Unit 10	Major Public Policy Issues as Controversies in Contemporary American Society	221
Unit 11	American Women	248
Unit 12	The American Family and Community	286
Unit 13	American Environmental Issues and Protection	323
Unit 14	American Popular Culture	362
Unit 15	American Sports Culture	396

Unit 1 Land and Cultural Regions

1 The Face of the Land

The continental US lies in central North America with Canada to the north, Mexico to the South, the Atlantic Ocean to the east and the Pacific Ocean to the west. Alaska borders northwestern Canada, and Hawaii lies in the central Pacific, some 3,200 kilometers from the US mainland. The United States covers an area of 9,327,000 square kilometers and ranks the fourth largest country in the world after Russia, Canada and China.

Covering a vast expanse of land, the physical environments of the United States range from the rolling countryside of the Penobscot River Valley in central Maine to the snow-capped peaks of the Cascade Mountains in western Washington state and from the palm-fringed beaches of southern Florida to the many-colored deserts of Arizona. From east to west, the continental United States spans across physiographic areas including the Atlantic-Gulf Coastal Plain, the Appalachian Highlands, the central lowlands, the Great Plains, the Rocky Mountains, the Inter-mountain Region, the Pacific Mountain Ranges and the Pacific Coastal Plain. Two of the most important mountains as geographical boundaries on the American land are the Appalachians and the Rocky Mountains. The Appalachians separate the eastern coast from the central lowlands with a belt of subdued uplands that extends from northeastern Alabama to the Canadian border. The Atlantic-Gulf Coastal Plain extends along the east and southeast coasts of the United States from East Long Island to the Rio Grande on the

US-Mexico border. The Atlantic Coastal Plain widens in the south, merging with the Gulf Coastal Plain in Florida. The northeast coast has many fine natural harbors, such as those of New York Bay and Chesapeake Bay, while a principal feature of the Gulf Coast is the great delta of the Mississippi River. The Rocky Mountains, also known as the "Rockies," form the western border of the Great Plains and stretch from Mexico through Canada into Alaska. The Rockies have been known as the "Continental Divide," as they separate rivers that flow east into the Atlantic from those flowing west into the Pacific.

The Mississippi River, which means "father of waters" in the Native American language, is the longest river in North America and the second longest in the world. Of the nearly 250 tributaries that flow into the Mississippi, the Ohio on the east and the Missouri on the west are the two largest. Mississippi and its tributaries form a 19,000-kilometer system of waterways that are connected to the Great Lakes in the north by canals and drain about half of the nation. The Great Lakes north of the central lowlands, which include Lake Superior, the largest fresh water lake in the world, Lake Michigan, Lake Huron, Lake Erie and Lake Ontario, are the most important lakes of the United States. Joined to the Mississippi River and its tributaries by canals, the Great Lakes provide the world's longest inland waterway transportation and constitute the economic lifeline of the Midwest. On the Pacific side there are two large rivers: the Colorado in the south and the Columbia in the north. The Colorado River rises in the snow-capped Rocky Mountains and flows into the Gulf of California. The Columbia rises in western Canada and continues in the US Both rivers drain an enormous area and are of vital importance to the dry western states.

Extending more than 1,000 miles from the Appalachians to the Rocky Mountains and lying between Canada in the north and the Gulf Coastal Plain in the south are the great Central Lowlands with the Great Plains to the west. Between the Rio Grande in the south and the delta of the Mackenzie River in the north lie the rolling Great Plains, which have an area of approximately 1,125,000 square miles and are roughly one-third of the United States. Also known as the Great American desert, the Great Plains have some areas that are extremely flat, while other areas contain tree-covered mountains. Over much of the expanse of the Great Plains, cold winters and warm summers prevail, with low humidity, much wind, and sudden changes in temperature. From east to west across the Great Plains, the climate gets progressively drier.

Between the Rockies and the Pacific Mountain Ranges to the west is the Intermountain Region, an arid expanse of plateaus, basins, and ranges. The Columbia Plateau in the north of the region is drained by the Columbia River and its tributary the Snake River, both of which have cut deep canyons into the plateau. The Colorado Plateau, an enormous area of sedimentary rock, is drained by the Colorado River and its tributaries, and there the Colorado River has entrenched itself to form the Grand Canyon, one of the world's most impressive natural wonders.

Between the Intermountain Region and the Pacific Ocean, the Pacific Mountain ranges parallel the Pacific Coast. The Cascade Range, with its numerous volcanic peaks, extends South from Southwest Canada into North California, and is continued south by the Sierra Nevada. Mt. Whitney in the Sierra Nevada, which rises 14,495 feet high, is the highest peak in the continental United States. West of the Cascade Ranges and the Sierra Nevada are the Coast Ranges extending along the length of the US Pacific Coast and are separated from them by a structural trough. Within this trough lie the Central Valley in California, the Willamette Valley in Oregon, and the Puget Sound lowlands in Washington. The Pacific Coastal Plain is narrow, and in many cases the mountains plunge directly into the sea. Major harbors on the costal plains include those of San Francisco Bay and San Diego Bay.

2 Cultural Regions

The physical features of the American land, with various land forms from the coastal plains, central lowlands, to the Great Plains and the mountain ranges, have given rise to the diversity in the major industries, economy and regional cultures of the nation. From east to west, the United States could be divided into six broad cultural regions: the Northeast, the Midwest, the South, the Mountain States, the Southwest, the Pacific Coast and the New States.

2.1 The Northeast

The Northeast comprises two sub-regions: New England and the Middle Atlantic states. The New England states include Maine, Vermont, New Hampshire, Massachusetts, Rhode Island, and Connecticut. The Middle Atlantic states are New York, New Jersey, Pennsylvania, Delaware, and Maryland.

New England, as a small hilly region, doesn't have a large expanse of rich farmland or a mild climate yet it can lay a historic claim to have played a dominant role in the development of modern America. It is the chief center of the American War of Independence. From the 17th century into the 19th century, New England was the nation's preeminent region regarding economy and culture.

From the beginning of the settlement, New Englanders found it difficult to farm land in large lots, as was possible in the South. By the mid-18th century, many settlers had turned to other pursuits. Shipbuilding, fishing and trade became the major industries of the region. In the first half of the 19th century, New England became the center of America's industrial revolution. All across Massachusetts, Connecticut and Rhode Island emerged new factories producing clothing, rifles, clocks and many other goods.

The cultural life of the region was also very strong. Older colleges and universities blossomed, while newer ones sprang up. New England's oldest schools of higher learning, including Harvard, Yale, Brown University and Dartmouth College, were among the prestigious Ivy League Universities. During the 19th century, New England was also a source of pioneers for the westward movement. New Englanders transplanted many of their ideas to the northern Midwest, to the Pacific Northwest and finally all the way to Hawaii. The early westward demographic and ideological expansion of New England was very influential, which made it justifiable to call New York, northern New Jersey, northern Pennsylvania, and much of the Upper Midwest

Unit 1   Land and Cultural Regions

"New England Extended."

As some of the older stock of New England travelled westward, a newer stock gradually began to take its place. Immigrants from Ireland, Italy and Eastern Europe arrived in large numbers in the cities of the southern part of the region. Immigrants from French Canada moved into the mill towns of New Hampshire and Maine. The influx of immigrants that began in the 1830s had changed the New England identity, but much of the early traits of New England Yankee – self-reliance, thrift, inventiveness, and enterprise – had survived.

The Middle Atlantic region, otherwise known as the Midland, had been settled from the first by a much wider range of people than New England. Dutch made their homes in the woodlands along the lower Hudson River in what is now New York. Swedes established small communities in present-day Delaware. English Catholics founded Maryland and an English Protestant sect, the Quakers, settled in Pennsylvania. In time, the Dutch and Swedish settlements in the region all fell under English control. An ethnically diverse area, the Midland set the cultural pattern for the ethnic and religious mosaic of the Midwest and Northwest.

In the early years, the Middle Atlantic region was often used as a bridge between New England and the South. Philadelphia, Pennsylvania, a mid-point between the northern and southern colonies, became the home of the Continental Congress, the group that led the fight for independence. Philadelphia was also the birthplace of the Declaration of Independence in 1776 and the US Constitution in 1787. At about the same time, some eastern Pennsylvania towns first tapped the iron deposits around Philadelphia. Heavy industries sprang up throughout the region with the nearby natural resources. Such mighty rivers as the Hudson and the Delaware were transformed into vital shipping lanes. Cities along these waterways – New York on the Hudson, Philadelphia on the Delaware, Baltimore on the Chesapeake Bay – expanded into major urban areas. Late in the 19th century, the inflow of immigrants to the region swelled to a steady stream. In the 1890s and early 1900s, New York had been the main port of entry for millions of immigrants and ranks the nation's largest city, the hub of finance and a cultural center today.

The Midland is the most densely populated area of the United States. The commercial and industrial development of the area had given rise to a "megalopolis" along the Atlantic seaboard, with a cluster of large cities growing closer in economic linkage, commuting and communications. Megalopolis extends roughly from southern New Hampshire to northern Virginia and contains dozens of metropolitan areas. Essentially, the megalopolis centers up and down the East Coast, from Boston in New England to Washington D.C. and some people even call this metropolitan area extending from Boston to Washington "Boswash", which includes New York City, Philadelphia, and Baltimore. Freeways and goo rail transportation have increasingly made Boston and Providence, as well as Baltimore and Washington D.C., parts of the same functional area. Shared airports and sports teams help tie together once-distant cities.

Megalpolis contains over 50 million people, or close to one-sixth of the total US population. The historical leading role of Megalopolis can be seen in nearly every aspect of American life, from art, architecture, to education and industry. Midtown Manhattan remains, by far, the single leading concentration of office space in the nation while Boston's tally of prestigious universities is unmatched in the country. Megalopolis has other important cultural traits as well. As the powerful nerve center of the nation in banking, public policy, and education, it has always been an important gateway for the vast majority of immigrants. While immigration from Asia and Latin America has in recent years diminished the dominance of Megalopolis in this regard, its long-standing tradition of ethnic diversity is still being constantly revitalized by new arrivals. Megalopolis is also known for its intense interest in historic preservation, which creates a landscape of contrasts – a region of new and constantly changing symbols of power and ethnicity but also a land of careful heritage preservation. Throughout the region, and often side by side with the skyscrapers, there are preserved neighborhoods, such as Society Hill in Philadelphia, South Baltimore, Greenwich Village, Georgetown and Capitol Hill, North Boston and the Boston Common, and hundreds more in big cities and small towns alike.

The defining of the Megalopolis region has, in turn, given rise to the specification of "Rustic Northeast" as a recreation area for Megalopolis. The Rustic Northeast thus includes not only the portions of the traditional New England states not identified as parts of Megalopolis, but also parts of upstate New York and northeastern Pennsylvania and New Jersey. Extending from the beaches of Cape Cod and the coast of Maine to the wooded uplands of central Pennsylvania, it has become a sort of cultural attic where the activities and conventions of the past are stored. The Rustic Northeast is known as "Fall Color Country", a land of countryside landscapes ideal for a variety of rustic activities, from picking apples to watching the production of maple syrup. As much of the Rustic Northeast acts as a retreat for Megalopolis, the region plays the role of the small, homogeneous, quaint, picturesque, and out-of-the-way to Megalopolis's role as the central, powerful, diverse, and blatantly historical.

2.2 The Midwest

The Midwest, which lies midway between the Appalachians and the Rocky Mountains and north of the Ohio River, includes Ohio, Indiana, Michigan, Illinois, Wisconsin, Missouri, Iowa, Minnesota, Kansas, Nebraska, and North and South Dakota. At the end of the 18th century, when the early frontiersmen crossed the Appalachians and settled in this area of the rolling central lowlands, they called the area the West. When the Far West was settled, however, this northern interior region of the country came to be known as the Midwest.

In the early years, the mighty Mississippi River served as a lifeline of the area, moving settlers to new homes and great amounts of grain and other goods to market. The humid continental climate, the rich soil, the ample rainfall and the long growing season in the central lowlands created favourable agricultural conditions for crop and livestock farming; and its natural system of waterways, helped by manufactured canals, facilitated both the movement of people to the west and the transportation of resources. All these made the Midwest the most important agricultural area in

America. Midwestern farmers produced more than half of the nation's corn, wheat, and oats and raised nearly half of its cattle and dairy cows. For this reason, the region was known as the "corn belt" of the US and was also nicknamed the nation's "breadbasket."

The combination of the abundant mineral resources in the Appalachians and well-developed waterway transportation of the Great Lakes enabled the industrial expansion of the Midwest at the turn of the 20th century. During the WWII era, the regional economy was fueled by a robust manufacturing sector and high demand for steel. With the thriving steel, coal and manufacturing industries in the region, the Midwest became known as the "Industrial Heartland of North America". By the 1960s and 1970s, though, the increased globalization, competition from overseas factories, and the rise of the high-tech industry in the nation had led to the decline of the region, characterized by the shrinking of its once-dominant heavy industry and manufacturing sector as well as the population loss to "the Sunbelt States" in the South and West. The term "Rust Belt" originated at this time because of the deterioration of the industrial region. Some major industrial cities of the Rust Belt include Chicago, Baltimore, Pittsburgh, Buffalo, Cleveland, and Detroit. The decline of the industrial Midwest also relates to key aspects of the region's identity as the land of overspecialized cities. The Midwest Heartland has more specialized industrial cities than any other region and with the decline of many of the industries associated with those cities, the region as a whole has not prospered. In a sense, the relatively specialized nature of places in the Midwest Heartland is what gives the region its identity. While northeastern cities such as Boston and New York have tended to be diverse historically, serving as ports, industrial centers, financial centers, university towns, and state capitals, the cities of the Midwest tended to push one dominant identity. It was in the Midwest that the idea of special-function cities was perfected and materialized, for instance, the city of Akron made tires, Canton made roller bearings, Toledo made glass, and Findlay was the home of Marathon oil, while Muncie made transmissions and Battle Creek specialized in cereals. Mining towns and steel towns were also specialized.

Many of the more specialized cities thus have a built-in inflexibility that makes it hard to compete in a modern world economy. Today, many cities of the Midwest Heartland have been developing new industries to replace the shuttered steel mills and manufacturing plants, nevertheless, the region is still facing challenges in its continuing economic regeneration.

2.3 The South

The South stretches from Virginia south to Florida and then west as far as central Texas, with its northern border roughly following the fall line through Alabama. The region also includes North Carolina, South Carolina, Georgia, Mississippi, Kentucky, Tennessee, Arkansas, Louisiana and Oklahoma. The South has its most distinctive regional culture and the most basic difference between the South and other regions is perhaps geographic. The South has mild temperature, plentiful rainfall and fertile soil, and it is often described as a land of yellow sunlight, clouded horizons and steady haze. The first Europeans to settle in this region were, as in New England, mostly English Protestants. These early settlers were Anglican rather than Calvinist, however, and few of them came to America in search of religious freedom as settlers in New England. Rather, many sought the opportunity to farm the land and live in comfort. The southern settlers' early way of life resembled that of English farmers and the South emulated England as much as New England prided itself on its distinction from it.

In coastal areas some southern settlers established large cotton farms called plantations, which required the work of many laborers. To supply the labor needs, plantation owners came to rely on black slaves shipped from Africa with the transatlantic slave trade. From the beginning of the 19th century, the interests of the industrial North and the more agrarian South began to diverge in obvious ways. The North became increasingly industrial while the South was wedded to the land. From the mid-19th century, as more states were admitted into the Union with the westward expansion, slavery became a focal point of division between the North and the South, which amounted to a national political crisis in 1860. Eleven southern states from Virginia to Texas left the federal union to form a nation of their own, "the Confederate States of America." The southern secession resulted in the American Civil War (1861 – 1865). The South finally surrendered and the Civil War brought an end to black slavery. The southern Reconstruction lasted officially until 1877, during which the Republican Party in the national government planned to rebuild the South by putting black southerners on an equal footing with whites and redistributing old plantation lands. For a time, black Americans gained a voice in southern government. By the end of the 19th century, however, southern towns and cities refined and legalized the practice of racial segregation. Blacks attended segregated schools from whites, rode in segregated railroad cars and buses, and even drank separate water fountains. In the early 20th century, many black Americans began moving from southern farms to the cities of the industrial North, which was known as "the Great Migration" in American history. Great changes took place in the 1960s, after years of black protests in the Civil Rights Movement, the landmark *Civil Rights Act of 1964* and *Voting Rights Act of 1965* were passed, which brought an end to obvious forms of racial segregation in public places. For the first time since southern Reconstruction, blacks gained a greater voice in local government in the South. The struggle of black Americans for equality hadn't ended, though, as the racial tension still tend to run high in the region in general.

  The unique culture traits of the South have remained largely rural. Most southern cities were designed more for genteel living than industrial efficiency. Today, there are large cities, such as Atlanta and Charlotte on the edge of the region, but most southerners prefer the image of slow-paced, gracious living in small towns. In recent years, the South has been renamed "the Sun Belt." Much of the growth in the Sun Belt is due to overflow from the high-cost regions to the north. As industries have sought to relocate away from high taxes, high lands and labor costs, many have taken close looks at the small and medium-sized towns and cities of the South. Domestic and foreign automobile plants have located in Kentucky and Tennessee, where labor and the community are perceived to be more flexible than in the big cities in the North. A significant return migration of southerners from such places as Detroit and Chicago is also fueling population growth in the Sun Belt. More recently, a variety of resort and retirement communities have sprung up throughout the region to take advantage of mild winters and the low cost of living. Indeed, while many writers have suggested that this term extends across the country from Florida to California, it is in the South where the term itself is most common. Today, the term Sun Belt appears in phone books and business directories all across the South.

The cultural influence of the American South in tropical Florida, nevertheless, has been quite marginal. The essential characteristics of the region are derived from two migration streams: the earlier stream of tourists and retirees from America's colder areas, and the later stream of Latino immigrants from the Caribbean and South America. The cultural landscape of north tropical Florida is tourist-oriented and exotic with a Mediterranean tropical look and south tropical Florida has been under a strong Hispanic cultural influence, with Cuban, Puerto Rican, Mexican, and Haitian immigrants transforming the region.

2.4 The Mountain States

The Rocky Mountain States comprise Colorado, Wyoming, Montana, Utah, Idaho and eastern Nevada. In many areas the population is sparse. The region occupies about 15 percent of the nation's total land area, yet it has only about 3 percent of the national population. In the Mountain States, rural settlement is discontinuous and spotty, with agriculture, in most areas, playing a secondary role in mining, mountain recreation, or grazing. In fact, the region is also characterized by cultural diversity. The mining towns of Montana and the Mormon settlements of southern Utah, for instance, have little in common culturally except for a certain remoteness and conservative tradition of self-reliance. The Mormon culture region, which dominates the center of the Mountains, stretches from northern Arizona through Utah and eastern Nevada to southern Idaho and exhibits a cultural unity in stark contrast to the rough-

and-ready mining towns and lumber camps that dominate the periphery of the region. Different from the grazing economy of most western lands, the Mormons raise crops on irrigated land. While the population tends to be dispersing in many eastern regions, the population is still imploding in the Mountains. A large proportion of the people live within 100 kilometers of either Denver or Salt Lake City. The Salt Lake City metropolitan area, although smaller than the more peripheral Denver-Boulder area, has a population of more than 1 million and is becoming an important transit hub.

The Mountain States have always been a region associated with recreation. In recent decades, the region has become a resort for the residents of the booming urban centers around it and people from around the world. Scenic wonders such as Yellowstone, Grand Teton, Zion, Bryce Canyon, Grand Canyon, and a variety of other national and state parks have become popular tourist destinations. Similarly, Aspen, Vail, Snow Bird, Brian Head, Sun Valley, and hundreds of other downhill and cross-country ski resorts have boomed in recent years. Indeed, the Mountains may become the last frontier in mainland America – a place to visit for the mythical, old-fashioned America of forests and farms.

2.5　The Southwest

The Southwest is composed of western Texas, New Mexico, Arizona, western Nevada and the southern interior area of California. Today, three southwestern states lie along the Mexican border – Texas, New Mexico and Arizona. All have a larger Spanish-speaking population than other regions except southern California. Much of the Southwest has a strong Hispanic heritage. Spanish explorers linked the Upper Rio Grande Valley with Mexico at an early point in time, and such cities as Santa Fe were more similar to Mexico City than to Boston. There is also much heritage in the Santa Fe-Albuquerque-Taos area that is a unique hybridization of American Indian and Spanish influences. Texas also has part of the Hispanic culture realm, while Texas has had a much greater influx of outsiders over the years than has New Mexico, many traditions remain. San Antonio is considered to be the epitome of the

Mexican-American Southwest as it is home to many Mexican-oriented products, such as salsa, and it is also the focal point of major migration routes between the border and northern metropolises such as Chicago. Another major center of Hispanic culture in the Southwest lies along the US-Mexico border from Brownsville to El Paso. Throughout much of this zone, there is not much cultural difference between one side of the border and the other. The influences of both nations converge here and permeate everything.

Most of the rapid population and economic growth in the Southwest has occurred in the large metropolitan areas that encircle the region. Dallas-Fort Worth, Houston, Denver, and Phoenix all lie on the edge of the Southwest and share some aspects of its culture. Much of the regional dress associated with the cowboy look of Texas originated in the Spanish-Mexican tradition. The boots, hats, chaps, spurs, bandanas, and guitars that have come to symbolize the cowboy were not part of the Anglo migration into Texas from the eastern regions but from the Spanish-Mexican tradition.

Over the past decades, white and black Americans from eastern regions have poured into the Southwest to participate in the energy booms. The Southwest began its serious trek toward urbanization and industrialization with the discovery of vast oil reserves during the 1930s. There was a great culture shift over the decades of the 1930s and 1940s, as much of the population of the Southwest went to California alongside the mass migrations into the region from the South. World War II brought a massive demand for petroleum products as well as the construction of a number of military bases from Texas to Arizona. By the 1950s, regional growth had reached phenomenal proportions. Today, in keeping with the tradition of mobility and change, many of the cities of the Southwest have pioneered new forms of urban growth.

2.6 The Pacific Coast and the New States

The Pacific Coast region extends along the Pacific Ocean all the way from Canada to Mexico and comprises Oregon, Washington, and California. The long narrow region is a land of varied scenery of wave-swept rocky cliffs, curving sandy beaches, forests of giant trees, snow-capped mountains, and barren deserts. In Washington, Oregon and northern California, the mountain ranges present some startling contrasts. To the west of the mountain ranges, winds off the Pacific Ocean carry enough moisture to keep the land well watered while to the east, the land is very dry. Parts of western Washington receive 20 times the amount of rainfall received in eastern Washington. The wet climate near the coast supports great forests of trees such as redwoods and firs. The region is also a land with a wealth of natural resources – forests, underground minerals, rivers and a bordering ocean, and fertile lowlands. For a long time, lumbering, mining, fishing, and farming were the major industries. In recent years manufacturing has become increasingly important in the region.

Traditionally, the northern part of the Pacific Coast states from central California through Oregon to Washington, has often been referred to as "the Northwest." Temperatures in the Northwest, as well as rainfall, make the climate different from that of the central farming region on the Pacific Coast. Because of the heavy rainfall and the mild winters in the northwestern lowlands, the pastures remain green much of the year and there is a heavy growth of grass and hay. Dairying is thus well developed and becomes the most important farm work in the Northwest. Fruit growing is also important in the Northwest. Apples, cherries, pears, apricots, and other tree fruits are grown and sold in large quantities. While the Northwest is not growing as rapidly as the Sun Belt, many of its cities have boomed in recent decades. The Seattle-Tacoma area has grown rapidly and constituted one of the major metropolitan areas in the nation today.

The core of the Pacific Coast in southern California is another "megalopolis" stretching from Santa Barbara in the north to San Diego in the south. This giant urban complex contains nearly 20 million residents and is the second "megacity" of the nation in rivalry with the megalopolis in the Northeast. California coast has become the dominant area for media with not only its long-standing Hollywood movie industry, but also the television and music industries. It is also an economic powerhouse in terms of industry and corporate headquarters. A high rate of migration

Unit 1 Land and Cultural Regions

from other parts of the nation and immigration from overseas over the years have resulted in the visible cultural diversity of the Coast. Some school districts have student populations from various countries, often speaking a total of 70 or more languages. With the teeming ethnic mix and diversity, there is thus much talk of the Coast becoming a "majority minority".

Lying beyond the Pacific Coast states are the states of Alaska and Hawaii. Both of these states were admitted to the Union in 1959 and are known as "the New States". Alaska is far to the Northwest on the American continent while the Hawaiian Islands lie many miles out in the Pacific Ocean. There are many contrasts between Alaska and Hawaii. With regard to size, the Hawaiian Islands could be fitted into Alaska ninety times over yet have about four times as many people as Alaska.

Alaska was purchased from Russia in 1867. Americans began to move to Alaska when the first big discovery of gold was made in the Klondike region of Canada near the Alaskan border in 1897. More and more people travelled northward with each new discovery in Alaska. Today, mining has continued to be important in Alaska. In addition to gold, there are rich deposits of copper, silver, and petroleum. While many Alaskans work in mines, a far greater number are fishermen as fishing constitutes the most important industry in Alaska.

Many Alaskan residents came from other parts of the US. Many are workers in mines or canneries, farmers, doctors, lumbermen or businessmen. About a third of the people of Alaska are American Indians and Inuits. The Indians live in small villages scattered about the interior and along the southern coast. Old customs and crafts of hunting and fishing of Indians are still kept in a few villages, though, most of the Indians earn a living as fishermen or cannery workers. The Inuits live along the western and northern coasts and their way of living is also changing. While some Inuits live on hunting and fishing much as their ancestors lived, many others work in canneries or at army and navy bases. Some Inuits still live in sod huts, but many have homes of wood. Often, away from the main streets, the homes are a mixture of old and new, with wooden frame houses standing next to log cabins.

The state of Hawaii is composed of four large islands and many smaller ones. The largest island is called Hawaii, from which the whole group of islands takes its name. Honolulu, the capital of the Hawaiian Islands and a chief seaport, is located on the island of Oahu, the most populous among the Hawaiian Islands.

Farming is the most important occupation on the Hawaiian Islands and most of the farming is done on plantations owned by business companies. Sugar cane is the leading crop of Hawaii and pineapple is another important crop. Trade is important between Hawaii and the mainland of the US. Hawaii sends raw sugar, pineapples, flowers and other products to the mainland and manufactured goods are shipped from the mainland to the Hawaiian Islands. Hawaii is an increasingly important link between Asia and Washington D.C. Its language is from Malaysia; much of its work force came originally from China, Japan, or the Philippines; its capital investment now comes from a variety of Asian as well as American sources; and tourists arrive from across the world. Just as East Asian food is served along with burgers and fries at fast food chains, and the music and dance traditions are remotely connected to those of Java and Bali with songs sung in English, the Hawaiian native Polynesian traditions have been long mixed with Asian and European practices.

Today, with the construction of new cities, resorts, and communication networks, there are ever-changing regions that rise and fall, however, regardless of the strong tendencies toward cultural homogenization and place obliteration, regional culture and identities persist, and different cultural regions of the United States continue to have their own characters and senses of place.

Essay Questions:

1. What is a cultural region? And what are the things, as you perceive, that give regions a unique sense of place and characters?
2. Discuss how the prominent physical features of different regions impact the major industries, economy and culture of each region.

Unit 1　Land and Cultural Regions

3. What are the distinctive characteristics of Megalopolis and what is its relationship to the Rustic Northeast?
4. What stand as the distinguishing traits of the Midwest as the heartland of America?
5. The cultural traits of the American South are much more homegrown than the other regions. What are the geographical conditions and historical factors that combine to produce an original cultural set of the South?
6. What does it mean to say that there is no single American West but an assortment of different Wests? Discuss the cultural traits that define the Southwest, the Mountain States and the Pacific Coast.

Unit 2　The People: Racial and Ethnic Diversity

　　The United States is a nation that has been built and developed by immigrants and their decedents for centuries. The diversity of immigrants makes America a multi-ethnic, multi-racial and multi-culture society. Though "Out of Many, One" has long been upheld by Americans, diversity now becomes an irresistible historical trend in the US. It not only helps shape American history, but emerges as a salient phenomenon in today's America as well. Admittedly, diversity has contributed to the development of American society and culture, but it has also posed a challenge to ethnic policy-making and state governance of the US.

1　A Nation of Immigrants

　　Immigrants from around the world arrived in the US at different times. A long time ago, nomadic hunters from Asia came to the Americas. After that, Northern and Western Europeans settled in the New World. Hundreds of years later, Southern and Eastern Europeans swarmed into the US. At present, spurred by the *Immigration and Naturalization Act of 1965*, an increasing number of Asians and Hispanics have become Americans. While the immigrants' place of origin is expanding from Europe to the whole world, the US grows from a white-dominated country to a multi-ethnic and multi-racial nation.

　　Before Europeans set foot on the American continent, Native Americans had lived on the continent for hundreds of thousands of years. They were the first immigrants and real masters of this land. About 30,000 years ago, nomadic hunters from Siberia crossed an ancient land bridge over the Bering Strait into what is now Alaska. In the following centuries, they spread into North, Central and South America. Around 12,000 years ago, with the Ice Age ended and the land bridge disappeared, the migration from Asia to America stopped. In the beginning, the Siberian nomads who had reached the Americas depended upon hunting for deer and birds, as well as gathering fruits and grains. Approximately 9,000 years ago, they learned to plant seeds and produce food, such as pumpkin, corn, squashes, beans, chili peppers, etc. Agriculture made it possible for them to settle down, form stable communities and develop common ways of life 5,000 years ago. According to the statistics, when European settlers landed on the American continent at the end of the 15th century, there were roughly 900,000 to 18 million Native Americans. They belonged to different tribes, speaking different languages and living different life styles. For example, for those who lived along the Pacific Coast, they caught fish with nets; for those who lived in the Southwestern United States, they invented ways of irrigation to farm the dry land in the desert. After European settlers started to colonize the American continent, more and more clashes happened between the colonists and Native Americans. As the settlers desired more land and natural resources, Native Americans were driven from east to west and even slaughtered by colonists. By the mid-19th century, Native Americans in the US had been forcibly relocated to Indian reservations in the barren deserts or mountainous areas.

Columbus' discovery of the New World in 1492 triggered a great tide of emigration from Europe to America. Two years later, Portuguese colonists gained control of Brazil. By 1574, Spanish settlers had occupied almost 1/3 of the American continent, with an immigrant population of 150,000. In 1607, English merchants and adventurers, who looked for gold and attempted to develop trade, built the first permanent settlement in Jamestown, Virginia. Decades later, due to political oppression and religious prosecution in England, a growing number of English people left for the US. Before the Independence War, 13 English colonies were established along the east coast. Between 1607 and 1776, more than one million Northern and Western Europeans came to the US. During this period, no efficient means of transportation were available to European immigrants. Thus, they had to sail across the Atlantic Ocean, which was a perilous journey of more or less two months. The majority of these immigrants hailed from Great Britain, Germany, Ireland, France, Sweden, Netherlands, Denmark, etc. They constituted the major group of immigrants from colonial times to the end of the 19th century. Compared with Native Americans and European whites, black people bought and shipped from Africa were the only involuntary immigrants in the US. As the plantation in the American South was in great need of cheap labor, the 18th century witnessed a surge in the black population in North America. As many as over 3 million black people were sold to America by English slave traders in this century. By 1776, blacks had made up 20 percent of all immigrants in the US, becoming an important part of the American population.

Starting in 1820, the US implemented the immigration registration system. Ever since then, the country had kept an accurate record of immigrant population growth. According to the record, from 1820 onwards, another immigrant wave continued well into 1890. Between 1820 and 1890, about 15 million immigrants flooded into the US, with 4/5 of the immigration population from Northern and Western European countries. From 1880 to 1965, the number of immigrants reached 32 million. These immigrants were mostly from Southern and Eastern European countries, such as Russia, Poland, Italy, Czech, Hungary, Greece, etc. At the same time, the number of immigrants from Northern and Western Europe experienced a steady decrease. Up till 1965, white people played a dominant role in American immigrants, and formed the foundation of the white population in modern America.

The postwar economic development and the new *Immigration Act of 1965* allured more people to immigrate to the US, profoundly changing its demographic picture. Beginning in 1965, there came a new immigrant wave. Between 1965 and 2019, about 43 million people from every corner of the world poured into this country. At present, the American immigrant population is four times larger than that in the 1960s. Among all immigrants, white people from European countries account for roughly 12 percent, while people from Asia and Latin America respectively make up 37 percent and 45 percent. The rapid increase in the number of Asian and Hispanic immigrants leads to a steady growth in the population of American ethnic groups.

In 2000, the population of Hispanics for the first time surpassed that of African Americans. Since that year, Hispanics have become the largest ethnic group in the US. In some cities like Los Angeles, the proportion of Hispanics reaches 47 percent of the total population. Why did so many people from Latin America move to the US? And why do they still keep moving? For one thing, because of economic poverty and political chaos, some Hispanics hope to seek better opportunities and improve their life in America. For another, it is associated with the American immigration policy. In 1924, out of diplomatic concern, the US started to place strict limits on immigration from the Eastern Hemisphere, but carried out a relatively loose immigration policy for immigrants from the Western Hemisphere. Therefore, it was easier for Hispanics to emigrate to the US from the 1920s to the mid-1960s. However, the *Immigration Act of 1965* began to limit immigration from Latin American countries. Surprisingly, the act sped up both legal and illegal immigration from Latin America, because a great number of Hispanics fretted about a much lower chance of immigrating to the US in the future.

A large number of immigrants from Asia to the US began during the California Gold Rush in the 1840s. The gold mines fueled the influx of Asians like Chinese, Japanese, Koreans and Filipinos who carried the American dream with them. But seldom did they make a big fortune. Most of them ended up taking labor-intensive jobs. For instance, they built the transcontinental railroad, did the farming and mining work, ran the restaurant and provided domestic services. With an increasing number of Asian immigrants, Americans feared that these people would pose a threat to white Americans in terms of competing for job and education opportunities. In addition, white Americans viewed people of Asian descent as inferiors, because they belonged to a different race from the white race. Hence white Americans' intermarriage with Asians would inevitably stain their superior white blood and therefore should be banned. Furthermore, Americans generally believed that, since these immigrants had different bloodlines and held different values and beliefs, it would be extremely hard to assimilate them into mainstream America. Under such circumstances, American society turned notoriously unfriendly to Asian immigrants. White American racists burnt and looted shops and restaurants run by Asians. At the same time, the US Congress passed a series of anti-Asian ordinances and legislation. Among them, the *Chinese Exclusion Act* (1882), which suspended Chinese laborers for a period of 10 years, was the first major legislation to restrict immigration into the US. Afterwards the *Immigration Act of 1924* finally closed the door to all Asian immigrants. It was up until 1943 when the US and China became allies that the US repealed the exclusion act targeting at the Chinese. In the wake of WWII, the US loosened the restrictions on immigrants from other Asian countries step by step. In this social milieu, Asians enjoyed the same opportunities to emigrate to the US as people from other places in the world. The *Immigration Act of 1965* further spurred the inflow of immigrants from Asia. In the 1970s, a great number of immigrants and refugees from Southeast Asia flocked in. It should be noted that, in the postwar era, when Asians move to the US, they usually come with their family, relatives and even friends. That is because Asians value the blood relationship and extended family. All of the above-mentioned factors make Asians one of the fastest growing ethnic groups in postwar America.

    Undeniably, immigrants have made immense contributions to the prosperity of the US. As for the economic aspect, immigrants put their labor, talents and funds into industrial, agricultural and technological progress as well as infrastructure construction. A case in point is that immigrants from Western and Northern European countries were dedicated to the US Industrial Revolution and agriculturalization in the American West. Another example is that immigrants from China and Ireland were devoted to the construction of transcontinental railroads and canals in the 19th century. As for the political aspect, immigrants defended the nation and its unity during the Independence War and the Civil War, promoted the labor movement and enhanced political democracy. For example, immigrants from Germany unswervingly supported the Union and the abolishment of slavery in the Civil War. Moreover, immigrants introduced Marxism, organized Marxist groups and planted the seed of scientific socialism, which fueled the labor movement. Furthermore, ethnic groups like Mexican Americans fought for their equal citizenship and political participation in the Latino Civil Rights Movement. The increasing number and power of ethnic groups make it less likely for American political parties to ignore their influences. As for the cultural aspect, the fine traditions and splendid cultures brought by immigrants from different countries greatly enrich American culture, shaping a unique multi-culture society. For instance, blues and jazz created by African Americans are now recognized as hallmarks of American music. Ethnic neighborhoods like China town, little Tokyo, little Italy and little Ethiopia fully display the diversity of American culture.

Overall, the place of origin for US immigrants expands from Europe to the whole world, which adds a cosmopolitan feature to its present demographic composition and ethnic structure. In fact, the expansion of place of origin keeps pace with the expansion of economic globalization, which expanded from Europe to other places like America, Asia, Oceania and Africa. Meanwhile, immigration in the US remains a thorny issue to be resolved. In the past few centuries, how to integrate newly arrived immigrants into mainstream society was the government's big concern. Since the 1980s, the influx of illegal immigrants and refugees has become a big headache for the American government. After the September 11 attacks, American immigration policy put more emphasis on the protection of national security. As the number of immigrants from Latin America and Asia increases dramatically and the crude birth rates of ethnic groups are higher than whites in the US, the ethnic structure now has experienced unprecedented changes. On the one hand, the proportion of the white population is constantly declining. On the other hand, the proportion of ethnic groups is steadily growing. Currently, the proportion of the non-white population attains about 40 percent, and this percentage is still increasing. In many ways, the changing ethnic structure exerts huge influences on American politics, economics, culture and diplomacy.

2 Racial and Ethnic Groups

As a nation of immigrants, people of hundreds of world ethnic groups ancestry live in the US, which makes the US a racially and ethnically diverse nation. Basically speaking, race and ethnicity have different connotations. Race emphasizes the common physical features of a group of human beings, e.g. skin color, while ethnicity stresses the common cultural traditions of a group of humankind, e.g. beliefs, values and customs. Hence, they have been used separately on official occasions. At present, the US Census Bureau generally recognizes six racial categories. They are white Americans, African Americans, Asian Americans, American Indians and Alaska Natives, Native Hawaiians and Other Pacific Islanders, and people of two or more races. According to this categorization, Hispanics are not identified as a race, nor are Arab Americans. Instead, they are treated as ethnicities. According to the US Census Bureau, as of 2019, 60.1 percent of Americans claimed themselves to be Non-Hispanic whites, 18.4 percent Hispanics, 12.2 percent African Americans, 5.6 percent Asian Americans, 0.7 percent American Indians and Alaska Natives, 0.2 percent Native Hawaiians and Other Pacific Islanders, and 2.8 percent multiple races. As for the stability and development of the US, all racial and ethnic groups are invaluable assets to the American nation.

2.1 Non-Hispanic Whites

The US Census Bureau generally defines Non-Hispanic whites as those who have origins in Europe, the Middle East or North Africa. In other words, the official definition of Non-Hispanic whites does not count in white people of Hispanic or Latino ancestry, like Mexican Americans and Puerto Ricans. Since Colonial America, European Americans have constituted the majority population of Non-Hispanic whites and America. As of 2017, they accounted for more than 40 percent of the US population. According to a survey in 2016, German Americans (13.9%) were the largest group of European ancestry, followed by Irish (10%), English (7.4%),

Italians (5.2%) and Polish (3%). Due to their predominance in the Non-Hispanic white population and long historical presence in North America, European Americans' experiences, to a large extent, reflect a major part of Non-Hispanic whites' life and form the basis of American culture.

As early as the 17th century, European settlers began to organize emigration to the New World. But in the 17th and 18th centuries, restricted by weather and traffic conditions, their immigration was on a small scale. About 1 million immigrants arrived in the US before the American revolution. They were principally from Northern and Western Europe, such as England (24%), Ulster Scottish-Irish (14%), Germany (11%) and Scotland (5%). The American government welcomed immigrants in the first two decades after the American revolution, because the newly-founded country was in great need of the labor force. But out of the concern for national security, the US second president John Adams signed the *Alien and Sedition Acts* into effect so as to limit immigration. Between 1784 and 1793, no more than 4,000 immigrants came to the US each year.

From the 19th century onwards, there were three waves of immigration from Europe. The first wave happened between 1820 and 1890. During this period, the total immigrant population reached 15 million. More than 80 percent of these immigrants hailed from Northern and Western European countries like Germany, Ireland, Great Britain and Scandinavia, roughly the same places as those during the era of colonial immigration. The second wave occurred between 1890 and 1930, witnessing a surge to 22 million and a shift in the country of origin. In this particular period, about 70 percent of US immigrants came from Southern and Eastern Europe, such as Italy, Greece, Poland, Russia, Bulgaria, Czech and Hungry. The Great Depression and WWII dramatically reduced the number of European immigrants, and it resumed a steady growth from the Postwar era until the early 1960s, standing between 100,000 and 125,000 annually. Afterwards the biggest proportion of immigrants arrived from Asia and Latin America rather than Europe.

With diverse backgrounds and various experiences, European immigrants came to the US for the following reasons. First, political oppression and religious prosecution in European countries drove a large number of people into America. Religious intolerance, and frequent revolutions and wars in Europe made Europeans believe that America was a promised land. For instance, the Pilgrims in the early 1600s sought to enjoy religious freedom in the New World. Likewise, due to the European Revolutions of 1848, political exiles from Germany, Poland and France as well as British Chartists searched for political asylum in the US. Second, industrial development and westward expansion in America provided unprecedented opportunities and thus attracted European immigrants to emigrate from their home countries. In comparison with European nations, America was scarce in population but rich in land and natural resources. In the 19th century, while America badly needed large numbers of laborers, the Industrial Revolution which gained momentum in Britain, France, Germany and Russian devastated the traditional economy and uprooted surplus labor. Under such circumstances, European unemployed skill workers and poor farmers were able to find more job opportunities, higher wages and better living conditions in the US. Third, natural disasters like the Great Famine in the mid-19th century forced people, the Irish in particular, to leave their homelands for America and start a new life. Just within 5 years between 1846 and 1851, approximately 1 million Irish arrived in the US. Last, continuous improvement in the means of trans-Atlantic transportation gave an impetus to immigration from Europe. The duration of travel decreased from two months of sailing in Colonial America to 10 days of voyage in the 19th century to less than half a day by air in the 20th century. And the enhancement of both the safety and comfort of the transportation means further encouraged European immigrants to set out.

  In general, pragmatic and enterprising, European immigrants inject vitality into the American nation. Economically speaking, European Americans made tremendous contributions to America's transition from an agrarian nation to an industrial power. They brought state-of-the-art technology to the US, facilitating the innovation of technology and the development of productivity in America. In the 18th and 19th centuries, the agricultural and industrial technology of Europe were well ahead of that of the US. Thus, numerous inventions made by European immigrants and their descendants, e.g. Thomas Edison, Alexander Bell, Samuel Slater, played an important role in advancing American agriculture, industry and transportation. Moreover, European whites offered a lot of cheap labor and skilled workers, who helped speed up the industrialization and construction of the US. For instance, Irish and Italians were the chief forces in railroad and canal construction, while Irish, Greek and French Canadians were the majority of textile workers in New England.

As a whole, American culture, to a great extent, is influenced by European culture, British culture in particular. The cultural ties to Britons beginning from colonial times have laid the groundwork for the shaping of American English, the US economic, political, legal and education systems as well as its cultural traditions. For instance, the American legal system rests on Anglo-American Common Law, following the doctrine of precedent. In addition, first created and observed by English colonists in 1621, Thanks-giving Day has become a national holiday widely celebrated by generations of Americans. Furthermore, the influences of the British music, sports, architecture styles and food can be felt in the everyday life of Americans. At the same time, American mainstream values are imprinted with WASP (White Anglo-Saxon Protestant) culture. Because in most of American history, WASPs hold national strength in national politics, economy, wealth, education and social status. Broadly speaking, WASPs refer to Northwestern European American elites with Protestant beliefs, such as Protestant English Americans, German Americans, Dutch Americans and Scandinavian Americans. They traditionally put emphasis on work ethics, individualism, community spirit, education, self-discipline and democracy, which have been commonly recognized and held by all Americans.

Nevertheless, the influences of white ethnic Americans should never be underestimated in American society and culture. Different from WASPs in geographical location, religion and culture, white ethnic Americans mostly come from Central, Southern and Eastern European countries. In contrast with the Protestant majority, white ethnics are more likely to take Catholicism, Judaism or Eastern Orthodox as their religious belief. Therefore, they maintain strong cultural identification with their national origins, and are hardly assimilated into the mainstream WASP culture. Such being the case, the unique heritage of white ethnic culture adds diversity and dynamism to America, making it a more pluralist and prosperous nation. Take food for instance. Not only are apple pies and hamburgers (respectively introduced by English settlers and German immigrants) well-known American foods, but also Polish hot dogs and Italian Buffalo wings become iconic symbols of American cuisine. In spite of their cultural distinctiveness, white ethnic Americans suffer long-standing discrimination throughout American history. When they arrived in the US in the 19th and earlier 20th centuries, most of them, particularly Irish, Italian and Jewish immigrants, were poor and undereducated peasants seeking a better life. They were largely relegated to the most menial and lowest-paying jobs, facing significant discriminatory treatment. They have been stereotyped as dirty, indecent, intellectually and morally inferior people by mainstream society. Currently, white ethnic Americans have already climbed out of poverty, and their household income and education levels have reached or even surpassed the average levels of Americans. With the rising economic status, white ethnic Americans gradually gain greater political power at both local and national levels, challenging the WASP-dominated political circles. To date, probably the most prominent white ethnic political figures are the 35th US president John F. Kennedy and the 46th US president Joe Biden, both of whom are Irish Catholics. In the next two to three decades, as Non-Hispanic whites continue to be the largest component of the American population, it can be predicted that the profound European cultural influences will still persist for years.

2.2 Hispanics

Hispanics, or Latinos, refer to those whose ancestors mainly came from Mexico, Puerto Rico, Cuba, and other Spanish-speaking countries in Central and South America. Broadly speaking, Hispanics also include people with French roots or of Portuguese origin in Latin America. Hence, this is a pan-ethnic heterogeneous group consisting of different national ancestries and races. Due to historical reasons, they share cultural and linguistic heritages to varying degrees. In 2018, of the total Hispanic population in the US, 61.9 percent were of Mexican descent, followed by 9.6 percent of Puerto Rican descent and 3.9 percent of Cuban descent. Mexican Americans are normally concentrated in the Southwestern region. Puerto Ricans are generally centered in the Northeastern and Southeastern regions. Cuban Americans mostly dominate the Southeastern, Northeastern and Southwestern regions. Among all 50 states, California, Texas and Florida have the three largest Hispanic populations. About 2/3 of Hispanics were born on American soil. Since 2000, thanks to large-scale immigration and high birth rates, the population of Hispanics has surpassed that of African Americans, and Hispanics thereby have become the largest minority group in the US. It is estimated that Hispanics will make up 25 percent of the American population by 2050. Currently, Hispanics are becoming an influential force in American social, economic, political and cultural life.

The ancestry of Hispanics can be traced to Spanish colonists as early as the late 16th century, when Spanish conquerors settled down in present-day Santa Fe, New Mexico. Before WWII, owing to the Mexican-American War (1846 – 1848), the Spanish-American War (1898), the Mexican Revolution (1910 – 1917) and labor shortage during two world wars, a great number of Mexicans and Puerto Ricans emigrated to the US. In the post-WWII era, pushed by the miserable life and such political turmoil as the Cuban Revolution (1953 – 1959) back at home, and pulled by American economic opportunities and political stability, Hispanics from many different Central and South American nations swarmed into the US. Within just half a century between 1970 and 2019, the population of Hispanics surged by 5.6 times. Most Hispanics settled in hub cities of the metropolitan area, and lived close to their family members in the Hispanic community. By and large, Hispanics traditionally vote for the Democratic Party, with the exception of Cuban Americans who normally stand for the Republican Party. According to a 2019 Pew Research study, 72 percent of Hispanics identify themselves as Christians, with 47 percent as Catholics and 24 percent as Protestants. Most of them take Spanish as their mother tongue, and speak Spanish at home. 80 percent of the second-generation Hispanics and 40 percent of the third-generation speak fluent Spanish. With the growing number of Hispanics, Spanish has become the most commonly spoken language other than English in the US.

Greatly affected by Spanish cultural traditions and Catholicism, Hispanics attach great importance to tradition values, e.g. the emphasis on the extended family and motherhood. Hence, the birth rate of Hispanics has always stayed high. According to a survey, the ratio of Hispanic families with three children or above is much higher than that of black families and white families. On the one hand, the high birth rate means the growing Hispanic population, which in many aspects could enhance their social influences. On the other hand, bearing and rearing more children inevitably increase the burden on Hispanic families, which is likely to throw them into poverty. Besides, the idea on hierarchy is deeply entrenched in Hispanic cultural traditions. It has been revealed in their views of skin color and gender roles. Like European Americans, Hispanics utilize skin color to define one's social class, regarding white skin as superior. As Hispanics are a heterogeneous population with a mixed ancestry of different combinations, their skin colors vary from person to person. Such being the case, in mainstream society, light-skinned Hispanics are better treated and accepted by white Americans. For instance, they can find more respectable and better-paid jobs, and gain higher social status than dark-skinned Hispanics. Meanwhile, in the Hispanic community, dark-skinned Hispanics are generally discriminated against and rejected by light-skinned ones, which causes division within the Hispanic ethnic group. As for gender roles, culturally speaking, Hispanics still follow their patriarchy traditions, i.e. male dominance and female subordination. But in reality, due to their elevated social, economic and political status, Latinas are able to win a bigger say in family matters and thus higher family status.

As an integrated part of American society, Hispanics have exerted significant influences on American economic development. First, the growth of the Hispanic population results in an increase in both laborers and consumers, which indicates their rising economic influence. Hispanics chiefly take low-paid and labor-intensive jobs that are barely preferred by white laborers, such as builders, miners, servants, fruit or vegetable pickers, etc. The Hispanic labor force grew by 22.5 million workers between 1976 and 2016, and it is expected to grow in the following decades. In terms of Hispanic purchasing power, it rises at a fast pace, increasing from $ 210 million in 1990 to $ 1.7 trillion in 2017. Second, the growth of Hispanic-owned businesses far outpaces that of businesses owned by other ethnic groups. Statistics show that Hispanic-owned companies grew by 190 percent from 1992 to 2019. Presently, almost 1 out of every seven enterprises is owned by a Hispanic. Third, Hispanics including foreign-born immigrants contribute enormously to US tax revenues. As of 2015, they contributed approximately $215 billion in nationwide tax payments.

In addition to positive economic influences, Hispanics also have favorable political effects on American political progress. They play an increasingly active role in promoting political rights for ethnic groups and combatting injustice against minorities in America. In the 1960s, the outburst of the civil rights movement led by African Americans inspired Hispanics to launch their own civil rights movement. They strived for better living conditions, more laborers' rights and the empowerment of the Hispanic community. Their efforts led to the passage of the *State and Local Fiscal Assistance Act of 1972*, which provided better housing and welfare to all Americans irrespective of race, gender and religion. It should be noted that, there is a rising number of Hispanics who are elected and appointed officeholders in federal, state and local governments. As of 2016, there were more than six thousand elected officials in the US who were of Hispanic heritage. Meanwhile, with the increase in the Hispanic population, the number of Hispanic registered voters keeps growing, which impacts government policies at all levels and even the presidential election. The electoral college increases the importance of votes from populous states like California, Texas, New York, Florida and Illinois, which are dominated by Hispanics voters. That explains why the presidential candidates always spare no effort to seek Hispanic votes.

Furthermore, Hispanic culture adds a splendid color to the American cultural landscape. For instance, many places in the Southwestern and Southeastern regions were first named by the Spanish colonists, such as Los Angeles, San Diego, San Francisco, Las Vegas and Florida. Aside from this, a number of Hispanic music forms like salsa, hip-hop, reggaeton, and ranchera are introduced to enrich American music. Furthermore, Hispanic cuisine, Mexican cuisine in particular, is one of the most popular and varied cuisines for Americans. Tortillas, salsa, guacamole and enchiladas have become common dishes in the daily life of Americans, just like ketchup, sandwiches and hamburgers. Therefore, it has profoundly influenced American food culture and changed their eating habits.

However, the influx of Hispanics also gives rise to a series of social problems. As Hispanic Americans are generally under-educated and mainly manual workers, they are apt to lose their jobs during globalization and economic recession. In 2020, the unemployment rate of Hispanic Americans reached 10.4 percent, 3.1 percent higher than that of non-Hispanic whites. By the same token, they live in worse housing and have smaller health insurance coverage than non-Hispanic whites. In addition to suffering low economic and social status, Hispanics, especially illegal immigrants, are subject to racial hostility. They are often blamed for the aggravated joblessness and economic decline by conservatives, which triggers numerous incidents of violence and harassment against Hispanic immigrants. From the 1990s onwards, a number of immigration control laws, especially the *Illegal Immigration Reform and Immigrant Responsibility Act of 1996*, have been made to impose stringent controls on immigration and implement harsh punishments on illegal immigrants. The number of Hispanic immigrants was strictly limited during the Trump administration. It is worth mentioning that, in the 21st century, the rising number and influence of Hispanics lead to conflicts between African Americans and Hispanic Americans. Because Black Americans tend to view Hispanics as a treat to their employment, survival and development. Meanwhile, segregation and discrimination against Hispanic Americans still exist in education, housing, employment and law enforcement, which intensifies racial tension and enlarges the racial divide. Under such circumstances, crime and drugs are infesting the Hispanic community. Accordingly, Hispanics, children in particular, are more likely to develop a sense of insecurity and inferiority, which can negatively impact their mental health.

In the future, while struggling for better employment, education and living conditions, Hispanics yet have to continue fighting for equal rights and social justice through political participation, legal means and probably, working with other ethnic groups.

2.3 African Americans

Following behind Hispanics, African Americans are regarded as the second largest minority group in the US. Like other ethnic groups, African Americans have gone through numerous hardships and obstacles, while striving for American citizenship and equal rights, including property rights, voting rights, legal rights, etc.

As early as 1502, Africans were kidnapped, enslaved and sold from West Africa to the Caribbean by Spanish settlers, so as to meet the demand for labor required by the booming colonial economy. In the next three centuries, apart from the Spanish, Portuguese and Dutch, English and French merchants were the foremost transatlantic slave traders. Generations of Africans contributed much to the survival and development of the New World. The first Africans were imported to North America by a Dutch ship in 1619. Initially, they were by no means permanent slaves. Instead, they worked as indentured servants under almost the same contracts as early poor European laborers. According to the contracts, black laborers worked for employers for a fixed term of servitude, usually five to seven years. Upon the expiration of their terms, they were expected to work for themselves, start their life anew and occasionally get a piece of land. However, in order to protect their profits and reduce conflicts with blacks, white Americans enacted laws to deprive black people of legitimate rights step by step, like the right to appear as a witness, the freedom of marriage, suffrage, etc. From 1641 onwards, the slavery system was gradually legalized in British colonies.

It was until the 1670s that hereditary slavery was perpetuated. Two decades later, the treatment of enslaved blacks as chattels of white people was written into legislation, which symbolized the official formation of the slavery system. Ever since then, there had existed a deep racial line between whites and blacks. Consequently, though African Americans mainly served as the important labor force on southern plantations throughout the 17th and 18th centuries, they were degraded to an inferior status and lived a hard life. For example, they were not allowed to learn reading and writing, and black families were more likely to disintegrate because of the sale or forced separation of family members.

After the Independence War, the institution of slavery was tacitly kept and acknowledged by the US Constitution. In the Constitutional Convention of 1787, southern states tried to count slaves for the purpose of gaining representation in Congress, but northern states rejected it and argued that enslaved Americans should be counted for the purpose of taxation. Neither of the two sides agreed to grant slaves the right to vote. Ultimately, both sides gave consent to *the Three-Fifths Compromise*, which counted each enslaved person as 3/5 of a free individual for both representation and taxation. Besides, the Congress decided not to intervene in the slave trade until twenty years later. To a large extent, the American revolution propelled Americans, particularly social activists and intellectuals in the North, to rethink the existence of slavery. Americans of social conscience started the abolitionist movement and called for the end of the institution. By 1804, slavery had been abolished in all northern states. Four years later, the slave trade was outlawed by the Congress. Nonetheless, viewed as essential to southern economies, slavery remained widespread in the South. In addition, with the invention of the cotton gin, the southern reliance on slaves was reinforced, which fueled the domestic slave trade. The critical issue of whether slavery should be kept in the US exacerbated sectional divisions. Sectional tension reached a new height in 1820, when disputes over whether new states should be admitted as slave states or free states arose. Although the tension was temporarily resolved by the implementation of the Missouri Compromise, the escalating national rift over slavery finally culminated in the breakout of the Civil War between the North and the South. The Lincoln Administration issued the Emancipation Proclamation in 1862, and made it official in 1863. The document set free those who had been held as slaves in the rebel states. About 3 million enslaved people benefited from it.

During the Reconstruction period, with the passage of the 13th, 14th and 15th Amendments, not only was slavery officially abolished in all states, but African Americans obtained US citizenship and won the right to vote. However, the emancipation and enfranchisement of black people met strong opposition and resistance from white people, especially white racists. The state legislatures of the South made local laws to disfranchise African American voters. For instance, African Americans were asked to pay poll taxes or pass literacy tests before exercising their voting rights, which was beyond the ability of the poor and illiterate blacks. Besides, such racist groups as the Ku Klux Klan (KKK) were organized to intimidate, attack or even kill African Americans, preventing them from political participation. Lynching of African Americans, which killed black people by hanging them without legal process, was common in the South. Aside from political obstructions, there were economic difficulties for African Americans. Without any effective economic help or supply of the essentials from the government, newly freed black people had almost nothing to start their life. Hence, most of them had no choice but to work as sharecroppers or domestic servants on former plantations. From the 1870s until the 1960s, racial segregation was practiced in virtually every social sphere across the nation, completely removing the rights of citizenship from Black Americans.

Due to the enactment of a series of Jim Crow laws by southern legislators, African Americans were denied access to certain residential areas (e.g. white-dominated blocks), facilities (e.g. public parks, libraries, restaurants, swimming-pools, theaters, cemeteries), and institutions (e.g. schools and churches). "Whites-Only" signs were put up in public facilities. Tennessee was the first state to enforce segregation in public transportation in 1875, and then other states followed suit. In 1890, the Louisiana legislature passed the *Separate Car Act*, restricting black people to separate public accommodations when they took buses or trains. Shortly afterwards, a mixed-blood descendant of white and black ancestry was charged under Louisiana law, because he took a seat in the whites-only compartment of the train and refused to relocate himself to the blacks-only compartment. When his case *Plessy v. Ferguson* was appealed to the US Supreme Court in 1896, the Supreme Court made the ruling that the *Separate Car Act* was constitutional. In other words, the local act did not violate the 14th Amendment and thus segregation was legal. The "separate but equal" decision further codified the segregation principle and worsened the circumstances of racial segregation in the US. At the turn of the 20th century, almost all southern states passed laws to forbid interracial marriage between whites and blacks and require separate public education and housing for colored people. Before WWI, all American states made laws to implement strict racial segregation.

Meanwhile, African Americans never gave up their struggle for freedom and equality. They established the National Association for the Advancement of Colored People (NAACP) in 1908. With the support from the NAACP, they fought for eliminating segregation and discrimination on the basis of race as well as improving the well-being of African Americans. Their efforts were productive, and they made impressive breakthroughs in the 1950s and 1960s. School segregation was first struck down through the case *Brown v. Board of Education* (1954), which was related to a black child's rejection by the nearby all-white school. The Supreme Court overturned the "separate but equal" doctrine, holding that it was in fact unequal. The landmark case established the precedent that segregation in education and other public services was inherently illegal, laying the cornerstone for the Civil Rights Movement. Dr. Martin Luther King Jr., together with other social activists, led countless protesters to launch primarily non-violent boycotts and sit-ins against racial segregation. The movement achieved significant gains, which facilitated the signing of the *Civil Rights Act of 1964*, the *Voting Rights Act of 1965* and the *Fair Housing Act of 1968*. Protected by new legislation during the civil rights era, de jure segregation and formal discrimination were curbed. Since the 1970s, African Americans have gained a greater foothold in government and multiple professions. large numbers of African Americans have been elected or appointed to important offices on the federal and state levels. The African American House of Representatives rose from 5 in 1965 to 57 in 2021. Up till now, the most prominent black political figures probably have been former US president Barack Obama and current US vice-president Kamala Harris. In present times, African Americans not only work in the sports, music and entertainment fields, but also work as lawyers, doctors and businesspersons.

In the first two decades of the 21st century, overt racial discrimination and segregation seldom exist, but systemic racism, one of the legacies of slavery, remains deeply entrenched. The lingering racism and discrimination in subtle patterns set up roadblocks to full equality for African Americans, and cause an enlarging racial divide between Black and White Americans. In addition, violence against African Americans, police brutality in particular, frequently happens, which triggers the Black Lives Matter movement in recent years. Undoubtedly, for African Americans, the process of achieving equality has been and will continue to be a long and arduous journey.

2.4 Asian Americans

Asian Americans refer to a pan-ethnic heterogeneous group consisting of people who come from more than fifty countries across East Asia, South Asia and Southeast Asia, such as China, Japan, Korea, Vietnam, India, Thailand, Singapore, the Philippines, etc. As a diverse group, they have big differences in historical experiences, socio-economic backgrounds, cultural traditions, languages and religions. Chinese Americans have been and are still the largest Asian ethnic group in the US, accounting for about 1/4 of the Asian American population. California, by far, has been inhabited by the largest number of Asian Americans among all states. In 2019, about 1/3 of Asian Americans lived there.

According to the historical record, in the 16th century, Filipinos arrived in the US and they were regarded as the first Asian Americans. However, early immigrants of Filipino ancestry were just in small numbers. Actually, the first Asians who emigrated in large numbers to the US were the Chinese and Japanese in the 19th century. Driven by the scarce opportunity and hard life back at home and attracted by the abundant opportunity and well-off life in America, Chinese immigrants set foot on the west coast and established the Chinese American community in California during the Gold Rush in the 1840s. Known as Chinese coolies, they took a few labor-intensive jobs. For example, they worked in the gold mines, constructed the railroad, ran the restaurant, and offered domestic services. A significant number of the Japanese, mostly Japanese rural farmers, travelled to the American West after the 1868 Meiji Restoration. Like early Chinese immigrants, they also hoped to find a better job and life in the US. They tended farmlands, growing rice and fruits in California. As early Chinese and Japanese immigrants had no intention of living permanently in the US, the majority of them were males who came alone.

Since European Americans assumed that Asian Americans were aliens with inferior cultures, Asian Americans became frequent targets of racial discrimination and violence. Adversely affected by this, Chinese Americans were not allowed to take up certain occupations and thus were prevented from obtaining economic success. Besides, they were segregated from the white community and forced to live in their own communities. Furthermore, many states put a ban on intermarriage with Chinese Americans. The passage of the *Chinese Exclusion Act* in 1882 worsened the circumstances of the Chinese American community, which restricted immigration from China for decades of years. Such being the case, Chinese Americans were not able to start a family and sustain the family line. At the same time, regarded as "yellow peril," Japanese Americans could only do farming and gardening work and provide domestic services. They were not permitted to get farmland ownership, and their children had to attend a different school named "the Oriental School" from white children. Though the immigration of the Japanese was not restricted, strict limits were set on the number of Japanese immigrants in accordance with the Gentlemen's Agreement (1907) between the US and Japan. Subsequently, the *Immigration Act of 1924* completely stopped Asian immigration to the US. WWII slightly improved the social status of Chinese Americans, because China and the US cooperated against Axis. In order to maintain wartime friendship with China, the US Congress rescinded the discriminatory *Chinese Exclusion Act*. Meanwhile, the surprise attack at Pearl Harbor launched by the Japanese put Japanese Americans in an even worse situation in the US. More than 120,000 Japanese Americans were forcibly relocated from the West Coast, and detained in concentration camps in the deserts of the Western United States.

After WWII, the enactment of the *1952 McCarran-Walter Act* revised the US immigration legislation and modestly increased the number of Asian immigrants. It was the landmark *Immigration and Nationality Act of 1965* that led to a surge in Asian immigration. According to the statistics, the population of Asian Americans soared from 1.4 million in 1970 to 12 million in 2000 to 19.36 million in 2019. About 80 percent of these immigrants were from China, Korea, India, the Philippines and Vietnam. First, as the largest Asian ethnic group in the US, different from early Chinese immigrants, Chinese immigrants in this phase were better educated, thereby engaging in mental work, such as scientists, engineers, doctors and accountants. Second, the Korean War and the *Immigration Act of 1965* promoted the development of the Korean American community. With the influx of Korean immigrants who held the same religious belief, Korean national cohesion was greatly enhanced. Third, mostly highly educated, Indian immigrants held hi-tech-related jobs and lived a respectable life in America. For this matter, they were the wealthiest among all Asian ethnic groups. Fourth, there were big distinctions among Southeast Asian immigrants. As the Philippines was colonized by the US in 1898, the majority of Filipinos had a good command of English and were familiar with American culture and customs. With certain skills, relatively higher educational attainment and fewer cultural barriers, Filipino immigrants were easily assimilated into mainstream society, becoming specialists, professionals and even entrepreneurs. Thus, immigrants from the Philippines reached a new height in the postwar time. Starting from the mid-1970s, because of war, starvation and political chaos, refugees from Vietnam, Laos and Cambodia fled to the US. Lack of funds, skills and education, most of them had to rely on aid provided by the US government. Meanwhile, a number of Vietnamese immigrants who came from the elite class in Vietnam gained a comparatively higher social standing in the US.

Generally speaking, immigrants from Asia, for the most part, are young adults between 20 and 39. The median age of Asia Americans is 33, two years younger than that of all Americans. As Asians value family and kinship, the marriage ratio of Asian Americans is higher than that of average Americans. The share of college-educated Asian Americans is almost twice that of college-graduated average Americans. With educational success, they are more likely to hold management and professional jobs, obtaining higher household income than the American general household income. In spite of their prominent educational and economic achievements, Asian Americans have long been victims of stereotypes and discrimination. For example, they were subject to the label of "model minority" between the 1960s and 1990s. They were first described as a "model minority" by the US mainstream media in 1966. At that time, the mass media reported the social-economic accomplishments of Japanese and Chinese Americans, and spoke highly of their hard work, adherence to traditional values and contributions to America. Twenty years later, the reports for "model minority" revived, with a focus on Korean, Indian, Filipino and Vietnamese Americans. Like before, the success of Asian Americans was attributed to their family and cultural values. At first glance, "model minority" is the recognition of Asian immigrants by the whole society. But actually it covers many facts. First, while extolling Asian Americans' success, it fails to reflect the experiences of all Asian Americans. Though an increasing number of Asian Americans rise into the middle class and live a well-to-do life, a substantial number of them, especially refugees and newly-arrived immigrants, lead a hard life and live in a bad environment. Hence, it, to a certain extent, misleads the policy-makers about the necessity of social aid to Asian Americans. Second, although Asian Americans are generally better educated than African Americans, Hispanics and even European Americans, their incomes are lower than those of the latter with the same educational attainment. Third, there lies "a bamboo ceiling" for Asian Americans. Normally, Asian Americans are more likely to become teachers, engineers, technicians, professors, doctors and librarians, but less likely to become managers, administrators and supervisors. Because they are considered too obedient and too introverted to take the leadership role. In addition, some of them are thought to be unable to communicate well in English. Taken together, "model minority" misrepresents the whole picture of Asian Americans' real life, and thereby hinders their social and economic development.

    Even if "model minority" has already become a myth, deep-rooted discrimination and unfair treatment still exist in a subtler way. Under such circumstances, Asian Americans stand up and work together to defend their rights. For instance, in terms of the affirmative action program which intended to redress education and employment inequalities caused by racism, there was a clash of views on the program among Asian Americans. On the one hand, they hoped to equalize educational or employment opportunities for minority groups. On the other hand, as Asian Americans had a better performance in education and employment than other ethnic groups, they were concerned that the implementation of the affirmative action program would adversely reduce the opportunities for them. So, in 1996, they started the California Civil Rights Initiative, known as Proposition 209, which called for the end of governmental and institutional preferential treatment on the basis of race. The constitutionality of Proposition 209 was upheld by the US Supreme Court one year later. So far the initiative has been supported by European Americans and Asian Americans, but has met great challenges from other ethnic groups like Hispanics and African Americans. Through industriousness, perseverance and great efforts, Asian Americans get established on American soil. Nonetheless, there is an urgent need for them to reinforce political participation and empowerment so as to eradicate stereotypes and achieve full equality.

2.5 Arab Americans

Arab Americans are generally defined as American citizens of Arab ancestry. Their countries of origin are diverse, including 22 Middle Eastern and North African Arabic-speaking nations, namely Lebanon, Egypt, Syria, Iraq, Somalia, Palestine, Morocco, Jordan, Yemen, Algeria, Tunisia, Saudi Arabia, Kuwait, Libya, United Arab Emirates, Oman, Bahrain, Comoros, Djibouti, Mauritania, Qatar, and Sudan. As of 2021, there are more than 3.5 million Arab Americans in the US, accounting for 1 percent of the total American population. Though a relatively small ancestry group, the current Arab population has been four times larger than that three decades ago. According to the US Census Bureau, in 2017, the five largest subgroups of Arab Americans were Lebanese (25%), Egyptians (12%), Syrians (8%), Somalians (7%) and Iraqis (6%). Presently, Arab Americans live across the nation, and as high as 94 percent of them live in metropolitan cities. They concentrate in such states as California, Michigan, New York, Texas, Florida, Illinois, New Jersey, etc. As for religious affiliations, over 3/5 of them are Christians, with 35 percent Catholics, 18 percent Orthodox, 10 percent Protestants, and 1/5 Muslims. In recent years, with the rising number and influence of Arab Americans, they have made great efforts to make themselves a separate ethnic categorization from the non-Hispanic white group. However, they have met with no success. Hence, they are still classified as non-Hispanic whites by the US Census Bureau.

Arabs began immigration to the US before the Independence War in the 18th century. Immigrating individually, they were small in number. All through American history, there have been altogether three recognizable immigration waves of Arab Americans. The first wave happened between the late 19th century and the end of WWI. An estimated 110,000 Middle Easterners left the Greater Syria province under the rule of the Ottoman Empire for America. Their homeland encompassed present-day Syria, Lebanon, Palestine, Iraq and Jordan. The majority of them were young illiterate Christians, who were driven away by religious prosecution, scant opportunities and economic hardships at home. They planned to stay temporarily in the US and came back after they made some money. Thus, they were largely single males, resulting in a high disproportion of Arab men to Arab women in the Arab American community. As they were almost uneducated and spoke little English, early Arab American immigrants usually became peddlers in large cities like Los Angeles, Detroit and New York, selling handicrafts, baked food and religious items. After they saved enough money, they usually started small businesses or even invested in the garment industry. During the period of the first wave, they were categorized as "Syrian" or "Turk" instead of "Arabs", because they were viewed as subjects of the Ottoman Empire.

The second wave lasted from the 1920s to the 1960s. After the decrease in the number of Arab American immigrants during WWI, large-scale Arab immigration to the US resumed in the 1920s. Different from the first-wave Arab immigrants, the majority of the second-wave Arab immigrants were Muslims. Besides, many of them were related to those who had already settled down and lived a better life in the US. The success of their relatives or friends allured them to emigrate. It was estimated that, towards the end of the 1920s, a total of 250,000 Lebanese, Syrians and Palestinians were in America. A significant number of them did business, setting up their own stores and importing Middle Eastern items to the American market. The Great Depression and WWII acted as setbacks to Arab immigration, cutting it down to no more than 1,000 Arabs each year. The Arab-Israeli War of 1948 proved a turning point. From 1948 through 1966, 80,000 Arab immigrants, predominantly Palestinians, arrived in the US.

The third wave took place from the mid-1960s to the 2010s. Due to the *Immigration and Nationality Act of 1965*, a new wave of Arab immigrants came to the US. They were mostly bilingual literate Muslims, who searched for better economic opportunities and quality education. From 1967 until 2003, more than 750,000 Arabs emigrated from the Middle East and North Africa, especially Palestine, Egypt, Syria, Iraq and Yemen, to America. Among them, the number of Palestinians was larger than any other Arab ethnic group. Palestinian immigration was spurred by the Six-Day War of 1967 and the intifadas of the 1980s and 1990s. Thanks to their particular experiences, Palestinian Americans came with strong ethnic and political awareness. Therefore, since the 1970s, the influx of Palestinians has greatly facilitated the formation of an Arab American identity and the political activism in the Arab American community. Under such circumstances, Arab American activists spared no efforts to establish Arab American organizations, such as the National Arab American Association, the Arab American Institute, the American Arab Anti-Discrimination Committee, etc. These organizations were founded to redress discrimination against Arab Americans, improve their images and protect their rights.

Presently, Arab Americans have contributed to every social aspect. Some hold important political office, some are famous actors and correspondents in entertainment, and others are prominent entrepreneurs and professors. Given the significant contributions of Arab Americans, the Arab American National Museum was opened to the public in 1995, in order to present and preserve the history and culture of Arab Americans. By the same token, the US State Department for the first time designated April as Arab American Heritage Month in 2021. Despite the increasing recognition of the contributions made by Arab Americans, Americans of Arab ancestry have been stereotyped as violent and threatening terrorists particularly after the September 11 attacks. In the wake of the event, Arab Americans have suffered more hate crimes like physical violence, hate mails, death threats, and racial discrimination like discriminatory practices in the workplaces and schools. Their situation deteriorated when the Trump administration issued a series of Muslim bans to block travel from certain Islamic countries. Such being the case, Americans of Arab heritage have become a leading force in fighting for equal rights and fair treatment over the past two decades.

2.6 Native Americans

Native Americans (also known as American Indians), real owners of the Americas, once created splendid civilization on the land. Their techniques of planting and irrigation have fostered early agriculture. Their oral tradition and vivid imagination have enriched American literature. Their skills in pottery-making, quilting, rug-weaving and silverwork-producing have beautified American people's life. The rhythm and melody of their music have been interwoven into the fabric of American symphony and opera. A great number of American places, rivers, mountains, animals and plants have been originally named by Native Americans. In spite of their great contributions, Native Americans were granted American citizenship as late as the 1920s. In addition, they have long been reduced to an inferior status in the society since the settlement of European colonists.

    When European settlers arrived on the American continent at the end of the 15th century, there were an estimated 900,000 to 18 million Native Americans. American Indians relied on hunting, fishing, gathering or extensive farming. Their society defined itself by bloodlines, consisting of thousands of tribes. The main tribal activities included hunting, wars between tribes and religious ceremonies. There lay an evident sexual division of labor between Native American men and women. Normally, men were in charge of hunting and wars, while women were responsible for farming, child bearing and rearing, and domestic chores. They believed in animism, i.e., all nature was alive with a spiritual power. As an integrated part of living beings on the earth, the mankind should live in harmony with nature instead of over-exploiting it. Human relations were characterized by love, sharing and mutual-help. Different from private ownership practiced by the mainstream society, Native Americans valued communal and tribal ownership, under which tribal resources like land, hunted animals and agricultural products were shared by all tribal members. In general, as Native Americans tended to put the collective well-being above personal interests, they were economically equal. As for the maintenance of tribal order, they took collective actions like driving someone out of the tribe or condemning someone together, rather than making mandatory laws or establishing legal systems. They boasted the qualities such as bravery, integrity, and self-esteem, as well as full of responsibility and sympathy.

With advanced technology and weapons, white settlers intended to exploit land and resources, accumulated wealth and achieved expansion in the Americas. Besides, bearing a sense of white supremacy and cultural prejudice, they stereotyped Native Americans as savages, and tried to subdue and transform these savages. Intense clashes inevitably erupted between whites and Native Americans. By the 1850s and 1860s, Native Americans had been totally defeated and dispossessed. Up until the 1930s, forced assimilation had been the major Native American policy implemented by the American government. Measures concerning education, religion, land privatization, economic development, customs of Native Americans were carried out to compel them to abandon their cultural traditions. For instance, after dividing tribal lands into either farmland or grazing land, *the Dawes Act of 1887* allotted the individual plots to the Indian household heads, and sold the remaining tribal lands to whites at a cheap price. Meanwhile, the government made great efforts to teach Native Americans skills in agriculture, husbandry and manufacturing and make them give up their nomadic life. However, Native Americans did not henceforth become self-sufficient farmers, nor were they assimilated into mainstream society. Lands owned by American Indians experienced a dramatic decline from 138 million acres in 1887 to 48 million acres in 1934. Those Native Americans who did not conform to the assimilation policy were either exiled or incarcerated.

As a whole, Native Americans were ready to accept technology and weapons introduced by whites, e.g. horses and guns, but rejected the system, values and customs of white people. Within the tribe, there was a great deal of divided opinion on the assimilation policy. Normally, biracial white and American Indians held positive views, while full-blooded Native Americans mostly refused to embrace it. Due to hunger, wars, diseases and slaughter, the Native American population dropped sharply from 1-2 million in 1500 to 600,000 in 1800 to 250,000 in 1900. After the enactment of the *Dawes Act*, American Indians who lost their land fell into poverty, and thus an increasing number of them left their tribes to seek jobs in the cities. Nonetheless, it was hard for them to find jobs and adjust to city life. Therefore, unemployment, school dropout, heavy drinking, suicide and crime were common in the Native American community. At the same time, blood ties were weakened in Native American tribes, and hundreds of tribal languages disappeared.

In order to address the problems caused by the *Dawes Act*, the *Indian Reorganization Act* (IRA), known as the "Indian New Deal", was passed in 1934 to end the forced assimilation of Native Americans and offer them a higher degree of self-government. Moreover, funds were distributed to improve living conditions for Native Americans and revive their cultural heritage. But the act was not able to solve all the problems faced by Native Americans, the loss of land and unequal treatment in particular. In 1953, House Concurrent Resolution 108 was introduced to terminate the supervision and control of the American government on Native Americans. However, from 1952 to 1956, 1.6 million Native American lands were still sold to whites by the government, and funds allocated to Native Americans by the "Indian New Deal" were frozen. The 1960s witnessed the rising national awareness of Native Americans and their continual struggle for civil rights. Responding to this, the American government placed "self-determination" as the new aim of the Native American policy, and took an active role in improving Native Americans' living standards and educational attainment. Shortly afterwards, a series of Native Americans self-determination laws were enacted and put into effect in the 1970s, affirming the self-government of tribal governments. Nevertheless, the Reagan administration in the 1980s cut back on social spending, which used to be used for improving Indian reservations and the life of Native Americans. In spite of setbacks, Native Americans have won more recognition and protection of their political and cultural rights in recent decades, e.g. religious freedom and protection for their arts and crafts.

At present, Native Americans depend on agriculture, husbandry, tourism, and mining for their livelihood on Indian reservations, and they are mostly workers and employees in the cities. In terms of the economic system, tribes remain to have the lion's share of land, resources and property of the reservations, and take a leadership position in the economic life of Native Americans, even if private ownership has been expanded on their reservations. Although their living conditions are improved, Native Americans are still plagued by such problems as racism, poverty, under-education, under-employment, substandard housing and ill health. As for Native Americans, there lies a dilemma: on the one hand, they demand self-government and self-determination; on the other hand, due to a lack of economic power, more often than not, they have to resort to the federal government while addressing their own issues. In this connection, the conflicts between the mainstream society and the Native American community are likely to continue into the foreseeable future.

3 Multicultural America: From "Melting Pot," "Salad Bowl" to "Tapestry"

Throughout centuries, the arrival of immigrants from around the world has profoundly changed the American racial and ethnic structure. While contributing to the diversity of American culture, the existence of different races and ethnic groups also results in clashes between mainstream culture and subculture. Such being the case, American national culture policy has been shaped and reshaped by its changing racial and ethnic circumstances, experiencing the development from Anglo-Conformity to Melting Pot to Cultural Pluralism to Multiculturalism. Meanwhile, American culture is vividly characterized by such metaphors as "melting pot," "salad bowl" and "tapestry".

In Colonial America, immigrants in the thirteen English colonies were predominantly from Great Britain. Due to the support of the English government and the preponderance of English immigrants, English became the most commonly-used language by all immigrants. At the same time, the English systems, religious beliefs, customs and way of life turned into social norms in everyday American life. While conquering the New World, settlers in the English colonies gradually formulated distinctive values, way of life and national identity, distinguishing themselves from Europeans. As the majority of the colonists were WASPs, WASP culture naturally played a dominant role in American culture, serving as the measurement of the American identity. For the time being, American colonists bore an ambivalent attitude toward immigrants. On the one hand, in order to promote the development of the

American continent, they welcomed newcomers to join them in the exploration of colonies and enjoyment of abundance in the land of America. On the other hand, they were concerned that the inflow of immigrants and the growing influence of immigrant culture would pose a threat to the dominance of WASP culture, which was likely to invite fundamental changes in American culture and life. Therefore, from the early 17th century to the early 20th century, colonial governments and the US government carried out the policy of forced assimilation to defend the superiority of WASP culture. Externally, all immigrants were required to give up their own languages, cultural practices and regious beliefs. Instead, they were expected to identify with the WASP-centered American identity politically, culturally and emotionally. Internally, droves of Native Americans were disposed of their land and forced to live on Indian reservations and embrace the WASP way of life. All of these means aimed to prompt the homogeneity of the American nation on the basis of WASP culture. In other words, all Americans, immigrants and Native Americans included, were to be molded to speak the same language, practice the same religious belief and embrace the same way of life. This constituted the core of Anglo-Conformity, reflecting an overt racist flavor and the sense of might culture in many aspects.

Before Anglo-Conformity completely retreated from that stage of history, the "melting pot" became the leading national culture policy in the US. Arising upon the founding of the US, "melting pot" took shape in the 19th century and declined in the 1960s. Different from Anglo-Conformity which emphasizes forced assimilation in accordance with Anglo-American culture, "melting pot" gives priority to natural assimilation and adjustment of ethnic cultures to the American way. During the process of assimilation, all ethnic groups are expected to lose their original ethnic identities, and blended to form a distinctive American nation. The idea of "melting pot" was first put forward by Hector St. John Crevecoeur, an emigrant French writer, in his *Letters from an American Farmer* (1782). He believed that individual Americans were "melted into a new race of men." But the new race mentioned by Crevecoeur did not include Black Americans or Native Americans. In fact, only those who shared great similarities with WASPs in terms of race and culture could be melted. Standing on the shoulder of Crevecoeur, American great thinker Ralph Waldo Emerson described the US as a more tolerant melting pot, whites, blacks and Polynesians all included. At the end of the 19th century, American historian Frederick Jackson Turner pointed out in his "frontier thesis" that the American West was the melting pot of the American nation. He held that, it was during the development of the American West that people from every corner of the world learned from each other, made compromises and formed a new culture. When Southern and Eastern European immigration to the US reached a peak in 1908, Israel Zangwill's play *The Melting-Pot* opened and made success, popularizing the metaphor and thesis – "melting pot." It was a modern version of *Romeo and Juliet*. The Russian American lovers who came from feuding families finally got married in America, but their marriage would be impossible if they still stayed in Russia. The happy ending tried to show that differences between American ethnic groups were effectively resolved through the edifying of American culture. As a cultural metaphor, the implications of a "melting pot" are evident. First, America is compared to a big pot where newly arrived immigrants are melted to form a new nation – the American nation. Second, since WASP culture is a dominant ingredient in the melting pot, the new nation is the recasting and reshaping of WASP culture. Third, the cultural features and traditional values of ethnic minorities melt away in the pot. Shortly after the success of the play, the "melting pot" thesis was utilized by the US government to promote Americanization activities in the early 20th century. Meanwhile, "melting pot" was used by scholars and thinkers to refer to American national culture policy. Though popular among the public, "melting pot" was not without criticism. Some assumed that ethnic minorities could better enrich American culture through their uniqueness instead of homogeneity. Others argued that the ingredients of ethnic minorities were experiencing gradual changes rather than being totally melted. Both arguments conveyed the message that it was both unrealistic and impossible for immigrants to completely abandon their former customs and values or to be fully Americanized. In the wake of WWII, with the influx of immigrants from

Latin America and Asia, the ethnic structure became increasingly diverse, and the cultural differences between ethnic groups were more salient. In this social milieu, "melting pot" began to fade away.

    Actually, while "melting pot" was still the prevailing vision of the US at the beginning of the 20th century, Cultural Pluralism came into being. As a new solution to deal with cultural differences and reflection of racial tension caused by force assimilation, Cultural Pluralism was first set forth by American philosopher Horace Kallen in the late 1910s and 1920s. He stood in opposition to taking Anglo-Conformity and "melting pot" as the norms and ideals of American society, and recognized the value of each ethnic culture. In his view, like orchestral music performed by different music instruments, American culture was created by different peoples. Besides, he thought that as a republic country, the US was committed to protecting the rights and culture of all Americans, each ethnicity included. Hence, he suggested that the coexistence and mutual development of each ethnic group and their culture should be advocated. It is worth mentioning that, Cultural Pluralism does not support independence or self-determination, which is apt to incur the division of the American nation. The precondition of Cultural Pluralism lies in adherence to the American system. In other words, a nation's unity rests on cultural differences and political identification. However, Cultural Pluralism did not receive much acceptance until the rise of the Civil Rights Movement in the 1960s. At this particular moment, with the awareness of ethnic rights aroused, immigrants sought equal opportunities and representation in society. Meanwhile, immigrants still kept their languages and cultural practices after generations in America. Under such circumstances, "melting pot" was no longer applicable. Instead, Cultural Pluralism gained ground, becoming the guidance for American national cultural policy. Following the prevalence of Cultural Pluralism, the "salad bowl" metaphor was put into use in the 1970s, which compared America to a big salad bowl. In contrast with "melting pot" which lays emphasis on cultural assimilation and homogeneity, "salad bowl" stresses the integration of different cultures and the maintenance of distinct qualities of each culture. Like the juxtaposed ingredients in a salad bowl, each ethnic culture preserves its distinctive values, traditions, religions and ways of life instead of becoming one and the same. The metaphor is more widely known as "cultural mosaic" in Canada, which also features the diversity of cultures. With the growing diversity in the US, the "salad bowl" found general acceptance among the public, and was clothed in political correctness. Nevertheless, Cultural Pluralism and the "salad bowl" are not flawless. Though Cultural Pluralism delineates the peaceful coexistence of different cultures, it does not make clear the status of each culture. While underscoring separate identities of different cultures, "salad bowl" fails to show the cohesion of American national culture.

The 1980s saw the replacement of Cultural Pluralism with Multiculturalism. Arising out of the increasing number and changing demographic composition of immigrants in the post-WWII era, together with the rising awareness of the political rights of ethnic groups, Multiculturalism emphasizes political recognition and equal status of different cultures. Specifically speaking, it calls for the acknowledgement of equal values of different cultures, and the bestowal of equal political, economic and cultural status upon all cultures. In order to realize these goals, governments at all levels and social institutions ought to take an active part in removing barriers and discrimination. For instance, Multiculturalism supports bilingual education for ethnic groups and preferential treatment of minorities during employment. In addition, Multiculturalism is dedicated to deconstructing the discourse of mainstream culture and constructing the discourses of subcultures. For example, African American Studies, Asian American Studies, Hispanic Studies, Women's Studies, Gender Studies, Ethnic Studies, etc. have been set up in American colleges and universities. Hence, it challenges WASP-dominated culture, dissolves white supremacy and promotes the establishment of a democratic society. There are both positive and negative influences of Multiculturalism. On the positive side, it increases social tolerance, reduces social conflicts and enhances national cohesion. Besides, it protects the rights and interests of minority groups, and improves their political participation, employment and education. On the negative side, the over-emphasis on cultural differences is likely to cause and intensify conflicts, which further weakens national unity and identification. Moreover, while upholding equality and justice, it gives rise to new inequalities and undemocratic practices, creating new racial divisions. For instance, the preferential treatment for minorities in the field of employment and education is regarded as reverse discrimination against white people. Furthermore, it leads to radical ideas. For example, when American history is told, the historical status and role of ethnic minorities are overstated.

In response to the new situation of immigration and the strong momentum of multiculturalism, American conservatives and nationalists express deep concern over the future of American national identity and the unity of American society. A case in point is the publication of *Who Are We? The Challenges to America's National Identity* by American political scientist Samuel Huntington. In this book, He urged Americans to strengthen their identification with WASP-centered national identity. Apart from conservative and nationalist views, there have been a group of scholars who put American cultural realities in perspective. They put forward a compromise metaphor to illustrate American culture. In 1998, the metaphor "tapestry" was first used by American sociologist Mary Deegan in her book *The American Ritual Tapestry* to describe American culture. According to Deegan, "tapestry" was crafted by different rituals and thus formed the social fabric. Today, "tapestry" has been infused with rich connotations. Different from "salad bowl" which puts emphasis on the distinctiveness of each culture, "tapestry" not only stresses the individual thread, but also highlights the interwoven picture that the finished tapestry presents. According to the metaphor "tapestry," each culture is an invaluable and vital thread in the colorful tapestry, which portrays the unified image of America as a multi-ethnic and multi-cultural society. So far, it has been accepted with fewer disputes.

Taken together, Since Colonial America, the American national culture policy and the depiction of American culture have been changing over time. But during the process, one fact never changes: immigrants create America, and America reshapes immigrants.

Contemporary American Society and Culture

Essay Questions:

1. Trace the historical development of American immigration from colonial times to the present. Then examine the political, economic and cultural impacts of immigrants on American society.

2. There have been such metaphors as "melting pot," "salad bowl" and "tapestry" to depict America as a nation of immigrants. What's your understanding of the visions of the American national identity as embodied in these metaphors?

3. Some scholars claimed that the election of Barack Obama as America's first black president symbolized America's entry into "the post-racial era." Based on the historical experiences and current circumstances of African Americans, do you think "the post-racial era" is a myth or a reality?

4. What are your perceptions of the prospect of multi-culturalism in American society?

Unit 3　Political System and Government Mechanism

The United States is a federal republic in its system of government. It is essential to interpret the key principles of the US Constitution in order to understand the American political system and government mechanism. Two fundamental principles were embodied in the US Constitution: federalism and separation of powers.

1　American Federalism

The US Constitution divides governmental powers between the central, or national government and state governments, giving substantial functions to each. Both national and state governments derive power from a common source, the Constitution, and neither receives its power from the other. This constitutional distribution of powers cannot be changed by the ordinary process of legislation, for example, by an act of either a national or state legislature. Further, both levels of government operate through their own agents and exercise powers directly over individuals.

There is a clear distinction between a federal system and a confederation. Whereas the former has "coequal" governmental units, the latter doesn't. In a confederation, there are also two levels of government, national and state, but the states basically hold more powers than the national government. The national government of a confederacy is thus largely an entity of the states and derives its power from the states, which means that the national government in a confederation is weak. In a federal system, both levels of government have a direct relationship with the citizens. In a confederation, the national government might be able to operate directly, but usually it will reach the citizens through the various states, even on such important matters as levying taxes, recruiting an army, and so on. The United States had a confederate system under the Articles of Confederation before the US Constitution was made in the Philadelphia Convention in 1787. The framers of the Constitution assembled in Philadelphia to create a stronger national government within the framework of a federal system and with enough authority to meet the needs of all times.

1.1 The Constitutional Framework of American Federalism

The formal constitutional framework of the US federal system could be summarized as: the national government has only those powers, with the one important exception of foreign affairs, delegated to it by the Constitution. The states have all the powers not delegated to the national government except those denied to them by the Constitution. But within the scope of its operation, the national government is supreme.

The Constitution, chiefly in the first three articles, delegates legislative, executive, and judicial powers to the national government. Article 1 sets forth the *express powers* granted to Congress. These are spelled out in various sections, but most notably in Article 1, Section 8, where the Constitution specifically stipulates that "Congress shall have power to": "lay and collect taxes, borrow money, regulate commerce with foreign nations and among the several states, establish post offices, declare war, raise and support armies, provide and maintain a Navy". In Article 2, the Constitution states that "the executive power shall be vested in a President." and Article 3 stipulates that "judicial power" would be vested in the Supreme Court and other lower courts that Congress might subsequently establish. In the field of foreign affairs, the national government has *inherent powers* that do not depend on specific constitutional grants, the national government has the same authority in dealing with other nations as it would have if it were a unitary government.

Notably, Article 1, Section 8 lists seventeen specific things Congress can do.

Then comes the clause that states "[The Congress shall have power] to make all laws which shall be necessary and proper for carrying into execution the foregoing powers, and all powers vested by this Constitution in the Government of the United States, or any Department or Officer thereof." This has been referred to as "the elastic clause". Here lies the essential question of what constitutes "necessary and proper" legislation, which entails the *implied powers* of the national government. Indeed, there are some things the national government can do which are only implicitly stated in the Constitution. These implicitly stated implied powers of the national government have led to much debate in the history of American federalism.

One of the most famous examples of implied powers involved the express grant of power to Congress to lay and collect taxes and to borrow money on the credit of the national government. Yet the Constitution says nothing about whether this also meant that Congress had the power to establish a national bank. However, two years after the new Constitution was adopted, a national bank was chartered for twenty years. Alexander Hamilton, the nation's first secretary of the Treasury, was the main proponent of the institution. The national bank became a competitor of several large state banks, as state banks sought the privilege of serving as government depositories, and hoped to see their own bank notes circulate widely in place of those of the national bank. When the charter of the national bank came up for renewal in 1811, it was not approved by Congress and intense political resistance over political and economic concerns had gradually built up. When the war of 1812 between the United States and Great Britain broke out, there was no national bank to provide financial support, and this put a heavy strain on the state banking system. The state banks suspended specie payments, and their bank notes circulated at depreciated figures, varying in terms of institutions and the distance from the issuing banks. As the bank notes lost much of their value when moved from the vicinity of the issuing bank, the government could only transfer money from one section of the country to another at the expense of a high depreciation cost. Finally, a second national bank was established in 1816, but the opposition from the states persisted. The state of Maryland levied a tax of $15,000 per year against the Baltimore branch of the national bank. McCulloch, the cashier of the bank, refused to pay on the ground that a state could not tax an instrument of the national government. While Maryland sued on the ground that the Constitution did not expressly authorize Congress to establish a national bank, the national government defended the bank as a reasonable exercise of Congressional power under the elastic clause.

In *McCulloch v. Maryland*, the Supreme Court decided that the establishment of a national bank was, indeed, an act that came within the "necessary and proper" clause of the Constitution. A national bank, therefore, could be established under the implied powers of the Constitution. Having thus established the doctrine of implied powers, the Supreme Court set forth the doctrine of national supremacy. Article VI of the Constitution states: "This Constitution, and the Laws of the United States which shall be made in Pursuance thereof: and all Treaties made... under that Authority of the United States, shall be the supreme Law of the Land; and the Judges in every state shall be bound thereby; any Thing in the Constitution or Laws of any State to the Contrary notwithstanding." This clause is known as "the National Supremacy Clause." All officials, state as well as national, are bound by constitutional oath to support the Constitution. States may not use their reserved powers to frustrate national policies.

The Constitution reserves to the states all powers not granted to the national government, subject only to the limitations of the Constitution. There are many areas of activity that lie within state control. States run educational systems, have considerable power over criminal laws, health services, roads and highways, recreational lands, and levy taxes. States can charter corporations and regulate industries. Not all of these activities are under the exclusive control of states, though, in many cases their leeway to act is great. In practice, powers that are not by provision of the Constitution or by judicial interpretation given exclusively to the national government may be concurrently exercised by the states, as long as there is no conflict with national law. There are powers that both levels of government can exercise at the same time over the same subject, for instance, levy income tax or taxes on gasoline.

These simple statements about the *concurrent powers* of the states and the national government, however, conceal difficult questions: for instance, a state may levy a tax on the same item as the national government, but a state cannot by a tax "unduly burden" a function of the national government or interfere with the operation of national law or abridge the terms of a treaty of the United States. As regards whether a state tax is an "undue burden" on a national function, it is the Supreme Court that ultimately decides. The issues became even more complicated in the area of interstate commerce. For instance, as regards state regulations designed to guard the public health, or collect a fair share of taxes from those who use state facilities, if there is no clear congressional direction, the Supreme Court must decide whether such regulations are within the reserved powers of the state, whether they come into conflict with federal regulations, or whether they unduly burden interstate commerce.

1.2 The Growth of the National Government

The outline of the constitutional structure of federalism, in reality, oversimplifies the division of powers between national and state governments. The formal constitutional powers of the national government are essentially the same today as they were in 1789, but the ways in which the powers are applied have changed greatly over time. Overall, the development of a national economy and the nation's international involvement have contributed to expanded national government activities, creating new political relationships within the American federal system. The expansion of national government functions has rested on three major constitutional pillars: the war power, the power to regulate interstate and foreign commerce, and the power to tax and spend.

Regarding *war power*, the national government is responsible for protecting the nation from external aggression and, when necessary, waging war. The national government has the power to wage war and to do what is necessary and proper to wage it successfully, which calls for the government power to mobilize the nation's industry and to apply its scientific knowledge to the tasks of defense. Congressional authority also extends to all commerce that affects more than one state and to all those activities, whose control is necessary and proper to regulate interstate and foreign commerce. The *commerce clause*, which entails the production, buying, selling and transporting of goods, has profound constitutional implications. As there are few aspects of the national economy today that do not involve interstate commerce, the national government has been able to expand its power in regulating a wide range of human activities. In addition, as Congress has *the power to tax and spend*, by attaching conditions to federal grants, Congress may regulate what it cannot constitutionally directly control. Thus, by withholding or threatening to withhold federal funds, the national government can influence – or control – state operations and regulate individual conduct.

These constitutional powers have made possible a tremendous expansion of federal functions and the growth of the national government. WWII brought national regulation of wages, prices and employment, alongside national efforts to allocate resources, train manpower and support engineering and inventions. After the war, the national government helped veterans and inaugurated a vast system of support for university research to develop high-tech weaponry and national defense. And during peace times, the nation has maintained substantial military forces. Moreover, in a globalized world today, only the national government can supervise relations between an internationally organized industry and its thousands of employees organized in national unions. Big business, big agriculture, and big labor all added up to a big national government. The growth of a national economy, and the creation of a national transportation and communications network, have all contributed to the expansion of federal power.

Further, the increasing economic activity of the national government has given rise to increased federal involvement with the states and localities. Through the transfer of funds from the federal treasury, the states and localities receive grants for such activities as education, police and fire protection, infrastructure building, recreation, job training, community development, etc. This form of "fiscal federalism" has substantially impacted the theoretical structure of American federalism.

Unit 3 Political System and Government Mechanism

Today, different from the founding years of the American nation, restraints on federal power stem from constitutional provisions that protect civil liberties rather than from those relating to the powers of state governments. While the national government may regulate state affairs by attaching conditions to federal grants to states, states may also resist national regulations on the ground of protecting civil liberties. So despite the growth of federal power, states are vital and active governments backed by significant social forces including civil liberties Union, minority rights associations and lobbies. In reality, oftentimes, in the battles over the implementation of laws passed by Congress, the greater political power may be with state and local officials rather than with national government enforcers.

1.3 Interstate Relations: "Horizontal Federalism"

Relations between the national and state government are often referred to as "vertical federalism" while the relations among the states as defined by the US Constitution are referred to under the term "horizontal federalism." Article 4 of the Constitution contains three provisions relating directly to "horizontal federalism."

First, each state must give "full faith and credit" to the "public acts, records and Judicial proceedings of every other state." The *full faith and credit clause* is one of the most technical provisions of the Constitution. In general, it requires each state court to enforce civil judgments of other state courts and to accept their public records and acts as valid documents. As it does not require states to enforce criminal laws of other states, the clause applies especially to noncriminal judicial proceedings.

Second, each state must extend "all privileges and immunities" to citizens of other states that it extends to its own citizens, including the protection of laws, the right to engage in peaceful occupations, access to the courts, and freedom from discriminatory taxes. Further, a state may not withhold political rights from US citizens who move into the state by imposing unreasonable "durational residency" requirements.

Third, Article 4 provides for extradition. The Constitution stipulates that a state shall deliver to proper criminals who have fled from another state when requested to do so by the government of the state from which the criminals have fled. Congress has supplemented this constitutional provision for *extradition* by making the governor of the state to which fugitives have fled the responsible agent for returning them. The governor, however, can decide not to honor the demand for return if it appears the fugitive will not be treated fairly after being returned. Normally, extradition is handled in a routine fashion. Further, Congress has made it a federal crime for a felony to flee from one state to another for the purpose of avoiding prosecution and has ordered to hold the federal trial in the state from which the person has fled.

There is considerable contact and cooperation among the states, most of which result in "interstate compacts" whereby the states agree to work together on particular projects. Interstate compacts should be approved by Congress before becoming binding on all signatory states and may be used to establish interstate agencies and to solve joint problems.

1.4 Structure of State and Local Governments

Each state has a governor, who shares executive powers with other elected officials, such as the lieutenant governor, attorney general, and secretary of state. The governor has the responsibility for preparing the state budget, which must be approved by the state legislature. The governor also has the important power of veto and notably, in forty-one states, governors have the power of "item veto", which means that the governor can reject only a part of a bill, and approve the remainder. Today, some states provide four-year terms for the governor and others two-year terms. In some states, especially in the South, governors cannot succeed themselves; in others, they can serve no more than two terms consecutively.

Most state legislators in the state House of Representatives serve two-year terms and four-year terms in the state Senate. State legislatures have undergone changes in recent decades. With the increase of state business, state legislatures meet much more often than in the past and now the trend is toward annual sessions which can last up to six months, alongside possible special sessions called by the governor.

Unit 3 Political System and Government Mechanism

Each state has a court system with normally three levels of jurisdiction: the lower, district trial courts; the court of appeals or superior courts with varying titles, which hear cases brought from the lower courts; and the Supreme Court, the highest state court. In the 19th Century, most state judges were elected, and their terms vary two to four years. Today, most state court judges are appointed by the governor, which has been seen as a move to "depoliticize" the judiciary but also as one that raises questions of political partisanship in appointments.

States have complete control over the subdivisions within state borders, which consist of counties, cities, townships, villages, and towns. Each state has a legislature composed of elected representatives from local senatorial and assembly districts, who represent their localities in the state capitols. While the most visible local officials are the chief executive or mayors of the large cities, the officials of the other units also wield considerable power. Some mayors have powers to choose other executives, veto local bills, appoint minor officials, and prepare budgets, while some localities are managed by a local commission and a professional city manager, in which case the role of the mayor is mainly ceremonial. Some cities are granted what is called "home rule" by their states, which means that the cities have substantial authority over local matters. In addition to a state judicial system, virtually every local government has the power to operate a court system with jurisdiction over certain criminal and civil cases. In general, local governments serve as important units of direct contact with local residents in such matters as education, police and fire protection, housing, and other matters with a direct impact on day-to-day life.

2 Separation of Powers

In addition to the diffusion of power on the levels of national and state government, powers were also divided among the three separate branches of government – the executive, legislative and judicial branches. The framers of the US Constitution allocated constitutional authority to each of the three branches and each branch is given some role in the actions of the others. Thus, Congress enacts laws, but the president can veto them. The Supreme Court can declare laws passed by Congress and signed by the president unconstitutional, but the president appoints the justices with the Senate's approval. The president administers the laws, but appropriations of funds are legislated by Congress. The Senate and the House of Representatives have an absolute veto over each other in the enactment of a law, as bills must be approved by both houses. Further, not only does each branch have some authority over the actions of the others, but each is politically independent of the others. The president is popularly elected in the General Election. Senators are elected by voters in each state, and the members of the House by voters in their Congressional districts. Although federal judges and Supreme Court justices are appointed by the president with the consent of the Senate, they hold terms for life once in office. The framers also ensured that a majority of the voters could win control over only part of the government at one time. A popular majority might take control of the House in a non-presidential off-year election, but the president representing a previous popular majority would still have two years of office. Further, senators are elected for six-year terms, with only one-third being selected every two years. Such a system of "checks and balances" put a premium on political processes of bargaining and compromise. Different decision-makers would have to reach an agreement on the policies. A politics of consensus, therefore, would be perceived as necessary, at least among those involved in the political process.

2.1 Presidency

The Constitution states that president "shall take care that the laws be faithfully executed." As the chief executive, the president must preside over the executive branch, which includes a vast bureaucracy of civilian employees. The growth of the federal role in domestic and economic matters has enlarged presidential responsibilities and contributed to the expansion of the presidential establishment. As a result, the number of employees in the presidential entourage has grown steadily since the early 20th century. Today, the institutionalized Presidency is composed of two layers: the White House staff, and the Executive Office of the president.

The White House staff consists of a group of advisors including the press secretary, appointments secretary, counselor to the president, special assistant to the president, legislative liaison officer, and speech writers. All of these have assistants, deputy assistants, and secretarial support staff of their own. The president appoints these advisors personally and does not need Senate approval for the appointment. White House staff members engage in the entire range of activities for the president: gathering information, contacting and lobbying Congressmen, meeting the press, and soliciting advice from various sources.

The Executive Office is more formalized than the White House staff. It is organized into several units developed along specific policy lines: the Office of Management and Budget (OMB), the Council of Economic Advisers (CEA), the National Security Council (NSC), the Office of Science and Technology, the Council of Environmental Quality, Office of the Special Representative for Trade Negotiations, and Intelligence Oversight Board. Although the units are equally important, some are more in the limelight than others and the three most prominent are OMB, CEA and NSC. The OMB continues to be the central presidential staff agency as it prepares the final budget the president sends to Congress for enactment. The OMB must approve all department legislative proposals that call for spending money and each agency has to clear its policy recommendations to Congress through OMB first. The CEA consists of three professional economists, whose job is to keep the president informed of economic trends and to interpret the potential economic consequences of certain acts. The president's appointments of these economic advisers, which must be confirmed by the Senate, usually signal the policy orientation of his administration on economic matters. The NSC is composed of the president, the vice-president, and the secretaries of state and defense. The president may invite others, who have the requisite security clearance, to attend the meetings. The closest person to the president on a day-to-day basis in security matters is the National Security Adviser, whose job is to advise the president daily on important matters of military and international concern, and to help the president with long-term policy issues.

Section 2 of Article II of the Constitution reads that "The President shall be Commander in Chief of the Amy and the Navy of the United States, and of the militia of the several states when called into the actual service of the United States." As commander-in-chief, the president is the head of military personnel. In this role, the president must be constantly informed of sophisticated new weapons, size and deployment of military forces, and he must assess where and when to use those forces to protect national security. In fact, over two centuries of national expansion and recurrent crises have increased the military powers of the president beyond those specified by the Constitution. As the complexity of Congress's decision-making procedures, its size, and its constitutional tasks make it a more deliberative and divided organization than the Presidency, Congress has granted president-wide discretion in initiating foreign policies, for diplomacy requires quick action, and often delegates authority to the president when crises occur. Ever since the US's permanent involvement in international affairs after WWII, the president's function as commander-in-chief has become increasingly important.

As the chief diplomat, the president is the central focus of American foreign policy. Congressional leaders, reporters, concerned citizens, and foreign governments all look to him and his office for the policies, signals, and negotiations that pertain to international affairs. The president appoints and receives ambassadors, and he can take the very important step of recognizing or breaking off relations with another country, which are all presidential initiatives taken in the president's capacity as chief diplomat. Another means presidents use in foreign relations is the executive agreement, an arrangement that, unlike foreign treaties, does not require approval by the Senate. The use of executive agreements has grown substantially over the years as it allows the president to bypass the Senate and enter into formal agreements with a foreign nation. In general, presidents have more leeway in foreign and military affairs than in domestic matters, which is partly due to grants of authority stipulated by the

Constitution, and partly due to the character of diplomatic and military activity.

In addition, the Constitution gives the president certain specific functions and powers in the legislative process. He can, for instance, veto bills passed by the Congress. Congress can override a veto by a two-thirds vote of each house, though, this is seldom done in practice. Indeed, the president's signature is required, if the bill is to become law. If he doesn't sign the bill within ten days and Congress is still in session, the bill becomes law without his signature. Yet if Congress adjourns before the ten-day period expires, the bill dies. This is known as a "pocket veto". The president's role as the "initiator of legislation" is defined in the constitutional phrase: "He shall from time to time give to the Congress information of the State of the Union, and recommend to their consideration such measures as he shall judge necessary and expedient." The president uses the State of Union address to set forth what he believes are the nation's major issues, and he lists, in general terms, the subjects he wants Congress to address. This general outline is followed by a series of specific messages, proposals and drafts of bills later sent to Congress.

From the early 1930s to the mid-1970s, Congress passed about 500 federal statutes collectively giving a president extraordinary powers. Once a state of national emergency was declared, for instance, a president could seize property, organize and control the means of production, seize commodities, assign military forces abroad, declare martial law, and control all transportation and communications. Overall, presidential power is greater today than the earlier times, however, as the chief executive and priority setter, a president must share power with members of Congress and bureaucrats.

2.2 Congress

Article 1 of the Constitution outlined the structure, powers and responsibilities of Congress, giving it "all legislative powers herein granted." Among these powers are the power to spend and tax in order to "provide for the common defense and general welfare of the United States," the power to borrow money, the power to regulate commerce with foreign nations and among the states, the power to declare war, raise and support armies, the power to provide and maintain a navy, the power to establish post offices and post roads, and the power to set up the federal courts under the Supreme Court. Further, the Constitution gave Congress the right to "make all laws which shall be necessary and proper for carrying into execution" the powers set out. Some non-legislative functions were also granted, such as participating in the process of constitutional amendment and impeachment. Overall, Congress performs these important functions: representation, lawmaking, consensus-building, overseeing, policy clarification and legitimizing. Representation is expressing the diverse and sometimes conflicting views of the economic, social, racial, religious, and other interests making up society. Lawmaking is enacting acts to help solve substantive issues. Consensus-building is the bargaining process by which these interests are reconciled. Overseeing the bureaucracy means seeing that laws passed by Congress are faithfully carried out. Policy clarification, or "policy incubation," is the identification and publicizing of issues. Legitimizing is the formal ratifying of policies through proper channels.

Congress is a bicameral, two-chamber legislature, composed of the 435 people in the House of Representatives – plus three additional nonvoting delegates from Washington, D.C., the Virgin Islands, and Guam – and the 100 in the Senate. Basically, the organization of Congress is achieved through three mechanisms: political parties, formal leadership positions, and committees and subcommittees. Each chamber devises its own formal and informal rules for regulating these mechanisms and maintaining order.

Most members of Congress are affiliated with one of the two major political parties and only occasionally will an Independent be elected to Congress. When a new member is sworn in, he or she is assigned a seat on one side of the aisle or the other according to party affiliation. And he or she automatically becomes a member of the overall party *caucus* for Democrats in the House or party *conference* for Republicans in the House and Democrats and Republicans in the Senate. These broad party groups designate their formal leaders and assign their members to the Congressional committee. The two major political parties thus are the first and major means of organizing Congress.

The *speaker* is the presiding office in the House of Representatives. The speaker of the House, who is usually a member of substantial seniority of the majority party, is selected by the majority party and formally elected by the House. The routine powers of the speaker of the House include recognizing members who wish to speak, ruling on questions of parliamentary procedure, and appointing members to temporary committees and conference committees. In general, the speaker directs the business on the floor of the House. The speaker is assisted by a *majority floor leader*, who helps plan party strategy, confers with other party leaders, and tries to keep members of the party in line. The minority party elects a minority floor leader, who usually takes the office of the speaker when his or her party gains a majority in the House. Assisting each floor leader are the party *whips*. The whips serve as liaison between the House leadership of each party and other House members and their job is to corral support from their party members for certain measures.

The vice-president of the United States, by constitutional mandate, serves as the president of the Senate but has little influence as he or she can vote only in case of a tie and is seldom consulted when important decisions are made. The Senate also elects from among the majority party a president pro tempore, who is the official chairperson in the absence of the vice-president. The real Senate leadership, however, is lodged in the Senate majority leader, assisted by a small circle of whips of committee chairpersons. In consultation with the minority floor leader, the majority leader determines the agenda of the Senate and has much to say about committee assignments for members of the majority party.

The basic work of Congress is conducted in committees and the main struggle over legislation takes place in committees and especially in subcommittees. Each chamber has standing committees, 22 in the House and 15 in the Senate; and there are 149 subcommittees in the House and 100 in the Senate. In addition, there are 4 joint committees and 13 special or select committees. The standing committees focus on major areas of concern, such as appropriations, judiciary, international relations, government operations, finance, agriculture, and human resources. Subcommittees deal with more specialized subjects within the broad committee topics, such as the Senate subcommittee on welfare reform within the Senate Finance Committee, and the House subcommittee on Africa of the House International Relations Committee. In addition to committees and subcommittees, there are special-issue caucuses, which are based on issues, regions, ethnicity, and gender. These organizations are not as strong as the more formal Congressional committees and leadership, but they are an important aid to legislators. Caucuses have been developing rather rapidly over the last few decades and the newly established caucuses tend to be more single-issue oriented than the older ones. This indicates that legislators are becoming more issue-oriented, more specialized and that they feel the need for an organization beyond the broad committees and even subcommittees to work for their particular goals. Further, as an agreement between both houses must be reached before a bill could be passed, a conference committee, a special committee of members from each House, will be established to settle the differences if neither house will accept the other's bill. Both parties are represented in the committee, with the majority party having more members. The proceedings of the conference committees are usually an elaborate bargaining process, as conference committees integrate the houses, help resolve disputes, and make compromises.

Since the 1930s, the pressure of a decade-long economic depression, WWII, the Korean War, the Vietnam War, periodic recessions, as well as the struggle for equal rights by racial and gender minorities, have given rise to a strong executive leadership of the Presidency. Further, the growth of the American nation into a world power since the 1930s has called for increased presidential activism. Although Congress did not enter into a complete eclipse, it hardly resembled the Congress of the 19th century. The presidential conduct during the Vietnam War and the corruption of Watergate in the early 1970s, however, aroused public concern about the alleged too-powerful

Presidency and the role of Congress. The growing public support for Congress had in turn given Congress the opportunity to reclaim its policy-making powers. In 1973, in the highly charged atmosphere of the widespread discontent over the Vietnam War, Congress passed the *War Powers Act* to limit the president's power to commit military forces to combat without Congressional consent. In 1974, the *Budget and Impoundment Control Act* was passed, which sought to give Congress greater resources in dealing with the budget and also restricted the president's power to impound funds appropriated by Congress. In addition to these acts, Congress has taken steps to curb presidential action in regard to emergencies as well as in connection with intelligence-gathering activities. In 1976, Congress passed the *National Emergency Act*, stating that an emergency declared by the president ends in one ear unless Congress is advised otherwise by the president. Furthermore, when the president declares an emergency, he must inform Congress of the specific laws under which he intends to act. Nevertheless, while there has been a new posture in Congress toward the executive leader, the chief policy-initiator role of the president will not be substantially altered. Still, it is significant that Congress has increased its activity in a number of areas to become involved in the governing process.

2.3 Judiciary

Article 3 of the Constitution establishes the existence of the highest court in the land – the United States Supreme Court. Congress is given the power to set up other "inferior" courts, i.e., lower courts, which it has done from time to time. Basically, there are three levels of federal courts in the national judiciary. The Supreme Court is at the top, consisting of nine justices serving for life, who are chosen by the president and approved by the Senate. On the next level are the courts of appeal, which are the most important judicial policymakers. The United States is divided into thirteen judicial circuits, with Washington, D.C. counting as one. Each has a court of appeals consisting of from four to twenty-three permanent circuit judges. Circuit judges are appointed for life by the president with the consent of the Senate. The United States courts of appeals have only appellate jurisdiction. They review the decisions of the district courts within their circuit and also some of the actions of the independent regulatory agencies. Each court of appeals normally utilizes planes of three judges to hear cases and less than 1 percent of the cases from these courts are scrutinized by the Supreme Court. Then there is the level of federal district courts with ninety-four districts in the fifty states, Washington, D.C., and Puerto Rico. District courts are trial courts of original jurisdiction. Although a few kinds of district court decisions may be appealed directly to the Supreme Court, most decisions must first be appealed to a court of appeals. In fact, most district court decisions are not appealed and for those that are, the court of appeals is generally the court of last resort.

In addition to the complex structure of federal courts, each of the fifty states maintains a complete judicial system of its own. The two court systems are related, but they do not exist in a superior-inferior relationship. The Supreme Court is the only federal court that may review state court decisions and it may do so only under special conditions.

The president also has the authority to appoint, with the consent of the Senate, the United States attorney for each federal district court along with several assistant US attorneys. These officers serve four-year terms as the government's lawyers by prosecuting and defending cases. The attorney general is the highest law enforcement officer in the country and head of the Justice Department. The primary function of the office is to decide which cases to prosecute when there is evidence of a violation of federal law. The deputy attorney general is the top assistant in the Justice Department. The solicitor general in Washington, D.C. is another important position in the federal judicial system, as the third highest job in the Department of Justice behind the attorney general and the deputy attorney general. This officer, appointed by the president with Senate approval, functions as the national government's top lawyer, deciding what cases to argue on behalf of the United States before the Supreme Court.

Article 3 of the US Constitution states: "The judicial Power shall extend to all Cases, in Law and Equity, arising under this Constitution, the Laws of the United

States, and Treaties made, or which shall be made, under their Authority," and Article 6 states: "This Constitution, and the laws of the United States which shall be made in pursuance thereof; and all treaties made, or which shall be made, under the authority of the United States, shall be the supreme law of the land; and the judges in every state shall be bound thereby, anything in the Constitution or laws of any State to the contrary notwithstanding." From this language, the Court has interpreted its right to exercise "judicial review," i.e., in the process of deciding a case or controversy, the Court can declare a law unconstitutional if the Court believes the law to be at variance with the Constitution. The matter of judicial review received its most forceful affirmation from Chief Justice John Marshall in 1803 in *Marbury v. Madison*. This was the first time in the country's history that the Supreme Court declared a provision of a Congressional act unconstitutional. To this day, constitutional authorities still debate Marshall's ruling, though, the debate is really academic, as judicial review has been firmly established in the American political system.

On the other hand, the Supreme Court has developed four important rules for exercising judicial review. These rules, which were cogently stated in 1936 by Associate Justice Louis D. Brandeis in a concurring opinion, are intended to exercise "judicial self-restraint": First, the Supreme Court will not anticipate a question of the constitutionality of a law; the question must be necessary to decide the case. Second, the constitutional ruling will be stated as narrowly as possible, confining itself to the precise facts of the case before the court. Third, if the case can be decided on grounds other than by ruling on the constitutionality of a law, those other grounds will be used. Fourth, the Court will take almost extra pains to construe a law in such a way as to avoid ruling it unconstitutional. The opposite of judicial self-restraint, however, is known as "judicial activism." In practice, some judges do not hesitate to involve the Court in a range of issues others might feel are beyond the purview of the judiciary. A court with "judicial activism" will thus constantly find itself involved in making decisions that border on policy-making.

There have always been critics of judicial activism, especially among those who do not embrace the decisions the judges are making. Critics contend that even if courts make the "right" decisions, it is not right for courts to take over the legislative responsibilities of the popularly elected representatives. Moreover, the contention is that as partisanship and ideology are important factors in the selection of federal judges at all levels, the judges' judicial attitudes and views might be affected by certain partisan policy preferences. Despite the criticism of an activist judiciary, it is important to note that the Supreme Court and the entire judicial system must derive support from the other branches and the general public, as the Court can only deliver opinions, and it has neither its own mechanisms for enforcing decisions nor the capacity to raise its own funds to operate. Ultimately, a continuing question of importance to the judiciary is the reconciliation of the role of the judges as independent and fair dispensers of justice for the political parties before them, with their vital role as interpreters of the Constitution.

Essay Questions:

1. What are the defining features of American federalism? And how is federalism represented in the American political system?
2. What might be the problems arising from the American federalism? Give examples to illustrate your point.
3. Does the Constitutional separation of powers between the president and Congress create an inefficient system in view of partisan politics and political polarization?
4. What's your perception of the criticism of "judicial activism"?

Unit 4 Political Parties and Electoral Politics

American political mechanism is characterized by two-party politics. The present party system in the United States, which consists of the Democratic Party and the Republican Party as two major parties, has roughly undergone three phases of development in American history: the first phase with Federalists and Democratic-Republicans as two major parties from 1790 through 1816, the second with Democrats vs. Whigs from 1828 through 1854, and the third with Democrats vs. Republicans from 1854 to the present.

1 The Development of the American Party System

In fact, the party system was by no means contemplated at the founding of the nation. George Washington, Alexander Hamilton, James Madison, Thomas Jefferson – none of these influential political figures were much concerned about a structured party system. Nevertheless, a two-party system evolved largely out of practical necessity for policy-making. As the first administration under George Washington had to build a kind of coalition among factions, Treasury Secretary Alexander Hamilton built an informal Federalist "team." In 1790, Hamilton developed a set of proposals about economic growth, which appealed to commercial and manufacturing interests. Secretary of State Jefferson and other officials disagreed with Hamilton's inclination toward a strong national government and favored an agrarian society of small farmers with minimum central government control. In the early years of the American republic, the Federalists dominated the government, and they began to reach out into the states to enlist people supporting their cause. Jeffersonians also set out to establish their own political network known as Jeffersonian Republicans or Democratic-Republicans. With Jefferson's election in 1800, a two-party structure was largely in place. The Democratic-Republicans were so successful that by the end of the second decade of the 19th century, with the election of James Monroe in 1816, the Federalists had faded as a party during the long period of Republican dominance. Historians have referred to this period with one-sided Republican victories as "the era of good feelings."

This "era of good feelings" for the Democratic-Republicans, however, lasted no more than a decade. By the 1824 presidential election, the party had broken into quarreling factions with John Quincy Adams leading one group and Andrew Jackson, a frontiersman and military hero, leading another. The ensuing political contention of the two groups reveals sectional conflicts. Northern interests favored protective tariffs, a US bank, and policies helpful to a growing industrial society. The South was opposed to the tariffs, which, southerners believe would hurt agricultural production. The newly developing West, however, wanted internal improvements and fewer governmental controls. After Andrew Jackson won the presidency in 1828, two distinct parties emerged: the Democrats and the Whigs, which developed as an opposition to Jacksonian democrats. Whigs took the name to imply that they were opposing "King Andrew," much as the Whigs during the Revolution had opposed King George III. The Whig was a mixture of slave owners and abolitionists, industrialists and farmers, who, despite their differences on many issues, were united in their common resentment of Jackson. The party Jackson and his colleagues organized is considered the direct forerunner of the present-day Democratic party, making it the oldest political party in the US history. By the time Van Buren succeeded Jackson in the White House in 1837, the Democrats had become a large, nationwide movement with national and state leadership, a clear party doctrine, and a grassroots organization. The 1830s and 1840s saw the flowering of the party system. Whigs and Democrats competed strenuously, reaching out for supporters and helping broaden the franchise by gradually lifting property qualification on voting. They developed the national convention, party platforms, and strong party leadership in the Houses. Still, the Whigs never achieved as broad and durable a coalition as the Democrats and neither party was strong enough to cope with the mounting sectional conflicts over the issue of slavery in the mid-19th century.

In 1854, the Republican Party, which consisted of antislavery forces, some Whigs, and some members of the minor parties, was founded and ultimately became known as the "Grand Old Party." The newly founded Republicans represented northern and western industrial interests and became identified as the party to save the Union. The Democrats, associated with the South and pro-slavery, were supported by the Southern planters and slave owners. As the party of the Union, the Republicans won the support not only of financiers, industrialists, and merchants but also of large numbers of white and newly freed black male workers and farmers. For fifty years after 1860, when Abraham Lincoln won the presidency, this Republican coalition won every presidential race, except for Grover Cleveland's victories in 1884 and 1892. The Democrats were unable to build a durable winning coalition until 1932, when the Democrats and Franklin D. Roosevelt, in the midst of the Great Depression, fashioned a new electoral coalition that won the presidency. Roosevelt put together a "grand coalition" of farm-labor-southern alliance with unemployed middle-class persons and racial minorities. This coalition led to the reelection of Roosevelt three times and brought presidential victories to the Democrats for two decades. From that point to the present, the two parties have seesawed back and forth in presidential elections. Today, as in the past, the two major parties will frequently attempt to bring within their fold diverse groups and individuals with ideological and policy differences in the interest of putting together a winning coalition.

2 American Party System: Key Features and Party Structure

The American party system is essentially two-party politics. There are a number of small, minor parties, which are often referred to as "third parties," though most of the time on both national and state levels, only two parties makes difference. Two-party politics is largely decided by the nature of the electoral system. Congressional districts have a single incumbent, and the candidate that carries the most votes wins. As only one candidate can win in the single-member district, the largest and second-largest parties will always dominate the elections. The House of Representatives is composed of 435 seats representing 435 separate Congressional districts, and to win the district seat, the candidate only needs to win a plurality of votes, not a majority. The same rule applies to the one hundred Senate seats with two from each state. In addition, the system of presidential election operates in this way on a national scale, further reinforcing the two-party dominance.

As political parties tend to be structured around elections and officeholders, the character of the parties will be affected by the character of the government positions they seek to control. With the federal system setting up elections and offices on a national-state-local basis, parties are organized in a similar way. Given the decentralized structural characteristics of federalism and separation of powers, the major parties are also decentralized and fragmented. One party, for instance, can be in the majority in Congress, but not control the Presidency, likewise, the Republicans can control some state legislatures and the Democrats others. This fragmentation is further represented in the varying constituencies at different levels of government: A senator serves an entire state and is electorally accountable to it while a representative serves a Congressional district. The presidential election runs in all states. Depending on the positions sought, politicians must appeal to different sets of voters, which decentralizes the party system. Therefore, rather than national parties, America has "nationwide parties", parties that are located in every state under the same banner of Democratic and Republicans.

In both major parties, the supreme authority is the national convention, which convenes every four years to nominate candidates for president and vice-president, ratify the party platform, and elect officers and adopt rules. Delegates to the convention perform these functions. In practice, however, the national convention has limited power, as the delegates have no ongoing functions after the convention adjourns and many key decisions have been made ahead of time. The convention usually ratifies the presidential candidate already chosen in the presidential primaries and caucuses during the preceding months.

The national committee is more directly in charge of the national party. The national party committee is composed of one woman and one man from each state, from Washington, D.C., Puerto Rico, the Virgin Islands, and certain territories. Each party has included state chairpersons, governors, members of Congress on the committee as well. The national committee members are chosen in various ways: election in primaries, state conventions, or by the state committees. Committee members meet once or twice a year and the normal meeting agenda is concerned with party rules and preparing for the next national convention. The national committee also chooses the national chairperson. In reality, the national chairperson is the choice of the president. If the party does not control the Presidency, the national committee will make the selection and the presidential nominee is given the courtesy of designating the chairperson at the close of the convention. The main job of the national committee chairperson is to manage the presidential campaign. As the chairperson is expected to take the lead in reconciling conflicting interests as a party unifier, he or she should not be too closely identified with one party faction or another. There are, in addition, three national vice-chairpersons, who are normally representatives from certain prominent segments of the party: labor, women, racial groups, and geographical regions. It is the national chairperson, backed by the president, that gives the party certain unity and direction when the party is in power. Whereas, when a party loses a presidential race, it often has no central leadership as the defeated presidential nominee usually has little power over the party.

The state committees are at the next lower level, which are similar to the national committees but are filled by members chosen locally. Most state committees are dominated by governors, senators, or coalitions of strong local leaders. In some states, the chairperson can be an important figure. The state chairperson often works very closely with county chairpersons throughout the state, which provides him or her with ample opportunity to get to know the political needs of each county and to satisfy those needs on a bargaining basis. Below the state committees are district and county committees, which are composed of representatives from the towns and cities and vary tremendously in functions and powers. In a few places, the local committees do countless favors for constituents, but most are small and inactive except during the few weeks before election day.

3 Minor Parties

As the two major parties seek to carve out wide middle-ground positions to bring into the fold many different groups, there is often some room left for the development of minor parties. Minor parties have basically taken three forms. One type breaks away from one of the major parties as the faction leaders usually fail to get their programs adopted within the major party. As a result, the faction left the parent party and established its own party structure. Among such secessionist minor parties are the Progressive "Bull-Moose" party of 1912, which broke away from the Republicans and the Dixiecrat that broke with the Democrats in 1948. One of the serious problems faced by this type of minor party is that it is neither likely to build the extensive nationwide voting apparatus that the parent party has, nor has enough patronage base to attract and hold party workers. It is thus unlikely that they will survive very long. The second type of minor party starts on its own as it normally takes social and economic positions that cannot be accommodated by either of the major parties. There are several small labor and socialist parties on the left and conservative parties on the right. Their programs are usually stated in doctrinaire terms, and they are not willing to compromise with the two major parties. They run their own candidates, but will not likely have the financial resources to run candidates at each level of government. The third type of minor party arises over a particular issue and dies as the issue is resolved or fades away. Several such third parties, such as the Free Soilers, rose and fell before the Civil War. The Progressive parties of Theodore Roosevelt in 1912 and Robert La Follette in 1924 challenged corporate monopoly and the political power of big business. George Wallace's American Independent Party (AIP) won about 13 million votes in 1968 over desegregation and other race issues but was evidently fading even before Wallace was badly wounded in an assassination attempt in 1972.

Minor parties have had a significant indirect influence. They have often drawn public attention to controversial issues the major parties wish to evade. And they have organized special interests and serve as "party-pressure groups" by pressuring the major parties and policy-makers. Whereas, minor parties have never won the presidency or more than a handful of Congressional seats and have never shaped national policy from inside the government. Overall, their influence on the platforms of the two major parties and the policy-making has been limited.

4 Congressional Elections

Every two years members of the House of representatives and one-third of the Senators stand for reelection. In general, there is a relative lack of competitiveness in congressional elections, as defined by the closeness of the vote between the two major parties. The lack of competition is largely due to the strength of incumbency. An incumbent House representative or a Senator can use the powers and privileges of office to raise campaign funds, particularly from interest groups whose positions they favor, and maintain the support of the constituency. Further, for the House election, as those House representatives in office serve the day-to-day needs of their constituents, often in ways quite detached from national politics, incumbent officeholders are often viewed favorably by those they represent. The favorable impressions, combined with the considerable electoral assets an incumbent House representative can amass, often make it difficult to unseat incumbents. As a result, a high percentage of representatives running for reelection retain office and likewise, incumbency weighs heavily in Senate elections. Candidates for the Senate, however, are far more visible than those for the House and they find it more important to take positions on national issues.

On the other hand, presidential performance also affects both House and Senate elections. Even in mid-term elections, some presidential candidates affect voter's attitudes in ways that help determine who wins congressional races, which is known as the "coattail effect." To a considerable degree, the votes cast in congressional elections seem to be a judgment or referendum on the performance of the president. Compared to the previous on-year election, the ruling party's share of the nationwide congressional vote almost invariably declines in the mid-term elections, though, the magnitude of that loss is substantially smaller if the president has a high level of popular approval.

5 Presidential Elections

There are three stages in presidential elections: primaries or caucuses, national convention, and the General Election campaign.

State presidential primaries are the main methods of choosing delegates to national conventions. Presidential primaries serve as "the popular contest" in which voters indicate their choice for president, usually from a list of candidates on a ballot, and the results of this vote are used to select the actual delegates to the national convention. There are presently two main systems of allocating delegates. First, in the proportional representation of voters' presidential preference, delegates are allocated on the basis of the votes won by the candidates in the popular contest. This system has been in use in most of the states. The second system is the winner-take-all policy, i.e., the winner of the presidential preference vote wins all the delegates in that state or district. Presently, only the Republicans have this policy while the Democrats banned it in 1976. Most primaries are closed primaries, i.e., only those citizens who have preregistered as members of a particular party may vote in that party's primary. Some states have a semi-closed primary system, which requires the voters to declare their party affiliation when they go to vote. There are also open primaries, whereby any voter can vote in any primary without declaring a party membership. The open primary of one party thus has the risk of being "raided" by members of another. For instance, registered Republicans can take part in the Democratic primary and possibly, vote for a weaker candidate to run against the Republicans later in the General Election. For this reason, some people feel the open primary is not a good way to hold the party system accountable. The increase in the number of presidential primaries has put considerable strain on potential nominees. They start early, having lecture tours across the country, making appearances in primary states and trying to get local media coverage. New Hampshire, for instance, is the lead-off state in February primaries, and carefully guards that role since being first gives the state special political prominence. All eyes are on the lead-off state to get some hints about who is the "front-runner" and shows surprising strength. Leading candidates thus tend to concentrate on the contest in the lead-off states, giving these states significant influence. States in turn have moved their primary dates to early in the process in order to get increased attention to their contests. As a result, the entire nominating process becomes "front-loaded".

Some states use a caucus and convention system rather than primaries for choosing delegates. In principle, the caucus-convention system is far simpler than the primary. Delegates to national conventions are chosen by delegates to state or district conventions, who are chosen in earlier county and precinct caucuses or at other local meetings. The selection process thus starts with precinct meetings open to all party members, who discuss and take positions on issues and elect delegates to the next higher caucus. This process is repeated at higher levels until delegates to the national convention are chosen. There are many varieties of the caucus-convention system, as they are regulated by different state parties and legislatures. For over half a century, Iowa caucuses in February have opened the official nominating season, followed by other state caucuses in the ensuing sixth months.

Since the 1980s, some states have banned together to hold their primaries and caucuses on the same day – normally the first Tuesday of March, which is known as

"Super Tuesday" – to maximize their influence. As many of the Super Tuesday states have small populations and few delegates, by holding their contests on the same day, they can have a greater effect collectively on selecting the presidential nominee. In addition, as many Super Tuesday states are in the South, they often have similar concerns on national issues. Super Tuesday states play a big role in choosing each party's standard-bearer and also serve to narrow the field of contenders. A number of candidates who perform poorly in Super Tuesday contests can be expected to drop out of the race, either because they see a slim chance of winning, or because they will find it more difficult to raise campaign funds or attract media coverage thereafter.

The second stage is the national convention. For the presidential nominee, the objective of the national convention is to win a straight majority of votes of delegates. The makeup of the state delegations is thus a key factor. Each party convention represents the states roughly in proportion to the number of voters in the state, but there is a bonus for states where the party is especially strong. The two major parties have often revised their rules for dividing the votes among the states in an attempt to satisfy both criteria.

An important function the convention delegates perform is to adopt a party platform, which is a statement of achievements, goals, and general policies that the party publicizes to the electorate. It is, above all, a campaign document to appeal to as many elements of the voting public as possible. Whereas, as the platform invariably leans toward those groups making up the party's core support, it may identify the party's most influential factions. For instance, the southern delegates walked out of the 1948 Democratic convention and formed a third party as the platform included a plank for black civil rights. On the other hand, political candidates sometimes use the platform to highlight how they differ from their opponents.

Over the years, the choice of the vice-presidential nominee has become increasingly important. Almost no one actually runs for the vice-presidential nomination, as the just-elected presidential nominee dictates the choice of a running mate. After the presidential and vice-presidential candidates deliver their acceptance speeches to the delegates, the presidential nominee may choose a new party chair, who usually serves as the presidential campaign manager. Then the candidate spends the final days of the summer planning campaign strategy and gearing the party for action. By early fall the presidential race for the General Election is on.

Throughout the presidential campaign, there is always the need to work on the image of the candidate – how he or she appears and sounds in the mass media, and on TV in particular. In the past few decades, presidential TV debates have enlivened the campaigns and become the focus of public attention. During three successive TV debating sessions in the election year, voters have a chance to see the candidates debating issues of public concern. The candidates respond to a wide range of questions from panelists, and they were given brief opportunities to respond to each other's answers. The format is more like a dual press conference than a debate, though, the viewers are able to see how each candidate reacted to intense pressure. After each debating session, there will be media comments on which candidate scored the most points, often followed by public opinion polls of the approval rating of candidates.

6 Electoral College System: Mechanics and Concerns

After presidential candidates have campaigned for months, the voters cast their ballots on – or ahead of, in some states – the General Election day, i.e., the first Tuesday in November. When US citizens vote for president and vice-president every election year, although ballots show the names of the presidential and vice presidential candidates, voters are technically electing a slate of "electors" that represent them in each state. The electors from every state combine to form the Electoral College. The Electoral College was established in Article II, Section I, of the United States Constitution, and was later modified by the 12th and 23rd Amendments, which clarified the process. Under the Electoral College system, each state is allocated a number of electors equal to the number of its US senators (always two) plus the number of its US House representatives (according to the size of each state's population as determined in the national census). Each political party with a candidate on the ballot designates its own set of electors for each state, usually at the state party conventions, matching the number of electors they appoint with the number of electoral votes allotted to the state. Electors are typically strong and loyal supporters of their political party, but can never be a US senator or representative. After the election, the party that wins the most votes in a state appoints all of the electors for that state. This is known as a "winner-take-all" policy, which became the norm across the nation by the 1830s, with the only exceptions of Maine and Nebraska currently. The electors for each state are required to cast their votes in mid-December, after which the votes are sent to the president of the Senate. The electors cast individual votes on separate ballots for president and vice-president, which has become important in several elections where electors voted for candidates other than those they were pledged to. On January 6 following the election year, the president of the US senate opens all of the sealed envelopes containing the electoral votes and reads them aloud. To be elected as president or vice-president, a candidate must have an absolute majority, i.e., 270 electoral votes for that position. If no presidential candidate obtains a majority of the electoral votes, the decision is deferred to the US Congress. The House of Representatives selects the president, choosing among the top three candidates, and the Senate selects the vice-president, choosing between the top two candidates. In the House selection, each state gets only one vote and an absolute majority of the states, i.e., 26, is required to elect the president. If a majority is not reached for president within the House by January 20, the day the president and vice-president are sworn in, the elected vice-president serves as president until the House can make a decision. If the vice-president has not been elected either, the sitting speaker of the House serves as acting president until Congress can make a decision. If a president has been selected but no vice-president has been selected by January 20, the president then appoints the vice-president, pending approval by Congress.

In effect, the Electoral College was a compromise adopted by the Founding Fathers, as some wanted the president elected directly, while others preferred selection by Congress. The Electoral College allowed for the election of a president who has the support of the national electorate. However, if several candidates split the national vote and no candidate gets the majority vote, the election is sent to the legislature. There are other factors in the adoption of the system as well. For one thing, in the 18th century, the Electoral College allowed the compromise between the slave states in the South and the free states in the North to be carried over into the election of the president. Southern slave states had no intention of allowing their slaves, who are counted as 3/5 a person, to vote in federal elections, however, they wanted the slave population to count towards representation to avoid domination from the North. Creating an electoral system that was based not on individual votes but on congressional representation thus gave the South an expanded role in choosing the president. For another, many of the founders were also concerned that poor communications technology in the 18th century would make it difficult for Americans to know enough about candidates from different regions of the country to make informed electoral choices. In this case, the founders assumed that under the national popular election, voters of most states would vote for their favorite sons, thus by dividing the national electorate between a number of candidates, none of the candidates would be able to approach a majority of the popular vote.

There have been some concerns with the Electoral College. First, the Electoral College gives disproportionate voting power to the states, favoring the smaller states with more electoral votes per person. By dividing the population by electoral votes, states with smaller populations have an "elector" for much fewer people than states with larger populations, which means that each electoral vote in smaller states carries more weight. The original intention of this system is that small states were given additional power to prevent politicians from only focusing on issues which affect the larger states. The concern was that without this additional power, politicians would often ignore small states and only focus on big population states. Whereas, in practice, with the winner-take-all method of distributing electoral votes under the Electoral College system, some states are still excluded from the campaign, which is not necessarily the small states, but rather the states that are not viewed as competitive. Since states allocate their votes in a winner-take-all method, a candidate often lacks incentives to campaign in a state that clearly favors one candidate. As an example, Democratic candidates have little incentive to spend time in solidly Republican states, and conversely, Republican candidates have little incentive to campaign in solidly Democratic states, rather, both parties will naturally focus on those swing states as "battleground states." Further, the winner-take-all rule often results in lower voter turnout in states where one party is dominant, as each individual vote will be overwhelmed by the majority and will not count in effect if the winner takes all the electoral votes. Second, there's a risk of "faithless electors." Presently, in 21 states, electors are not obligated by law to vote for the candidate for whom they were selected. Even in the 29 states where electors are obligated by law or pledge, they can often still vote against their party without being replaced. Some states issue only minimal fines as punishment. Other states instigate criminal charges varying from a simple misdemeanor to a 4th-degree felony. In fact, since the founding of the Electoral College, 157 electors have not cast their votes for the candidates they were designated to represent. Third, if no candidate receives a majority of the electoral votes, the presidential vote is deferred to the House of Representatives and the vice presidential vote is deferred to the Senate, which could easily result in a purely partisan battle. If the Senate and the House of Representatives have divided party control, they would naturally select members of opposing parties for the presidency and vice presidency. This potential opposition in the presidential office would not be good for the stability of the country or the government. The focal point of controversy around the Electoral College, however, has been the possibility of electing a "minority president" with the winner-take-all policy, i.e., the presidency can be won without winning the popular vote. This has happened 5 times since the founding of the Electoral College, in 1824, 1876, 1888, 2000 and most recently in 2016. In every one of these elections, more than half of the voters voted against the candidate who was elected.

    With the concerns of the Electoral College, a number of alternatives have been proposed to the Electoral College system. The most obvious alternative would be to switch to a system of direct election of the president, by counting the votes cast nationwide. Others claim that the best alternative would be a system in which the slight advantage to the small states by awarding them electors for their two Senators would be maintained but the electoral votes should be awarded proportionally to reflect the popular vote in the state rather than a winner-take-all policy.

In practice, numerous variations of each of these alternatives have been proposed. Whereas, even if consensus could be reached, political realities argue against a shift to direct election. Some small states would resist change. Despite the small number of electoral votes in total in these small states, closely contested small states in close elections often receive much more attention than they otherwise would. State representatives want to keep the small advantage they have. More importantly, with the winner-take-all policy, minor parties could hardly secure a win in states. Overall, the allocation of electoral votes is in line with the state representation in Congress, as an embodiment of the federal system of government. While reformers will continue to agitate over the Electoral College system, it is unlikely that any significant change is on the horizon.

Essay Questions:
1. What are the historical development of the two major parties in the US?
2. What are the key features of the US party system? What are the shaping factors of a decentralized party structure?
3. How does the Electoral College system work? What are the main concerns with the system?
4. In what sense does the Electoral College system of the American General Election constitute the basis of the two-party political system and the federal system of government? How do you perceive the alternatives to the Electoral College and the prospect of such reform proposals?

Unit 5   Technology and Industry

The United States has the largest economy in the world. According to the statistics of the International Monetary Fund (IMF), its overall gross national product (GDP) in the year 2019 is $21.427 trillion (calculated by purchasing power parity (PPP) method), around 1.5 times as much as the GDP of China, the second largest economy. Also, it ranks eighth in the world in terms of per capita GDP (PPP method calculation). It is almost universally recognized by the world as the technologically most advanced country, owning many hubs of research and development for cutting-edge technologies such as the world-famous silicon valley, and ranking first of the globe in total amounts of venture capital and research funding. It parallels China as the world's largest trading nation and ranks the third largest manufacturer in the world economy, although the total number of labor force employed in manufacturing has been on a continuous decline since late 1990s.

 The US Economy: An Overview

After the end of the Cold War in 1991, the United States experienced a long-term prosperity propelled by a high-level growth rate due to the upgrading and wide applications of information and communication technologies (ICT). The average GDP growth is 3.4% during the period from 1990 to 2000, and 2.5% in the years from 2001 to 2007, which is relatively high in the developed world. However, the subprime credit crisis of 2007 – 2008 expanded into a worldwide financial storm unexpectedly that imploded both the US economy and the whole globe. Continuous bankruptcies and closedowns of major investment banks and other financial firms formed a domino effect that destroyed many firms and sectors, creating a large-scale disruption that paralleled the Great Depression of 1929 – 1933. Therefore, the continuous negative growth and decline during 2008 and 2009 was named "the Great Recession." From late 2010 all the way to 2019, the US economy gradually regained its momentum and performed better than most of the western advanced economies. The IMF statistics revealed in late 2016 that the US GDP's share in the world total was increased by a fraction of 1.26% from 2008 to 2015, while all the other countries of the G-7, namely, Canada, the United Kingdom, France, Germany, Italy, and Japan got their GDP shares decreased in the total GDP of the whole globe. Furthermore, the US has been leading the latest round of development of new technologies in the past decade, in the fields of artificial intelligence (AI), quantum computing, digital platforms of big data analysis, and new branches of ICT. As a result, the European Union and its major member states such as Germany and France, are now shocked by and imploring for the dramatically widened US-Europe gap of productivity and technological progress.

Nevertheless, the COVID-19 pandemic has brought a huge blow to the US economy since late February and early March of 2020. The latest data from the Bureau of Economic Analysis of the US Department of Commerce indicates that the US GDP shrank by 5% in the 1st quarter and by a phenomenal 31.4% in the 2nd quarter of the year 2020. Personal incomes are also in slumps, while the unemployment rate has been kept at a high level since the beginning of 2020. This pandemic has put havoc on the overall ecology of business operations and social lives. The real effect of this disruption has not been fully revealed as the situation of the pandemic is still fluctuating and developing forward.

Rising rapidly in the second half of the 19th century and dominating the world economy since then, the US economy is viewed as a structural factor that has been shaping and may continue to shape the grand trends of the globe. In fact, this economy is not only unique for its sheer size and fast changes, but also characterized by several features that are unparalleled in the world:

First, high-speed technological development is integrated with dynamic business through a powerful financial sector. Britain is the first industrialized country in human history. It built an industrialized economy around the 1820s with its industrial production mechanized by applications of large-scale machineries and steam engines. Its technologies were absorbed by the United States very rapidly and American entrepreneurs created their own industrial productions through a process of adapting and upgrading these British technologies. Based on this process, from the 1840s on, Americans began to invent new technologies by themselves and created a momentum to establish a complex industrial production and transport system that was no less efficient than the British one. Amazed at the rapidity of learning and renovating in the US industry, the British termed the dynamics of US economy of the US "the American System." Ever since the 1840s till now, this "American System" had led almost every wave of surging of high and new technologies in the world, including the widespread application of electricity and oil in the early 20th century, the invention of semiconductors and aerospace equipment in the 1950s – 1960s, the phenomenal progress of ICT led by the "internet boom," and the current development of AI and big data platform.

Thanks to its highly developed finance sector and a culture of advocating business adventure in unchartered new industries, ingenious scientists and engineers from all over the world have immigrated to the United States and formed close relations with bold investors through a variety of institutionalized financial links, such as "initial public offering" (IPO) mechanism of traditional stock exchanges and private equity funds that inject venture capital into highly risky projects of research and development. The unparalleled strengths and liveliness of the US financial sector have always provided a powerful force that not only pushes forward the imperative of technological innovations but also integrates them with business and turns them into profits.

Second, the US government plays an important role in shaping and promoting its technological development and economic growth. Although the US private sector driven by market demands is a fundamental engine for technological and industrial upgrading, the public sector, in other words, the government, is also an outstanding player that shapes the path dependency of US technological development as well as the evolution of its industrial and economic structure. Traced back to the time of Alexander Hamilton in the late 18th century, this newly-born republic on the Atlantic coast was already practicing a kind of "national security capitalism," which means government deliberately nurtured the establishment of domestic manufacturing industries, particularly textile and arms productions, through subsidies and protective tariffs. Throughout the whole 19th century and the first half of the 20th century, protectionism was normalcy. The 1828 *Abominations Act* uplifted US average tariff to a record level of 61.7%. From the 1870s all the way to the 1920s, in pace with its development into the largest industrial economy of the world, the US not only continued its protectionism, which was embodied in the "tariff policy complex" of the Republican Party, but also deliberately input a large quantity of fiscal resources into railway-related industrial sectors. Without governmental support, it is unimaginable that the transcontinental railways and related heavy and chemical industries could expand at such a high speed. After the Second World War, it is the "Defense Advanced Research Projects Agency" (DARPA), an institution funded and supported by the military, that shaped the technological path of the US semiconductor industry as well as the strategic directions of its ICT sector. Integrated with market demands and private entrepreneurs' drive for profits, governmental policy is an indispensable catalyst of technological innovations.

Third, the resilience of the US economy is maintained through a constant change of its comparative advantages and the speculative volatility of its financial sector. Starting from a relatively small agrarian economy on the Atlantic coast and expanding outward to more and more virgin lands of this new continent, the US has always restlessly adapted itself to internal and external changes brought by continuous immigration, technological innovations, and territorial expansions. In pursuit of more incomes, wages, and profits, millions of pioneering farmers and workers and adventurous businessmen converged their desires into a powerful strength that determined the US comparative advantages and disadvantages. From colonial time to Gilded Age, the abundance of natural resources formed the basic comparative advantage of the US while the scarcity of manpower and capital was the disadvantage. Therefore, American entrepreneurs tended to adopt large sets of labor-saving large machinery more easily and invested better-quality raw materials into industrial productions, compared to their British counterparts. This unique situation laid the foundation for its industrialization and nurtured its leading role in the inventions related to electricity and the automobile during the period of the 1870s – 1890s. Since the 1920s capital became increasingly more abundant and began to be viewed as a comparative advantage by economists. After the Second World War and particularly since the 1960s, the capacity of technological innovations and entrepreneurship entered the list of US comparative advantages and since then have been regarded as its core competitiveness, while labor is still a disadvantage, not for its scarcity, but for its relatively high cost. The new circumstances outlined the US path towards a service-sector-dominated post-industrial economy.

Also, the US economy has been repeatedly molded and remolded by financial crises, because the volatility created from financial speculations has become an inherent nature of its culture and social life. When the US gained its independence from Britain in the 1780s, the financial sector that was represented by an embryonic stock market under a buttonwood tree of Wall Street, which later developed into the world-famous New York Stock Exchange, already took a definite position in the US economy. The fevers of waves after waves of new settlers for making quick money turned the financial sector into the beating heart of the business, simultaneously pumping endless money into the real economy and manufacturing bubbles that would inevitably burst. Since the 1792 Panic, major financial crises, followed by recessions, unemployment, and bankruptcies, appeared almost every 20 – 40 years before the Second World War and almost 10 – 20 years after it. However, financial crises are also viewed as a herald for "creative destruction," a term coined by the Austrian economist Joseph Schumpeter to describe the replacement of obsolete machineries and technologies by new ones through economic cycles, because the clear-out of old and inefficient enterprises would make room for newer and more competent businesses, and the resources of old industries that suffered exponentially decreasing profit rates could be moved to new sectors that may contribute to the core international competitiveness of the US. In this sense, the volatility of the US financial sector is part of its dynamics of pushing technology and economy forward.

2 The Shift of Leading Technologies and Industries

Leading technologies refer to cutting-edge technologies that may bring a dramatic transformation of the whole economy by creating the highest level of efficiency and the fastest speed of growth of profit rate for businesses, while leading industries are those that are based on and structured by these new advanced technologies. When the newly born United States signed a peace treaty with Britain in Paris in 1783, it was an agrarian society with over 80% of its population bound to cropland. Nearly 110 years later, the net value of the output of manufacturing industries surpassed agriculture for the first time in the US in 1890. Almost another 100 years later, in 1979, the US became the first post-industrial advanced economy of the world because the share of net added value of its service sector to the total GDP reached the level of 70% while the manufacturing industries shrank to the second position. All these thorough and phenomenon changes were initiated by the leading technologies and pushed forward by leading industries, time and again. Therefore, it is meaningful to draw a big picture of the evolutionary path of the leading technologies and industries.

2.1 Labor-Saving Technologies and Industries, the 1770s – 1860s

The original 13 colonies on the Atlantic coast, which formed the earliest United States, were all agricultural societies with underdeveloped industries. However, as British colonies were always highly commercialized and intricately connected to the world markets and especially the European market, commerce and foreign trade were prosperous on the North American coast. Stimulated by continuously increased demands from overseas markets, the manufacturing industries were also initiated in the northeastern states, which were called "New England" at that time. From the 1770s to the 1820s, the manufacturing productions were operated by family-run craft-shops and mills that were driven by water power. In 1791, the US treasury secretary Alexander Hamilton delivered to Congress a report on manufactures, which was a landmark historical record of the beginning stage of US industries. According to an estimate in this document, 2/3 or 4/5 of US clothing was made by household businesses.

The transfer of British industrial technologies and the widespread of large factories transformed the northeastern and mid-Atlantic states of the United States. Thanks to the close cultural, ethnic, and business connections to Britain, those technologies to mechanize labor-intensive manufacturing industries and related energy supply, invented in Britain during the "first industrial revolution" in the late 18th century and early 19th century, were all transferred to the United States quickly during the period of 1790s – 1820s. As early as 1789, a young mechanic named Samuel Slater built the first water-driven mechanized spinning mill in Rhode Island after he had worked in England's textile firm for over 10 years. Since then, the globally-advanced British technologies were all brought to the east coast of the United States and became widespread in the New England area. In the hand of skillful American technicians and entrepreneurs, these British-originated technologies were adapted and even reinvented to become more labor-saving, because of the labor scarcity on the new continent at that time. As the US federal government was deliberately constructing a "national security capitalism" and input a substantial amount of fiscal resources to subsidize textile and arms production, the labor-saving technologies connected to textile and energy-supply, such as mechanized spinning loom, steam engine, and locomotive, were especially welcome in the US and became the leading technologies, while textile and arms-making became the leading industries.

The introductions, renovations, and spread of these advanced technologies and industries also transformed the organizational forms of production and business operations. Family mills were replaced by factories in New England during the 1810s – 1820s. Benefiting from the abundance of land and other natural resources, the American factory systems were much larger in size and more complex in structure than their British counterparts. Also, American engineers and businessmen invented two American-style techniques for organizing production: standardized interchangeable parts and a continuous flowing process for assembly lines. When these two techniques became common norms of the gigantic and complex factories in the US, they formed an industrial superiority over Britain within less than two decades. The British were impressed and amazed by the US industrial achievements when they saw its exhibition at the Crystal Palace Exposition of 1851, and started to summarize the US industrial operational model as "the American System."

2.2 Nationwide Industrialization, the 1820s – 1910s

During the 1870s, the expanding network of trans-continental railways and the integration of western states into the unified national market of the US provided a new momentum for sustained economic growth. New demands, new markets, and new resources formed a potent stimulus to the industrial capital in New England and the five great lakes area. Fast transport of cargo through railways and quick transmission of messages through telegraph wires lowered the cost of long-distance connections between various sites of production and sales, thus expanding the scale of mass production in manufacturing industries. All these changes accelerated the technological developments and gathered the new technological and industrial imperative that was later termed "the second industrial revolution" by historians.

While the majority of new technologies of the first industrial revolution were invented by British engineers and technicians in labor-intensive industries such as textile during the 1750s – 1820s, those of the second industrial revolution were almost exclusively developed in the United States, in capital and technology-intensive industries such as iron and steel, non-ferrous metal, metalworking machinery, machine tools, new energy sources, and automobile. From the 1890s on, machine tools began to be applied in a more automatic and speedy way due to the introduction of electricity, and the machine tool industry became the hub for nurturing and diffusing new techniques and skills. In the early 1900s, the invention of the combustion diesel engine catalyzed the birth of the automobile industry, and in turn added enormous momentum to the expansion of the oil industry. Electricity and diesel engine gradually replaced steam engine as the major source of power to drive machines, locomotives, and vehicles. High-quality steels cast though the more automatic machineries were widely applied in construction and propped up a new kind of building that changed the skylines of New York, San Francisco and other major cities: the skyscrapers.

Moreover, as mass production became the normalcy of the US manufacturing industries, new management techniques for organizing industrial productions also appeared. Developed from interchangeable parts and a continuous flowing process, a set of rigorous procedures, regarded as "scientific management methods", was created to standardize every move of various production processes in workshops and put all the moves together to establish more efficient flowing lines and optimum quota of production for each worker, based on a meticulous cost-benefit calculation. Because this set of procedures was originally summarized by Frederick Taylor, they are also termed as "Taylorism" and were widely applied in big factories with a complex of flowing lines, such as the Ford Corporation.

All in all, the US achieved nationwide industrialization during this period. Before the 1880s, agriculture still produced the largest share of the net value of output and income in the total GDP and national income of the U.S. In 1890, for the first time in history, manufacturing industries produced more income and output than agriculture. In the year 1900, the annual value of the output of manufacturing industries was twice as much as that of agriculture. In 1910, the US became the largest industrialized economy in the world, its manufacturing industries produced a total output twice as much as that of Germany, the second-largest industrial power. And in 1913, the total output of US manufacturing industries accounted for 1/3 of the world's total.

2.3 The Standardized Mass Production and the Dominance of Consumerism and Fordism, the 1920s – 1970s

During the 1870s – 1890s, there was already a trend that industrial and financial capital and labor were increasingly concentrated into a few monopolistic firms, due to the law of economy of scale and the relentless desires of businessmen for higher profit rates. Through complex measures of merges and acquisitions, different forms of large corporations that were capable of monopolizing over the majority of the production process of a whole industry appeared, such as trust and holding companies. Originally there were horizontal mergers that combined rival firms producing identical or similar products, and the archetype was the Standard Oil Company operated by John D. Rockefeller. Then during the first decade of the 20th century, more and more vertical mergers appeared, which means a single firm controlled most or all of the stages and links of a complete production process of an industry. Economist historian Alfred Chandler argued that only in those industries in which continuous flow line technologies could be effectively applied was it meaningful and profitable to establish vertical merger, which is called "the Chandler Thesis." The archetype of this kind of merger was the steel company run by Andrew Carnegie. The concentration of capital in a few large firms laid the foundation for mass production and consumption in the 1920s – 1960s.

During the "Golden Decade of Prosperity" of the 1920s, these industrial giants developed forward even further, as "Taylorism" was enforced widely in industries. Although the Great Depression and the Second World War brought huge disruptions to the American manufacturing industries, the tremendous productive capacity of US industries recovered and further expanded in the 1950s and 1960s, until it was dealt a fatal blow in the early 1970s owing to the collapse of the Bretton Woods system and the energy crisis. Ever since the 1920s, the unparalleled and unprecedented manufacturing power of the US was upgraded and strengthened by two factors, one cultural and the other one technical: consumerism and Fordism.

Consumerism refers to an ideology that believes in the goodness of continuously increasing mass production to deal with the complexity and volatility of consumer demands. It emphasizes that demands from consumers should be viewed as the supremacy of both private businesses and the government's policy-making in the economy. Therefore, it advocates relentless upgrading of the efficiency of mass production in large-scaled monopolistic firms and encourages short-term consumption of common people. To increase consumption, it also argues for the key role of the market and puts stress on the business resilience structured by marketing techniques and intangible assets such as brands, in contrast to the production-prioritized Stalinism. Based on this ideology, ever since the 1920s, the US developed a consumerist culture connected to market fundamentalism, vastly different from the Stalinist culture that worshiped heavy industries and tangible industrial products.

Stimulated and promoted by consumerism, Fordism formed in the US in the 1920s. Henry Ford, the founder of the Ford Corporation coined this term to express his ideas for running his gigantic automobile corporation and dealing with the market, consumers, and society at large. Fordism advocates for a flow-line-based mass production system that involves technically complex combinations of synchronization, precision, and specialization, with the purpose of producing cheap and sturdy consumer goods at high speed, to dominate the market. The Ford Model T car was the most typical example of this kind of production. Also, Fordism argued for decent wages and welfare for all manual workers so that common people can keep their capacities for mass consumption, which was a direct echo of consumerism. Combined together, consumerism and Fordism offered cultural, ideological, and technical supports to the sustained development of mass production and economic prosperity in the US during the 1920s and 1950s – 1960s.

2.4 The ICT Technologies and the Rise of Silicon Valley

The development of information and communication technologies started at the end of the Second World War, when the first modern computer was built in 1946 at the University of Pennsylvania. During the 1950s – 1960s, not only the electronic computing facilities were continuously invented, improved, and upgraded, the original integrated circuits were also created due to the breakthroughs in semiconductors, particularly technological advances in metal-oxide-silicon semiconductor device fabrication. In pace with the growth of market demands, firms producing integrated circuits have been consistently upgrading the functions and performance of their products, managing to manufacture new circuits increasingly smaller in size and more and more powerful in performance. In 1965, Gordon Moore, the director of research and development of the Fairchild Semiconductor Company raised the idea that the number of components of transistors on an integrated circuit would be increased by a factor of two every year while the costs would be reduced in proportion. This is the famous Moore's Law. Although it is not a rigorously calculated rule, it turned out to be something like a self-fulfilling prophecy. The ICT-related industries and sectors have indeed developed forward at roughly this rate of growth.

ICT technologies drastically transformed the landscape of the US economy, especially after the energy crisis of 1971 – 1973. The soaring of the fuel price dragged the U.S. economy into a trap of "stagflation", which means a combination of economic stagnancy and inflation that pulled the economy and society to a sticky point. As a result, traditional industries of mass production had to handle this hard time of rising costs uplifted by sustained inflation and decreased revenue caused by stagnancy. Dissatisfied with consistentl slumps in profit rates in these traditional industries, American investors turned to look for investment opportunities in more knowledge-intensive industries and sectors that might cost far less than mass productions of traditional manufacturing industries but still bring high-profit rates. They became more and more interested in ICT industries and firms, particularly those that produced integrated circuits, computer hardwires and software and those that specialized in related research and development.

Right at the same time when the energy crisis rocked traditional manufacturing industries, the financial sector in the US was also getting through a transformation, because the investment banking system was regrouped at that time and new forms of investment for highly risky projects of new and high technology development, such as hedge funds, venture capital, and private equity firm, emerged and began to inject enormous resources into ICT research and development. It was no coincidence that "Silicon Valley," an area near San Francisco Bay where ICT-related research and development institutes and business firms producing computer hardware, software, and components are now concentrated, stood out as a global center for ICT-related innovations in the early 1970s. Ever since then, well-educated and ingenious students and scholars of science and engineering majors from all over the world have been swarming into this area in pursuit of careers and fortunes. Since the 1970s, two more turning points have made ICT-related industries even more prominent and strategic in the US economy. One is the early 1990s, when the internet commenced to work as the foremost means for American firms to get information and transmit messages. The other one is the several years since 2010, as artificial intelligence became more mature and began to be applied to digital platforms such as social media. In pace with this progress, the ecology of the US corporate world has also experienced a series of changes. Taking the place of traditional giant corporations of mass production like GM or GE, or traditional investment banks, new upstart enterprises in the ICT-related fields, such as Microsoft, Apple, and Google, has become the centers of fortune and power at the present.

3 The Industrial Hollowing and the Industrial Structure

Industrial hollowing has become an outstanding and ever-lasting trend in the evolution of the US economy for almost four decades, ever since the beginning of the 1970s, and has transformed not only its overall economic structure, but also its social relations and the constellations of its political forces in a very dramatic way. It is safe to say that one can never have a deep understanding of the rise of American populism in the last decade without establishing a full picture of the industrial hollowing in the US.

3.1 The Energy Crisis of the Early 1970s

A steady and sustained operation of the manufacturing sector always needs continuous inputs of raw materials and fuel, which had been pretty normal before the 1970s. According to US official statistics, the total output of production reached an unprecedented peak in the late 1960s. However, the third Middle East War broke out in 1973 as the Arab-Israel conflict re-intensified. At that time, Israel was a strategic ally of the United States because it played a pivot role in the resistance to Soviet influence in that region. In order to protest the US military and political support to Israel and to tip the balance of war toward the Arab side, members of the Organization of Arab Petroleum Exporting Countries (OAPEC), a branch of the Organization of Petroleum Exporting Countries (OPEC), declared an embargo of oil toward the U.S. and some other western countries in October 1973, which lasted until March 1974. This embargo created a ripple effect to the whole industrialized world as it drastically uplifted the price of crude oil and in turn increased all the prices of fuel and raw materials along the supply chains of industrial production. In 1979, the Iranian Revolution created a second wave of energy crisis. The regime change in Iran in that year disrupted the overall oil production of the world and forced the oil price to rise. These two energy crises brought destructive impacts on the US economy and made the entire 1970s a "lost decade" for the United States. Repeated ups and downs of oil prices inevitably pulled the US economy, and particularly its industrial production, into roller-coaster-style instability. The price of fuel soared, the production cost became unpredictable, and the whole manufacturing sector was irreversibly harmed. Recessions and unemployment became widespread.

3.2 The Decline of Traditional Heavy Industries

Just in pace with these energy crises, the competition from West European and Japanese manufacturers turned out to be ever more intensive in the world market. On the car market, German companies such as Volkswagen and Japanese car-makers such as Toyota, Honda, and Nissan grew into formidable rivals of American automotive companies, and forcefully encroached upon market shares that had originally belonged to American companies. In 1970, the UK, France, and West Germany jointly founded the Airbus Industrie GIE consortium, a multinational airliner manufacturer. In the following years, it developed into a strong competitor against the American aviation industry. Also, the "four Asian tigers" were vigorously taking away the world market for labor-intensive products such as textiles and apparel.

The continuously rising production cost triggered by energy crises and the ever more fierce international competition from America's rivals who enjoyed some advantages that were not owned by US businesses, such as cheap and plentiful labor force, or more agile and resilient economic structure, forced American manufacturers to adapt themselves to these heavy pressures. From the early 1970s, American factory owners gradually moved their production lines, workshops, or even the whole of their businesses to other countries where the production cost might be lower. Also, outsourcing became a normal practice for American businessmen as they may purchase their supply from abroad at a much lower price. In this way, the 40-year-long "Industrial Hollowing-out" began in the United States. For example, in the early 1970s, the mayor of Camden, a once prosperous industrial city in New Jersey, described his city's industrial district as "a rat-infested skeleton of yesterday, a visible obscenity of urban decay." In the mid 1970s, Hugh Carey, then governor of New York, already noted the draining of governmental fiscal income because of the moving-away of industrial production.

If the 1970s witnessed a tremendous decline in American labor-intensive industries that produced consumer goods of low-profit rate, the 1980s became a period when American heavy and chemical industries started to be pulled into a long-term trap of decline and hollowing-out. In the 1980s, economic globalization gained momentum because of the acceleration of the European integration process, and China's initiation of reform and opening. Under such circumstances, outsourcing and move-away of the manufacturing sector came to be even more serious. From 1977 to 1987, in Youngstown of Ohio, a traditional smokestack city specialized in the steel industry, over 50 thousand jobs were lost, and business bankruptcies spread out like wildfire. Following the close-down of steel plants, community institutions, including families, churches, and even the city government itself, collapsed.

3.3 The Accelerated Industrial Hollowing from the 1990s

In the 1990s, this trend of de-industrialization was pushed forward even further at a higher speed. In 1995, the World Trade Organization was established and the rule of trade liberalization was enshrined by the political establishments of the west as a panacea for carrying forward economic growth. This situational change caused an enormous flooding of foreign products into the domestic market of the United States and dealt an especially fatal blow to American manufacturing sectors. Those cities in the eastern and southern Great Lakes area, which had specialized in the production of heavy and chemical industries, had to struggle with nightmare-like conditions, suffering population loss, draining-away of tax revenue, rising poverty rates, high rates of unemployment and crime, widespread drug abuse and domestic violence, and swelling welfare rolls. Therefore, "the Rust Belt" came into shape in the eastern Great Lakes area. In the Rust Belt, large-scaled manufacturing plants were demolished or abandoned, and those industrial communities, which had fairly flourished in the past, changed into ghost towns. This trend of decline, dilapidation, and deprivation extended to the first two decades of the 21st century. Almost all the major cities in this area experienced serious population loss. For example, from 1970 to 2006, Cleveland, Detroit, Buffalo, and Pittsburgh lost about 45% of their population.

3.4 The Transformed Industrial Structure

Actually, in pace with the development of de-industrialization and the shaping of "the Rust Belt," the economic structure of the United States has also been transformed dramatically. Before World War II, the US was an industrial power with a tremendous capacity for manufacturing industrial goods as well as consumer goods. Its capacity of heavy and chemical industry was particularly prominent and it was this capacity that it was honored as the "Arsenal of Democracy" that contributed to the victory of allies against the Fascist countries. The 1950s and 1960s witnessed another grand expansion of its industrial production and at the end of the 1960s, its industrial capacity reached the peak. Since the 1970s, due to the industrial hollowing-out, the manufacturing sector has accounted for a less and less share of its total output and GDP. At the end of the 1970s, the service sectors already surpassed 70% of its total GDP while the agricultural and manufacturing sectors combined took only less than 30%. In the year 2019, the net output of agriculture was only 0.8% of the total GDP of the US while manufacturing accounted for 11%.

Nevertheless, the new and high-tech parts of manufacturing have been retained in the US and the absolute volume of its manufacturing capacity is still astonishingly large. The 2014 data shows that its total manufacturing output in 2013 was still larger than those of Germany, France, India, and Brazil combined, reaching the level of 2.4 trillion US dollars. Airplane production is the largest portion of its manufacturing. Ever since 2011, the manufacturing sector has still taken a share of 18% of the world's total.

4 The Evolution of US Industrial Policy

Ever since the independence of the United States from the colonial rule of Great Britain in 1783, its political elites and many of its businessmen advocated for a strong government intervention in its industry and economy for the purpose of protecting its infant manufacturing sectors from the more competitive imports of European countries, particularly from Britain, which was already an industrial power at that time and would soon complet 1st industrial revolution. Since then, industrial policy has always been an important part of the US official economy policy and has always been playing an outstanding role in its economy, shaping the path of its technological innovation, industrial structuring, and overall economic development. Through the form of government subsidy, tax exemption, protective tariffs, public and military procurement contracts, and government funding for research and development in selected sectors and industries, industrial policy has been employed as an effective and forceful tool by American political elites to upgrade US capacity of producing high-quality civilian and military equipments and facilities with cutting-edge technologies. Although industrial policy has been regarded as anti-market, counter-productive, and inefficient by neo-liberalist economists since the late 1990s and retreated from mainstream economics textbooks, it has always occupied a position in the toolkit of the US top-level policy-makers. It is for this reason that the United States government is termed "the developmental state in disguise." Therefore, the US industrial policy deserves special attention when one is studying technologies and industries in the US.

4.1 The Hidden Developmental State of the US in History

In 1791, just 8 years after the formal independence of the United States, Alexander Hamilton, the first secretary of the US treasury, worked out the first official document of industrial policy in the US history: the *Report on the Subject of Manufactures*. He argued in this document that without government support to domestic manufacturing sectors, not only was it impossible for the newly-born United States to fully develop its economic potential on this new continent, but its material base for building up a strong military to protect itself would be seriously damaged. Therefore he advocated for strong protective tariffs and government subsidies for the purpose of promoting the development of textile and arms-making, the two most important industries in his view. During the 19th century, the US maintained a very high level of tariffs, to protect its infant industries of textile, machinery, iron and steel, ship-building, and other heavy and chemical industries. By 1820, the average tariff level had already reached 40%. In 1828, the US Congress passed the *Tariff of Abominations Act*, uplifting the average tariffs to 61.7%. In addition to protective tariffs, Abraham Lincoln pushed forward private investment in railroad construction in the 1860s through government loans at favored interest rates. The Civil War also nurtured government procurements that injected enormous resources into private businesses of military-related industries. During Franklin Roosevelt's time in the 1930s, "special measures" were employed by his administration to revive the US economy from the havoc of the Great Depression, including government investment in public projects of infrastructures, public procurements, and relaxation of antitrust measures.

4.2 The Military-Industrial Complex

After World War II, the Cold War brought a new wave of industrial policy that adapted the US to the unprecedented tension with the Soviet Union in the strategic competition for developing new and high-tech industries at that time, such as aerospace, airplane production, nuclear energy, and computing, and telecommunication. During the Cold War years, government funding, particularly funding and intervention from the military, became an important source of support to industrialists of the private sector in their efforts to establish a capacity of developing cutting-edge technologies and producing advanced equipments. Through this continuous support, military leadership and industrialists coordinated with each other and formed an especially close relationship, which was termed as "Military-Industrial Complex." From the late 1950s all the way to the 1990s, the Defense Advanced Research Projects Agency (DARPA) of the US Defense Ministry funded military-related research intensively, igniting the sparks of all the most frontier technologies in the latest technological revolutions, particularly in the field of telecommunications and aerospace. In this sense, military and government support have never been absent from the continuous evolution of the US technology and industry.

Essay Questions:

1. Why does the economy of the United States enjoy a financial sector that is much more powerful than Japan and European continental economies? What is the driving force that helps to create the trend of financialization in its economy?
2. When did the industrial hollowing begin and why? What changes in the world economy and international economic competitions accelerated this process?

3. The 1970s has been regarded as "the lost decade" in the US economic history. What are the major crises during this period that contributed to the recession of the US economy during this decade, and how?
4. Why is the United States termed as a "hidden developmental state" by some economists and historians?
5. Why is the rise of populism attributed to the industrial hollowing and "the Rust Belt"?

Unit 6　Trade and Investment

　　Even before the independence, the 13 British colonies along the Atlantic coast already got deeply involved in the international trade of the mid-18th century, which was expanding and flourishing due to the commercialization of European-controlled colonies and was supported by the then-prevalent ideology of mercantilism. Therefore, outward trade and investment have been engrained into the inner mentality of American people as a more efficient way to generate wealth than autarky. On its full independence in 1783, the newly-born United States was very eager to establish its own network of foreign trade. Particularly, attracted by the vast potential of the trading market in China, an American sailing ship named "Chinese Empress" started out from Boston and arrived in Canton (now Guangzhou), the regional capital of South China and the only port opened to the west at that time. The foreign trade of the US increased continuously in pace with its industrialization during the long 19th century and early 20th century as it grew into the largest industrial power in the world. After World War II, as the Bretton Woods System of international finance kept the exchange rates stabilized for over 20 years and mitigated the monetary risks of the trade, the US foreign trade grew forward and prospered for almost two decades. However, impacted by the collapse of the Bretton Woods System and the two energy crises in the early 1970s, the industrial hollowing-out occurred and spread. This change turned its merchandise trade from a surplus into a deficit. 1975 was the last year in which the US merchandise trade had a net surplus. Since then, the US merchandise trade has stayed in a permanent deficit for over 45 years, which has inflated irreversibly. This process of deficit inflation became more accelerated since the mid-1990s, as the Soviet bloc disintegrated and the seemingly unstoppable marching of globalization was widely regarded as a zeitgeist of that time.

This trend has created two effects. On the one hand, with the faster move-out of labor and resource-intensive manufacturing sectors since mid-1990s, the US has come to concentrate on very risky high-tech sectors that demand huge amounts of pre-investment and very long processes of intensive research & development. The idea of knowledge economy has been gradually substantialized. The US has established its advantage on cutting-edge technology and specialized knowledge in many professional fields, and enjoyed a substantial surplus on service trade since the mid-1980s. In other words, its trade has been structurally transformed into a "post-industrial" and "post-modern" system. However, on the other hand, trade issues turn out to be increasingly politicized since the late 1990s as the multilateral trade system led by the World Trade Organization came into effect in 1995. Workers and small businessmen of grassroots society were more and more exasperated at the flooding-in of cheap foreign goods, which, according to WTO rules, should enjoy free entry into America's domestic markets, while at the same time, large corporations and venture capitalists have taken away the lion's share of the net wealth created by the globe-wide liberalization of trade. Trade politics has developed into a very acute and controversial arena.

A diversity of interest groups are fiercely competing against each other in this arena. Those interest groups in support of protectionism and those in advocacy of free trade doctrine are fighting against each other almost permanently, which is been frequently interpreted by the media and academics as a confrontational dichotomy of winners vs. losers of globalization. The Seattle Riot of 1999, a landmark incident showing grassroots indignation toward the elites and revealing the emerging of American populism in the post-Cold War era, revealed the inherently conflicting nature of globalization and persistent endogenous instability of the US-founded multilateral trading system. Since 1999, populism has been emerging from these groups and now occupies an unneglectable force in US politics. It is widely agreed by both economists and political scientists that American trade politics determines not only trade policy but also the long-term path and pace of its macro-economy.

On the other hand, as service sectors have replaced manufacturing as the dominating force driving the US foreign trade, finance, one of the service sectors that used to be developing in parallel with manufacturing, is gaining more weight and enjoying more advantages in the US economy. Supported and accelerated by the globalization that integrates the US finance sector with other economies at an unprecedented pace, more and more foreign investors, including both foreign private institutional investors and sovereign wealth funds controlled by foreign governments, have been pouring their money into the financial assets inside the US, with a hope to reap the benefits provided by its dynamic technological innovations and matured financial markets. Therefore, there has occurred a trend of net capital inflow into the US In pace with this development of the more domineering role of finance and banking in the US economy and the continuous decline of manufacturing in both GDP and merchandise trade, financialization has become an inevitable trend that has not only transformed the US economic structure and its foreign economic relations, but also brought prosperity as well as volatility and chaos to the world economy. In other words, financialization in the US economy has made both its own economy and the economy of the whole world tremendously more complicated and unpredictable.

1 The Trade

The US enjoyed a substantial surplus of trade in goods for almost 20 years since the end of the Second World War. The Bretton Woods System of the 1950s and 1960s established a very stable international financial infrastructure that almost eliminated the risk brought by the volatility of the exchange rate. The industrial goods produced by US manufacturing was gladly accepted by its allies in West Europe and Asia-Pacific region because of the unrivaled technological edges and cost advantages that the US enjoyed at that time. Nevertheless, this tranquil "golden age" was unexpectedly disrupted and overturned in the late 1960s and early 1970s. The Vietnam War, the collapse of the Bretton Woods System, and the repeated energy crises all contributed to this sudden destruction of the old order. At the same time, US manufacturing began to decline unavoidably as German and Japanese firms gained more technological edges in some traditional capital and technology-intensive sectors such as automotive and electronics.

1.1 The Deficit of Merchandise Trade

Since 1970, the stable surplus of merchandise trade was replaced by fluctuations between deficits and surplus for five years. The year 1975 was the last year in which the US enjoyed a surplus in its trade of goods. From the end of 1975 till now, a sustained deficit has been staying in the US merchandise trade and its size has been increasing relentlessly. The huge deficit of merchandise trade has kept the US current account of its international payment negative for over 45 years. Although the US service trade gradually develops an annual surplus, its margin has never been large enough to offset the deficit of trade in goods, as the international multilateral trading system and the global governance frameworks have not been able to create much room for cross-border service trade. However, due to the convenience created by the US dollar hegemony in the world economy and the lucrative potentials of high-tech innovations, foreign investors have always been interested in US domestic financial assets and investment opportunities. Their money has been pooled into the US continuously and offsetting its trade deficits, forming a weird equilibrium between the over-consumptions of Americans and the expanding credits of foreigners.

The statistics of the United States Census Bureau indicate that the deficit of US merchandise trade reached $ 861.515 billion in the year 2020, while its service trade surplus was totaled $ 285.174 billion. Putting together all the numbers of cross-border trade of goods and services as well as the relevant capital transfers, the US had a current and capital account deficit of $ 621.582 billion. However, on the other hand, the total net inflow of foreign money in its financial account during 2020 was

$ 652.985 billion, more than offsetting this deficit. In the year 2019, its current and capital account deficit was $ 478.589 billion while its net borrowing in the financial account was $ 480.377 billion.

1.2 The Major Sources of Expanding Trade Deficit

The constantly expanding size of the trade deficit of the US is a permanent characteristic shaped by its post-industrial and post-modern economic structure, which is a result of a complex mechanism of interactions between its natural economic evolution and official macroeconomic policy. All in all, the expansion of the trade deficit can be explained by the following factors:

1) The unrestrained consumerism in the US and the marching of economic globalization. The economic financialization began to develop at the same time when the industrial hollowing-out occurred. The applications of electronic technologies in the sectors of banking, insurance, and securities, such as credit cards and electronic computing devices, accelerated this trend and expanded the total scale of credit to an unprecedented degree. Suddenly it became very easy for common citizens to expand their consumption through credit borrowing, and consumerism became a mainstream mode of life. Driven by unrestricted desire for consumption and easy credit, ordinary Americans created an aggregate demand for consumer goods that apparently outsides the overall capacity of supply from US manufacturing, which is on a path of shrinking. During 1951–1955, the net output of US manufacturing accounted for around 27% of its total GDP. In 1999, it accounted for 15%. Now it is barely above 10% of total nominal GDP. Almost all the industries experienced a substantial decline in terms of the percent of their value-added to the total GDP and percent of employment to total jobs, except for the industries of computer and electronics. Obviously, this decline means American manufacturing becomes less capable of meeting domestic needs and Americans have more demands for import.

On the other hand, the US capacity of export of manufactured goods is also on the decline. During the 1960s and 1970s, western Europe and Japan successfully developed their capacity of producing sophisticated goods, such as automotive, electronics, machineries, transport equipment, chemicals and pharmaceuticals, which were regarded as products of traditional capital-intensive sectors. Since the 1990s and especially since it entered into WTO in 2001, China has developed into a new manufacturing center of mass-producing consumer goods. Dragged by its disadvantages in labor cost, land price, gradually dilapidated infrastructure, and stagnancy of traditional technology, the US has lost its competitiveness in these labor-intensive sectors or "heavy and chemical industries." Operating through a "flying geese model", East Asian countries have sliced away the US shares on the international markets of these sectors and industries.

2) The imbalance between saving and investment. The US has a very dynamic system of technological innovations. Every year there are hundreds of new proposals for high-technology development that are initiated from innovative new ideas and may contain tremendous potentials for market shares and profits. In order to substantialize these new ideas, scientists, entrepreneurs and businessmen need to make investments and thus create a huge demand for capital. They not only crave money-form capital, but also desire capital goods. In other words, they need to make fixed asset investments in the form of high-end equipment, appliances, machinery, and facilities to carry forward their technological research and development and to apply these new and high technologies to business. In theory, the capital for investment in an economy is mainly converted from domestic savings, which is the extra money deposited in the banking sector by enterprises and common citizens. However, as above-mentioned, saving takes less and less share in the total net wealth of the whole country as people become less reluctant to deposit their income due to the influence of consumerism and expansion of easy credit. In this way, there has occurred a gap between insufficient saving and ever-increasing demand for capital, including industrial goods for fixed asset investment. Stimulated by this gap, net import will increase.

3) The relatively liberalized international capital flow. The constant increase of the US aggregate demand for goods and capital, the loss of competitiveness

of its export, plus the relative decline of its domestic manufacturing capacity and savings, generate a wide gap between a huge annual outflow of money for paying for import and an inadequate inflow of its external revenue obtained from export and other channels of income. This gap has to be filled through an inflow of foreign money. Fortunately, the US enjoys a great reputation as a good destination for foreign investment and has been consistently attracting foreign capital ever since the end of the Second World War. This capital inflow finances the import-export gap and injects huge resources into its economy.

Its attractiveness to foreign capital can be explained by the following reasons: 1) It has a mature and stable legal and executive system that is relatively friendly to foreign investment. With most of its institutional frameworks administrating and regulating private businesses and financial markets already established at the end of the Second World War, it provides a stable and business-prone context for foreign businessmen and capital to operate. 2) It has a dynamic and innovative mechanism to nurture new technology that may offer above-average returns to those risk-prone venture capitals. The development of "Silicon Valley" in the past 70 years is a good case showing the potential and the flexibility of its mechanism for the research, development, and commercial application of new and high technology, which attract a large amount of capital that is willing to take extra risks for the possibility of gaining extraordinary profits. 3) It has a highly developed and complex system of financial markets that connects its dynamic real economy and offers tremendous potential for profits to foreign investors. On its financial markets, it is always easy for foreign investors to find investment opportunities that give satisfying returns. 4) The international financial hegemony of the US dollar means foreign investors can always obtain a premium of convenience if they invest in financial assets within the US. This egemony was originally established through the Bretton Woods System and became sustained until now. 5) The flexible floating exchange rate and the globalization in financial markets.

Therefore, for over 45 years, annual inflow of foreign capital has propped up the driving force of its technological development, industrial upgrading, and economic growth, which could have been drained by the continuously expanded merchandise trade deficit. Whereas capital inflow does fuel its domestic demands for imported manufactured goods and entrepreneurship for new technology and business, it also makes the macroeconomic policy more volatile and more prone to financial crisis and economic shock.

2 The Inward and Outward Direct Investment

The US is the largest country in the world in terms of its total scale of inward and outward cross-border direct investment. On the one hand, it has always been regarded as one of the top places attracting foreign direct investment from entrepreneurs, businessmen, and institutional investors of various kinds, due to its dynamic technological innovations, mature and stable legal and executive frameworks, fluctuating but flexible financial markets that may contain plentiful resources for financing, and the sheer size of its economy that has a huge potential to provide promising business opportunities. The countless inflow of foreign money fuels its technological and industrial upgrading. On the other hand, it is also the top country in the world making direct investments abroad. Yet the profound impact brought by the COVID-19 pandemic transforms political leadership's perceptions and creates new trends in its foreign direct investment. Now a heated debate is emerging among both top-level politicians and businesses about trade with some newly-emerging economies, as they are concerned with the "security of supply chains." It is anticipated that although it may be difficult to alter those existing supply chains, which are partly supported by overseas direct investments of American corporations, there would inevitably emerge new changes in the volumes and directions of both inward and outward foreign direct investments.

2.1 The Inflow and Outflow of Foreign Capital

For each year an enormous amount of foreign capital flows into the US and is used to purchase some substantial assets. These assets are directly owned, controlled, and operated by foreign investors for substantial business activities, such as establishing or running branches or subsidiaries for foreign corporations, or operating productions in plants. Therefore, it is called "foreign direct investment" (FDI). According to the *World Investment Report 2021* issued by the United Nations Conference on Trade and Development (UNCTD), the US received an inflow of foreign direct investment of $156 billion in the year 2020, still the largest recipient of the world, and the outflow of its direct investment to foreign countries in 2020 was $93 billion, ranking the 4th in the world. Yet the total amount of this inflow in 2020 was 40.2% smaller than that of the year 2019, which was $261 billion, whereas the outflow of 2019 was $94 billion, showing only a slight reduction. Apparently, the outbreak of the COVID-19 pandemic dealt a heavy blow to the US economy and divert foreign investors' attention. The last shock of such scale was the international financial crisis of 2008. According to statistics from both the US department of commerce and UNCTD, the last low point of foreign direct investment was in 2009, when the inflow and outflow of foreign direct investment in the US in 2009 were only $150 billion and around $ 310 billion respectively. It took more than five years for the US to recover the scale of annual FDI inflow to the level before the 2008 financial crisis, whereas its annual FDI outflow never restored to full momentum before 2007. Now the COVID-19 outbreak pulled them down again and completes a ten-year cycle.

2.2 Inward and Outward Foreign Direct Investment

There are several factors determining the direction of foreign direct investment. The gravity model of international trade was first introduced in the mid-1950s, which roughly stipulates that the amount of bilateral trade flow between two countries is proportional to the overall weights of their economies and inversely proportional to the distance between them. Foreign direct investment is widely regarded as a complement and booster to international trade, so this gravity model is also widely applied in the analysis of foreign direct investment. Further studies reveal that the directions and volumes of foreign direct investment are determined by a series of more specific factors, and among them, the most important ones are market size, infrastructure availability, and trade openness. In brief, the less geographically distant and more developed a foreign economy is, the more likely that an American corporation would consider investing in that country, and vice versa.

Empirical data verify this theoretical assumption. Europe has always been the largest recipient of US capital and also the largest source of FDI inflow into the US, as Europe is not only nearer to the US than the most dynamic economic powerhouses in the Asia-Pacific region, but also outstanding in economic weight and development level. A comprehensive report issued by the US Bureau of Economic Analysis (BEA) on July 22nd, 2021 reveals that in the year 2020, US FDI outflow to Europe accounted for 84.8% of its total FDI outflow that year, while the FDI inflow from Europe into the US was 63.6% of the total. Although US media frequently talked about the dynamic growth and great potential of the Asia-Pacific countries, the US FDI outflow to this region only took 14.9% of the total and the FDI inflow from this region into the US was 16%. In the same year of 2020, US outward FDI into Latin America was 12.8% of the total while the inward FDI into the US from Latin America accounted for 13.9% of the total.

In terms of the overall position of FDI of the US in the 2020 and 2019, in other words, the accumulative stock of capital outflows from and inflows into the US, Europe and the Asia-Pacific region always rank 1st and 2nd on the list, whereas Latin America ranks 3rd on the outflow side and 4th on the inflow side, while Canada ranks 4th on the outflow side and 3rd on the inflow side. Other countries and regions are insignificant on the US FDI maps. More specifically, the United Kingdom has the largest stock of US FDI outflows in 2020 ($890.1 billion), the Netherlands ranks 2nd ($844.0 billion), Luxemburg the 3rd (759.4 billion), Canada the 4th ($422.2 billion) and Ireland ($390.3 billion). These five countries absorbed more than half of all the outbound direct investment of the US capital. On the top list of largest sources of FDI inflows into the US, it is quite interesting that Japan was the largest investing country, having a capital stock of $647.7 billion, while Canada ranks 2nd ($490.8 billion), the United Kingdom the 3rd ($486.9 billion), the Netherlands the 4th ($484.0 billion) and Germany the 5th ($411.3 billion). Altogether the capital inflows from these five countries accounted for more than half of all the FDI inflows.

As for the industry distribution of US inward and outward FDI capital, manufacturing and finance (including insurance) are the two most important industries in which both American investors and foreign investors poured most of their money. From 2017 to 2020, the amount of outflowed American capital invested into these two industries of foreign countries always accounted for roughly 30% of its total FDI outflows. Of all the foreign manufacturing industries that absorbed US capital during 2017–2020, "chemicals" and "computer and electronic products" were the two most important ones that swallowed 45% of total US direct investment in foreign manufacturing. Whereas, of all the foreign FDI money that flowed into the US during the same period, 63.6% flowed into manufacturing, finance (including insurance), and wholesale trade, which ranked the top 3 American industries that absorbed foreign capital.

Also, in academic literature, FDI is usually divided into two types: 1) "horizontal" or "market-seeking" FDI. Foreign businessmen duplicate the whole process of production in almost identical new plants in a host country to localize production and sale on markets, to circumvent trade barriers, reduce relevant costs in labor or transport, and become more competitive through more nimble adaptation to local customers' preferences. 2) "vertical" or "production cost-minimizing" FDI. Some large-scaled multinational corporations tend to deconstruct the whole process of production into many interconnected chains and make cross-border relocation of some of them for the purpose of reducing labor costs or obtaining raw materials more conveniently. From the 1950s to the 1970s, when those American manufacturing giants established their affiliates in Latin America or Asia-Pacific, which were underdeveloped regions at that time, most of their direct investments were conducted in the "vertical" form, as they planned to take advantage of plentiful resources of local places, be it human or natural resources. Whereas at the same time, American multinational companies operated more or less "horizontal" FDI in the West Europe and Japan, for the purpose of taking larger shares of already developed local markets. However, both Latin America and Asia-Pacific region went through profound transformations in pace with the waves of economic globalization and regional integration from the late 1970s, and American companies had to adjust their investment strategies. Vertical supply chains still operate in the largest American multinational companies across the world. On the other hand, as former developing economies of Latin America and East Asia have gradually uplifted their technological level and upgraded their industrial structure, US FDI in foreign countries becomes more and more "horizontal"-oriented.

3 Domestic Political Dynamics on Trade Issues

Foreign trade has never been a pure economic or technological issue that only involves cold calculation of data. In the US, it is always a political battel field that stimulates tense policy debates and fierce competition between a variety of interest groups, political parties, and political forces. The trade politics in the US, including trade policy, policy-making, and relevant political fights, is closely connected to the political ebbs and flows of the whole American society and the power struggles in the corridors of government institutions in Washington, D.C. It is safe to say that all the forces across the whole ideological and political spectrums are involved in trade politics to some degree.

Furthermore, a retrospection over history reveals that there is a political pendulum swaying permanently along the left-right nexus of these spectrums. Whenever the US economy is dominated by a momentum of fast growth and prosperity, the political pendulum of the US is usually turning leftward with stronger intellectual and political voices for more progressive efforts to promote trade liberalization, economic globalization, and regional integration with the external world. During these periods, people are self-confident and tolerant toward the imported foreign products or inflow of foreign capital, and free trade doctrine, which is normally embodied in ideas of eliminating tariffs and non-tariff barriers, would be intensively advocated by businesses and supported by many different social groups. Under such circumstances, top political leadership would stipulate more liberalization-oriented trade policy and sign more potent bilateral or multilateral free trade agreements. The leftward turns of the US political pendulum could be found during the period of the 1890s – 1910s, when the US rose as a new and largest industrial power in the world, and the period in the 1990s, when its economy was accelerated by the ICT revolution.

On the other hand, whenever the US economy is slowing down along a path of slumps and declines, dragged by serious crises, recessions, and depressions, the political pendulum would turn rightward with more potent requests from various social interests for economic nationalism, protectionism, and state mercantilism. People of different walks of life become increasingly intolerant toward foreign products and capital and come to be more averse to international competitions. Under these situations, political leadership would adopt a more protectionist trade policy, building up tariffs and other sorts of trade barriers. External negotiations for free trade agreements and efforts to construct a multilateral trading system would be stalled. Trade war would sometimes break out and damage the world economy. In history, the US political pendulum turned rightward during and after the Great Depression of 1929 – 1933. And since 2016, again it has turned rightward with more and more protectionist and nationalist measures on external economic relations.

The US has had a persistent deficit in merchandise trade ever since 1975, and the overall volume has been increasing continuously for over 4 decades. The growth and expansion of this deficit is in pace with the industrial hollow-out, the decline of manufacturing, and the emerging of economic financialization. Furthermore, this deficit also nurtures and helps to create a huge annual inflow of foreign capital and make the international finance and US financial system even more volatile and complicated. Also, this deficit is interpreted as an enormous loss of jobs to working-class people. As the imbalance of trade is permanently creating profound impacts on US economy and social life, it has always been treated as a hot issue in American politics and debated permanently in media and election campaigns. Although trade and relevant economic issues themselves are highly technical with a plethora of monotonous data and statistics, their social and political implications are far-reaching and fundamentally controversial and dividing. From the mid-1970s till now, intellectuals and political forces across the full ideological and political spectrums have been actively participating in the political debate of trade imbalance. It is interesting that professional economists and business elites from large corporations are normally optimistic toward this imbalance and regard it as natural and beneficial to the US economy and society, while populist politicians, trade unionists, activists of civil society, and intellectuals from the fields of humanity and political science frequently criticize it in a strong and harsh tone.

Some think tank experts in advocacy of liberalism or specialized in economic policy research are on the optimistic side of these debates and argue for a tolerance of merchandise trade deficit and a continuation of free trade and near-zero tariffs. Starting out from the opinions of the classical free trade doctrine of Adam Smith, David Ricardo, and David Hume, they hold that trade deficit is the natural consequence of US economic transformation and may be beneficial to the efficiency of its economy and social life. The basic point of their arguments is that trade would lead to a natural transnational specialization that pushes each country to concentrate its resources and labor force on the production of those goods and services in which they enjoy the highest level of efficiency. In other words, each country would take full advantage of its own comparative advantage and produce more products with fewer inputs, and in this way, more products would be churned out in each sector of the whole world economy and the global-wide economic efficiency would be uplifted. They further argue that a merchandise trade deficit means the US could concentrate its capital on the sectors of high technology development and its consumers would benefit from low-cost consumer goods imported from labor-plentiful countries. Thomas L. Friedman's best-seller *The World Is Flat: A Brief History of the 21st Century* (first published in 2005) and Handel Jones's best-seller *Chinamercia: Why the Future of America Is China* are the most well-known representative works showing this optimism and enthusiasm for pushing forward globalization and liberalization of trade and investment for sake of global-wide economic efficiency.

However, many politicians, practitioners, activists, and some economists disagree with this optimism. The Seattle riot of 1999 already indicated the potential danger of deep social divisions and class warfare if the trade deficit grows persistently without being politically checked. Since then, and particularly in the past decade from 2010, many scholars and civil society activists have argued that the key damage brought by this unchecked trade deficit is not the industrial hollowing-out per se, but the serious loss of jobs of working-class people and the shrinking of local communities in the "Rusty Belt," which means destruction of the very fabrics of American middle-class society and democracy. Those optimistic economists who propose to leave the trade deficit alone and advocate globalization think that the net gains of American economic efficiency would compensate for the loss of jobs and the move-out of traditional manufacturing. They argued that government could reap part of these net gains to re-train those who were laid off and the market would reallocate new jobs to them. However, as many scholars and politicians pointed out, that is not the case. This rosy assumption that increased economic efficiency would naturally close the rich-poor gap and rectify the inequality between the privileged few and common people turns out to be a utopian myth. It proves to be very difficult for those American workers of traditional sectors of manufacturing to locate new jobs or start a new life and career, and some traditional industrial towns or cities are stepping onto an irrevocable path of decay. From 1999 to 2002, standing at the crossroad between the 20th and the 21st centuries and already witnessing the 1999 Seattle riot, some economists such as Dani Rodrik and Joseph E. Stiglitz warned of further social unrest in the US ignited by imbalanced trade, but the mainstream neoliberalist elites did turn their ears to these voices. In the following two decades, these prophecies turned out to be real and precise. Grassroots populism emerged and developed into an unneglectable force as people from the underclass tried to make their voices heard.

The Seattle riot of 1999 marks the rise of anti-globalization politics. Since then, the seemingly irresistible momentum of globalization has fundamentally transformed the domestic social lives and external strategic environment of the US and brought it a string of unprecedented challenges. Within the US, distrust and disbelief of rank-and-file Americans toward the elites have increased, because the working class and even the middle-class felt that they were helplessly underprivileged, underrepresented, and finally unemployed, and that political and business elites fail to deliver the promises of rescuing disadvantaged citizens in the process of trade liberalization and economic globalization. Outside the US, there is a fast shift of economic weight and power from the developed world to those "newly-emerging" economies. Such changes were fermenting dissatisfaction and nurturing the anti-globalization politics in American society and politics as well.

On the other hand, suspicions of the promises of neo-liberalist economics have provided theoretical support to the anti-globalization requests. In the mid-1990s, the international relations theorist Susan Strange already criticized the unchecked globalized financial markets as "casino capitalism". After the breakout of the 2008 financial crisis, more and more scholars crated introspective theories on the inherent defects of unchecked market-oriented globalization. In 2011, Harvard scholar Dani Rodrik proposed the concept of the "political trilemma of globalization" in *The Globalization Paradox: Democracy and the Future of the World Economy*. He argued that it is not possible for the world to maintain the three different systems of nation-state, hyper-globalization, and democratic politics altogether simultaneously, any two of them may coexist at the price of undermining or even destroying the third one. In his opinion, hyper-globalization, which is a term that he coined to refer to the high-speed development of globalization since the 1980s, may help to establish some global-scale democracy, but in this way, it would inevitably restrict and weaken the independent sovereignty of the nation-state like a "golden straitjacket." Nation-state could establish domestic democratic politics, but has to do so at the price of slowing down hyper-globalization, otherwise the rules of global governance would bend or twist a nation's democracy to benefit from globalization. In other words, this is a trilemma. In his 2012 book *The Price of Inequality: How Today's Divided Society Endangers Our Future*, Joseph Stiglitz pointed out that globalization entered a very dangerous stage, as US macroeconomic policy and its central bank now only work for the top 1 percent elites who are reaping the extra profit brought by the increased economic efficiency in globalization. In the following decade, a large body of literature of both rigorous academic research and commentary works talked of the "dark sides" of globalization and offered a variety of theoretic explanations and political advice. In all these works, concerns about the devastating blows brought by the imbalanced trade on workers and industrial communities form an important part of their themes.

Enlightened by these theories and reckoned by academicians, some civil society activists and politicians rose up and initiated campaigns or movements in defense of the weak and the "losers" of globalization. On September 17th, 2011, a multitude of protesters came to the Zuccotti Park in New York and launched the "Occupy Wall Street" movement. They then walked into Wall Street and other areas where the largest investment banks and other financial institutions in the US were concentrated. Shouting the well-accepted slogan "We are the 99%," they successfully attracted huge numbers of working-class and mid-class people who were disadvantaged and dissatisfied with the enormously widened rich-poor gap in the US since the financial crisis. Within one week the movement spread all across the whole America and developed into the "Occupy Movement." Grassroots people who lost their jobs, fortunes, residences, or careers in the financial crisis and the subsequent years of the Great Recession took to the street and protested this harsh reality of inequality in the US, where people once had had the American dream of "from rugs to rich" but only came to find an insurmountable barrier to affluent and decent lives. Protesters rallied before the financial districts of almost every major metropolis of the US or protested in front of the gates of major investment banks and giant corporations, shouting slogans and distributing flyers. Later protesters in the Zuccotti Park in New York even disseminated free tabloids, newspapers, and magazines promoting this movement. Within half a month this "Occupy Movement" surpassed the national border of the US and expanded into many developed countries and areas of West Europe and Asia-Pacific regions. It is estimated that the "Occupy Wall Street" movement appeared in over 600 communities in the US while the "Occupy Movement" spread to over 951 cities in 82 countries. This movement lasted for a year and created widespread influence in both the developed and developing world. Although the identities of participants of this "Occupy Movement" were rather versatile and their political goals were more or less divergent, they all expressed suspicions or aversions on unchecked globalization.

After the outbreak of the financial crisis in the Autumn of 2008, US federal government carried out expensive schemes to bail out those investment banks and big corporations from bankruptcy, so as to prevent the contagion of the crisis from destroying the whole national economy. These bailout plans ignited public anger. Common people were losing their jobs during this crisis and the subsequent recessions and Wall Street financial sharks obtained huge severance packages even if their recklessness triggered this crisis. Yet the federal government still chose to support these "too big to fail" banks and corporations through taxpayer-funded schemes. On February 19th, 2009, CNBC reporter Rick Santelli criticized government's tax-funded bailout schemes and proposed that perhaps people should form something like a modern "Boston tea party," referring to the historical movement of American grassroots movement against British Crown's tax in mid-18th century before the American Independence War. Responding to this call, conservative activists rallied and initiated a series of protests, demonstrations, and meetings in advocacy of lower taxes, smaller federal budget, and less national debt. In this way, the "Tea Party Movement" emerged and began to play a role in American politics. Participants of the Tea Party expressed a strong anti-establishment mood, showing suspicions and disaffections on neo-liberalist elites. Furthermore, just as Historian Walter Russell Mead analyzed in *Foreign Affairs* in 2011, this Tea Party movement shows an isolationist and anti-globalization orientation. Inheriting the spirit of the Boston Tea Party of the 1750s, they advocate that the US shall retreat from a chaotic outside world.

There is a large body of English literature devoted to US trade politics. Within this literature, some works calculate the economic benefits and losses of specific trade policy, some concentrate on a particular field of US trade relations with foreign countries, such as the US-China trade relations, whereas others highlight the structure and process of US policy-making, especially the president-congress relations on some trade issues. Moreover, some research works analyze the domestic political dynamics influencing the formulation of US trade policy, from the perspective of interest groups, political parties, or other kinds of political actors. Among all these researches, the model of "two-level game" has attracted the most attention and become the most widely applied analytical framework.

The "two-level" game was originally explained by American scholar Robert Putnam and then got more and more detailed elaborations by successive scholars. This model argues that any trade policy-making, and especially the policy-making for external trade negotiations, should be viewed from two levels. The upper level is the interactions between US top political leadership in charge of trade policy and their foreign counterparts, which reveals the international environment and foreign pressures that US federal leadership has to take into consideration for a sensible and feasible strategy, and also indicates US external economic relations. On the other hand, the lower level of this model is the interactions between US political leadership (including congress, the president, cabinet departments, and political parties in congress) and its domestic political forces of non-top-level, such as interest groups (including those groups of businesses, trade unions, and professionals), lobbies, advocacy groups, and other forms of civil society organizations. It is on this level that the most intricate and profound characteristics of US trade politics can be located and depicted. By sorting out the power structure and dynamics of interactions on this level, the interrelations of different forces of US trade politics can be drawn out, their relative positions within the whole system can be precisely figured out, and the mechanism of their influences on US trade policy can be finally worked out. Now this "two-level" game model is viewed as a basis of the whole edifice of knowledge of US trade politics.

4 The Trade Defense Instruments and Investment Screening System

Trade defense instruments are one of the most important parts of US trade policy. Douglas A. Irwin argued in his 2017 book *Clashing over Commerce: A History of US Trade Policy* that the US trade policy has been used to achieve three objectives in history: 1) From independence to the end of the Civil War, US trade policy was used to raise revenue for the federal government, mainly through the tool of tariffs. 2) From the end of the Civil War in 1864 to the end of the Great Depression in the 1930s, it was applied to restrict imports for the purpose of protecting domestic commerce. 3) Since the end of the Second World War till now, it is utilized to establish reciprocity for bilateral or multilateral free trade systems. Thus in his opinion, the overall objectives of US trade policy can be summarized into "three Rs: revenue, restriction, and reciprocity". His argument contains some truth because the main purpose and core mission of US trade policy evolved and transformed during different historical periods. Nevertheless, one part of US trade policy has survived the whole history and still plays a very important role in its overall framework of trade policy. That part is the trade defense instruments.

In December 1791, only eight years after the independence of the US, Alexander Hamilton, one of most outstanding founders of this newly-created country on the Atlantic coast, issued "the Report on Manufactures", which laid the earliest foundation of the American trade defense instruments to protect its infant domestic industries from competitions of imported foreign goods. Influenced by the European mercantilism of the 16th – 18th century, Hamilton's policy package included subsidies on domestic industries, tariffs, and technical standards as non-tariff barriers. In the first half of the 19th century, Congressman Henry Clay inherited Hamilton's thoughts and developed them into the "American System," a set of policies that contained three mutually-supported columns: high-level tariffs to prevent import from damaging America's domestic industries, a national central bank to fund internal commerce, and federal subsidies to accelerate the development of transport and other infrastructures that may facilitate nationwide market system. From then on, trade defense instruments were not only regarded as an indispensable part of US trade policy, but also incorporated into its toolkit of national macroeconomic policy.

Among these instruments, the tariff was and is still the most frequently used policy tool of the US to carry out top leadership's political will on trade issues. The Tariff of Abominations of 1828 reached a level of over 60%, the highest one in US history, while the *Smoot-Hawley Act of 1930* created the second highest level of tariff in history, only slightly lower than the level of 1828. As neoliberalist economics became the mainstream ideology in the developed world after the end of the Cold War in the early 1990s, and particularly after the establishment of the World Trade Organization in 1995, major developed countries reached a consensus that tariffs should be gradually eliminated in the future. However, this consensus dissipated during the second decade of the 21st century. Unlike its European counterparts who relegate tariff to the rank of an obsolete policy tool that conflicts with the contemporary value of trade liberalization, the US leadership still applies punitive tariffs frequently for the purpose of protectionism, and even keep a punitive tariff on the products imported from one of their closest allies, the European Union, which baffles the European leaders.

4.1　The US System of Anti-Dumping, Countervailing, and Safeguards

At present, the US trade defense instruments contain three major categories of measures: anti-dumping duties (AD), countervailing (also referred to as anti-subsidy) duties (CVD), and safeguards. The prototypes of these three categories already appeared in the Title of VII the *Smoot-Hawley Act of 1930*. After the Second World War, the US led many rounds of multilateral negotiations over half a century and finally achieved the objective of establishing the World Trade Organization. Under its promotion, a matured and detailed system of rules for these three categories was established in the rulebook of the WTO and became part of the international economic law, in which some fundamental concepts and preferences of US law are incorporated. To be precise, WTO's general rules for a national government to conduct proper anti-dumping, countervailing, or safeguards actions are set forth in the "Multilateral Agreements on Trade in Goods," which is the Annex 1 of the "Uruguay Round Agreements," one of the core legal texts of WTO. Nevertheless, the US retains the power and right to interpret these WTO rules, which may inevitably bend them to its own purpose and interests. Furthermore, it has a complex system of domestic law that regulates and stipulates the actual procedures and process for judicial investigation, judgment and ruling on the charges of these three categories.

WTO rules stipulate the definitions of these three categories as follows: 1) "Dumping" refers to the activity that a company exports a product at a price lower than the price it normally charges on its own home market. 2) "Subsidy" refers to a financial contribution or a form of income or price support provided by a government that creates substantial benefits to domestic industry or enterprises. 3) "Safeguard" refers to government measures to restrict imports of a specific product if the domestic industry manufacturing the same kind of product is seriously injured or threatened with such injury. According to WTO, a government or a public body (such as the European Union) shall first conduct proper actions to confirm that dumping or subsidy does exist, and it does inflict some injury on domestic industry and enterprises, before it is entitled to take any anti-dumping or countervailing measures. As for safeguards, WTO also stipulates that substantial evidence of injury or threats of injury shall be clearly found before any action could be taken.

In US domestic law, a set of procedures are clearly defined for an operable process to conduct investigations on charges of anti-dumping, countervailing, and on evaluation for possible safeguards. According to US law, any American enterprise that thinks itself harmed by dumping, foreign subsidy, or suffering from substantial injury inflicted by some imported product shall present a petition to the Department of Commerce, then the International Trade Administration (ITA) of the Department of Commerce evaluates the petition and determines whether to file this petition as a case and initiate an investigation. Once an investigation begins, it is the ITA of the Department of Commerce that determines the existence and amount of dumping and subsidy and it is the US International Trade Commission (USITC) that determines whether a US industry does suffer some material injury. If both the ITA of the Department of Commerce and the USITC make affirmative determinations, then the ITA will direct the US Customs and Border Protection (CBP) to collect punitive duties on imports. Just as mentioned above, the tariff is still attached with the greatest importance in the tool box of US trade regulation.

4.2 The Section 301, 201, 232

WTO only provides general rules to member states for conducting trade defense actions, which are rather vague and difficult to be effectively implemented. That partly explains why the Trump administration openly expressed disdain on WTO and declared that the US would not be directly subject to its jurisdiction in the 2017 and 2018 Trade Policy Agenda. The US has its own complex system of domestic law that directs the application of trade defense instruments for protecting its market and industry from being harmed by imports. Of all the US domestic rules, laws, and regulations for trade defense, three specific sections of law occupy the most outstanding position of the whole system and are most frequently applied. They are the sections 301, 201, and 232. Each of these three sections performs a specialized function. Section 201 and 301 are part of the *Trade Act of 1974*, while section 232 was created in the *Trade Expansion Act of 1962*.

Section 232 of the *Trade Expansion Act of 1962* granted president of the United States the power to impose tariffs to block the import of a certain kind of product if the US Secretary of Commerce recommends him to do so based on substantial evidence that the import of that kind of product "threatens or impairs the national security." National security is the most concerned interest of Section 232 and of the *Trade Expansion Act of 1962*, which was passed as law in October of that year, only one week before the breakout of the Cuban Missile Crisis. At that time, the US was in full confrontation with the Soviet Union at the peak time of the Cold War and national security inevitably became a focus of legislators. Although the concept of national security is not specifically or precisely defined in this piece of legislature, it obviously refers to the US's capacity to produce military-related materials, devices, or equipment. Since 1962, Section 232 was repeatedly applied either under requests from business interest groups, or by some executive officials, such as the president, the Secretary of Commerce, the Secretary of the Treasury, or the Secretary of Defense.

From 1962 to 2020, the Department of the Treasury, Commerce, and Defense launched 31 investigations under Section 232 altogether. In 14 investigations of all these 31 cases, the executive institution of the US government, either the Department of the Treasury or the Department of Commerce, determined that a threat or impair to US national security did exist and presented their judgments to the president, while the president took actions to block import in 9 cases, through punitive tariffs, or some other tools of trade barriers such as coercive quotas or foreign countries' voluntary export restraints. Another 11 cases of investigation were launched by the president and his trade representative, with various conclusions. The protected industries in these investigations included crude oil and petroleum products, iron and steel, chemicals, strategic raw materials such as uranium, and high-tech products of that time such as the making of watches.

The Trade Act of 1974 was passed when the irrevocable process of decline and hollow-out of traditional manufacturing began in the US Also, it was created to grant the president a maneuvering power to make US preference for trade barrier issues incorporated into the agreements of the Tokyo Round multilateral trade negotiations. In essence, this act built fast-tracks for the US president to take action to block imports under urgent situations, and the Sections 201 and 301 are the most important boosters on the fast tracks. Section 201 stipulates that if a US executive institution, usually the US International Trade Commission (USITC), determines that a specific kind of imported product poses serious injury or a threat of serious injury to a US industry after filing a petition from US domestic businesses, trade unions, or their interest groups, the president shall take actions to provide domestic industries with "temporary relief" from imports so that they can readjust themselves in the face of foreign competition. These actions are usually conducted through safeguard procedures and processes and result in high-level tariffs or quotas. The process of Section 201 investigation is initiated by the USITC itself, upon a petition, or at the request of the US Trade Representative (USTR), or the US Senate Finance Committee, the Ways and Means Committee of the US House of Representatives.

While Section 201 is only targeted at a certain kinds of foreign products and grants the president the power to take technical measures, Section 301 is targeted at a foreign government that is allegedly behaving to "distort the international market" and harm the US business interests in general, such as subsidizing a foreign industry "unfairly," or maintaining high-level tariffs or non-tariff barriers, or some other policy or practice that violates its obligations of the international trade agreement. According to Section 301, these "misbehaviors" of a foreign government justifiy the US government to take any necessary retaliatory actions, including technical measures such as tariffs and strategic actions such as sanctions, which may alter US foreign relations dramatically or ignite international conflicts in a much broader way. Therefore, Section 301 may be viewed as the last resort of trade defense and the heaviest weapon of protectionism. Section 301 stipulates that, upon filing a petition or self-initiating by the USTR, the USTR shall establish a self-led "Section 301 committee" to conduct public hearings and work out a special report on that targeted country. Based on this report and its recommendations, and directed by the president, the USTR negotiates with the foreign government for compensation, take unilateral retaliatory actions, or launch dispute settlement proceedings at the WTO.

4.3 The CFIUS

The US government established the Committee on Foreign Investment in the United States (CFIUS) under the directive of president Gerald Ford in 1975. At that time, some member states of the Organization of the Petroleum Exporting Countries (OPEC) suddenly got very rich due to the sharp increase in oil price during the energy crisis, and their investment in American portfolio assets (such as treasury bonds and corporate stocks) grew up very rapidly. The US Congress felt uncomfortable with them and worked out more restrictions on foreign investment, while president Ford took a mixed attitude toward it because of the economic slow-down in the US The CFIUS was established as a compromise between the Presidency and the Congress. After the 9·11 terrorist attack in 2001, the American public became more alert toward investment from the Islamic world, and CFIUS's role became more outstanding. In 2006, the plan of a Middle East State-owned Enterprise "Dubai Ports World" to purchase important facilities of six US ports stirred up a roar of suspicions in US public and put CFIUS under the spotlight of harsh criticism. Pressed by public dissatisfaction, the *Foreign Investment and National Security Act of 2007* emerged and gave a clarified legal status to the CFIUS, largely uplifting its position within the labyrinth of the US executive structure.

During the decade after the 2008 international financial crisis, investment was more and more regarded as an alternative to trade. As protectionism became more entrenched and exclusive framework of regional economic integration such as the European Single Market gained more advantages, cross-border investment was accelerated. Nevertheless, as inward foreign direct investment, especially those "greenfield investments," came to be more prevalent, there was a continuous growth of foreign investors' capacity to directly control or even dominate the pace and path of the host country's industrial and economic development. Therefore, US political leadership turned out to be more and more concerned with the national security threats imposed by inward foreign direct investment. It was out of this concern that the *Foreign Investment Risk Review Modernization Act of 2018* came into effect that broadens the jurisdictions of CFIUS and uplifted it to a much higher status. According to this act, mandatory declaration to CFIUS is required on certain non-share-controlling foreign investment transactions related to "critical technologies" and some types of real estate transactions involving foreign persons, and the term "critical technologies" is also redefined in this act, which virtually expands the power of CFIUS.

> **Essay Questions:**
>
> 1. Why was the US merchandise trade turned from surplus into deficit in 1975? What are the domestic and international structural factors that led to this historical turnover?
>
> 2. Why could US maintain its balance of international payment despite huge volumes of trade deficits in the past 45 years? Why could it manage to keep a strong inflow of foreign capital?
>
> 3. What is the "Flying Geese Model" of the East Asia? And how is this model connected to the "lost decade" of the US in the 1970s?
>
> 4. What the differences between the Section 201, 301, and 232, in terms of their targets, procedures, policy tools, and institutional actors?
>
> 5. How is the US social pendulum swaying along the left-right nexus of US political spectrum in relation to the changes of its trade and economic relations?

Unit 7　The Finance

Finance is always regarded as the backbone of the economy that provides production and commerce with necessary capital and funds to drive forward their operations. Particularly, the United States is viewed by many economists and historians as the "financial capitalism" that concentrates a large proportion of its resources on the development of finance-related sectors, with its manufacturing declining irreversibly. When the earliest American gurus of neoliberalist economics such as Milton Friedman rose in the mid-1970s to offer solutions to the persistent stagflation of that time, they sold to the political leadership and public a refreshing idea that the cumbersome fiscal policy of Keynesianism should be replaced by monetarism, a term they invented to emphasize the importance of "natural increase" of money supply and flexible monetary policy. They argued that in order to maintain an energetic market and the health of growth, government fiscal interventions should be as little as possible. Since then, the finance sector took a more and more prevalent position and expanded at an unprecedented speed. Now it is almost anointed with a golden aurora by university graduates when they are seeking a job.

　Driven by technological advances, monetarist policy, and waves of globalization, economic financialization has become a permanent trend in the US since mid-1970s that shaped the path and pace of its growth. Each sector, industry, and enterprise of the US economy is strongly impacted, driven, or manipulated by the ubiquitous financial capital, and any fluctuation in the financial markets must be taken into consideration by corporate and political leaders as important factors restricting their decisions. Even non-financial corporations, particularly those manufacturing giants, got more and more involved in financial activities to increase and diversify their revenues. Therefore, a study on the US finance sector is of special importance if one wants to establish a fine-grained panorama of its economy.

The US finance sector of the present time is marked by two characteristics:

1) The real estate sector is increasingly viewed as an interconnected and integral part of the financial sector in the broad sense. In the past two decades since the beginning of this new century, real estate development is closely connected to the finance sector, as those real estate developers borrow enormous amounts of loans from banks and other kinds of financial institutions for large-scaled pre-investments of purchasing lands and constructing real estate projects. In other words, real estate developers obtained more and more powerful financial leverages to expand their businesses, which of course, made them much more closely connected to or controlled by financial institutions. Therefore, current American and British official statistics often put the sectors of normal finance (banking and securities), insurance, real estate, and rent and leasing into a general broad category that is abbreviated as "FIRE."

2) Non-commercial banking sectors, particularly those of financial brokers (such as investment banks, hedge funds, or other kinds of securities dealers) are much more active and influential in the US financial system. A commercial bank usually accepts deposits and offers loans, earning profits from the interest rate gaps in between, while a non-commercial bank institution such as an investment bank usually works as an intermediary broker that mediates between investors who seek a good return from their capital and entrepreneurs who seek funding to start up their venturing projects. The major business of an investment bank or other kinds of financial brokers includes: underwriting debts or securities for their customers, helping them to get listed in the major stock market (which is normally termed as Initial Public Offering (IPO)), or managing mergers and acquisitions for them. Endeavoring to create capital for customers in much more flexible and speedy ways than commercial banks do, these financial brokers are pumping funds into the most innovative and riskiest businesses that often contain the sprouts of newly emerging high-tech industries. It is this reason

that makes them more influential and more important than traditional commercial banks.

1 The Sustained Financialization of the US Economy

Economic financialization has become a general trend in the US economy ever since the mid-1970s. Its momentum reached a full-fledged stage before the 2008 financial crisis, and still increased after the crisis. This trend is embodied in two characteristics:

1) The total scale of the broad-sense financial sector (FIRE) has been expanding and its weight in the overall economy has been continuously increasing in the past 45 years. The percent of added-value of the broad-sense financial sector in the total GDP was around 13% in the mid-1970s. It increased to around 18% in 2001 and 19.9% in 2005 – 2007. The broad-sense financial sector's profits accounted for over 40% of the total profits of all firms in the US in 2001, which was a stunning rise from the level of 15% – 17% in the mid-1970s, whereas the ratio of manufacturing sector's profits to the total plummeted from 40% in 1974 to less than 10% in 2001. In the meantime, the average daily volume of transactions in the New York Stock Exchange was increased by 320 times from a meager 50 million shares in 1974 to 1.6 billion shares in 2006.

The widespread and internationalized sub-prime credit crisis lowered the ratio of financial sector to GDP from 19.9% in 2005 – 2007 to around 18% at the end of 2008. However, after 2008, the financial sector regained its advantageous position very quickly and expanded even further. The statistics of the Bureau of Economic Analysis of the US Department of Commerce reveal that in the past decade of 2010 to 2020, the percent of the added value of narrow-sense financial sector (banking, securities, and insurance) in the total US GDP still rose from 7% to around 9%, while the proportion of broad-sense financial sector (FIRE) to the GDP rose from 19.6% to around 22%. In contrast, during the same period, the manufacturing's share in the total US GDP fell from 12% to around 10.5%, although both Obama and Trump administrations worked out a large number of mercantilist and economic nationalist measures to reinvigorate

US industries.

2) Non-financial corporations are more and more involved in financial activities and their portfolio returns have occupied a principal position in their total revenues. Nowadays non-financial corporations in the US are very active in financial or capital operations, such as offering mortgage loans to consumers in money markets or investing in stocks or bonds in capital markets, which were originally auxiliary activities to support their major businesses or supplement incomes from sales of products, but later developed into important businesses. In parallel with the expansion of the financial sector in the US economy, the portfolio returns (which means incomes from a combination of different kinds of financial assets, such as stocks, bonds, loans, or insurance instruments) of these non-financial corporations gradually took much larger percentages of their total cash inflows than their revenues from mainstream businesses, and therefore the financial sections gained the largest weights in the organizational structures of these corporations. For example, some scholars revealed in 2006 that the Ford Auto Company, a traditional American corporation specialized in producing automobiles, obtained the majority of its profit not from car sales, but from selling auto loans to customers. Actually, the portfolio income's overall ratio to the total cash inflow of US manufacturing firms rose from a little more than 30% in the mid-1970s to a staggering 95% in 2001, which partly reflected the slumping profit rate of traditional manufacturing and partly indicated the financial bubbling in the US at that time.

2 The Assets, Instruments, Markets, Institutions, and the Operating Mechanism

2.1 The General Categories of Assets, Instruments, Markets, and Institutions

The US has the largest and the most complex financial system in the world, which consists of different kinds of markets operated by a variety of profit-seeking institutions and supervised by regulatory agencies that establish rules and govern the activities of different players in all of the financial markets. Financial markets play the function of channeling funds from the places where there is a surplus of money that is saved from consumption to the places where people and institutions spend more than their incomes. Therefore, there are three kinds of players in the financial markets: 1) lender-savers who have surplus money in hand and want to lend it out for some returns; 2) borrower-spenders who are in need of money for consumptions, investments, or other purposes; 3) financial intermediaries that are brokering between lender-savers and borrower-spenders and making profits from their brokerages. It needs to be pointed out that both lender-savers and borrower-spenders include households, business firms, government, and foreigners. Before the emerging of economic financialization in the mid-1970s, households had been the principal lender-savers, and businesses and government had been the principal borrower-spenders. As mortgage loans for purchases of cars, houses, or high-value consumer goods became more and more prevalent from the mid-1970s, households also took up the role of borrower-spender gradually. Since 1985, the United States has been on the status of debtor nation for over 35 years, meaning its position on the financial account of its balance sheet of international payment has been negative for over 35 years with the total value of its foreign-related liabilities surpassing its assets in foreign countries. Both its federal government and its common citizens are accustomed to borrowing money with their future incomes as collateral, thanks to the highly developed US financial markets and the hegemony of the US dollar in world economy. There are many criticisms and pessimistic anticipations on the huge debt of the US, federal government, but the US national debt in the form of its treasury bonds is still regarded as one of most stable and safe instruments of financial investment on international markets, because of its economy's resilience and powerful capacity to generate new wealth from its constant technological innovations.

In the US, financial assets and instruments are most frequently classified into three categories:

1) Debt. This category of financial assets and instruments includes loans, bonds, and mortgages. Unlike loans or mortgages which are established on relatively fixed lender-borrower relations and difficult to be transferred, bonds are the most transferrable form of assets that can be easily sold and purchased in the market, so it has the highest level of liquidity. Businesses or individuals can issue a bond on financial markets for gathering funds, not only promising to not only repay the whole principal of this debt, but also obligated to pay interest after a fixed regular interval time and time again, until it expires.

2) Equity. When an investor purchases an equity issued by a business firm, he nominally owns a share of that firm's total capital and is entitled to a return in the form of a dividend from any direct increase of that firm's net profit. The most common form of equity is stocks that can be purchased and sold on stock exchanges. And there are other forms of equities in the capital of a corporation that may be restricted from being easily transferred. It is estimated by economists that the total market value of debt instruments is normally 2.5 – 2.6 times as much as that of the equities in the US, although the later has always been much more well-known and more closely observed by common citizens. Particularly, the markets of US treasury bonds are very prosperous and consistently attracting foreign institutional investors.

3) Derivatives. In the US, a derivative is a set of rights and obligations that are "derived" from a substantial asset (such as a bond or a stock) or a set of assets (such as the form of an index). These rights and obligations are normally embodied in a contract based on underlying assets. The most frequently traded derivatives in financial markets are forwards, futures, options, and swaps. Derivatives are viewed as the most typical embodiment of "fictitious economy" that results from the deepening of financialization and they have been proved to be the most volatile and riskiest instruments traded in markets. The swaps are especially risky and locked by some scholars as the culprit that triggered the 2008 crisis. Also in the US, bonds, stocks, derivatives, and other financial instruments are generally termed as "securities" as

long as they can be traded easily. In brief, all the financial assets and instruments in the U.S. can be classified into three basic types: debt, equity, and derivative, so all the financial markets also roughly fall into these three categories.

From the perspective of the organizing and operating of markets, the US financial markets can also be classified into Primary vs. Secondary Markets. On the primary market, a new stock or bond is issued by the government or a business firm for the first time. The initial issue of these securities on primary markets is usually conducted behind closed doors far away from organized stock exchanges such as the New York Stock Exchange (NYSE). In the US, it is the investment banks who are playing a major role in the primary markets for the new issue of securities through an operation of underwriting, which means an investment bank guarantees a price on the securities of a firm and sells them to the public by taking advantage of its broad network of connections.

On the other hand, when stocks or bonds are already issued, they will be further traded on the secondary markets, which are highly organized mature systems with large scales and great reputations. Not only stocks and bonds, but also futures, foreign exchanges, and options are traded on the secondary markets. Financial brokers and dealers work in these secondary markets selling and buying securities for customers at their requested prices. According to American economists, although secondary markets do not provide direct convenience to the new issue of securities, they can increase the liquidity of these securities that may promote the issuing firm's sale in the primary market, and more importantly, they help to determine the price of a newly issued security through the call auction mechanism that involves huge numbers of participants. In this sense, secondary markets are much more flexible, resilient, and sensitive to the actual demands of the economy than primary markets.

Secondary markets include two categories: 1) Exchanges. These are highly organized places with complete facilities and devices that offer convenience to the trading of certain types of financial instruments or assets and disseminate relevant information instantaneously. Because trading of securities can be concentrated within these exchanges at a regular time based on a uniformed set of rules, the effects of the economy of scale are achieved and the efficiency of transactions is improved. 2) Over-the-Counter Market (OTC). In an OTC market, sellers and purchasers at scattered and distant locations can make sporadic deals through computers and other kinds of modern communication tools. In the US, most stocks are traded in exchanges, while most bonds are traded in OTC markets. This is because bonds have a larger diversity of qualities, yields, and maturities than stocks, so they are more difficult to be standardized like those listed stocks in exchanges. The US government bond market is one of the most famous OTC markets, whose yearly trading volume even surpasses that of the NYSE. Because OTC markets are much more sporadic and scattered in nature than exchanges, they can keep away from the media spotlight and are less susceptible to news or situational changes.

Financial intermediaries are playing an indispensable role in US financial markets. Their most important function is to reduce transaction costs for those buyers and sellers of financial assets and instruments so that the market can allocate capital and money much more efficiently and quickly. They have several advantages to achieve the improvement of the efficiency of transactions, such as store of data and professional expertise, economy of scale based on their sizes, and networks of widespread connections to various parts of the whole financial system. The Federal Reserve of the US divides all American financial intermediaries into three general categories: 1) Depository Institutions that absorb deposits from the savings of households and business firms and earn net revenues from the interest rate gap between deposits and loans. Within this general category, there are commercial banks, the most traditional form of financial institution that lend corporate and consumer loans, issue mortgages, and sell US government bonds. Besides commercial banks, there are some mutual savings banks, credit unions, and other specialized institutions that are formed by specific social groups for certain purposes of financial guarantees. 2) Contractual Savings Institutions that pool money from people of certain social groups or professions and transfer the money into portfolio investments for the purpose of increasing its total value after a long time. A large number of these institutions are insurance companies that collect fixed amounts of money after each regular interval of time, which are called "premium of insurance policy" and convert these premiums into investments in securities, particularly government bonds and mortgages. The most active insurance companies in the US are life insurance companies and fire and casualty insurance companies. A variety of pension funds, particularly government-supervised retirement funds, also fall into this category. 3) Investment Intermediaries. The most famous type in this category is the investment banks, because they were put under the spotlight of the media as the ones who opened Pandora's box in the 2008 financial crisis. Furthermore, within this category, there are mutual funds and finance companies that provide loans to consumers who want to purchase high-value goods such as automobiles but do not have sufficient money. Ford Motor Credit Company is an example of finance company.

2.2 The Symbols of the Vitality and Resilience of US Financial System: NYSE and CME

Millions of financial transactions happen every day in the US. The fluctuation created from each of these transactions would contribute to the overall volatilities and disruptions of the whole system of financial markets and finally form a systemic risk that may lead to a crisis. In order to monitor the instantaneous ups and downs of these transactions, both regulatory agencies such as the Federal Reserve Board and the Securities Exchange Commission and the media are always keeping a close observation on the financial markets, especially the securities markets where the largest proportion of all transactions of financial assets and instruments are conducted. There is a saying in the circle of financial professionals, which says: "Money never sleeps." It never sleeps because the whole system of securities markets in the US keeps operating. However, this system is too enormous, complex, and fluid to be precisely observed as a whole, so both media and regulatory agencies focus their attention on a few organized exchanges that are the largest and the most comprehensive ones viewed as the crucial pivots of the whole financial system. The most important of these pivots are the New York Stock Exchange (NYSE), the Exchange of the US National Association of Securities Dealers Automated Quotation System (NASDAQ), and the Chicago Mercantile Exchange (CME, which is the largest organized market of futures and options in the world).

The New York Stock Exchange (NYSE) is the oldest organized exchange in the US and the largest one in the world in terms of its market capitalization, average daily trading value, and average daily trading volume. Before the universal application of the computerized electronic trading system, NYSE's main trading activities happened on the trading floor, which was inside a very spacious hall. At this place, traders from different financial intermediaries initiated and implemented transactions of stocks on behalf of investors. On every working day, traders usually entered the trading floor at 9:30 eastern time when NYSE's opening bell rings. They gathered around an appropriated post where there was a specialist broker who was employed by an NYSE member firm and working as an auctioneer that tried to match traders who wanted to buy stocks with those who wanted to sell, through an open outcry auction method. All the trading would be closed at 4:00 pm. The invention of the internet brought dramatic changes to stock trading. In September 1995, an unmanned and automated electronic system was applied to NYSE's trading for the first time. In January 2007, NYSE established the electronic hybrid market system. In this system investors either trade by themselves through NYSE's electronic system that makes matches automatically and enforces trading orders swiftly, or send their requests and orders to the trading floor. In NYSE, trading activities are conducted in a continuous auction format. After all the trading parties declare their offers of prices and numbers of specific stocks that they want to purchase or sell, matches are made through the automated electronic system or manned auction by prioritizing the sellers and buyers who have the smallest price gaps in their offers and make bids first. Since 1987, the NYSE adopted trading curbs to restrict over-volatile speculations. Since 2011, it has been practicing a circuit breaker mechanism that halts trading automatically when the margin of average price slump exceeds certain levels.

NYSE has a long history. The earliest stock trading was conducted under the buttonwood trees along Wall Street. In May 1792, 24 financial brokers signed the Buttonwood Agreement that set up a uniformed floor commission rate that these brokers would charge their clients. This agreement created the organizational foundation for NYSE. In the following years, trading was often conducted in some coffee houses or other kinds of public places. In 1817, the New York Stock and Exchange Board was organized for setting and implementing new rules to govern increasing speculative activities. In 1865, the office of this board moved to the location where the NYSE stands now. NYSE's quick adaptation to the application of the electrical telegraph in the 1900s offered it an unbeatable edge over its major rival, the Philadelphia Board of Brokers. Nevertheless, it also became the epicenter of the financial storm that triggered the 1929 – 1933 Great Depression, so an overhaul was made on its operating and trading mechanism during the 1930s. After the Second World War, it experienced the Black Monday of October 19th, 1987 when the Dow Jones Industrial Average Index took a free fall, which initiated a serious recession at the end of the 1980s.

The Chicago Mercantile Exchange (CME) is the largest market in the world that is specialized in the trading of futures, options, and other related financial derivatives. It was established in 1898 as the "Chicago Butter and Egg Board", an organized exchange trading agricultural products in the form of futures. In July 2007, it merged with the Chicago Board of Trade, which was another major future-trading market. In August 2008, it also merged the New York Mercantile Exchange (NYME) and the Commodity Exchange Inc. (COMEX), which had been an important market for the trading of futures and options of precious metals and minerals, such as gold, silver, copper, aluminum. Like NYSE, the CME practiced the open outcry method for matchmaking in trading before the adoption of the automated electronic trading system. It even developed a complex system of hand signals for traders in the 1970s which was also adopted by the NYSE. In 1992, it established the first globe-wide electronic trading platform on which futures contracts could be traded in large numbers. Later this platform was developed into the CME Globex Trading System, which is the core of CME nowadays. Over 90% of the total volume of trading in CME is conducted through this electronic online system.

3. The Governmental System of Fiscal and Monetary Policy-Making

Fiscal and monetary policy are the two most important and fundamental types of macro-economic policy that are stipulated and implemented by the US government for the purpose of regulating and adjusting the economy. Fiscal policy includes tax, fiscal transfer in the form of social welfare, government-led investment in public projects, and other means that directly increases or decreases the volumes of government income and spending. It is usually drafted by the Treasury Department of the US federal government and approved by Congress, as Congress controls the "power of the purse." Whereas the monetary policy refers to the government regulation of the overall quantity and speed of money circulating in the economy through interest rates and central bank supply of money through open market operations. In the US, the de facto central bank is the Federal Reserve Board.

Both fiscal and monetary policy is closely connected to the US financial system, either shaped by or shaping and in turn, influencing the whole economy. For example, whenever the president of the US decides to adopt an expansionary fiscal policy, which means lowering tax rate and increasing federal spending for the purpose of creating more consumptions and investments, the Treasury Department would have to issue bonds and increase the US national debt, so that more money could be raised to compensate for the decreased fiscal income and maintain government schemes. In this way, the efficiency and steadiness of the US securities market are coupled with the federal fiscal policy. This situation occurred during the years of the Reagan and Trump administrations when they both raised a huge amount of income through national debt for funding the development of new and high-tech sectors. During the two terms of Ronald Reagan, the US national debt held by the public got nearly tripled from $738 billion to $2.1 trillion, while Donald Trump was nicknamed "king of debt" because he increased the national debt by almost $7.8 trillion. The incremental add-up of national debt changes both the general price-level and investors' expectations on US securities markets, particularly the bond market, and makes the financial system more fragile to disruptions. On the other hand, whenever the Federal Reserve declares its plan to lower interest rates, just like what it has been doing since the outbreak of COVID-19 in early 2020, there would be an anticipation from the general public that overall price-level for securities, particularly stocks, would rise because lower interest rate reduces investors' evaluation on bank deposits and pushes them to move money to securities markets. In this way, it is likely that some bubbles (which means large-margin uplifting of the prices of financial assets above their intrinsic value) may occur due to raised demands for securities and more frequent speculations. All in all, the role of the US government and its policy are quite important and deserve close observation.

3.1 The Treasury Department and the US Fiscal Policy

The US Department of Treasury is in charge of all incomes and spending of the federal government and is responsible for drafting and enforcing the federal fiscal policy. Therefore, its role in the US macroeconomy is unneglectable and crucial. It oversees the federal mint and other relevant agencies that are assigned with the work of printing paper money or minting coins. All the US federal taxes are pooled into the Treasury Department through the US Internal Revenue Service (IRS), which is a section of it. In addition to the mission of collecting federal taxes, it also manages the instruments of US national debt, administrates banks and other saving institutions by supervising their operations and issuing or revoking their licenses, and advises Congress and Presidency on macroeconomic and fiscal issues. Supported by around 10 bureau-level subsidiary institutions, it is led by the Secretary of Treasury. It is also playing an outstanding role in the US foreign economic policy as it can offer precise data about the US foreign debt and international debt market. Created by Congress in 1789, its original role was to manage federal revenue when the tariff was almost the single most important source of income for the federal government. When Alexander

Hamilton swore into office as the first Secretary of Treasury in 1789, he was faced with the very weak financial capacity of George Washington's cabinet to carry forward its administration on the US economy. Therefore he took an effort to strengthen the status and functions of the Treasury Department in the federal bureaucracy. He established the earliest operational mechanism in the Treasury Department to enforce administration, regulations, and guidance on federal tax, national debt, and management of financial markets. And it is Alexander Hamilton who formulated the earliest set of industrial policies through the tax-raising and spending function of the Treasury Department. Under Hamilton's leadership, the Treasury Department entrenched its position as the major and most professionalized US federal institution in the management of fiscal and debt affairs.

A sophisticated system of fiscal policy of the US federal government had not existed before the 1929 – 1933 Great Depression. Before the Civil War, tariffs had been the single most important source of federal income and the power of the Presidency on tax collection and spending had been relatively weak due to tough checks of Congress. Staggering fiscal basis and strong restrictions from Congress on tax issues impeded the Presidency from formulating consistent fiscal policy to adjust or stimulate macroeconomy. In the Civil War, the federal executive branch obtained stronger leverage on fiscal affairs because there was a very urgent need to fund the war. Taking advantage of this opportunity, the Presidency and the cabinet successfully brought into effect the *Legal Tender Act of 1862* and the *National Bank Act of 1863*, which formed a set of practices that substantially increased their power to determine tax issues and print paper money. After the Civil War, the US government began to play a more active role in the management of the national economy. It subsidized private companies to accelerate the construction of railways, roads, and canals, thus helping to establish a nationwide network of transport that facilitated a national system of markets and speeded up the process of industrialization. However, influenced by the ideology of laissez-faire that dominated the Anglo-Saxon economies, the US federal government largely got its hands off most of time.

A historical turning point came when a financial storm broke out in 1929 that triggered the Great Depression. Faced with unprecedented levels of unemployment and decline, the Franklin D. Roosevelt administration had to take unusual measures to intervene in the economy. It worked out a package of "New Deal" that contained a set of expansionary fiscal policies to increase government spending, invest in a number of public projects, and establish a social security framework that could provide relief to unemployed workers. The New Deal changed the role of the federal government in the economy forever, because since then the ideological and perceptional barriers to more initiative governmental role in the economy were removed. Fiscal policy came to be employed as an effective tool to stimulate or stabilize the macroeconomy. During and after the Second World War, the US government further consolidated its role of economic administration and carried forward a series of federal schemes for the purpose of increasing production and jobs. Also in the 1950s and 1960s, the theory of Keynesianism, which advocates outstanding government role through initiative fiscal policy, became matured and provided theoretic support and guidance for federal leadership to intervene in economy. Mostly it adjusted and regulated the economy through a fine-tuned system of regulations, supervisions, and interventions in the form of tax and public scheme investment.

The beginning of the 1970s witnessed a series of structural changes in the world economy, as the financial crisis of 1969 – 1970, the collapse of the Bretton Woods System, the energy crisis, and the stagflation stepped onto the world stage one after another. Also, Keynesianism's influence was declining as it could not offer an effective solution to these economic disruptions and a new theory rose up in the name of Monetarism, which developed into neoliberalist economics and took the position of mainstream ideology for the three decades since the early 1980s. Under such circumstances, fiscal policy's status fell off bit by bit in the overall system of the US macroeconomic policy and monetary policy got to be more important and prevalent, as neoliberalist economics opposes direct government intervention and advocates for indirect monetary adjustment through interest rate and money supply.

Nevertheless, monetary policy-making is actually determined by the Federal Reserve, not the president or his cabinet. So the president and his team members, including the Secretary of the Treasury Department, still rely on fiscal policy to realize their wills and orientations on the economy. As Gerald T. Fox argued in his 2015 book *U.S. Politics and the American Macroeconomy,* nowadays there are electoral political-business cycle and partisan political-business cycle that operate through fiscal policy. Before a general election, a president hoping to win a second term always enforces some expansionary fiscal policy that increases jobs but creates some degree of inflation. After winning a general election and before the mid-term Congressional election, an incumbent president always adopts contractionary fiscal policy to stabilize the economy. This is the electoral political-business cycle. Also, a Democratic Presidency is very likely to take up expansionary fiscal policy that regards unemployment as a priority in the list of problems waiting for solutions, which will most probably uplift the price-level in the long run. Whereas a Republican Presidency always tends to carry out contractionary fiscal policy to stabilize price-level but worsen the situation of unemployment. This is the partisan political-business cycle. These two cycles offer a generalized picture that defines the position of fiscal policy in the US politics and macroeconomy.

3.2 The Federal Reserve and the US Monetary Policy

Operating as the central bank of the US and largely independent from the Presidency and the cabinet, the Federal Reserve system occupies a top position in the US overall structure of macroeconomic administration because it has the full power to determine the monetary policy, which usually includes measures to regulate or adjust the interest rate, money supply, and availability of credit. Although it is the US president who has the nominal power to appoint or discharge its chair or important members of its board of governors, and the president may also express his concerns and dissatisfactions on monetary policy, which are usually unneglectable and inevitably creates some influence on the Federal Reserve's policy-making, the president or his cabinet member can not alter the Federal Reserve's decision, nor can they intervene in its daily operations or internal management. This relative independence guarantees the professionalism of the Federal Reserve and the reliability of US monetary policy.

It was stipulated in the 1913 law for creating the Federal Reserve that the function of this institution is to maximize employment and stabilize price-level through long-term management of interest rates. As the US economy becomes more and more volatile and complex, its functions and jurisdictions have been expanded continuously. Now it is also responsible for supervising the US banking sector, overseeing financial markets, and supporting federal and state-level public finance. More specifically speaking, it works as the "lender of last resort" to all commercial banks, depositary and saving institutions, and federal government institutions. Whenever a financial crisis broke out and disrupted the whole financial system, it is the Federal Reserve that is obligated to intervene in the chaos and offer financial or political support to markets and private financial institutions to stabilize the situation.

The organizational structure of the Federal Reserve contains several levels. On the top are the chair and the board of seven governors who are all appointed by the president and approved by the Senate. The chair and the governors have a term of 14 years, but they can not take a second term. And the board that is obligated by the law presents a report to the Speaker of the US House of Representatives annually. It has 12 regional Federal Reserve Banks located in 12 crucial cities in the US economy, for the purpose of supervising private commercial banks. It also has a "Federal Open Market Committee" consisting of all the governors of its board and the president of each regional Federal Reserve Bank. This committee is the operating body that sets up specific targets of monetary policy and takes actual decisions to achieve these targets. It also has many advisory councils. Because all the private banks are required to put a deposit into the account of a Federal Reserve Bank, it pools a huge reserve which is called the "federal funds." The federal funds work as a reservoir for private banks or other financial institutions to lend and borrow from each other for the purpose of meeting the federal requirement that each private bank should keep a proportional reserve in the Federal Reserve for the safety of the deposits that they hold. The interest rate that a private bank pays for borrowing a part of the reserve of another private bank that is deposited in the federal funds is called the "federal funds rate." Regulated by the board of the Federal Reserve through its "open market operations" (OMO) that indirectly changes the total amount of money circulating in the economy, this interest rate is termed the "benchmark rate" that links and determines all the commercial interest rates of private banks or other kinds of financial institutions. In other words, it is a financial thermometer revealing the trend of expansion or contraction of total credit and a fundamental tool of the US monetary policy.

4. The Evolution of the US Financial System

A retrospect on the evolution of the US financial system reveals several characteristics: 1) There is a permanent cycle of boom and bust in the US financial history. A period of exuberance always leads to overheating of the economy and then to crises, which in turn would trigger a period of recession. In other words, there are always endless macroscopic ups and downs in the economy. Sometimes termed "business cycle" by media and scholars, this process always gets through ups and downs like a roller-coaster. The theory of "Bounded Rationality" is now employed to explain the psychological basis of cyclic financial crises. It points out that it is impossible to keep the economy operating on a steady track because of the deep-rooted human nature of restlessness, recklessness, and impulsiveness for more satisfaction. Despite all these theoretic explanations, financial crises in the US seem to be more dramatic and ferocious than those in other developed countries, which might be explained by the deepened financialization of its economy compared to those of other countries. 2) Non-bank financial brokers have taken up an outstanding role in US finance that is much more influential and powerful than those of their counterparts in other countries. (It should be pointed out that investment banks are not real banks but securities brokers and dealers. Every source of American literature on finance confirms this point.) These brokers' sophisticated and excessive exploitations of leverages have been increasing the volatility of the US financial markets. Also, their skillful activities of lobbying and campaigning have magnified their influence exponentially. 3) The monetary policy carried out by the US government also increases and multiplies the roller-coaster effect of its financial and business cycle. Ever since the fading of Keynesianism and the rise of monetarism in the early 1970s, the US political and policy leadership have gradually formed a preference for monetary policy rather than fiscal policy to stimulate and sustain economic growth in the long-run. Because of its highly financialized economic structure in which the broad-sense financial sector has accounted for over one-fifth in the past two decades, monetary policy could achieve a long-term effect on its macroeconomy that is both potent and nuanced. Whereas on the other hand, it also largely intensifies or even exacerbates the expansionary and contractionary pace of the cycle.

4.1 The Evolution of the US Banking and Securities Sector

Before the 20th century, commercial banking was the most important part of finance, because of their total weight in financing both government and big industrial corporations. Since the 1920s however, securities, particularly stocks and derivatives, turned out to be more and more prevalent because they could provide the real economy with more plentiful financial resources in a more convenient and swift way than the traditional banking sector. After the Second World War, research and development of new and high technology became the most eminent engine that kept up the growth of US economy. However, technological innovations were highly risky and volatile, and needed large amounts of fast and flexible pre-investment. Risk-prone venture capital provided by the non-bank financial intermediaries on the securities markets could adapt themselves to this need more easily than those offered by the traditional commercial banks, so it became unavoidable that traditional commercial banking declined as non-bank financial intermediaries specialized in the issue and trading of securities and derivatives prospered. The structural shocks that terminated the Bretton Woods System in the early 1970s accelerated this trend. From the year 1974, all the way throughout the 1980s and 1990s, commercial banking's share of the total US financial assets was decreasing continuously, reflecting a sustained decline in parallel with the industrial hollow-out. The number of commercial banks also fell down with capital of the banking sector more and more concentrated into a few large banks. At the same time, non-bank financial intermediaries working as securities dealers and brokers developed quickly. Pushed by increasing demands from high-tech industries and the real estate sector, a momentum of "securitization" emerged since the late 1960s. This momentum is still developing forward at present. In the meantime, derivatives experienced extraordinary growth during the first decade of the 21st century, and their development has slowed a bit since the Great Recession triggered by the 2008 financial crisis.

Derivatives also speeded up their development since the late 1960s. In 1968, a new set of rules on commodity future trading was passed and incorporated into the *Commodity Exchange Act*, which requires that each future merchant commission should own a minimum amount of capital before he started to run a commodity future business. The enforcement of the future contract is also under more detailed supervision since then. As speculations on futures of agricultural commodities became more reckless in the 1970s, the *Commodity Futures Trading Commission Act of 1974* was passed to further refine the rules and put trading of commodity futures under direct federal supervision. In the mid-1990s, assisted by the newly-emerging internet and information technology, traders of non-bank financial brokerage institutions invented a kind of derivative called "credit default swap" (CDS), which mitigated the risk of a single lender for not getting repayment from a borrower on a loan or a mortgage. The CDS was gladly accepted by investors who lent money in the form of long-term credit and soon became the most widely adopted form of credit derivative in the US. It is estimated by the US Comptroller of the Currency (which is the currency administration authority of the federal government) that CDS trading takes a share of 88% in the total market value of credit derivatives in 2020. However, CDS also creates a vast network of mutually connected long-term debts that have to be paid on pre-defined conditions. It was viewed as the major technical trigger of the 2008 financial crisis.

4.2 The US Central Bank System and Executive Financial Administration

When the US achieved independence in the late 18th century, there were only three small banks were unable to concentrate sufficient financial resources to fund its commerce and industry. It was Alexander Hamilton that proposed to establish a national bank with a strong capacity to fund and support US entrepreneurs, particularly those early-time industrialists in New England. In 1791, Congress approved the establishment of the First Bank of the United States, which ran business as a quasi-commercial bank, not a central bank. Partly controlled by the federal government and partly owned by private share-holders, it was viewed as one of the three major expansions of federal power in economic administration, together with excise taxes and a federal mint. After the War of 1812, private banks prospered and developed very quickly, creating the first financial crisis in US history, the Panic of 1819. In 1817, the Second Bank of the United States was created, which was still a quasi-commercial bank that provided the federal government with the services of depositing and managing its revenues. Then in 1833, president Andrew Jackson ordered the disbanding of this Second Bank of the United States. Since then, the US banking sector entered a period of free development with no central executive administration. By 1860, nearly 8000 state-level banks were operating in the US, each issuing its own paper money. During the rest time of the 19th century, the idea of building a federal-operated national bank to fund domestic industrialization and regulate the financial system was raised time and time again by a variety of politicians, but to no avail. Without a centralized monetary authority, private financial institutions grew up and expanded wildly. But a lot of chaos appeared when the US converted its currency system from bimetallism to the gold standard. After fierce debates, the US finally established the gold standard through the *Coinage Act of 1873*, in order to end chaotic conditions of the private banking sector.

The Panic of 1907 was the catalyst that led to the creation of the Federal Reserve system. Faced with this crisis and the subsequent waves of bankruptcies of state-level banks and private businesses, the federal government came to realize that it was absolutely necessary to create a federal-controlled "lender of last resort" to offer rescues and stop the domino effect of a financial storm. It was out of this consideration that the *Federal Reserve Act of 1913* was passed by Congress and the real modern central bank was established in the US. The 1929 – 1933 Great Depression further strengthened the power of the Federal Reserve and expanded its jurisdiction. In order to calm down bank-runs and rebuild public confidence in the banking sector, the Federal Reserve was authorized with more decision-making power and resources for the work of reorganizing financial markets and the commercial banking sector. Particularly, the *Banking Act of 1935* granted the Federal Reserve Board more discretionary power on credit management and supervision of banks. During this period the US also abandoned the gold standard, adding more leeway for the US Presidency and the Federal Reserve to take monetary decisions. After the Second World War, the gold standard was partially recovered by the Bretton Woods System. However, this system was maintained for only 25 years and terminated by president Richard Nixon in 1970. During the 1980s and 1990s, a series of executive measures and legislative activities, such as the repeal of the *Glass-Steagall Act* in 1999, formed a tide of deregulation on the whole financial system that created a set of hidden systemic defects like burying a ticking bomb. In 2008, this ticking bomb exploded into crisis and recession. For the purpose of remedying and rectifying these defects, the *Dodd-Frank Wall Street Reform and Consumer Protection Act* was enacted in 2010 and largely tightened regulations and supervision of financial intermediaries. Nevertheless, in 2018 a set of new regulations was signed into effect by president Donald Trump that loosened regulations on the US financial sector and partly offset the effect of the *Dodd-Frank Act*.

5. The Financial Crises

The perpetual cycle between prosperity and recession is a permanent characteristic in the US economy and the pivot that converts boom into bust is always a financial crisis. The US economy is based on a free market system that has to achieve a clearing of all goods and services through a pricing mechanism, and "bounded rationality" as mentioned above determines that irrational and even fanatic decisions are normalcy in trading. Irrational decisions in markets create distortions of price and create bubbles. This distortive effect would accumulate and surpass a certain threshold that triggers an unstoppable plummet in price. And then a recession emerges. According to the National Bureau of Economic Research (NBER), a top think tank of economic policy in the US, a recession is a nationwide significant decline of economic activities across all sectors and industries that lasts for at least half a year with drastic falls in GDP, real income, employment rate, and of added value in commerce and industry. As the financial sector has always occupied the most outstanding position as the thermometer of the whole economy and the blood vessels of other sectors, a crisis in the US always appeared on a financial market first, be it a debt market or a stock market, and then led to a bank-run, which usually triggered a widespread panic that created surges of bankruptcies and led to a momentum of economic slow-down. The history of the US financial crisis could be traced back to 1785, only two years after its formal independence, when a bank-run suddenly happened because of bank failures triggered by federal default of war debt. Since then, financial crisis occurred every 5 to 10 years and a large-scale fierce crisis that would drag the national economy into a long-term recession time happened again and again for every 20 years at the most.

5.1 The Banking Crises in the late 19th Century

The Panic of 1837 was the first major crisis in the 19th century that profoundly transformed patterns of industrial production and financial markets. In 1833, president

Andrew Jackson disbanded the First Bank of the United States, which was both a quasi-commercial bank and a prototype of federal monetary administration authority. That year was followed by three consecutive years of economic growth, industrial exuberance, and credit expansion. At that time, British industrialization created huge demands for American cotton, prosperous international trade increased the import of silver, and relaxed federal supervision of financial markets also absorbed European capitals into investment in the US transport projects. Nevertheless, improved transport in the US increased the efficiency of the production and supply of cotton, resulting in a sharp fall in cotton prices. As a large number of merchants, plantation owners and workers depended on the sale of cotton for profits and repayment of their bank loans, the continuous fall of cotton prices caused widespread debt default. Faced with a higher and higher risk of failure of repayment, when banks in New York raised interest rates and decreased lending by a large margin, indirectly leading to a dramatic plummet of the prices of stocks and other securities that were connected to cotton producers, thus lowering cotton prices even further. Crisis broke out simultaneously in the debt market and in cotton production, which developed into a 4-year recession that devastated the whole economy. This crisis and recession reshuffled the banking sector and made cotton production more agile to the changes of demands.

The Panic of 1873 was another major shock to the US economy in the 19th century that contained historical significance. The *Coinage Act of 1873* established the gold standard in the US which changed the ecology of finance and trade in the US dramatically. This change forced silver to retreat from US financial and credit system and dealt a huge blow to some banks, mines, and farms that used to build their profits on circulations of silver, which was made even worse as a series of disruptions occurred in Europe due to the termination of the Prussia-France war. Domestic and international disruptions and disturbances halted the boom brought by the transcontinental railway construction and put many overexpanded businesses under stress. In September 1873, Jay Cooke & Company, one of the largest financial intermediaries of the US failed to sell new bonds of Northern Pacific Railway, a project that it had invested heavily in the hope that the "railway boom" would continue. This failure led to its bankruptcy and initiated a locked-in effect that toppled many banks and financial brokerage institutions and also triggered a collapse in the stock market. Even the New York Stock Exchange was closed for some time. Unemployment spread out like wild fire from the banking sector to the manufacturing industry. The labor-business relations got constantly deteriorated and led to many strikes. This recession destroyed the hope of the American south to improve its infrastructure and speed up industrialization, widening the North-South gap in the fields of industry and transport.

5.2 The Great Depression and the New Deal

The financial crisis that happened in 1929 and the subsequent recession that persisted for almost ten years were termed "the Great Depression", which was one of the most significant and decisive stages in the history of the 20th century. It dealt a huge blow to the US society and profoundly transformed the ideology of its political elites and the life style of common people. On the Black Thursday of October 24th, 1929, an intensive wave of selling occurred in the New York Stock Exchange right after the opening bell, which immediately shocked the stock market and triggered a wave of panic. In the following week, prices took a free fall constantly and millions of dollars of market value evaporated in just a few days, despite a joint effort made by some of the most powerful tycoons of that time to prop up stock prices. Medium and small investors who were common people from middle class or working class found their savings wiped out almost overnight because they invested most of these savings into stocks. They had to reduce their consumption to the utmost degree and soon were forced to confront unemployment because this crisis pulled many companies into bankruptcy. Waves after waves of bankruptcies and close-downs swept all over the country. A strong sentiment of indignation and despair spread across every section of American society and the US entered the darkest time of the 20th century.

British economist John Maynard Keynes attributed this crisis to severe insufficient demands created by the serious decline in labor's income relative to profits of capital and the incapacity of the government to increase consumers' demand through budget deficit and spending. He proposed a set of expansionary fiscal and monetary policies that was summarized as Keynesianism several years later. In echo to this rise of Keynesianism, US president Franklin D. Roosevelt formulated a series of laws, regulations, and measures to intervene in the economy collectively called "the New Deal," which stood as a sharp contrast to the laissez-faire policy held by his predecessor, Herbert Hoover. F.D.R. raised a huge amount of national debt through Treasury bonds and spent it on large public projects, so as to provide laid-off workers with relief and jobs and create new demands to recover the economy. He also passed a set of laws and regulations to establish a social security system that might cushion the shocks brought by waves of bankruptcies of businesses. In the meantime, he also took an effort to reshuffle the banking sector and reorganize the system of financial markets. From 1933 to 1935, he managed to put into effect a series of laws that reformed the whole financial system, such as the *Emergency Banking Act* that eliminated poor-quality banks and reshaped the banking sector, and the *Glass-Steagall Act* that separated traditional commercial banking from securities brokerage. He pushed the US government to abandon the gold standard to increase the political leadership's capacity to handle international monetary situations. Through his new deal and thanks to the stimulation of war-time production initiated in 1940, the US finally stepped out of the dark time of the Great Depression. From then on, the American political elites no longer regarded the perception of "laissez-faire" as a divine principle for managing a free market economy and began to accept the doctrine of Keynesianism that emphasizes the necessity of government interventions in a market economy.

5.3 The Great Recession and the 2008 Financial Crisis

Since the early 1980s, new waves of globalization was emerging after the profound structural transformations of the world economy in the 1970s, and the US domestic economy went through a process of deregulation and liberalization influenced by the fading of Keynesianism and the rise of neoliberalist economics. These two trends helped to create breakthroughs in information technologies and brought into the US a ten-year boom during the 1990s. However, the overexpansion of deregulation and liberalization also fermented a new round of bubbles and crises. Particularly, the repeal of the *Glass-Steagall Act* in 1999 dramatically expanded the business scope of securities brokerage institutions such as investment banks. These institutions began to delve into unregulated and less supervised fields with a desire for extraordinary profits. Partly pushed by some investment banks' impulsive to expand the housing mortgage business through a new financial alchemy called "mortgage-based securities" (MBS), nurtured by the inconsiderate housing policy of the George H. W. Bush administration that increased real estate-related credit by several times, a housing bubble gradually appeared in the US in the mid-2000s.

Irrational exuberance pushed risk-prone investment banks and other financial brokerage institutions to increase the amounts of their credits and accelerate the issue of their mortgage-based securities. Just at that time, newly invented financial derivatives, such as the Credit Default Swap (CDS), were introduced into the securities market and widely adopted by institutional investors and financial brokers for the purpose of getting more effective collaterals for their own risky investments. The combination of mortgage (which is a traditional form of debt) with securities generated an innate destabilizing effect on the securities markets, because the shocks from a defaulted mortgage would be magnified by the speculative effect of securities markets. What was even worse was the connections of CDS with MBS since CDS itself always develops into a vast network of collaterals among a diversity of investors and brokers. Therefore, when the housing bubble burst in 2008 due to a sudden and ferocious plummet of real estate prices, the subprime credit of housing mortgages became defaulted in large quantities and produced a domino effect through complex chains of MBS and CDS that magnified, intensified, and prolonged the destabilizing and destroying effect originating from the price plummet in real estate markets.

In this way, the 2008 financial crisis was triggered and spread all over the US. As a result, the most serious recession since the time of Great Depression of the 1930s occurred in the last years of the first decade of the 21st century and dragged the whole world into a period of slow-down and decline. As if the Pandora's box was suddenly opened, this crisis initiated a locked-in process in the world economy and global politics. It directly ignited the European Sovereign Debt Crisis of 2009 – 2010 and indirectly facilitated the "Arab Spring" of 2010 – 2011. On the one hand, Europe became more and more disintegrated since the sovereign debt crisis and underwent a series of crises, such as the Ukraine crisis of 2014 – 2015, Brexit of 2016 – 2020, terrorist attacks of 2015 – 2017, and the rise of domestic populism since 2016. On the other hand, it also shifted the power distribution of the world and sharpened the big-power rivalries of the present day.

Essay Questions:

1. What is the difference between finance in a broad sense and in a narrow sense? How did the broad-sense finance in the total GDP of the US change in the past two decades?

2. Name different kinds of financial intermediaries in the US financial system and discuss the difference between commercial banking and investment banking.

3. What is open outcry auction? Why are there fewer open outcry auctions presently? How is the circuit breaker mechanism applied in the New York Stock Exchange?

4. Why is the rate of federal funds so important and so closely observed by almost all the economists and financial analysts of the US and the world?

5. What are the defining features of the US financial system? What led to the decline of Keynesianism and the rise of Monetarism in the early 1970s?

6. Why is the repeal of the *Glass-Steagall Act* in 1999 reviewed as a turning point that initiated the housing bubble of the first decade of the 21st century and the ensuing 2008 financial crisis?

7. When and why did the US shift from bimetallism to the gold standard and abandon the gold standard later? In what sense did the Bretton Woods System partially recover the gold standard and how did the System collapse?

8. What are the electoral political-business cycle and partisan political-business cycle? Can you name some historical cases of these two cycles?

Unit 8　Education

In the US, education has long been cultivating numerous talents and promoting progress in different dimensions. As the American economic, political and military strengths rest largely on education, the reform and development of education often go ahead of social transformation. In fact, great importance has been attached to education since colonial times. Upon setting foot on American soil, European settlers carried to the New World their tradition of prioritizing education, and made great efforts to set up various educational institutions. Later on, the founding fathers viewed education as the foundation of the nation. Though there have been considerable changes in educational thought and system, the emphasis on education has remained the same. Generally speaking, American education is comprised of preschool education, elementary education, secondary education and higher education. There are both public schools and private schools in each phase of education. By the 1960s, the American educational system had already developed into the world's largest and most comprehensive educational one, featuring the major characteristics of universality, decentralization, generalization and specialization.

1　Educational System

On the one hand, decentralization is practiced in the American educational system. Because of this, the US does not have a national school system administered by the federal government. Accordingly, the federal government has no power over school curricula or educational management in individual schools. Though the federal government has played an important role in promoting American education, it is the state governments that retain the right to establish and operate public schools. Besides, state and local school districts, as a rule, determine specific educational programs and policies for local communities. On the other hand, in accordance with the US Constitution, the educational systems of different states are virtually the same. Normally, the educational system of each state consists of such four phases as preschool education, elementary education, secondary education and higher education.

1.1 Preschool Education

Generally speaking, preschool education means any education that children receive before elementary education. In the US, it normally refers to education for children between 3 to 5 years of age. Before attending elementary schools at 6, American children experience three stages of development, i.e. infants (0-1 year old), toddlers (1-3 years old), and preschoolers (3-5 years old). As for children between 0 to 5 years of age, the majority of them receive education from nursery schools, day-care centers, children centers, pre-kindergartens (usually for 4-year-old children) and kindergartens (usually for 5-year-old children). American public elementary schools usually provide one to two years of free preschool education before elementary education. Hence kindergarten is considered the starting point of American public education. There are both publicly and privately funded preschool education institutions like public preschools and church-affiliated children centers. Private preschools can be further divided into two groups – non-profit and for-profit ones. Though most preschool educational institutions are privately operated, preschoolers from low-income families can receive free preschool education through the Head Start program funded by the federal government. In most states, preschool education is optional. About 64 percent of preschoolers receive preschool education, and a great number of 5-year-old children attend public kindergartens.

American preschool education emphasizes the development of children's learning and hands-on abilities, adaptability, interpersonal communication and teamwork spirit. Preschool educational institutions invariably give priority to children's safety, which has been written down in detail in their rules and regulations. Furniture, lockers and electrical appliances in the schools are equipped with protective devices, so as to prevent children from being hurt. For instance, the power supply of electrical equipment is wrapped with the insulation covering and the sharp corner of furniture is covered with the rubber cushion. During the children's learning process, teachers play an essential role. First, they vividly read stories to the children, organize various activities like role-play, handwork, drawing, singing and dancing. In this way, children learn knowledge through playing and doing. Second, they teach the children a rudimentary knowledge of reading and arithmetic as well as self-care skills, which prepares the children for study at elementary schools. Third, respecting children's different personalities, needs and choices, they give individualized teaching in accordance with children's aptitudes. In this aspect, a sizable number of skills are taught strategically in order to meet the diversity of children's learning. Fourth, teachers utilize a variety of methods to ensure the physical and mental health of the children. When children face difficulties and setbacks, teachers will encourage them not to give up or give in. If any children are misbehaving or naughty, teachers will communicate with them rather than scold or punish them. Fifth, teachers cultivate children's teamwork spirit and leadership. They will lead the children to realize the importance of cooperation, sharing and communication during the activities. Last but not least, teachers normally involve parents in children's early education. It comes as no surprise that, parents are informed of the children's performance at school by teachers when they pick up their children after school, or through parent-teacher meetings. Undoubtedly, all of the teachers' efforts are conducive to developing children's diverse interests and forming good habits, laying the ground for their long-term development.

1.2 Elementary and Secondary Education

Since colonial times, American elementary and secondary education have made considerable achievements, and played a crucial role in economic prosperity and social advancement. There lie historical, political and cultural reasons for this phenomenon. First, the US has a profound tradition of attaching great importance to education. When the early settlers, especially the Puritans, set foot in the New World, they placed emphasis on education and set up schools. Up till now, the tradition has been well kept. At present, it is still exerting huge influences on American society and people. Second, with disparate and flexible operating models, the educational system varies from state to state across the country. It is in line with the federalism applied in the US political system. Because of the division of power, the federal government is responsible for the macro-control of education, such as education legislation and providing funds for certain educational programs. By contrast, specific educational issues, such as school building and running, ought to be determined by each state. In addition, the coexistence of public, private and home schools accommodates the varied needs of students. Furthermore, educational programs, curricula and tests are determined in accordance with local wishes and market demands by the local community. Fourth, as a nation of immigrants, America makes full use of immigrants' talents, learns from their educational strengths, and takes their educational needs into consideration. This leads to the diversity of the student body and teaching methods in American education.

  Through centuries of ongoing reforms and consistent exploration, there have been well-developed and multi-functional elementary and secondary educational systems. As early as the 17th century, free public schools at public expense were founded in a few areas. In 1642, Massachusetts required local parents to provide schooling for their children. Five years later, it issued a decree that each town with over 50 families should provide a teacher, and each town with over 100 families should establish a school. After the founding of the nation, rapid industrialization and westward expansion fueled the movement for public education. In 1852, Massachusetts passed the first compulsory education law in America. The Post WWI era found the universality of compulsory education in elementary schools, and the Post WWII decade witnessed universal secondary education. Currently, all the states have enacted compulsory education laws, requiring the youth of school age to receive education at school or at least to be home-schooled. The compulsory education lasts from 11 to 13 years. There are altogether 12 academic years for elementary and secondary education in four different modes: 1) 8-year elementary school study plus 4-year high school study; 2) 4-year elementary school study, 4-year middle school study plus 4-year high school study; 3) 6-year elementary school study, 3-year junior high school study plus 3-year senior high school study; 4) 6-year elementary school study plus 6-year combined junior-senior high school study. When students graduate from high school, they are around 16 to 18 years old.

American educators generally hold that, as people are educational objects, students should be respected and understood during the educational process. With this as a consensus, American elementary and secondary education takes on distinctive characteristics. First of all, the ideal of humanistic education has been applied in elementary and secondary schools. It means that education is student-centered and people-oriented. Specifically speaking, the characters and privacy of students are fully respected and well protected, and their curiosity about and interest in the world are cherished and encouraged. For instance, a compact is made by all the students, and put up on the wall of the classroom. It is equal to one's self-discipline, calling students' attention to respect, responsibility, integrity and mutual-help in class. At the same time, schools provide all-round services for student's academic and social life at school. In order to secure the effectiveness of teaching, instruction is conducted in small classes. On average, there are 20 to 25 students per class in the public school and 15 to 20 students per class in the private school. Thus, teachers are able to give individualized instructions and adjust their teaching methods in accordance with students' performance. Additionally, school facilities are advanced, user-friendly and free of charge. School libraries usually have a rich collection of books, magazines and multi-media materials, which suit the varied learning styles of the students. School buses are available to ferry students to and from school. In some public schools, students from low-income families can even have free lunch.

Secondly, patriotic education has been reinforced and paid special attention to, especially after the 9·11 attacks. The American government takes every opportunity like the festivals and ceremonies to foster patriotism in the American heart. Independence Day, Flag Day, Washington's Birthday, Veterans Day, and presidential inaugurations are the best occasions to evoke the patriotic feelings of all Americans. Customarily, the inaugural speeches made by the presidents are permeated with a patriotic flavor, which is exemplified by the speeches of president Franklin D. Roosevelt, president J. F. Kennedy, and president Baraka Obama. Another important means to transmit patriotism is the Hollywood movie. In these movies, Americans are portrayed as the world's saviors and heroes, and American values are praised and propagated, as is shown in *Saving Private Ryan*, *Rocky* and *Mission: Impossible*, *Pearl Harbor*. Furthermore, through civic education in different phases, civic skills are cultivated, and a sense of citizenship is fostered. As a rule, children in elementary schools are taught to recognize various American symbols, acquire a rudimentary knowledge of American history, and have a perceptual understanding of democracy via the election of class leaders. In doing so, secondary schools usually bring home to students the rights and obligations of American citizens, the American political system and the US constitution and legal system. This, to a large extent, helps students develop a strong sense of civic responsibility. In recent two decades, due to the terrorist attack and globalization, American society has stressed historical education in and out of school. Schools invariably require students to learn important historical events or documents, such as the Independence War, the Civil War, the *Declaration of Independence*, and the US Constitution. Historic sites like the Independence Hall and the residences of the founding fathers are set aside and preserved as museums for public tours. Besides, students are exposed to the cultural values of different countries and ethnic groups around the world. Such being the case, students are more likely to realize the importance of communication, understanding and tolerance. Meanwhile, they are able to identify with American values while making comparisons between

American culture and other cultures.

 Thirdly, the courses of elementary and secondary schools lay emphasis on both fundamental knowledge and practical use, as well as project learning and hands-on abilities. The courses are divided into required subjects and electives. The core required subjects include English, mathematics, science, and social science, which account for almost half of the teaching hours. The required subjects should accord with the curriculum system designed in each state. Students are required to pass the final exams of these subjects before graduation. Apart from the required subjects, students are free to choose the electives that they are interested in. There also lies a great amount of flexibility in teachers. Normally, teachers are allowed to offer courses according to their strengths and local needs. If schools, during evaluation, find that the new courses are fit for students and conducive to their development, the new courses will be approved. There are at least dozens of different elective subjects up to more than one hundred, such as music, art, photography, penmanship, driving, gardening, cooking, programming, architectural design, etc. Students can either raise livestock on school farms, or work in wheat plots. The electives take the diversity and freedom of students into full account. On the one hand, they satisfy students' thirst for knowledge at different stages through playing, which cultivates their characters and develops their potential. On the other hand, they help shape students' in-depth perceptions and understanding of real life, laying the foundation for broad vision and their future careers. Furthermore, a large variety of clubs and students' associations are organized. Students can take part in these organizations in their spare time to enrich their lives and improve their abilities. What's worth mentioning is that, American elementary and secondary schools pay great attention to providing project learning opportunities to students. According to students' topics of research projects, schools will not only assign teachers who are familiar with students' research fields as mentors, but also invite experts in certain fields from society to give professional guidance. In order to collect first-hand materials, students have to go to the community, the lab, the factory, the store, etc. Consequently, students are able to acquire research abilities and master research methods.

Fourthly, cooperative learning and innovation are highly valued. Cooperative learning requires students to study in groups in class like group discussion and group reading, and do research projects after class. In doing so, students learn how to get along with their partners and solve problems. During the process, students also come to see the importance of mutual help, mutual respect and compromise-making, so as to achieve win-win results. While cultivating the spirit of innovation, teachers show students the process of inventing things, and introduce the fundamentals of invention. More importantly, teachers inspire students to think independently and critically, encourage them to ask questions and challenge ready answers. Furthermore, respecting students' subjectivity, teachers lead students to do the experiment on their own, experience the generation of knowledge, and finally come to their own conclusions through careful observation and analysis. By contrast, rote memorization of textbooks and deferent acceptance of teachers' answers are unwelcome and discouraged. Therefore, the class usually leaves enough time for students' reflection and discussion. As for elementary and secondary schools, apart from study in class, after-class study is equally important. Because such different activities in daily life as access to nature and social work will inevitably help students to discover problems, raise questions, and come up with solutions.

Fifthly, teaching approaches are flexible and diverse. As teaching is student-centered, teachers fully respect their students and communicate with their students on an equal footing. In class, students are motivated and encouraged to think outside the box and put forward their own ideas. If students have any questions, they feel free to interrupt their teachers and raise their questions in no time. Discussion sessions are set aside for group study, mutual learning and debates. Teachers try their best to design activities and questions, and make students feel at ease in class. As for homework, the workload is not heavy. Teachers assign the tasks with instructive and practical significance. In order to finish their homework, students need to observe nature and have a better understanding of society. It comes as no surprise that, taught in this way, students are more likely to build up confidence in their thinking and hands-on abilities. In addition, teaching can be carried out beyond the classroom. As organizers and instructors, teachers make good use of social resources to engage students in learning. For example, history teachers can take their students to museums or historic sites, where curators or guides provide more historical knowledge. Music teachers can take their students to concerts or invite certain musicians to talk with students in the cafeteria. In-class instruction and off-campus study broaden students' vision, enrich their knowledge, and enhance their sense of citizenship.

Finally, elementary and secondary schools have great autonomy in educational management, supported by parents and local communities. As there are no national textbooks or examinations, schools can make individual decisions about the textbook, the teaching and the examination. A great number of schools design their own curricula and programs to meet the needs of local communities. Teachers can adjust their teaching methods and content according to the acceptance of students, and then offer individualized teaching to students. Most teachers are dedicated to teaching with a strong sense of responsibility and a great passion for the job. The development of education is inseparable from parental and community involvement. The Parent-Teacher Association (PTA) has been established in almost every school. This organization serves as a bridge between families and schools. Parents can help schools raise funds, and participate in school activities and management. For instance, they can volunteer to help in the school library, or they can offer advice and suggestions on educational programs and reforms. Communities also provide financial and manpower support to advance local education.

1.3 Higher Education

Ever since the American first institution of higher learning, Harvard College (now Harvard University), was founded in 1636, US higher education has gone through centuries of development. It followed the British model in the 17th and 18th centuries, learned from German universities in the 19th century, and formed its own educational model and style in the 20th century, especially after WWII. At present, with the multi-level and multi-type operating model, the US is the world leader in higher education. This is evidenced by the largest number of the world's first-class universities in America, and the best quality of school-running among all the institutions of higher learning around the world. From the 20th century onwards, due to domestic and international situations, the American government has paid an increasing attention to higher education, by enacting educational laws and providing financial support. Through decades of development in the 20th century, American higher education has changed from elite education to universal education. Nowadays as many as 75 percent of American high school graduates can enter universities and colleges. Fundamentally speaking, the rapid development of higher education, together with the cultivation of large numbers of talents, can be explained as part of the reason why the US rises as a world giant in such a short time.

In general, contemporary American higher education has its own features. First, it adheres to the ideals of freedom, openness and inclusiveness. There are various schools of educational philosophy in America, with John Dewey's as the most influential in the 20th century. Dewey's educational philosophy is in essence pragmatism. On the one hand, it emphasizes practice, i.e. learning by doing. Not surprisingly, the social aspect of human nature has been given priority in this philosophy. Human beings are expected to improve themselves via their communication with others. On the other hand, it is people-oriented, which stresses adjusting education to real situations. Such being the case, education should cultivate students' abilities in accordance with their interests and nature. At the same time, education should serve for a democratic society and its development. Schools, viewed in such a context, should be the microcosm of society, rather than ivory towers divorced from reality. Taken together, education should have both flexibility and humanity, and combine liberalism with pragmatism.

Second, diversity and universality are the most prominent features. As the US Constitution reserves the administrative power of education to the states, the US does not have any national universities. It means that education is under local control. Even though founding fathers like George Washington once proposed a national university, they were unable to create one. Currently, there are various ways of founding universities and colleges. Either individuals, organizations, corporations, religious groups, or state and local governments are allowed to set up schools. Additionally, different institutions of higher learning vary from each other in educational ideologies, goals, methods and operating models. These circumstances are inseparable from the US democratic system. In Americans' view, the democratic system requires the devotion of knowledgeable persons, and school education can impart knowledge to students so as to promote democracy. Hence, schools are committed to constructing a more prosperous and harmonious society via the cultivation of democratic virtues. To this end, schools, institutions of higher learning included, should promote universal education.

The universality of American higher education means that Americans, irrespective of race, class, gender, sexuality, health, age, wealth, etc., have equal access to tertiary education. The democratization of American higher education started in the 1940s to the 1980s and 1990s. In 1944, the *Servicemen's Readjustment Act*, known as the "GI Bill of Rights," was passed to provide financial aid to the veterans of WWII to receive higher education or training. The law intended to reward those soldiers who had made great contributions in the war, alleviate the employment pressure caused by the influx of veterans into the job market. Besides, it was made to facilitate the cultivation of technicians and professionals, so as to meet the needs of economic growth. In 1946, veterans accounted for half of the students who got higher education. Within just a decade from 1940 to 1950, the number of college students doubled. Moreover, special programs such as Affirmative Action programs have been introduced to provide equal educational opportunities in American society since the 1960s. As the government shifted its attention from elite education to mass and universal education, its policies focused more on addressing education inequalities caused by racism, gender discrimination, poverty, physical limitations, etc. Consequently, schools and educational institutions funded by the government, in turn, carried out the

Affirmative Action programs in varying degrees. For example, while making admission decisions, they might give preferential treatment to minority students (e.g. members of ethnic groups and females) or even set quotas for these students. Furthermore, the development of American higher education was stimulated by the postwar technological revolution and the pressure from the Soviet Union. Sputnik, the first artificial satellite, was launched by the Soviet Union in 1957, which sent the US into panic. All of a sudden, Americans' sense of superiority in their science and technology vanished. Out of the need for national security, the US Congress passed the *National Defense Education Act* (NDEA). Recognizing the connection between education and defense, the law aimed to vigorously promote higher education. It stood as a milestone in the legislation of higher education, paving the way for universal education in postsecondary study. Last but not least, since the 1980s, there has been an increasing number of middle-aged and elder "returning students," who worked for several or many years before they returned to school. Besides, nowadays it is not unusual to meet part-time students who hold full-time jobs and study at school in their spare time. Therefore, student bodies have become more diverse.

Third, the development of institutions of higher learning is closely related to local needs. American higher education is oriented to the requirements of the market. Customarily, universities and colleges offer courses that reflect the needs of the students. As a result, postsecondary institutions create the credit system. Based on this student-oriented system, they build management and teaching systems. At the same time, university and college students are cultivated in accordance with the needs of the market. Since the US Constitution and tradition determine that education is a local matter, the federal government does not have the power of establishing and running schools across the nation. The goal of the US Department of Education is to ensure quality education and equality in education. In line with this goal, it is mainly responsible for providing federal financial aid to educational programs, gathering educational information such as teaching techniques and educational trends, and identifying key issues in education. State governments may play a role in deciding textbooks and taking charge of statewide standardized testing. It is the school board or the board of education in each school that guides and runs the school. Specifically speaking, it bears primary responsibility for making policies for the guidance of the school, developing the school curriculum, determining the direction of development, deciding the annual budget, appointing a superintendent, etc. As a rule, while setting the goals, the school board first analyzes the strengths of the school and the characteristics of population, economy and culture in local areas. And then it formulates its guiding principles to accommodate local needs. Needless to say, various requirements of the market bring about the diversity of the educational system of higher education. Linking up with the market, American postsecondary institutions develop quickly and significantly.

Last but not least, institutions of higher learning have undertaken reforms of specialization and professionalization. On the one hand, the management process is adjusted to match the teaching, operation and resource distribution of the school, becoming more specialized and professional. On the other hand, according to their own needs of development and requirements for teaching and management positions, postsecondary institutions have conducted the standardization of operation and management. They set standards for positions of different disciplines and fields, and determine the qualifications and promotion for teaching staff. Because the core of specialization and professionalization lies in the specialization and professionalization of the faculty, especially well-known professors and scholars. Reforms in these two aspects show the efficient and sound management of the American educational system.

All of these important features give an impetus to the development of contemporary American institutions of higher learning by leaps and bounds. In the 21st century, in spite of controversial issues and problems, American higher education keeps moving forward.

2 Public and Private Schooling

The US compulsory education law requires children of school age to attend a public or private school, or at least to be homeschooled for a certain period. The law shows that Americans have different channels of receiving education. According to the statistics, in the autumn of 2017, public elementary and secondary schools accounted for 75 percent of all elementary and secondary schools, while the proportion of private ones was 25 percent. In terms of enrollment, about 88 percent of American students went to public schools, about 10 percent attended private schools, and around 2 percent received homeschooling. As for postsecondary education, the statistics revealed that, in the fall of 2017, public postsecondary institutions made up 38 percent of all the institutions, while private ones accounted for 62 percent. But the enrollment of public postsecondary institutions was much larger than that of private ones, with 73.5 percent of university students going to public ones and 26.5 percent studying in private ones. The data indicates that most Americans received formal public schooling for both basic and higher education. In spite of this fact, public and private schooling remain the most common ways to receive education in the US.

2.1 Public Schools

Public school is the bedrock of American basic education, symbolizing the democratic system that Americans take great pride in. In the American cultural context, the public school, by definition, is the public-funded, government-administered school that takes charge of the education of all citizens. It commonly includes public primary and secondary schools, and public postsecondary institutions. But even if public institutions of higher learning are funded by public expense, attending such institutions is not free. Typically, students have to pay the tuition fee which costs 15,000 to 25,000 each year. Generally speaking, public school has the following features: 1) the public nature, which means that education can not only improve one's morality and manners but also have positive impacts on society; 2) commonality, which means that the public school can transmit the common values and beliefs as well as social ethics, so as to maintain social stability and national unity; 3) equality, which means that the public school education opposes the polarization and segregation of the rich and the poor, and advocates equal access to education; 4) the national nature, which means that the school is created and run by the government; 5) the school is primarily maintained at public expense supported by taxpayer dollars. How did the American public school come into being? What are the issues facing the public school today?

Ever since the first immigrants established the Massachusetts Bay colony, public schools have taken root on American soil. A number of town schools, the earliest form of public schools, were created, including Latin schools, reading and writing schools (also known as 3R schools) and dame schools. Latin schools were mostly funded by private contributions, while reading and writing schools and dame schools were both private and public funded. But none of them were tuition free. At that time, a lot of the teaching was done at home by parents or the tutors or masters of apprentices. Though children were not required to receive education at school, the elite class usually sent their sons to Latin schools for formal education. Besides, some women taught a group of children basic reading and writing at home and charged little. These women's houses were called dame schools. Furthermore, in reading and writing school, children learned reading, writing and arithmetic. In 1635, the first official public school – Boston Latin School was opened. Up till 1647, there were 11 town schools in 60 towns of New England. All of these schools were voluntarily set up by local residents with self-governance and self-financing. Although there were funding resources like donations and taxpayer money, most of the towns relied on charging the tuition fee. These early town schools laid the foundation for the practice of the Massachusetts education laws in the 1640s.

Regarded as the first education law in American history, the *Massachusetts Act of 1642* required parents or masters of apprentices to ensure the basic education of children under the supervision and control of the government. If parents or guardians did not fulfil their responsibilities, the government can send uneducated children to get an education. Five years later, the *Old Deluder Satan Act of 1647* was passed in Massachusetts. The law required towns of 50 or more families to hire a schoolmaster for the instruction of reading and writing, and towns with populations of 100 or more families to establish a grammar school for the preparation of students for higher education. Moreover, schools were operated at the local level and funded either by the tuition fee or by local public funds. The law was viewed as the earliest legislation on public schools, which resulted in the founding of public-funded schools in each town of Massachusetts. With these laws as the basis, other colonies in New England followed suit. Under such circumstances, basic education gradually became a mandated public responsibility in New England.

However, New England's efforts met setbacks in 1686 when Britain reorganized the Dominion of New England and cancelled all the laws relating to mandated public schooling in New England. At the same time, a series of changes emerged. First, in many towns, the dame school and the reading and writing school merged into the elementary school, which provided more formal teaching of reading, writing and arithmetic around religion. The Latin grammar school remained the same. All of these schools were supervised by some competent local residents. Second, the school district was created in New England and promoted across colonies. In 1766, the Connecticut Congress authorized the school district to set up the local school. In 1789, Massachusetts first recognized the legal status of the school district. As a result, the school district became the educational institution at the grassroots level. But actually from 1686 to the independence of the nation, public education was at a low ebb. With economic and social development, the public's requirements for education changed over time, but the teaching content and school system did not change much.

Public education made slow and steady improvements from the founding of the nation to the 1830s. After the revolutionary war, the founding fathers and the federal government attached great importance to education. For instance, George Washington suggested that a national university should be built to bring up political leaders for the New Republic. In addition, Thomas Jefferson proposed a bill for establishing a system of public education. In the bill, he was adamant that a formal education system supported by taxpayer money should be created. Congress enacted the Land Ordinance of 1785, which divided the newly acquired land into townships consisting of 36 one-square-mile sections. According to the ordinance, Section 16 was set aside to establish a public school. From then on, most of the new states would grant land for public schools and use the tax of public land to fund schools. To a large extent, the law laid the policy and material groundwork for public education. Meanwhile, states played an increasing role in public education. New York state was the first to establish the state-level administrative system of education. It also reorganized the Board of Regents of the University of the State of New York in 1787, which was in charge of secondary and higher education in the state of New York. In 1789, Massachusetts took the lead in passing the nation's first comprehensive education law. It required towns to establish elementary schools with a six-month school year and communities with more than 200 families to set up grammar schools. In addition, it made standards for teacher qualifications. Furthermore, though the proposal of a national university failed to be accepted by all Americans, state universities sprung up across the nation. The state of North Carolina founded the nation's first state university in 1795, and then other states in the south, west and east regions followed in its wake. By 1860, as many as 66 state universities were established across the country.

Apart from the efforts of the federal and state governments, Americans' perceptions of public education underwent sea changes. People began to take the promotion of public welfare as the major responsibility of the nation, and public education served as the means to achieve this goal. Additionally, along with industrial growth and economic development, people came to realize the importance of knowledge for the safety and happiness of the whole society. Furthermore, since the birth of the nation, the ideals of popular sovereignty, egalitarianism, humanitarianism and rationalism have taken hold in the New Republic. At the same time, beginning from the 18th century to the beginning of the 19th century, the charity school movement was launched. Out of humanity, the wealthy people who were concerned about social issues founded charity schools to remedy the defects of public-funded schools, so as to reduce poverty and crime. In other words, schools were used as a social means to help children adjust to the life of the industrial society and address social problems. It echoed the public's perception of public schools as the way to improve social well-being. Besides, the monitorial system (or Lancasterian system) that was extensively practiced in charity schools provided an efficient, low-cost and convenient teaching method for the expansion of the scope of public education.

From the 1830s onwards, the common school movement, led by Horace Mann and Henry Barnard, was prevalent across the nation. The creation of the nation's first State Board of Education in 1837 marked the beginning of the movement. The campaign arose out of a wide range of social backgrounds. The labor organization requested equal and public-funded education, because the charity school, though providing the poor with access to education, drew the line between the rich and the poor. The working class was also offended by the sympathy shown by the wealthy. At this particular moment, German public schools set a good example for Americans. Such being the case, government officials like governors began to advocate public education, and hundreds of organizations that supported free public schools were founded, such as the American Institute of Instruction and American Lyceum. In addition, education assemblies were held in all of the states to propagate public education and court the support for the establishment of free public schools. In 1840, there were dozens of education publications. Some of the most influential publications were the *American Journal of Education, Common School Assistant* and *Common School Journal*.

The movement worked toward several major issues. First, it helped build the state board of education in most of the states and reform the school district system. Hence it ended the lack of coordination under the school district system, and education was placed under the supervision and management of the state system in a more formal and systematic way. Second, the educational tax based on one's property was levied and public schools bolstered by the tax were set up. It enabled the rich to be clear that public schools served for the goods of both the poor and the rich. Because education could prevent crime and protect property. Third, a new model of public school came into being. It provided equal access to everyone, regardless of race, class, gender and religion. The new school also gave moral education, both religious and political education included, so as to form common views of religion and politics as well as maintain social stability. Due to the common school movement, public schooling became the majority form of schooling in 1860. Nevertheless, these public schools were not totally free. It is up until 1940 that free public education and public schools came to emerge. In 1852, the compulsory attendance act was passed in the Bay State of Massachusetts. It was the nation's first attempt to require the attendance of children between the ages of 8 and 14 at school. It also required each city and town of the state to offer elementary public schools. Following that, numerous states enacted similar laws concerning mandatory attendance for children. By 1918, compulsory education was implemented in all states. The compulsory education law, in large measure, facilitated universal access to basic education.

The common school movement indisputably sped up the establishment and development of the public education system. Though elementary schools were the main beneficiaries, secondary institutions also benefited from the movement. The post-Civil War era found the rise of public secondary schools. Just within two decades between 1870 and 1890, the public secondary school enrollment increased by over 150 percent. In 1930, its enrollment was almost 40 times bigger than that half a century ago. One of the important reasons for this phenomenon was the changing requirements of people for education. After the Civil War, with economic and industrial growth, Americans, the middle class in particular, were in great need of secondary education, which provided diverse and practical courses for the work in the field of industry, business, science and technology. Moreover, the legislation of compulsory education gave an impetus to the secondary school enrollment rate, which surged from 20 percent in 1910 to 95 percent in 1970. The US became the first country in the world to have universal access to secondary education. Furthermore, during the progressive movement, a reform movement to cure social ills at the turn of the 20th century, education was viewed as a mild and effective means for social reforms. In such social movements as the settlement house movement and the assimilation of immigrants, public schools were endowed with the responsibility of transforming society and disseminating American values. In American society, sweeping social changes and higher requirements for education led to the reform of the educational system. In 1867, the federal Office of Education (now the US Department of Education) was created to help states build effective public educational systems. Its duty continued to expand in the following decades to support postsecondary institutions and vocational education. In 1918, the Commission on the Reorganization of Secondary Education issued a thirty-two-page report named *the Cardinal Principles of Secondary Education*, which put forward the objectives of secondary education on the basis of individual differences. In addition, the report also listed the comprehensive high school as the major model of secondary education.

In the 20th century, American public education encountered several crises. One happened during the Great Depression. The economic recession resulted in the reduction in educational funds, which further invited tension among teachers, school administrators, labor unions and the government. The other took place after WWII. The Cold War and Civil Rights Movements prompted people to place high hopes on public education to address social problems, but the results turned out to be disappointing. As education was considered the cornerstone of science, technology and national defense, it was imperative to reform public education. In response to this situation, American educator James Conant wrote *The American High School Today: A First Report to Interested Citizens* (1959) and *The Education of American Teachers* (1963). He proposed required core courses such as mathematics, foreign languages, science, literature, art and gifted education (i.e. programs which can support gifted and talented students). Besides, he called for improving the teaching quality and reinforcing the training for teachers. These suggestions became the guidance for the public secondary education reform in the 1950s and 1960s. But Conant's focus was the comprehensive high school, and his emphasis was put on the cultivation of talent in science and technology. Hence other talent and academic fields remained unheeded. Moreover, in 1958, the *National Defense Education Act* was passed to assist both basic and higher education, private and public. However, money was not distributed to every school. Instead, the federal government funded certain educational programs that would directly benefit national defense. Furthermore, in the 1960s, American educator Jerome Bruner developed a landmark curriculum based on social science, which was influential on educational programs. Nevertheless, during its application, it was hard for parents to understand and thereby utilize it. Finally, the War on Poverty initiative introduced numerous educational programs to end poverty and promote school integration. Because it was generally believed at that time that poverty and discrimination hindered schools from providing qualified people for national defense and economic development. As part of a grander legislative reform – "the Great Society," the War on Poverty initiative enacted legislation to expand social welfare. For instance, the *Elementary and Secondary Education Act* was passed in 1965. The far-reaching law intended to support students from low-income families to have equal access to quality primary and secondary education. The policy-makers held that educational equity would lead to equal results and finally eliminate poverty. Even if lots of money and energy were invested in those programs, there was no considerable progress. What's worse, white people had grievances against those programs, taking them as reverse discrimination. As for the government's measure of involuntary busing, white parents chose to move to the suburbs, causing "white flight." Owing to the failures of public education reforms, the uniformity and democratic function of public schools were played down. But educational reforms did not stop.

Beginning in the late 1960s, the alternative school movement was in full swing until the 1970s. Learning from previous lessons, it intended to provide more options for teaching content, methods and programs and give parents enough choices in public schooling, so as to improve the quality of education and realize educational equity.

Magnet schools were products of the movement. On the basis of free choice, magnet schools were created in part to end school segregation in a voluntary way. What makes them alluring is their specialized and diversified curriculum, with a particular focus on math, science, technology, art, gifted education, foreign languages, career education, Montessori, etc. They are free and open to students who live in or out of the school district. Therefore, students with varying backgrounds are attracted to magnet schools and thereby magnet schools are more diverse than conventional public schools. By 2020, there are 4340 magnet schools across the nation with more than 3.5 million students, and thereby magnet schools have become one of the hottest choices among public schools. But a magnet school may not just be in one's school district. In that case, students have to travel long distances through complicated commutes, which inevitably costs more time and energy. Besides, magnet schools haven't truly addressed such problems as high dropout rates and racial integration. These are the shortcomings of magnet schools.

Despite the fact that public schools made consistent efforts in reforms, there was no improvement in public education. An educational reform report known as *A Nation at Risk: The Imperative for Educational Reform* was released, which gave an education warning of the worsening quality of public education. Spurred by these circumstances, the American government propelled a series of educational reforms through the privatization of public schools in varying degrees. Of all the new policies that have been implemented, two are the most common and influential. One is the school voucher. The school voucher is, in essence, a form of government subsidizes. It is issued to allow parents the ability to choose the best school for their children. So far, this is the most controversial educational reform. The other is the charter school. The charter is in fact a legislative contract. The charter school refers to a public-funded school that is governed by an individual or organization (such as a teacher group, community organization, parents, business group, etc.) under the charter with local school boards. The school is, to a large measure, independent from the rules and regulations that the school district set for other public schools. Therefore, the charter school emphasizes autonomy and it is accountable for students' academic performance. If it does not achieve promised results, the school will be closed. Ever since the founding of the first charter school in Minnesota in 1991, charter schools have grown fast and enjoyed popularity in the US. Due to the economic downturn, the charter school now faces the challenge of insufficient funding.

After making lots of exploration and experimentation, Americans have successfully developed the public school system and advanced educational reform. In the new era, Americans continue to grapple with a number of hot issues in public education. They include but are not limited to school violence, decreased funding, dropout rates, school choice, quality education, curriculum and textbook, and the assessment system of the quality of education. It remains to be seen what new measures American education is going to take.

2.2 Private Schools

In the US, private schools refer to private-funded schools that are created and administered by non-governmental entities, including for-profit corporations and not-for-profit organizations like the church. As an indispensable part of the American educational system, private education boasts a long history in America.

When European settlers arrived on the North American continent in the early 17th century, they transplanted the European tradition of private education on American soil. According to the historical research, the College of Henrico in Jamestown, Virginia founded by Anglican Church in 1618 was the first chartered private school in the English colonies. But because of the conflict between whites and Native Americans, the school was never opened. In spite of a temporary setback, henceforth different Christian denominations set up schools at different levels respectively. Not surprisingly, most of the schools at that time were privately-owned and permeated with religious influence. Besides, in the self-sufficient agrarian society scattered with villages and towns, the teaching content and school year were random, and school management was loose and informal.

As for institutions of higher learning, prior to the US independence, a total of nine colleges had been founded and chartered in the 13 colonies. These colleges include Harvard College (1636), the College of William & Mary (1693), the Collegiate School (1701, now Yale University), the College of New Jersey (1746, now Princeton University), King's College (1754, now Columbia University), the College of Philadelphia (1755, now the University of Pennsylvania), the College of Rhode Island (1764, now Brown University), Queen's College (1766, now Rutgers University) and Dartmouth College (1769). They were small in scale, with only a few teachers and students. Modeled on the curriculum of Oxford and Cambridge universities, they trained students in theology and classic studies. Due to the close relationship with churches, they generally prepared students to be clergymen. Most of the students were from well-off families.

At the end of the 17th century and the beginning of the 18th century, when the economy and society developed quickly, an increasing number of people hoped to learn practical knowledge and skills. But public schools in this period still focused on traditional subjects such as Latin and divinity, and prepared a small number of students for higher education, which could no longer accommodate social needs. In this social milieu, private primary and secondary schools, which offered courses like sailing, bookkeeping and geography in accordance with students' needs and requirements, gained momentum. In fact, both the teaching content and schedule were tailored to students. For instance, night schools and boarding schools were established for those who had special needs for education. Those schools gradually developed into formal schools with organized management. They were known as "academies."

In 1751, Benjamin Franklin founded an academy in Philadelphia, signifying the beginning of the academy movement. Apart from providing classic studies, academies also offered practical training programs relating to life and career. In order to attract more students, they recruited women students who were ignored by public education, and taught subjects that meet women's needs and fit their interests. Some academies were created by individuals, some by corporations, and others by churches and other religious organizations. Private as they were, they obtained support from states, counties and towns. For example, they normally got a permit for tax reduction issued by the government, or sometimes received financial assistance and land grant from the government. In addition, they were allowed to accept donations and raise funds via issuing lottery. All academies charged tuition and enjoyed autonomy, independent from the organization and management of states. Evidently, academies, in many aspects, laid a solid foundation for the shaping of present private schools. Between 1830 and 1860 when public secondary schools were still in their infancy, academies stood out as the most important educational institutions that gave secondary education.

After the founding of the nation, private postsecondary institutions entered a new age of development. The previous colleges successively changed their names to universities. Besides, the decision of *Dartmouth College v. Woodward* (1819) set the precedent for providing legal support to the original charter of the private school, which protected the legitimate rights of private corporations in operating schools. This resulted in the rise of private institutions of higher learning from 1820 to 1860. According to the statistics, of all the 182 postsecondary institutions in 1860, 116 were private. Meanwhile, professional education like medical and law studies were added to the curricula of private universities. In addition, more attention was given to science and practical knowledge. Hence, many private universities founded colleges of science and began to offer subjects relating to industry and agriculture.

Influenced by the Civil War, academies encountered the problem of lacking funds. In addition to that, the courses of academies did not make timely adjustments, thereby not suiting new social needs anymore. Therefore, academies declined after the Civil War and began to make reforms, while public secondary schools started to flourish. In the postwar period, keeping up with the times, private postsecondary institutions sought the opportunity to leap. Benefiting from the *Morrill Act of 1862*, the Massachusetts Institute of Technology (1861) and Cornell University (1865) were financed to become leaders in national industrial and agricultural research. In 1876, John Hopkins University, the nation's first research university, was established.

Learning from Germany's Heidelberg University, it set up a graduate school and advocated research and innovation, which in many aspects revolutionized American higher education. From then onwards, other universities, such as Harvard University, Yale University, Princeton University, Columbia University and Cornell University, all introduced advanced educational experience from Germany, including the elective system, the seminar system and graduate education. The experience of German universities offered tremendous help to American universities, which enabled them to become world-renown prestigious universities.

Apart from acquiring academic and innovation advantages of private schools, many families sent their children to private schools out of religious needs. The first Amendment to the US Constitution prohibited religious instruction and services in public schools. Thus, private schools became the first choice for religious families. The ruling of *Pierce v. Society of Sisters* (1925) served as a significant precedent for ensuring parents' freedom of choice for children's schooling. Equally significant, it recognized the legitimate rights of private schools. In other words, parents were permitted to send their children for private schooling, where religious instruction could be given and religious services conducted. At the same time, private schools were allowed to operate alongside public schools. More than five decades later, the decision of *Mueller v. Allen* (1983) opened the door for states to offer indirect means of support to private schools. Since then, government aid to private schools has been allowed if it meets all of the following conditions: 1) the purpose of aid is secular; 2) the aid does not advance religion; 3) the aid does not result in an excessive entanglement between government and church. Henceforth, private schools have enjoyed steady development. Currently, there are more than 30,000 private elementary and secondary schools, educating 10 percent of all school students. Of all the private elementary and secondary schools, about 50 percent are run by Catholic Church, 28 percent by other denominations, and 22 percent by non-religious organizations. And there are over 2600 private postsecondary institutions, serving 26.5 percent of all college students.

Spreading across the nation, private schools have taken on distinctive features through hundreds of years of development. First, almost free from the intervention of the government, private schools enjoy a great deal of autonomy in operation and management. As a rule, private schools hold distinguished educational philosophies and unique running models. And the government normally set laws and regulations for the taxation of private schools as well as the safety and health of teachers and students. Moreover, private schools could determine on their own the admission, recruitment and curriculum. Furthermore, teaching is conducted in small classes, with emphasis on the cultivation of students' characters and independent thinking. Finally, seminars and workshops are frequently used in class, so as to encourage students to think and express their opinions.

Second, both teachers and students achieve good performances. As for teachers, they feel free to play an active role in teaching, educational experiments and academic research. In addition, they are motivated to put forward their opinions on such important matters as school development, teaching assessment and curriculum formulation. Usually special attention is given to their ideas, which imbues them with a sense of achievement. As private primary and secondary schools place emphasis on the study of academic courses and offer a wide range of elective courses, students are able to choose more academic and elective courses, so as to be better prepared for college admission. Moreover, they set high standards for students' academic performance, so teachers are ready to offer academic assistance to students and give more home assignments. In private postsecondary institutions, intellectual freedom and research innovation are highly valued. In this case, students are motivated to come up with new ideas and achieve academic excellence.

Third, private schools not only stress intellectual education, but also pay great attention to disciplinary and moral education. Due to the small number of students at school, private schools can give strict supervision over students and harsh punishment against those who violate rules and regulations. In doing so, students can develop good moral codes and a strong sense of citizenship. Meanwhile, truancy, drug abuse and school violence can be prevented, and a good order and safe environment can be built at school. Thus, both teachers and students at private schools believe that their discipline is stricter and more effective than that in public schools.

In the new age, owing to internal and external reasons, private schools, especially private elementary and secondary schools, face serious challenges. First, the small scale of private elementary and secondary schools which facilitates their quality education also restricts their further development. Compared with public elementary and secondary schools which serve larger and more diverse student bodies, private elementary and secondary schools provide fewer educational services and programs. For instance, because of the small number of students, only one-third of private schools offer medical services, and school facilities like libraries are usually small in scale. Besides, as private elementary and secondary schools enroll fewer non-English-speaking students or students with special needs like physical handicaps, it is less likely for them to get government financial aid in special educational programs.

Second, private schools are criticized for exacerbating social stratification and segregation. The high tuition and fees are unaffordable for students from low-income families, thereby keeping them out of private schools. But wealthy families can send their children not only quality education but also the opportunity to associate with children from the same class, so as to maintain their social and class advantages. In addition, more than 3/4 of private elementary and secondary school students are whites, and non-white students are in very small numbers. This is quite unfavorable for school integration and social inclusion.

Finally, with the emergence of more choices in the education market, the competition for students becomes more intense, which poses a big threat to the survival and development of private schools. For instance, in recent years, such new models of basic education as chartered schools and home schools have attracted an increasing number of students. For one thing, these schools are more affordable than private schools. For another, they also hold distinguishing teaching philosophies, obtain rich curriculum resources and produce good teaching effects.

Overall, private schools made up for such shortcomings of public schools as lack of diversity and prohibition against religious instruction. Since early times, they have been providing more educational choices for parents, who hope to select quality education that are most suitable for their children. More significantly, private postsecondary institutions represent the academic strength and top level of American higher education.

3 Crucial Issues in American Education

3.1 Equality of Educational Opportunity: Race and Gender

As a fundamental part of the American dream, equality of educational opportunity refers to equal access to education for everyone. It includes a broad range of influential educational issues. For school-age children, it means that all of them have access to public schooling. For children who have already attended the school, it involves equal treatment at school, equal representation of the diverse student body in the curriculum and textbooks, and the acceptance and approval of students' varying backgrounds. Even if the struggle for equal educational opportunity never stops in the U.S., inequality in educational opportunity continues to be a thorny problem. In many instances, race and gender are important factors affecting the equal chance to get an education.

In a multi-racial and multi-ethnic society, ethnic groups, especially African Americans, have long been deprived of the right to education. After they obtained the right of education, most of them had no choice but to study in segregated schools with substandard facilities and low-quality teachers. In the first half of the 20th century, segregated schools were run under the doctrine of "separate but equal." It derived from the decision of *Plessy v. Ferguson* (1895), which acknowledged legal segregation in the US. It is the landmark case *Brown v. Board of Education of Topeka* (1954) that finally overturned the 1895 decision. The Supreme Court ruled on the case that segregated education was unequal education, which gave essential legal support to school desegregation. A decade passed before a significant achievement was made in federal legislation to end the segregated situation at school. In 1964, Title VI of the *Civil Rights Act of 1964* took effect, forcing American public schools to accept and enforce school desegregation. The federal government warned publicly supported schools of the termination of federal financial assistance if they still adhered to school segregation. This was an effective legislative act. Within a few years, many public schools, especially those in the South, changed their segregative policies and practices. Under the *Civil Rights Act of 1964* and *Executive Order 11246* in 1965, the Lyndon B. Johnson administration initiated affirmative action programs to equalize educational or employment opportunities for members of minority groups. Aiming at redressing centuries-long discriminatory practices, affirmative action policies were designed to give preferential treatment, like setting quotas, to all minorities who had equal qualifications for education or jobs. In 1971, through ruling *Swann v. Charlotte-Mecklenburg Board of Education*, the federal Supreme Court enacted the practice of mandatory busing to enforce desegregation in public schools. The highly controversial forced busing continued into the early 1990s. If busing is viewed as a practice of involuntary desegregation, magnet schools provide a means to achieve voluntary integration. With the emphasis on free choice, those schools use creative and distinctive programs and curricula to attract students with varying racial backgrounds. Thus, it has won wide support from the public, non-whites and whites alike. It should be pointed out that some measures for school integration do not escape controversy or criticism. For instance, affirmative actions have been accused of resulting in "reverse discrimination", which was another form of unequal treatment. Additionally, involuntary busing is blamed for violating individual freedom, which invited opposition from both white and non-white parents.

Evidently, the federal Supreme Court and legislature have made strenuous efforts to rectify forms of unequal educational opportunity. Apart from top-down endeavors, minority groups also take different political actions to obtain equal educational chances. They try to remedy their disadvantages and redress their grievances through social movements, educational engagement and the courts.

For example, aided by the Pan-Indian movement, Native Americans strove for the development and control of educational programs concerning their schooling, which led to the passage of the *Indian Education Act*. This law helped Native Americans get federal funds to develop their own educational programs. Likewise, spurred by the Mexican American Civil Rights Movement, Mexican Americans called for the introduction of educational programs like bilingual education, which met the specific needs of Mexican American students. In addition, ethnic and racial minorities tend to play a more active and influential role in the educational system, for instance, running for the members of school boards, and looking for jobs as school administrators and teachers. Research shows that the larger representation of ethnic minorities in the educational system in many ways facilitates desegregation and educational equity. Furthermore, legal means are widely used by ethnic groups to protect their educational interests. *Brown v. Board of Education of Topeka*, *Cisneros v. Corpus Christi Independent School District* and *Tape v. Hurley* are cases in point.

  Undeniably, considerable educational gains have been achieved for racial and ethnic minorities. Take, for instance, students who have received higher education for no fewer than four years. Between 1960 and 1995, the percentage of African American students surged from 3 percent to 13 percent. The progress is remarkable. But if it is compared with the percentage of white students in the same period, a wide disparity can be found. Because the proportion increased from 8 percent to 24 percent. In addition to the widening educational gaps between the whites and minorities, less visible forms of racial segregation still haunt American integrated schools. The tracking and ability grouping system is one of the most common ways to sustain segregation. Different races can be placed in separate curriculum tracks. Unequal treatment of white students and minority students within the same school or even the same class is another barrier for students to get equal educational opportunities. Normally, the punishment for students of color could be harsher than that for white students, even if they have committed the same offenses. Worst of all, the deep-rooted color line serves as an ever-lasting gulf that can hardly be bridged. Those who attempt to cross the line often end up being looked down upon by their folks. Thus, school integration leaves much to be desired.

Like racial and ethnic minorities, women have been and still are denied equal educational opportunities in the US. For example, in earlier times, when men were able to attend colleges and universities, the doors of institutions of higher learning were closed to women. While men were expected to be equipped with rich knowledge and dominate the world, women were supposed to learn a rudimentary knowledge of reading and writing as well as domestic skills for the purpose of serving the family. As a matter of fact, the expansion of female education opportunities in America is inseparable from every endeavor made by American feminist activists. As early as the women's rights movement (or the first-wave women's movement) which was launched in the 1840s, feminist pioneers put more options for female education high on the agenda of the movement. With the efforts of early feminists and the development of the public school system, the latter half of the 19th century witnessed big progress in equalizing female education opportunities. At that time, all the primary and secondary schools were open to women, and postsecondary institutions began to allow co-education. Hence there was a significant increase in the number of college-educated women.

In spite of all these improvements, gender discrimination remained to be prevalent in the educational system in the first half of the 20th century. It was not rare to see discriminatory practices in college admission and employment, educational programs and the awarding of scholarships and loans. In response to this situation, the second-wave women's movement of the 1960s gave priority to educational equity, while struggling for women's equal rights in the mainstream society. Women's activities spurred the introduction of *Executive Order 11375* in 1967, which added gender to the affirmative action programs as one of the protected groups. To further promote equal access to education, women's organizations pressured the government to pass Title IX of the *Higher Education Act of 1972*. The law required all educational institutions including preschool, primary, secondary and postsecondary schools to ensure equality treatment of women. Bolstered by these legal achievements, the campaign for equal educational opportunities for women made considerable breakthroughs. From 1972 onwards, segregated courses were cancelled, sex discrimination was outlawed in athletic programs, representation of women was added to textbooks, gender bias was redressed in the content of standardized tests. At the same time, an increasing number of women began to hold high academic and administrative positions in the educational system. Their presence set good examples for female students and changed the picture of educational inequity. Consequently, the percentage of women who received doctoral and professional degrees rose from 14 percent to 37 percent between 1971 and 1991. The number of women participating in high school sports increased eight-fold between 1971 and 1996.

Stepping into the 21st century, Americans continue to face various forms of hidden gender discrimination in education. Targeting eliminating gender discrimination and realizing educational equity, some feminist educators proposed the approach of gender-neutral education. Specifically speaking, teachers can give equal educational opportunities in the classroom. For example, they can distribute equal interaction with students of both sexes, use gender-neutral curricula and educational materials, and make discussion topics of equal interest to both male and female students. Besides, single-sex education was proposed. In the feminists' eyes, an all-girl classroom or school might make it possible for women students to get equal educational opportunities that used to be inaccessible to them in coeducation. The progressive approach has been countered by conservatives. They argue that all the progressive measures will hinder teacher freedom, violate students' rights, and destroy school operations. Moreover, the single-sex courses or programs actually prove the distinction between men and women, which will reinforce gender stereotypes. In their views, gender differences are the realities of life that need to be respected and extolled, rather than being ignored or hidden. It seems that Americans have to address the ever-lasting conflict over "difference vs. equality" before they resolve the above-mentioned dispute. At present, American women are still on the way to educational equity.

3.2 Multicultural and Multilingual Education

Multicultural education refers to the educational policy and philosophy that help students respect cultural differences, build cultural tolerance, learn about different cultures, and view the world from different perspectives. It aims to bring equal educational opportunities for diverse groups (racial, ethnic, religious, social-class and cultural groups) and create social justice in the society as a whole. Emerging in the 1970s, multicultural education borrowed inspiring ideas from the Civil Rights Movement, and initially paid attention to racial and class issues. Since the 1980s, it has expanded to cover more issues, for instance, gender, religion, language, health, sexuality and nationality, etc. Consequently, a comprehensive educational model of multicultural education took shape. Different from ethnocentric education which teaches and students from a particular ethnic cultural perspective, multicultural education educates students from multiple cultural perspectives, including ethnic cultural perspectives. Unlike bicultural education which gives students the knowledge of two different cultures, multicultural education exposes students to multiple diverse cultures.

In recent decades, continuous waves of immigrants led to the increasingly diverse population in the US. According to the US Census Bureau, in 1990, European Americans accounted for 71.3 percent of the total population, with African Americans 12.1 percent, Hispanics 9 percent, Asian Americans and Pacific Islanders 2.9 percent and Native Americans 0.8 percent and other races 3.9 percent. But by 2019, the demographic picture had changed enormously. The European American population reduced to 60.1 percent, while the population of ethnic minorities grew rapidly. 18.5 percent of the US citizens claimed themselves to be Hispanics, 12.2 percent African Americans, 5.6 percent Asian Americans and Pacific Islanders and 0.7 percent Native Americans and other races 2.9 percent. In addition, the arrival of immigrants greatly enhances the cultural diversity in America. As the immigrants are from every corner of the world, they are of different racial groups, speaking many languages, observing different traditions and practicing multiple religions. Their cultural differences and unique cultural heritages inevitably facilitate the shaping of a pluralist society. Thus, multiculturalists hold that it is imperative for school education to reflect the multicultural society and relate to the lives of a diverse student body.

In order to promote the reform in multicultural education, the federal government introduced programs that could bring equal educational opportunities to students with varying cultural backgrounds. It also kept the record of each state's performance in ensuring educational equity. In accordance with the guidance of the federal government, many states began to adjust the school curriculum and implement educational equity programs, so as to treat both majority and minority cultures fairly. In addition, from 1981 onwards, all the institutes of teacher education were requested to provide multicultural education to teachers. This policy was put forward to enable teachers to better understand the multicultural education philosophy and its specific measures, so that teachers can be put in a good position to communicate with students with different cultural backgrounds. In 1990, the National Association for Multicultural Education was established to advance educational equity and eliminate discrimination through multicultural education. This non-profit organization has already built a national network with local chapters across the country, bringing together individuals and groups from all walks of life who show interest in multicultural education.

While practicing multicultural education, multiculturalists call for multicultural representation and fair shares of the dominant and the dominated cultures in the curriculum. They argue that, in addition to formal school study, families and communities also have to create a favorable environment for students to experience and learn diverse cultures. For example, some parents teach their children the cultural traditions of their own ethnic groups at home. Or the community organizes some activities celebrating the traditional festivals of the ethnic groups that live in the neighborhood. The after-school activities can be viewed as the continuation of multicultural education. Furthermore, teachers are expected to bring home to students the interdependence of different cultures and the contributions of all Americans. In this way, students are able to see the richness and significance of diverse cultures, so as to develop respect, tolerance and empathy for different cultures.

Last but not least, bilingual education is implemented. Bilingual education means teaching students, newly-arrived immigrant children in particular, to be proficient in the use of both their native languages and English. Specifically speaking, bilingual education can be further divided into transitional bilingual, maintenance bilingual and two-way bilingual. Transitional bilingual programs first instruct students in their native language. After students learn English, classes are only conducted in English. Maintenance bilingual programs pay equal attention to students' native language and English, so students learn their native language while learning English. Tow-way bilingual programs give lessons in English and another language to English-speaking and non-English-speaking students in one classroom. Ever since the bilingual education movement was launched in the 1960s by Mexican Americans, bilingual education has become a controversial issue. As for proponents of bilingual education, closely related to the history and culture of a particular ethnic group, one's native language should be preserved and the rights of learning one's native language ought to be protected. Hence, if students receive education in a language that is beyond their understanding, they are deprived of part of their rights to education. Additionally, research findings show that the ability of reading and writing in one's native language will help one to learn English better. Because a solid linguistic foundation is beneficial for one's cognitive advancement in the future. Furthermore, bilingual education could increase students' communicative skills, so as to aid them in obtaining more career opportunities. Ethnic groups such as Mexican Americans, Asian Americans and Native Americans generally welcome the bilingual programs. However, bilingual education meets strong opposition from Conservative Americans. Opponents believe that bilingual education is unnecessary and detrimental to the central place of English. Because of this belief, they ask the government to stop the funding for bilingual programs, and instead make English the official language of the United States. At present, bilingual education is not accessible to every student. In spite of the disputes over bilingual education, some educators nowadays call for the introduction of multilingual education. For one thing, as a multilingual society, US education should reflect the reality of the society and promote multilingual communication. For another, equipped with multiple languages, students are able to develop a global vision and improve their cognitive proficiency.

Actually, apart from bilingual education, multicultural education is another contentious issue. Multiculturalists ask for the honest and fair representation of diverse cultures in every aspect of the school curriculum and a multicultural perspective in teaching and learning, so as to display the nation's diversity and democracy. They point out that, minority groups and their cultures have been underrepresented in the school curriculum and their contributions have been played down in the textbooks for a long time. What's worse, students are taught in a Euro-centric single perspective, which makes them less likely to form a complete and full picture of the world. Giving priority to the WASP culture, Conservatives strongly oppose multicultural education. In their eyes, giving representation to previously marginalized groups is no more than "the balkanization of the curriculum," and this will definitely invite the disintegration of the nation and the destruction of western civilization. Both sides agree that American culture is shaped and constituted by diverse cultures. Thereby schools should transmit all cultural heritages, and the school curriculum ought to manifest various cultural influences. The difference lies in the fact that conservatives hold tight to the central and irreplaceable place of European traditions and Western civilization. The conflicts between the two sides escalates into so-called "culture wars" from the late 20th century till now.

In general, the disputes over culture and languages can be reduced to a basic question: Who is an American? Currently, both the majority and minority groups are defending their own cultural values, and fighting for more share of their cultural representations in the whole society. It can be predicted that the contention over multicultural and multilingual education will continue into the years to come.

Contemporary American Society and Culture

Essay Questions:

1. Trace the development of American elementary and secondary education from colonial times to the present, and examine the lessons and experience from this development.

2. What are the contentious issues in contemporary American education and what are the social causes of these issues?

3. Explore how public schooling comes into being in the US, and discuss its strengths and weaknesses.

4. The American population projection has it that into the mid-21st century, non-Hispanic white Americans will become the racial minority. What impact will it have in turn, as you perceive, on multicultural education in the US?

Unit 9　Religion in American Culture and Politics

　　The US is a western country with a deep-rooted religious heritage. In comparison with European countries, the US has a greater number of religious adherents with much higher church attendance. The high levels of religious commitments of Americans are repeatedly noted by European observers. As perceived by the French sociologist and political theorist Alexis de Tocqueville in his ground-breaking work *Democracy in America*, "On my arrival in the United States the religious aspect of the country was the first thing that struck my attention, and the longer I stayed there, the more I perceived the great political consequences resulting from this new state of things." The number and variety of churches, religious schools, missionary activities, alongside the high levels of church attendance, are all expressions of the deep religiosity of the American people. Public Polls reveal that despite the steady decline of the Christian share of the population in the US over the past decades, today Christians still constitute about 2/3 of the American national population with little change in the rate of church attendance. In addition, non-Christian faiths represent around 10% of the national population, which means about 3/4 of the people in present-day American society affirm religious beliefs. A look into the role of religious thought and practice in American life thus helps reveal the diversity and complexity of American culture.

1　The Puritan Tradition

　　American religious heritage could be traced back to the early phase of colonial period. In 1620, a merchant ship named "Mayflower" set sail from England, with 102 passengers hoping to start a new life on the other side of the Atlantic. When the ship was anchored at Provincetown harbour, Massachusetts, 41 of the passengers as Puritan Separatists who sought to break up with the Church of England and establish a new church in the New World – whom today we often refer to as "Pilgrims" – signed a document they called *The Mayflower Compact*. The brief document promised to create a civil body politic governed by elected officials and any laws and regulations that would later be established "for the general good of the colony." The compact became the foundation of the government at Plymouth colony and remained in force until the colony was absorbed into the Massachusetts Bay Colony in 1691. Still, as noted by William Bradford, who drafted the compact and later became the governor of Plymouth colony, "As one small candle may light a thousand, so the light here kindled hath shone to many, yea in some sort to our whole nation", the Mayflower Pilgrims and their descendants remained convinced that they alone had been specially chosen by God to act as a beacon for Christians around the world. *The Mayflower Compact*, as an adaptation of the Puritan church covenant to a civil situation, was the first document to establish self-government in the New World on the basis of popular consent and this early attempt at democracy set the stage for future American colonists seeking independence from Britain.

  This conviction of the "God's chosen" held by early Puritan settlers in American colonies was best manifested in John Winthrop's famous speech "A Model of Christian Charity," also known as "A City upon a Hill." John Winthrop, who was selected as governor of the Massachusetts Bay Company in 1629, was given the task of leading a fleet of Puritan settlers to establish a community of their own in New England the following year. The speech was given to his fellow travelers on board as they prepared to sail from their native England. Winthrop's words laid out specific guidelines for living together in a Christian community to create a "holy communion" in their new Massachusetts Bay colony. Most notably, Winthrop compared this "holy communion" to "a city upon a hill," a city rising above the surrounding land, which is visible to all, and is destined to be subject to careful scrutiny. Winthrop suggested that if he and his fellow Puritans succeed in this "holy experiment," they would serve as a shining example for others to follow and if they fail, their failure would bring disgrace to Christians across the globe.

Throughout American history, the "A City upon a Hill" speech has been much cited in American political rhetoric to support the notion of American exceptionalism, which holds that the United States, with its unique formation and development, is essentially different from any other nation in the world. Supporters of American exceptionalism have used Winthrop's "city upon a hill" thesis to suggest that the United States – much like the original Massachusetts Bay colony – serves as a leading example for the rest of the world. The notion of American exceptionalism has thus often been used to justify American foreign policy and actions that might otherwise be viewed negatively, such as overseas military intervention and the appropriation of land from Native American tribes. In the mid-19th century, the belief in American exceptionalism also served as a moral justification for the westward expansion in that the western frontiersmen were believed to be entrusted with the "manifest destiny" to spread liberty westward as the "God's chosen." Overall, in different phases of national development, the religious convictions of early Puritan settlers have constituted a historical legacy with an enduring impact.

In the founding of the American nation, Puritanism, the body of beliefs that accompanied the Puritans to Massachusetts Bay, became one of those formative ideologies that contributed to the American national identity. As Alexis de Tocqueville observed that "the whole destiny of America is contained in the first Puritan who landed on these shores, because Puritanism was almost as much a political theory as a religious doctrine." While the essence of New England Puritanism is the covenant theology, their ideals and practices included a striving to achieve independence in their community life, the freedom of the conscience, self-discipline, and the moral conduct of individuals. These Puritan ideals stemmed from the ethics of Calvinism as an intensely religious movement within the 16th century Protestant Reformation.

Central to Calvinist belief was the elect, the "God's chosen" to inherit eternal life and who were thus predestined to this end. Calvinist teaching has it that the only evidence of being included as a member of the elect to have eternal salvation was in one's daily life and deeds, and success in one's worldly endeavors was a sign of possible inclusion. This "doctrine of the calling," which holds that faithful believers are called to work as the highest service to God and the good works are indispensable as a sign of election, was at the heart of the Puritan work ethic. To gain assurance of the well-being of their souls, individuals were thus strongly motivated to show progress in their work pursuits through worldly asceticism, devotion to their calling, self-discipline, and hard work. In this regard, vocational success and material wealth became the hallmark of individual achievement. Such individualistic values of self-fulfillment also find expression in Puritan belief in the "priesthood of all believers." Those early American Puritan settlers, who followed the Calvinist teachings of Protestantism, held private individuals as equals that stand alone before God, seeking salvation on their own rather than from a priest speaking in God's name. The affirmation of individualism constituted an integral part of Puritan heritage, which had an influence far beyond the Protestant church with a profound effect on the American national character.

2 No Established Religion

A distinctive feature of American religious institutions is the lack of an established church. The First Amendment of the US Constitution in the *Bill of Rights* stipulates that "Congress shall make no law respecting an establishment of religion, or prohibiting the free exercise thereof." Its precise meaning is that Congress shall not be allowed to establish a single national church or grant preference to any particular religion. This "separation of church and state" was largely an act to legalize the existing conditions of American society. From the colonial beginning, the American population had a heterogeneous religious composition with a variety of Protestant denominations and the colonies were simply too large for any single denomination to gain control over others. The idea that no single church should become the center of religious life in the nation became accepted and the result was a growth of different Protestant denominations and religious pluralism.

The Constitutional clause that "Congress shall make no law respecting an establishment of religion, or prohibiting the free exercise thereof," while prohibiting the establishment of a national church, entails the protection of individual rights to practice their own religious beliefs. Based on the idea of separation of church and state, there is the exemption of church property from taxation. All spending for church purposes is tax deductible, so far as federal income tax is concerned, which reveals a significant difference between the treatment accorded to churches and that given to businesses. Accordingly, the income tax advantages to pastors of all denominations and the tax-exempt status of the church constitute an important assistance to church finances.

In reality, the connections between church and state in the US are universal. Among the practical connections are the political conventions with religious rituals and services. The Senate and the House of Representatives regularly open with spoken prayers with those leading the prayer representing a variety of denominations. Chaplains of Congress in both houses are appointed and supported, and so are chaplains of the armed forces. The chaplains of armed services, whether Jewish, Roman Catholic or Protestant, are both representatives of churches and officers of the US government. In this regard, if "separation of church and state" is interpreted to mean that government should make no allowances for religion or belief, then the US is a long way from complete separation. From government chaplains, official prayers and proclamations to religious symbols on government documents, it is clear that the American government acknowledged the religious heritage of the nation. Essentially, the separation of church and state has not denied a religious dimension in the political realm. Personal religious belief and association are considered to be private affairs, though, there are certain common elements of religious orientation that the majority of Americans share, which have played a crucial role in the development of American political institutions and provided a religious dimension for the whole fabric of American life.

3 American "Civil Religion"

There is also a pronounced tendency in American political life to approach political issues in moral terms, which owes much to the Puritan tradition. American political rhetoric is often infused with religious symbols and references and debates about contentious policy issues are frequently framed in terms of competing moral values. This constant recourse to religious images and symbols in American political culture reveals what has often been called a public theology, a political religion, or most often, American "civil religion," as defined by the American sociologist Robert Bellah in his writings in 1967. The term "civil religion" doesn't refer to any formal code of beliefs that is fully developed and authoritatively specified in a single written document. It lacks the status of a state established religion and is neither the religion of a particular church nor a fully articulated religion that competes with existing denominations. Rather, by attributing a sacred character to the nation, civil religion serves as a unifying force to harmonize diverse faiths and political beliefs.

The American civil religion represents the religious dimension of public life, which is expressed in a set of symbols, beliefs and rituals. Notably, the words "in God we trust" on the American national currency, "Annuit Coeptis" ("God favors our undertakings") on the Great Seal, Pledge of Allegiance to "one nation under God," national anthem, legislative prayers, and oaths sworn in federal courts all make explicit reference to belief in God. In the presidential inauguration, the religious motif is apparent through the oath-taking on the *Bible* and the prominent participation of clergy in the ceremony, which reaffirms the religious legitimization of the highest political authority. Civil religion enables Americans to bring together secular politics and their religious society, so as to give religious sanctity to their patriotism and nationalist legitimacy to their religious beliefs. This mingling of religion and patriotism may help build support for and commitment to the nation. Civil religion, in this way, can build up symbols of national solidarity and mobilize personal motivation for the attainment of national goals.

American civil religion, however, has not always been invoked in favor of worthy causes as it can be explicitly or implicitly linked to the ideal of "manifest destiny" as moral justifications for the nation's imperialist expansion since the early 19th century. Civil religion can easily degenerate into mere religious nationalism, as an ideology that fuses God, country and national flag to counter any criticism of the nation's foreign policy. More importantly, while American civil religion is taken as a non-denominational, national religion, it is essentially Christian in its origins, content and tone. Today, the growing diversity in the ethnic composition alongside a decline in the Christian population of the American society have given rise to an increasingly diverse religious makeup, which provides a counter discourse to the American civil religion with Christianity as its core. The momentum of multiculturalism built upon this growing cultural diversity has posed further challenges to civil religion as public consensus of civic codes.

4 Religious Diversity

Religious pluralism stands as another distinctive feature of American religious institutions. The lack of an established religion, above all, provides a fertile ground for a flourishing of religious faiths in the US Further, the diverse racial and ethnic composition of the American people has also given rise to a diverse religious landscape. Religious diversity is, first and foremost, manifest in the numerous denominations of Protestantism, the most significant religious tradition in the US.

4.1 Protestantism

National surveys have revealed that over 40% of American adults currently identify with Protestantism. Historically, Protestantism in the US has three main traditions: mainline, evangelical and black Protestantism. In terms of theology, mainline and evangelical Protestants differ primarily over the three S's: scripture, sin, and salvation. The mainline Protestants stress Jesus's role as a prophet of social justice, and in this theological vision, emphasize both personal spirituality such as questions of salvation and engagement with social problems. In this tradition, which understands religious duty in terms of sharing abundance, mainline Protestants are inclined to accept many different sources of religious truths and biblical interpretations. Evangelicals, consistent with their view of Jesus as personal savior, assign the unique authority to the biblical scripture, and have the belief in the obligation to share their creed by bringing others to salvation through a personal embrace of God. Such views are widespread among Protestants variously described as conservative, traditional, or Pentecostal, holiness, and Adventist, as subgroups under the broad umbrella of evangelicalism. By contrast, the mainline Protestants are oftentimes labeled as liberal, moderate, historic, and mainstream. On the other hand, African American denominations in black Protestant tradition, manage to combine the evangelical emphasis on salvation with the mainline commitment to social action.

In terms of denominations, mainline Protestants usually include predominantly white groups such as the American Baptist Churches in the USA, Episcopal Church, Evangelical Lutheran Church in America, Presbyterian Church in the United States of America, Reformed Church in America, United Church of Christ, and United Methodist Church. Most white evangelicals may be found among Baptists, the southern wings of Methodism and Presbyterianism. Compared with mainline denominations, white and black evangelicals alike mostly subscribe to a literal interpretation of biblical scripture, and are more likely to draw a great deal of guidance from religion and have higher church attendance.

Demographic changes and the baby boom in the US in the years after World War II had brought numerical growth of mainline Protestantism and expansion of church facilities. Nevertheless, since the mid-1960s, mainline Protestant denominations have lost a significant proportion of membership. Some observers interpreted the decline of mainline membership in terms of parishioner resistance to the social activism characteristic of liberal Protestantism during the activist era of the 1960s. With the Rev. Martin Luther King, Jr. and his Southern Christian Leadership Conference in the forefront, a sizable share of mainline Protestant clergy engaged in the civil rights movement and called for an end to legalized racial segregation. The civil rights movement in turn spurred efforts among other minorities long consigned to the margins of Protestant life. Civil rights concerns gave rise to the second-wave feminism and its calls for the ordination of women, for inclusion of women in leadership positions at all levels. Yet many parishioners, who considered churches places primarily for fellowship and personal spiritual growth, held contrasting views and saw the social activism of their clergy as unwarranted political intrusions. Faced with the resistance from conservative congregations who gave priority to personal spirituality over civic engagement, many clergy sought appointments outside the local parish, in campus ministries, the seminaries, and other environments that were more supportive of political activism of church leaders. Other reform-minded members of the clergy, weary of the constant battles within the church, chose to leave the ministry for opportunities in secular agencies. As a consequence, social movements and calls for social change in the 1960s provided challenges to the membership and dominant influence of mainline Protestantism.

Further contributing to the decline in mainline Protestant membership were a drop in the birth rate among mainline Protestant adherents and the failure of mainline churches to retain participation of baby boomer generation as they came of age. Some baby boomers turned to new religious movements that flourished in the sixties counterculture. While the mainline churches attempted to reverse the decline by experimenting with new approaches to worship and new ways of organizing congregations in order to meet the perceived needs of persons unaffiliated with churches, experimentation in structure and worship failed to stem the decline.

On the other hand, the social movements of the 1960s that contributed to the decline of mainline Protestantism invigorated American evangelicalism. Feminist movement calling for "women's liberation" challenged women's roles as housewives confined to domesticity and subordinates to their husbands, alongside sexual revolution of the Hippies movement, and the increased activism of gay, lesbian and transgender Americans for full acceptance had altogether raised deep concerns of many evangelicals that marriage and family life were endangered. Evangelicals founded powerful organizations including Stop ERA and Concerned Women for America, and railed against the Equal Rights Amendment (ERA) to the US Constitution which was proposed to provide for the legal gender equality and prohibit discrimination on the basis of sex. Adding to the fears of many evangelicals were the challenges to legal authority implicit in both the Civil Rights Movement and the Vietnam War protest. Developing a conviction that these "menacing" social trends would dismantle the moral fiber of the nation, evangelicals began to apply to politics the same missionary zeal they had traditionally shown in converting individuals.

The mobilization of evangelicals to organized political action was represented in the rise of the New Christian Right (NCR), which has evangelicals as its primary constituency and draws support from politically conservative Catholics and Jews. The New Christian Right is an umbrella term for a host of religious organizations. The most prominent of the organizations, Moral Majority, was founded in 1979 by evangelist Jerry Falwell, the minister of the nation's largest independent Baptist church, in Virginia. Concentrated mostly in the southeastern states, Moral Majority drew most of its membership and leadership from other independent Baptist churches. Positioning itself as pro-family and pro-American, Moral Majority advanced conservative social values, notably opposing abortion, pornography, the ERA, and gay rights. Moral Majority energized a host of organizations sharing common agenda including Christian Voice, the National Christian Action Coalition, etc., which are collectively known as New Christian Right.

With political activism in voter registration, lobbying, and fund-raising, New Christian Right formed a powerful electoral constituency aligned with the Republican Party and its impact on American politics was almost immediate, claiming credit for the winning of Ronald Reagan in 1980 general election. The contribution to Republican victories in 1980 had brought NCR to national prominence. Leaders of the Republican Party granted considerable symbolic recognition to NCR, by featuring them at the Republican National Convention and adding to the party's platform calls for a constitutional amendment to restrict abortion, the legalization of religious prayers and meetings in public schools, and opposition to ERA. However, Republicans' pledge to advance NCR agenda proved to be more of a rhetoric and NCR had few policy accomplishments during Reagan's presidency. After a decade of work that turned out to have yielded little in policy changes, the Christian Right movement underwent a thorough transformation in the early 1990s. The movement began to concentrate energy at the state and local levels, building up mass-based support within the Republican Party and a network of local power centers. Most of the pioneering organizations including Moral Majority disbanded and in their place rose new mass-membership organizations with stronger local chapters, among which are the Family Research Council, the Traditional Values Coalition, and Citizens for Excellence in Education with renewed influence. Pat Robertson, a Southern Baptist minister who had an abortive run for presidency in 1988, founded the most prominent of the new organizations, Christian Coalition. By 1995, under the leadership of Ralph Reed, Christian Coalition claimed 1.6 million members in more than 1,600 local chapters, access to a network of 60,000 churches and $25 million in funds. Its annual conference became a mandatory stop for Republican candidates seeking the presidential nomination and for a time it became known as "the Republican Party's No.1 interest group." Christian Coalition aimed to advance the agenda of "Contract with the American Family," which included calls for abortion restrictions, pornography as well as laws to shield Christian schools from state regulation and to promote religious prayer in public schools and state funding of religious education. Notably, it gave equal weight to such social issues beyond religious and moralistic concerns as lowering taxes and dismantling welfare programs. In doing so, the second-generation Christian Right organizations had sought to expand the traditional agenda of the early-phase movement to appeal to a broader range of social conservatives. Since the 1990s, NCR has constituted a vital force in the winning coalition of Republicans, replacing the historical role of mainline Protestants as a major voting bloc and the core of the Republican constituency.

4.2 Catholicism

The mid-19th and early 20th centuries saw two major waves of early Catholic immigration to the US. In about three decades before the Civil War, millions of Irish came to the US and there were around two million Irish immigrants in the 1840s alone. By 1850, Catholics had constituted the largest single religious group in the US, and further, in the decades between the Civil War and World War I, there was another surge in Catholic immigration from southern, central and eastern Europe.

Early Catholic immigrants often took low-paying jobs in the nation's burgeoning factories. For nearly two generations, the educational attainment of Catholics lagged considerably behind that of Protestants. For two to three generations, Catholics were also under-represented in the ranks of business executives, political leadership, and other high-profile positions. Anti-Catholic sentiment was also responsible for some of the challenges that confronted early Catholic immigrants. Catholic immigrants often encountered hostility from American Protestants, who had long harbored a suspicion of Catholics and their faith. Many Protestants held Catholicism to be incompatible with democracy, believing that Catholic loyalty to church leaders – especially the Pope in Rome – superseded loyalty to the state. In addition, some Protestants believed that the Catholic reliance on the parochial or parish school system to educate children would never mold students into good citizens in a democracy.

On the other hand, as early Catholic immigrants – including Irishmen, Italians, Poles, Ukrainians, Czechs, and a host of others – tend to settle in ethnic enclaves with familiar surroundings, parishes took on ethnic dimensions, keeping alive folk traditions associated with places of origin. Overall, the distinctive character of Catholic faith and practice, Protestant hostility to hierarchical structure of Catholicism

Unit 9 Religion in American Culture and Politics

as an institution, as well as ethnic enclaves and parishes that grew along ethnic lines, combined to give early immigrant Catholicism what many historians have called a "ghetto" mentality.

As generations of Catholic immigrants sought to shed their identity as religiously and ethnically "other," the era of WWI marked the first move away from this state of marginalization. When Catholics largely supported the Allied cause in WWI, some suspicion abated. The beginning of the Cold War in the aftermath of WWII had further undermined the differences between American Catholics and Protestants, as in the US-Soviet Cold War rivalry, a shared American identity became an imperative to forge national consensus. By the mid-20th century, American Catholics had achieved parity with their Protestant counterparts in terms of educational attainment, type of employment, and family income. As Catholics took their place in the cultural mainstream, they not only looked more like their Protestant counterparts in terms of socioeconomic measures, but also garnered greater social acceptance. In 1960 general election, the victory of John F. Kennedy as a Catholic presidential candidate became a symbol of the social acceptance of American Catholicism.

The Catholic Church in the US, unlike mainline Protestantism, has continued to grow after WWII. Catholic growth doesn't come primarily from replenishment but largely results from the new waves of immigration that got underway in 1965 with major changes in US immigration laws. The *Immigration and Nationality Act of 1965* ended a system that placed quotas on both how many immigrants could enter the US each year and how many could come from any particular nation. The resulting new immigration included in those coming from Mexico, the Caribbean, other areas of Central America, and South America. The overwhelming majority of post-1965 Latino immigrants are Roman Catholics. With a birth rate higher than that of the general population, these immigrants are transforming the character of the American Catholic Church.

Latino immigrants' way of being Catholic has much difference from that of Catholics with European ancestry. Latino Catholicism has a rich historical heritage of blending traditional Catholic belief and practice with deeply embedded tribal cultures in the Americas. For tribal cultures, a vibrant sense of the supernatural expressed through exuberant song and dance shapes religiosity. As a consequence, Latino Catholicism has long been more emotionally energetic than European Catholicism that once informed the American church. This more lively approach supplements and enriches the sacramental life of the church and its cycle of rituals. In addition, Latino religiosity has nurtured a stronger individualism. Latino Catholics, as compared with European Catholics, are more liberal such matters of economic and social justice as immigration reform but are more conservative on some other issues including abortion rights and homosexuality. Overall, the Latino presence is reshaping the character of the American Catholic Church. With the continued Latino immigration, the Latino influence on American Catholicism will become ever more significant.

4.3 Judaism

As with Catholicism, American Judaism grew significantly with the immigration between the Civil War and WWI. Given the restrictions many European nations placed on Jews until well into the 19th century and the overt persecution in areas of Slavic and Russian Europe, Jews had little affective identity with their nations of origin but more with a complex religious and cultural heritage. Jewish institutions celebrated this shared identity in ways that cut across national boundaries, solidifying a Jewish cultural and ethnic heritage.

Adaptation occurred as Jews assimilated into American life, which was best represented in the changing role of home and synagogue. For centuries, Jewish practice highlighted what happened at home, not in the synagogue. Membership in a synagogue or attendance at services has thus never measured Jewish identity as much as in Christianity. In traditional Jewish life, home-based ritual and practice centered on the dietary guidelines prescribed in the Torah, from foods eaten to how foods are prepared and served. Many American Jews, however, in their adaptation to the American society, have relaxed such family observance. On the other hand, synagogues, once devoted to study of Torah and reflection on Jewish law, became religious institutions akin to Christian churches. As teachers of Torah, Rabbis gradually added to their role the pastoral functions of a minister or priest.

The greatest adaptation came when German Jewish immigrants in the 19th century spearheaded the movement known as Reform Judaism. In an effort to update traditional Jewish practice, Reform Judaism added English prayers to services, abandoned much of the Jewish kosher dietary guidelines, and made other accommodations to a predominantly Christian society.

Today, Jewish institutional life in the US has taken shape around four approaches: 1) Reform Judaism, which emerged in Germany and then in the US in the mid-19th century. 2) Orthodox Judaism, the branch of denomination adhering most closely to tradition and to the path set forth in the Torah. For the Orthodox, being Jewish is a matter of religious faith usually based on birth, not merely ethnic identity. Synagogue worship is likely to rely heavily on prayers in Hebrew, gender roles are more clearly defined, and observance of the Law is central for individuals in their pursuit of holiness. 3) Conservative Judaism, which also has mid-19th century German roots. Not as strict as the Orthodox, Conservative Jews believed that Reform Judaism abandoned too many essentials. With much importance placed on scripture, a trait shared with the Orthodox, Conservative Jews are generally open to critical, scholarly analysis of texts, a trait shared with Reform Jews. Conservative Judaism, because of its moderate, centrist position, became the largest branch of American Judaism. 4) Reconstructionist Judaism, which emerged in the US around 1920, tends to emphasize enduring Jewish ethical principles, but not traditional observance and practice, believing much is out of step with rational, modern understanding. Reconstructionist Judaism is the most liberal denomination most open to new ideas and to using knowledge from contemporary culture to understand faith.

The openness of both Reform and Conservative Judaism in the American context to some cultural adaptation resulted in the rapid increase in marriages of Jewish Americans to non-Jews. Intermarriage means that many persons of Jewish heritage are found in families blending multiple religious traditions. Some identify themselves as "secular" Jews and "ethnic" Jews, but not "religious" Jews, while many who are otherwise unobservant attend religious services on the Day of Atonement, the most sacred day in the Jewish religious calendar. The number of Jews in the US, nevertheless, has remained much smaller than the influence of the Jewish heritage on American life and culture, owing to extraordinary upward mobility, educational achievement, and success of the Jewry in professions ranging from business to politics, academia to popular entertainment.

4.4 Immigrant Religions

1965 had ushered in a new era when different religions assumed increasing importance. The passage of the *Immigration and Nationality Act of 1965*, which lifted the quotas based on nation of origin to favor a modest immigration from Northern and Western Europe, had resulted in a wave of new immigration that rivaled one at the start of the 20th century in scope and magnitude. The largest numbers of immigrants in the new wave came from Mexico, Central America, and South America. Immigrants from Africa, Asia and the Middle East also increased dramatically. Like earlier generations of immigrants, these "new immigrants" brought their religions with them. Asian Buddhists and Hindus came to America, fusing ethnic identity and religious practice in their new home. Smaller numbers of Sikhs and Jains joined them. There has also been a steady growth of Islam, reflecting the larger numbers of immigrants coming from Muslim nations in the Middle East, Asia, and Africa. Together, they created what some historians of religion called "a new religious America."

Among Asian groups, Buddhism has shown the fastest rate of growth because of immigration. Today, virtually every American city has Buddhist temples. Some serve the immigrant adherents based on national origin and ethnicity and others cater primarily to American converts. In every case, distinctive styles and practices reflect the place of practitioners' origins. For many American converts, the practice of meditation remains basic while for many immigrant Buddhists, regardless of land of origin, the rigors of meditation are reserved for monks rather than laypersons. Overall, temple participation has never been as central to being Buddhist in America in the way that participating in a congregation is central to most American Christians.

The Hindu tradition had also increased dramatically since 1965 and most US Hindus are recent immigrants and their descendants. Today, most American cities have at least one Hindu temple. Unlike temples in India, most Hindu temples in the US are also cultural centers, offering programs to sustain an Indian American identity and a Hindu consciousness that go well beyond religion. As a consequence, Hindu families in the US may in effect have greater association with a temple-cultural center than in India. Immigration trends suggest that Hinduism will grow at a more rapid rate than the general population. The same trend holds for two other religious groups with historical roots on the Indian subcontinent, Jainism and Sikhism, although their numbers remain small.

The change in the immigration law in 1965 had also brought a growing number of Muslim immigrants to the US. The American Muslim community is strikingly diverse, representing a mosaic of ethnic, racial, linguistic, and national identities. Muslims in the US come from more than fifty nations ranging from Africa to Southeast Asia. Arabs, African Americans, and South Asians constitute the three largest American Muslim groups. The majority of American Muslims are of the Sunni tradition, but every Islamic sect is represented in the US, including Shi'ites, Sufis, and the Druze. Much like Hindu temples, mosques in the US have often become Islamic cultural centers, embracing both Shi'ite and Sunni Muslims from a variety of national backgrounds.

Early immigrants that came primarily from Europe had brought the religious traditions that shaped earlier American culture and as a consequence, the dominant religious influences maintained a European focus. The new immigrant religion, however, undermines that European bias and a more diverse and global perspective, one oriented to Asia, Latin America, and Africa, is replacing the Euro-centric understanding of religion that has long impacted American life. In time, that will represent the most significant impact of religious diversity in the US.

Essay Questions:

1. What's the historical legacy of the Puritan tradition in the US and its impact on the American national character?
2. What's your understanding of separation of church and state in the US?
3. What is the American "civil religion"? How does it represent the mixture of theocracy and secularism in American religious tradition? And what are its implications for the American society?
4. What are the changes in contemporary American religious landscape and what are the implications of such changes?

Unit 10   Major Public Policy Issues as Controversies in Contemporary American Society

One of the most enduring features of the American society is the juxtaposition of deep divisions with a capacity for regeneration and renewal. Policy issues that top the agenda of election campaigns are often hotly debated divisive issues sparking national discussions in the United States. A study of the historical origin and cultural roots of these divisive policy issues as controversies, as well as the supporting and opposing social forces behind with competing claims and philosophies, provides insights into the changes and continuities of the American society in history and in prospect.

1 Gun Control

Gun control has been an issue of increasing public concern since the mid-19th century in the US and every mass shooting incident would put the issue at the forefront of national debate. The United States has about 5% of the total world population but the US residents own close to half of all the world's civilian-owned firearms. The number of private guns in the US, which stands around 400 million today, is about the size of its population. Presently, about 1/3 of adults in the United States personally own a gun and about half of the adult US population live in households with guns. Guns are prominent in contemporary US popular culture as well, appearing frequently in movies, TV dramas, pop music, books and magazines. The general requirements for private gun owners is over 18 for rifles and over 21 for handguns, with no crime records or mental illness, nevertheless, there's easy access to guns ranging from sports stores, gun shops, shooting ranges to gun shows, or one may have mail orders through a licensed agent.

The deep-rooted American gun culture is further represented in the American public conception of guns. Oftentimes, there's a notable increase, if not a surge, in gun sales after mass shooting tragedies, which became known as the "Sandy Hook Effect." In December, 2012, the gun massacre at Sandy Hook elementary school in Newtown, Connecticut took the life of 26 people including 20 children within the ages of six and seven. The tragedy sparked a nationwide discussion about imposing stricter gun control legislation on the nearly $32 billion firearms industry. Yet as the national debate on the possibility of new gun control laws unfolded in the wake of the shooting, gun sales surged in parts of the country as gun enthusiasts moved quickly to purchase new firearms, spurred on by the prospect of tougher gun laws.

The popular saying that "the US was born with a rifle in hand" reveals the historical roots of American gun culture in the colonial period. Guns served as essential tools for hunting and survival to early settlers. More importantly, private gun ownership provided the basis for militia as each colonized state set up militia for military defense and state security. In the War of Independence, guns became powerful weapons to resist colonial rule, tyranny and to fight for freedom. This notion of private gun ownership as a symbol of individual freedom of self-defense was then embedded into American culture and constituted the basis of the Second Amendment of the US Constitution.

The Second Amendment has it that "a well regulated Militia being necessary to the security of a free State, the right of the people to keep and bear Arms shall not be infringed." If the War of Independence is the overthrow of tyranny by gun, the Second Amendment is considered the deterrence to tyranny and violation of civil liberties. Regardless of many divisions of Federalists and anti-Federalists with their competing political visions at the founding of the American nation, there were consensus among Founding Fathers about the implications of private gun ownership and militia. Thomas Jefferson held that "no free man shall be debarred from the use of arms within his own lands or tenements" and "for a people who are free and who mean to remain so, a well-organized and armed militia is their best security." Alexander Hamilton thought that militia could be summoned immediately to counter conventional troops if the latter are in support of tyranny. James Madison believed that "Americans have the right and advantage of being armed – unlike citizens of other countries whose governments are afraid to trust the people with arms." Consensus among founding fathers provided the basis for the Second Amendment, which in turn created the constitutional basis and rationale for pro-gun lobbies and activists in defense of individual freedom of private gun ownership.

Gun culture was further entrenched in the westward expansion and opening up of the American western frontier in the mid-19th century. Amid the unfavorable environment and tough road conditions, as well as clashes with native Indian tribes, western frontiersmen used to carry pistols and guns for self-defense while riding a horse in the wilderness. In addition, hunting and shooting became their major pastime as there were at times shooting contests for boys. Guns were not only indispensible tools for survival but also symbols of masculine power and courage. Guns thus became associated with frontier spirit and cowboy culture as an integral part of traditional American culture.

During the Civil War in the 1860s, Lincoln administration promoted the manufacturing of guns as weaponry to arm the general public in the north. Millions of northern people became armed and learned to shoot and fight with guns. As political scientist Robert Spitzer comments: "Two elements of the modern American gun culture have survived since the earliest days of the country; the hunting/sporting ethos and the militia/frontier ethos." There remains a powerful central elevation of the gun associated with the hunting/sporting and militia/frontier ethos among the American gun culture. Though it has not been a necessary part of daily survival for over a century, generations of Americans have continued to embrace and glorify it as a living inheritance – a permanent element of the nation's style and culture. In his article, "America as a Gun Culture," historian Richard Hofstadter popularized the phrase "gun culture" to describe the long-held affections for firearms within the US, with many Americans embracing the association of guns with America's heritage. The right to own a gun and defend oneself is considered by some, especially those in the West and South, as a central tenet of the American identity.

With the historically rooted gun culture as part of American way of life, there have been basically no substantial government measures for gun control throughout the 19th century. Rather than being considered a danger and threat to social stability, gun has been taken as "a symbol of order" and "a totem for traditional values of freedom" by conservatives. Problems began to emerge, however, with lack of gun regulations. Campus shooting, increase in gun homicide and firearm-related violence, notably the assassinations of president John F. Kennedy, Martin Luther King Jr. and senator Robert Kennedy in the 1960s, raised increasing public concern for gun control. Amid the the liberal cultural climate of the sixties counterculture movement, the massive gun control movement became a major pushing force behind the passage of *Gun Control Act of 1968*, which stood as a milestone in gun control legislation. The act required gun dealers to have a license, restricted purchases by prohibited persons, including felons and minors, and generally prohibited the interstate sale of firearms. It also imposed more severe prosecutions for firearm-related crimes, ban on export of firearms except those for sporting purposes. It was known as the most substantial and restrictive gun control act since the 1930s, marking a big step forward as compared with previous gun control acts in the 1930s.

The Brady Bill, passed in 1994, was another major gun control act. It required dealers to conduct background checks and thus provided an enforcement mechanism for restricting purchases by prohibited persons. The bill was named after James Brady, the former press secretary for Reagan administration, who was permanently disabled as a result of an assassination attempt on president Ronald Reagan in 1981. The Brady Bill was largely pushed by Handgun Control Inc. (HCI) founded in 1974. As the most influential interest group for gun control, HCI saw an increase of interest and fund raising in the wake of the 1980 murder of John Lennon and 1981 membership exceeded 100,000. Following the 1981 assassination attempt on president Reagan, and the resultant injury of James Brady, his wife Sarah Brady joined the board of HCI in 1985. HCI was renamed in 2001 to Brady Campaign to Prevent Gun Violence and has been a top donor for gun control campaigns. Other major national gun control lobbies include Everytown for Gun Safety founded by former New York City Mayor Michael Bloomberg, Coalition to Stop Gun Violence, Sandy Hook Promise, the Violence Policy Center, and so on. It is important to note, however, that the overall campaign finance of federal elections by the major gun control lobbies taken together rarely rivaled that of the National Rifle Association of America (NRA), the top donor for gun right.

The National Rifle Association of America, founded in 1871, "promotes firearm competency, safety, and ownership, as well as police training, hunting and self-defense training in the United States" in terms of its mission statement. NRA's political activity is based on the tenet that firearm ownership is a civil right protected by the Second Amendment. NRA has a nearly century-long record of influencing as well as lobbying for or against proposed firearm legislation on behalf of its members, and calls itself "America's longest-standing civil rights organization". Observers and lawmakers see NRA as one of the top three most influential lobbies in Washington. Presently, NRA membership stands around 5 million. Former presidents that have had close linkages with NRA include John F. Kennedy, Ronald Reagan, George Bush and George W. Bush, who is a member of NRA. In 2005 the then president George W. Bush signed into law the *NRA- backed Protection of Lawful Commerce in Arms Act* which prevented firearms manufacturers and dealers from being held liable for negligence when crimes have been committed with their products. The *NRA-backed Disaster Recovery Personal Protection Act of 2006* prohibited the confiscation of legal firearms from citizens during states of emergency.

In addition to actively engaging in electoral politics and legislative process, NRA has also been campaigning against research projects on gun violence. In 1993, following the publication of a study funded by the federal Centers for Disease Control and Prevention (CDC) revealing that gun ownership increased the risk of homicide at home, the NRA successfully lobbied Congress to reallocate the CDC's budget for research on gun violence and to adopt the Dickey Amendment. The Dickey Amendment prohibited CDC from using federal funds to "advocate or promote gun control", which effectively prevented the CDC from funding research on gun violence in subsequent years.

With the anti-gun and pro-gun lobbies in contest, the sides of the gun debate are often described as "gun control" versus "gun rights" activists. Political arguments of gun politics in the United States center on disagreements that range from the practical, constitutional to the ethical. Political arguments about gun rights fall under two basic questions: 1) Does the government have the authority to regulate guns? 2) If it does, is it effective public policy to regulate guns?

The first category, collectively known as rights-based arguments, consist of arguments concerning Second Amendment freedom, state constitution, rights of self-defense, and security against tyranny and invasion. Central rights-based arguments of gun rights activists include: The Second Amendment of the US Constitution protects individual gun ownership; Gun control laws give too much power to the government and may result in government tyranny and the government taking away all guns from citizens; The Second Amendment was intended to protect gun ownership of all able-bodied men so that they could participate in the militia to keep the peace and defend the country if needed. On the other end of the political spectrum, gun control activists contend that: The Second Amendment is not an unlimited right to own guns; The Second Amendment was intended to protect the right of militias to own guns, not the right of individuals; Civilians, including hunters, should not own military-grade firearms or firearm accessories.

Public policy arguments, the second category of arguments, revolve around the reduction of gun violence and gun-related deaths, gun safety education, and the effectiveness of gun ownership for self-defense. Public policy-based arguments of gun rights activists against gun control laws often entail: Gun control laws do not deter crime, and it is gun ownership that deters crime; Gun control laws would prevent

Unit 10   Major Public Policy Issues as Controversies in Contemporary American Society

citizens from protecting themselves from foreign invaders; Gun control laws are racist as current gun control laws are frequently aimed at inner city, poor, black communities who are perceived as more dangerous than white gun owners; More gun control is not needed, rather, education about gun safety is needed to prevent accidental gun deaths. Gun control activists' conter-arguments, on the other hand, often entail: Enacting gun control laws such as mandatory safety features would reduce the number of accidental gun deaths; Gun control laws would reduce the societal costs associated with gun violence; Armed civilians are unlikely to stop crimes and are more likely to make dangerous situations, including mass shootings, more deadly.

Behind the gun debate was partisan politics entwined with interest group politics. On January 16, 2013, in response to the Sandy Hook Elementary School shooting and other national tragedies, president Barack Obama announced a "plan to reduce gun violence" for imposing stricter gun control in the United States, and providing greater access to mental health services. The plan included proposals for new laws to be passed by Congress, and a series of executive actions not requiring Congressional approval. After Obama signed 23 executive actions for his plan, gun enthusiasts joined in rallies across the United States to oppose gun control and protested that any attempt to impose new gun regulations undermined the right to bear arms under the Second Amendment. The proposals for new laws was also frustrated in Republican-controlled House. It was in fact not the first time for a gun control proposal to be thwarted in Congress. In 1994, president Bill Clinton pushed for passage of a landmark *Federal Assault Weapons Ban* (AWB), a subsection of the *Violent Crime Control and Law Enforcement Act*. AWB had a prohibition on the manufacture for civilian use of certain semi-automatic firearms it defined as assault weapons, as well as certain ammunition magazines it defined as"large capacity."AWB expired on September 13, 2004 and Legislation to renew or replace the ban was proposed numerous times unsuccessfully. Renewed efforts to pass a new federal assault weapons ban were made after the Sandy Hook shooting in December 2012. On January 24, 2013, Senator Feinstein introduced S.150, the *Assault Weapons Ban of 2013* (AWB 2013). The bill was similar to the 1994 ban, but differed in that it would not expire after 10 years. On April 17, 2013, AWB 2013 failed on a Republican-controlled Senate vote of 40 to 60.

Partisan divide on gun control was further represented in public opinion. Public opinion polls have revealed a stark contrast between registered voters in support of Democratic and Republican presidential candidates in their views of gun priorities – whether it is more important to control or protect private gun ownership, and the gap has been widening. It is notable that the public view of gun control is much confined to background checks for gun sales, prevention of purchases by prohibited people and those with mental illness, and creation of a federal database to track gun sales. When it comes to banning the assault-style weapons and high-capacity ammunition clips, however, the public became nearly evenly divided, which is parallel to the evenly divided general public views of gun priorities.

What further makes gun control a divisive issue is the regional differences. The Northwest and Western coast, with a concern for the rising firearm related crime rate in the region, are more supportive of gun control while the Southwest, West and Midwest, with their frontier tradition as historical heritage of gun culture, are generally known to be pro-gun states. In view of the role of the Midwest traditionally known as swing states in presidential elections, gun control can become a much delicate issue as the election race is likely to be decided largely by swing states where hunting is a popular pastime, like Missouri, Ohio or Pennsylvania. Candidates of both parties want to win over gun owners as voters, not alienate them. For Republican candidates, that means emphasizing their pro-gun credentials to win them over, but for Democrats, gun control could be a trickier issue as it often proves a hot button in the election campaign.

Given the regional differences and divided public opinion, the contest between pro-gun and gun control interest groups and activists in electoral and partisan politics, the gun debate rages on in the US.

Unit 10 Major Public Policy Issues as Controversies in Contemporary American Society

2 Affirmative Action: Fairness vs. Justice

Affirmative Action has been a contentious issue on the national, state, and local levels since its inception in the 1960s. Introduced during the Johnson administration in the 1960s, affirmative action is part of a long legacy of civil rights policies that date back to the post-Civil War period in the US. But unlike previous measures, such as the *Civil Rights Acts of 1964 and 1965*, which prohibited racial discrimination, the goal of affirmative action was to adopt a proactive approach to redressing past discrimination, to compensating for past sufferings of minorities, esp. African Americans for black slavery, racial segregation and racism. It encouraged employers and college admission officers to have active recruitment of racial minorities. State and local governments followed the lead of the federal government and began formal steps to encourage employers and public universities to take efforts to diversify their work forces and student populations.

In 1967, Affirmative Action was broadened to include women. The inclusion of women in Affirmative Action goals and programs at this particular moment reflected fruits of the second-wave of American feminist movement for gender equality in the workplace during the 1960s. Over the past decades, the implementation of Affirmative Action programs has revealed the complexity of race and gender as political categories. While at times Affirmative Action programs involve overlapping categories when the beneficiaries are black women as double minorities, more often, there have been more controversies around race-based Affirmative Action.

Fisher v. Texas was, among other lawsuits over Affirmative Action brought to the Supreme Court, a case that rekindled national debate on Affirmative Action in recent years. In 2012, Abigail Fisher, a white applicant for the University of Texas at Austin filed suit against the University on the grounds of "reversed discrimination" against Caucasian applicants, in violation of the Equal Protection Clause of the US Constitution. Fisher alleged that she was denied admission to the University's 2008 freshmen class while some less qualified applicants of racial minorities were admitted, given the race-based Affirmative Action programs of the University. The Supreme Court ruled in June 2013 in support of the University, yet the case was sent back to the lower court for further proceedings. In 2014, the District Court of the Fifth Circuit sided with the University and the Court of Appeals affirmed but ruled that "strict scrutiny should be applied to determine the constitutionality of the University's race-sensitive admission policy." Backed by Students For Fair Admissions (SFFA), a nonprofit organization of some 20,000 members as a counter-force to race-based Affirmative Action programs, Fisher appealed to the Court again and the case was headed back to the Supreme Court in 2016. The majority opinion of the Supreme Court upheld the University's admissions program, confirming that educational institutions may consider race as a factor when seeking to create diversity in study body. It also noted that the University should regularly evaluate available data on the diversity of student body resulting from Affirmative Action and "tailor its approach in light of changing circumstances, ensuring that race plays no greater role than is necessary to meet its compelling interest." The majority opinion reiterated that the University has an ongoing obligation to use available data "to assess whether changing demographics have undermined the need for a race-conscious policy; and to identify the effects, both positive and negative, of the affirmative-action measures it deems necessary." The Supreme Court justices, however, are also divided in their opinions. Justice Alito reiterated the circuit court dissent's claim that the Circuit Court majority believed that automatically admitted minority students were "somehow more homogeneous, less dynamic, and more undesirably stereotypical than those admitted under holistic review." Justice Thomas Clarence, as an African American, also authored a dissent. In this dissent, he reiterated the thoughts expressed in his concurrence in *Fisher v. Texas* I in 2013 that "a State's use of race in higher education admissions decisions is categorically prohibited by the Equal Protection Clause." The divide in the Court is in itself revealing of the controversies around race-based Affirmative Action as a focal point of national discourse on racial equality and social justice.

The central arguments against Affirmative Action entail: Affirmative Action violates ideals of color-blind public policies, offending moral principles of fairness and principles of equality of opportunity and due process enshrined in the 14th Amendment of the US Constitution. Opponents contend that Affirmative Action has often proven to be socially and politically divisive by alienating racial minorities from whites rather than integrating them. They further argue that the implementation of Affirmative Action for decades has not made things better: it does not work and it is not the key to raising the achievement level of racial minorities and females. They claim that Affirmative Action for African Americans mainly benefits middle-class, wealthy and foreign-born blacks rather than native blacks raised in socially, educationally or economically disadvantaged families. In addition, opponents believe that by compromising their self-esteem and self-respect, Affirmative Action stigmatizes its beneficiaries, who are conscious that they have been given preferential treatment simply because of their color or gender.

Opposition to Affirmative Action had its ideological origins in the rise of racial neo-conservatism in the early 1970s. The racial neo-conservatives were mostly those originally white moderates from the right of the Democratic Party and the left of Republican party, who were formerly supportive of black freedom struggle during the early phase of the Civil Rights Movement. After the passage of the *Civil Rights Act of 1964* and *Voting Rights Act of 1965*, and the abolition of racial segregation, however, they began to step back from their original position of support of black freedom struggle. The turn was largely derived from their dissatisfaction with the ruling Democratic Party's high tax and welfare spending, as welfare programs largely favored racial minorities, esp. Blacks. This discontent of government "tax and spend" politics have dual consequences: Firstly, it triggered a "tax revolt" party realignment of those originally southern white Democrats with Republicans; Secondly, it spurred racial conservatism. With an assumption that black equal civil rights became secured and institutional racism was eliminated in the post-civil rights era, racial neo-conservatives claimed that the American society had entered into a "color-blind society" free of racism, and barriers to social upward mobility of African Americans were being dismantled. The rise of middle-class African Americans in the post-civil rights era has, in the eyes of many racial neo-conservatives, provides a revealing example of the diminishing social barriers for African Americans in the "color-blind society." Accordingly, racial neo-conservatives advocated a laissez-faire approach to racial equality, and in turn, such government policies of Affirmative Action supportive of African Americans ought to be repealed. In this sense, racial neo-conservatives often tried to distinguish themselves from old-fashioned racists in the pre-civil rights movement era as they claimed to embrace the ideal of racial equality and positioned themselves as the true inheritor of the civil rights legacy. Thus a new "color-blind" racial discourse first fomented by racial neo-conservatives and policy advisers around the turn of the 1970s became the national majority consensus in the 1980s and 1990s and constituted a basic rationale for anti-Affirmative Action initiatives.

The 1990s represented a period of active, organized efforts on state levels to roll back Affirmative Action. In 1997, California passed Proposition 209 – the California Civil Rights Initiative or CCRI – the state ballot proposition which amended the state constitution to prohibit state governmental institutions from considering race, sex, or ethnicity, specifically in the areas of public employment, public contracting, and public education. Proposition 209 provided the first representative case of such a state effort, which effectively ended Affirmative Action in state and local agencies in California. The immediate impact of Proposition 209 was felt in the declining percentages of enrollment of underrepresented minorities, especially African Americans at public and private universities in California, and a decrease in the hiring of women faculty and racial minority faculty at these universities, as well as the failure to maintain the level of diversity in students and faculty as maintained under Affirmative Action. There followed similar developments in state of Washington with the passage of Initiative 200 in 1998 and Michigan with the Michigan Civil Rights Initiative (MCRI) in 2006 with Affirmative Action bans. In a Michigan lawsuit *Schuette v. Coalition* to Defend Affirmative Action in 2014, the Supreme Court ruled that there is no authority for the judiciary "to set aside Michigan laws that commit to the voters the determination whether racial preferences may be considered in governmental decisions, in particular with respect to school decisions." Thereby the Supreme Court upheld MCRI as the amendment to the state Constitution and that states had the right to ban Affirmative Action if they chose to do so through the electoral process.

Given the controversies around Affirmative Action, the remedial approach in an aim to compensate for past wrongs and injustices appear to be problematic as the approach raised questions of moral difficulty of inter-generational reparations. In this regard, diversity approach seems to provide more convincing rationale for Affirmative Action. The goal of Affirmative Action, as held by proponents of Affirmative Action, is to achieve positive social interactions among different ethnic groups, by way of promoting diversity in students, for the purpose of multicultural education. It is equally applicable to job employment, supporters argue, as diversity in the workforce helps developing intercultural competence essential in a globalized world. With the call for building a multicultural society amid the rising multicultural movement in contemporary American society, achieving diversity has become a basic rationale for supporting social forces behind Affirmative Action.

Essentially, as a hotly debated policy issue, Affirmative Action has revealed the tension between the notion of "justice/equality" and "fairness/liberty" as democratic goals of society and rationales for policies. The rationale of opposing forces to Affirmative Action has it that Affirmative Action endangers individual liberty in the sense that liberty entails equality of opportunity and due process. Supporters, on the other hand, hold Affirmative Action to be essential in achieving equality of opportunity for underprivileged minorities, who otherwise are unable to enjoy equal opportunities in education, job employment and other aspects of public life. They point to the persistent gap between non-Hispanic whites and African Americans in their overall socioeconomic conditions, regardless of the rising black middle-class in the post-civil rights era. Further, there remains a large black underclass who have been caught in the cycles of generational poverty, residential segregation, lack of educational opportunities and other life chances, job unemployment and criminal injustice. In the case of women, despite the elimination of institutional and legal sexual discrimination, it will be a long time before all traces of gender discrimination and injustices could be entirely eradicated. Affirmative Action are thus interpreted as essential government efforts to free those underprivileged minorities from restraints on their individual liberty. This interpretation of "justice/equality" as "fairness/liberty" is essentially in line with former president Franklin D. Roosevelt's vision of "freedom from want, freedom from fear" articulated on January 6, 1941. In the 1941 State of the Union address, FDR proposed four fundamental freedoms of people: freedom of speech, freedom of worship, freedom from want, and freedom from fear, which became known as "the second Bill of Rights". The underlying philosophy of FDR's Four Freedom Speech is that a "big government" that takes efforts to promote social justice and equality is essential to securing people's "freedom from want and fear", which is of equal importance to first amendment freedoms of speech and worship. Affirmative Action, in this sense, also represents the competing visions of "big government" and "small government" by the supporting and opposing forces. While the opponents advocate a laissez-faire approach by the government to racial and gender equality, supporters embrace a "big government" to protect underprivileged minorities from restraints on their life chances.

3 Abortion Rights: Pro-choice vs. Pro-life

Abortion rights, as the most divisive moral issue facing America today, also stands as a religious, legal, and in turn, a political issue that divides contemporary American society. Religious implications of the issue are derived from the religious conceptions of human life. Among the anti-abortion religious groups, Catholics are the staunchest opponents of abortion rights as the Catholic Church holds that "the first right of the human person is his life" and that life is assumed to begin at fertilization. As such, Canon 1398 provides that "a person who procures a successful abortion incurs an automatic excommunication" from the Church. Some major national anti-abortion, pro-life organizations are funded by the Catholic Church. The

Unit 10 Major Public Policy Issues as Controversies in Contemporary American Society

National Right to Life Committee (NRLC), founded in 1967 under the auspices of the National Conference of Catholic Bishops, is the oldest and the largest national pro-life organization in the US with affiliates in all 50 states and over 3,000 local chapters nationwide. American Life League, Inc. (ALL) is an American Catholic grassroots pro-life organization. The group opposes abortion under any circumstances and opposes all forms of contraception, embryonic stem cell research, and euthanasia.

In the 20th century, the debate over the morality of abortion became a major issue that divided Protestantism. Protestant views on abortion vary considerably with the "anti-abortion" and "abortion-rights" camps. Protestant supporters of abortion rights include the United Church of Christ, the United Methodist Church, the Episcopal Church, the United Presbyterian Church, the Presbyterian Church, and the Lutheran Women's Caucus. The Southern Baptist Convention, the largest Protestant denomination in the United States, opposes elective abortion except to save the life of the mother. The National Association of Evangelicals includes the Salvation Army, the Assemblies of God, and the Church of God, among others, and takes an anti-abortion stance. The Church of Jesus Christ of Latter-day Saints (the Mormon Church) opposes elective abortion based on a belief in the "sanctity of human life." During the early phase of American history, however, the influence of religious conservatism was manifest in the anti-abortion legislation of the 19th century.

In 1821, Connecticut passed the first state statute criminalizing abortion and every state had anti-abortion legislation by 1900. Rather than arresting the women having abortions, legal officials were more likely to interrogate these women to obtain evidence against the abortion provider in order to close down that provider's business. Roe vs. Wade in 1973 was a landmark case with the Supreme Court decision that restrictive state regulations of abortion violated a woman's constitutional right to privacy, which is implicit in the Due Process Clause of the Fourteenth Amendment. The Court deemed abortion a fundamental right under the US Constitution, thereby subjecting all laws attempting to restrict it to the standard of strict scrutiny.

By legalizing abortion on the federal level, *Roe v. Wade*, on the other hand, aroused national controversies on many fronts. A year after *Roe v. Wade* was passed, the first "National March for Life," sponsored by the March for Life Education and Defense Fund, was held in Washington, D.C. on January 22, 1974 and the March came down as an annually held tradition ever since. In response to Roe vs. Wade, furthermore, Illinois Congressman Henry Hyde introduced an amendment that would prevent federal funding for abortion. The Hyde Amendment was passed on September 30, 1976. Under this amendment, no federal funding could be used to pay for an abortion for any reason. Like all abortion-related policies, the Hyde Amendment is hotly contested, and subject to frequent protests. Pro-choice groups were concerned that the Hyde Amendment would cut off abortion access for low-income women. In response to this concern, some states instituted their own policies or funding resources to help low-income women access abortion services. By the 21st century, roughly one-third of the states had some form of state funding in place to make up for the lack of federal abortion funding. The Hyde Amendment, nevertheless, has constituted a legal basis for anti-abortion initiatives with its continued policy implications. In 2019, the Trump administration repealed the coverage of "elective abortion services" in health insurance plans included in the *Affordable Care Act* (ACA) of the Obama administration, based on a charge from some members of Congress and other pro-life leaders that "the hidden abortion surcharge" as a federal government mandate had violated the Hyde Amendment. Planned Parenthood Action Fund, a major national pro-choice organization, called the repeal "another direct attack at abortion access" as it could potentially cause some insurance plans to "drop abortion coverage altogether to avoid this administrative burden or raise costs."

  The strongest repercussions of *Roe v. Wade*, however, were felt in the rise of the "New Christian Right" in the 1970s as a major conservative force in American politics. The "New Christian Right" is an informal coalition formed around a core of evangelical Protestants and Roman Catholics. It draws additional support from politically conservative mainline Protestants, Jews, and Mormons. Pro-life campaigns, gay rights and sexual morality are among the core issues that motivated the New

Christian Right. The Roe vs. Wade supreme court decision provided a catalyst for the founding of the Moral Majority in 1979, the first national organization of the New Christian Right, and launched them into the political arena. The Moral Majority's impact on electoral politics was immediate as it became the single most important religious force behind the Republican candidate Ronald Reagan and contributed to his triumph in the 1980 presidential election.

Today, Democrats and Republicans have taken opposing stances on abortion rights. The Republican party becomes essentialized as the pro-life party and Democrats adopted the pro-choice identity. Republicans' pro-life position, however, is essentially a political strategy. When abortion first became a public policy issue in the 1960s, many Republicans supported the liberalization of state abortion laws, believing that abortion law reform was in line with the party's tradition of support for birth control, middle-class morality, and mainline Protestant values. Republicans shifted their position on abortion only after they decided to bid for Catholic votes, taking abortion policy as part of their "Catholic strategy." In addition, there were also signs that pro-life policy had broader appeal among a larger contingent of social conservatives who were turning against the idea of abortion based on their opposition to feminism and the sexual revolution. By the early 1970s the abortion debate had changed as feminists became the vanguard of the abortion rights movement in place of Republican-leaning members of the medical profession and the clergy. Abortion rights advocates such as the National Organization for Women (NOW) and the National Association for the Repeal of Abortion Laws (NARAL) called for legalizing "abortion-on-demand" in the belief that no woman should be forced to carry an unwanted pregnancy to term. As a consequence, the abortion rights movement moved away from its early association with Protestant-led birth-control campaigns, and became associated primarily with the feminist movement and the sexual revolution, both of which were disconcerting to many socially conservative Republican Protestants. Concerned that the increased availability of abortion might encourage premarital sex and out-of-wedlock pregnancy, social conservatives began to associate calls for the legalization of abortion with cultural liberals who were challenging the nation's social mores. Furthermore, when in the early 1970s Democrats moved to the left on women's rights issues including abortion and sexual revolution, Republicans reacted by distancing themselves from Democrats' alleged cultural liberalism. Abortion policy, in this sense, played a pivotal role in transforming Republicans from a predominantly mainline Protestant party into a party of conservative Catholics and evangelicals. Republicans' decision to adopt an anti-abortion platform in the 1970s created the basis for the party's outreach to social conservatives. The heavy concentration of evangelicals in the historically Democratic southern states made them an attractive target for Republican party activists who concluded that they had to win evangelical votes in order to win the south in the 1980 election. Reagan appealed to evangelicals and the leadership of the Roman Catholic Church on abortion to win their votes away from the Democratic party. New Christian Right activists lined up behind Reagan and became a significant source of political support for Republicans in the 1980 election.

In 1983, faced with the failure to pass a constitutional amendment banning abortion, however, New Christian Right responded to their failure at the federal level with renewed activism at state and local levels. The Supreme Court's 1989 decision in *Webster v. Reproductive Services* aided pro-life groups in their move to local activism as the Court ruled that states would be given wide latitude in determining how and when abortions are performed within their borders. The result has been a second explosion in the number of restrictive laws passed by state legislatures and the pro-life movement to push through state restrictive legislation on abortion has continued to gain momentum into the 21st century. In May 2019, Alabama Governor Kay Ivey signed into law the *Alabama Human Life Protection Act*, which bans all abortions in the state, except "when abortion is necessary in order to prevent a serious health risk" to women. The act criminalizes abortion procedure, reclassifying abortion as a Class A felony, punishable for up to 99 years in prison for abortion service providers. States including Tennessee and Ohio have passed similar restrictive legislation, which has reignited national debates and controversies on abortion.

Even though Republicans abandoned their attempt to pass a constitutional amendment against abortion after it failed in Congress in 1983, the Republicans' pledge to support a constitutional "human life" amendment remained part of the party's official platform throughout the rest of the 20th century, continuing its symbolic role as a beacon for social conservatives. By mobilizing rightist religious leaders and adopting conservative positions on such highly charged social issues as abortion rights and homosexuality, Republicans were able to bring into their party millions of New Christian Right, many of whom were Democratic converts from southern states. The political mobilization of religion and religious mobilization of politics have thus found expression in electoral politics with the partisan divide on abortion.

4 The Immigration Debate

As a nation of immigrants, the United States has more immigrants than any other country in the world. Today, more than 40 million people living in the US were born in another country, accounting for about one-fifth of the world's migrants. Immigration has been transforming the racial and ethnic composition and demographic landscape of American society. According to the much-cited population projections, if the current immigration rate continues into the mid 21st century, the foreign-born immigrant population of the US will nearly double the current size, and non-Hispanic white Americans will no longer be the majority, at least numerically, as African Americans, Asians, Latinos, and Native Americans will constitute over half of the population. This projected shift was seen by many as implying the possible revolutionary changes in the relationship between racial majority and minorities, including a decline of, or even an end to, European American social and cultural dominance and a flourishing of multiculturalism. The prospect of demographic changes brought by the immigration tide has raised concerns of social conservatives over a potential press on infrastructure and environmental building, a burden on social security benefits and a potential threat to the job market. Above all, however, was the anxiety of anti-immigration nativists about national identity, the fear that the American national identity would be in jeopardy with the immigration tides and demographic changes. The nativist position holds that immigrants would be inassimilable, and their customs and manners would endanger the American political institution, and that they would constitute a treat to the American national identity. Overall, anti-immigration sentiment is typically justified with arguments and claims including government expenses may exceed tax revenue relating to new immigrants; language isolates immigrants in their own communities and immigrants often refuse to learn the local language; immigrants often acquire jobs that would have otherwise been available to native citizens, thus depressing native employment; immigrants might create an oversupply of labor and depress wages; immigration tides might increase the consumption of scarce resources and make heavy use of social welfare systems, and moreover, can swamp a native population and replace its culture with their own.

Nativism, which defined the American identity in a restrictive sense, took root in the early phase of American history. The first wave of the nativist movement represented the strong anti-immigrant and especially anti-Roman Catholic sentiment that started to manifest itself during the 1840s. The Native American Party, an American nativist political party that operated nationally in the mid-1850s, was an outgrowth of the anti-Roman Catholic sentiment in the mid-19th century. The Native American Party, which believed there was a "Romanist" conspiracy by Catholic bishops and priests to subvert civil and religious liberty in the United States, sought to politically organize native-born Protestants in the defense of traditional religious and political values. As a national political entity, it called for restrictions on immigration, the exclusion of the foreign-born from voting or holding public office in the US, and a 21-year residency requirement for citizenship. By 1852, as the Native American Party was achieving phenomenal growth, it began to shed its clandestine characteristics and was renamed the American Party. When Congress assembled on Dec. 3, 1855, 43 representatives were avowed members of the party. That, however, was the peak of the party's power. At the American Party convention in Philadelphia the following year, the party split along sectional lines over the pro-slavery platform pushed through

Unit 10 Major Public Policy Issues as Controversies in Contemporary American Society

by southern delegates. Caught in the sectional strife, the American Party fell apart after 1856 when anti-slavery party members joined the Republican Party while southern members flocked to the pro-slavery banner still held aloft by the Democrats. Two other groups that took the name the American Party, however, appeared in the 1870s and 1880s. One of these, organized in California in 1886, proposed a briefly popular platform calling for the exclusion of Chinese and other Asians from industrial employment. The party's platform was rooted in the resurgence of nativism, which developed with greater intensity in the economic crisis of the 1880s accompanied by economic modernization. Nativist sentiments were particularly strong among the petty bourgeoisie and unorganized workers who were most threatened by modernization and they perceived early Chinese immigrants as posing threats to the workforce and their place in the American society. Anti-immigrant sentiments found expression in the passage of the *Chinese Exclusion Act* in 1882, which excluded Chinese laborers from immigrating to the United States and became the first immigration law passed by Congress that targeted a specific ethnic group.

The 1920s saw another wave of the nativist movement which focused on Catholics, Jews, Southern and Eastern Europeans, and nativists realigned their beliefs behind racial and religious nativism. The racial concern of the anti-immigration movement was linked closely to the eugenics movement that was sweeping the US in the twenties. Nativists launched a "100 percent Americanism" campaign based on a theoretical and scientific racism of eugenics, which cast the then immigrants from Eastern and Southern Europe – largely Jews and Italians – in a position of racial inferiority and projected a vision that the superiority associated with Nordic Americans – Western and Northern European Americans – would be drowned in a genetic flood unleashed by the new immigrants. The nativist eugenics movement culminated in the *Immigration Act of 1924*, which restricted immigration to the US through a national origin quota, i.e., 2% of residents of each nationality in the US based on the 1890 national census. The clear aim of the *Immigration Act of 1924* was to restrict immigration from Southern and Eastern Europe while welcoming a relatively large number of immigrants from Western and Northern Europe and the act effectively ended Asian immigration to the US.

Historically, nativists' conceptualization of the American identity and mainstream culture has evolved with the fusion of "ethnics" into the European white race. Since the mid-20th century, as the racial edge to the perception of ethnic differences among white Americans has disappeared, nativism began to define American identity largely in terms of European whites and sought to curtail colored naturalization and immigration. Today, right-wing social forces and white supremacists have formed a dissenting nativist faction in American society, but their outlook has been largely defensive and they are hardly as formidable as nativists in the earlier phases of American history. The immigration debate in present-day American society revolves around the issue of "unauthorized immigrants" as an overriding concern of policymakers, as the undocumented currently account for around a quarter of the immigration population, most of whom are from Mexico. In November 2014, president Barack Obama announced a series of administrative reforms of immigration policy, collectively called the Immigration Accountability Executive Action. The centerpiece of these reforms is an expansion of the Deferred Action for Childhood Arrivals (DACA) initiative created in 2012, which grants work permits to undocumented immigrants who arrived in the United States as children, and the Deferred Action for Parents of Americans and Lawful Permanent Residents (DAPA) initiative for the parents of US citizens and lawful permanent residents who meet certain criteria. Together, these initiatives could provide as many as 5 million unauthorized immigrants with temporary relief from deportation. The objectives of these reform efforts are that DAPA and expanded DACA would not only keep families united, but also increase US gross domestic product, tax revenue, and raise wages. Within hours of the announcement, however, Maricopa County, Arizona Sheriff Joe Arpaio challenged the Obama administration's plan to defer deportations in a federal court in Washington, D.C., in *Arpaio v. Obama*. Shortly thereafter, representatives of 17 states filed a similar case, *Texas v. United States*, in a federal

Unit 10 Major Public Policy Issues as Controversies in Contemporary American Society

court in Brownsville, Texas, with 9 other states later joining the lawsuit. On the other hand, a broad spectrum of supporters – including 15 states and D.C. – filed "friend-of-the-court" briefs supporting the Obama administration's plan. In 2017, the Trump administration's announcement to end DACA evoked renewed controversy with protest rallies of immigration rights supporters in D.C. and other major cities, placing the issue of "unauthorized immigrants" at the forefront of the immigration debate.

On the other hand of the political spectrum, cosmopolitan liberalism, as a competing vision with nativism, takes an expansive view of the American identity, and has confidence in the capacity of an inclusive American identity to absorb immigrants. In the vision of cosmopolitan liberalism, to be an American is to be loyal to core values of the American society, and an American nationality could therefore be claimed by those who adhere to it, regardless of their race, ethnicity, religion and origins. Nativism and cosmopolitan liberalism have competed with each other in the course of American history as cosmopolitan liberalism has, at various times, resisted pressures from American nativism by campaigning for open immigration and liberal naturalization procedures. WWII had a deep impact on the development of cosmopolitan liberalism, and WWII itself proved a singular manifestation of cosmopolitan liberalism with an aim to fight against Fascist racism. The Sino-US collaborations in the 1940s in the Chinese War of Resistance to Japanese invasion paved way for the *Magnuson Act of 1943*, which repealed the *Chinese Exclusion Act of 1882*. Further, cosmopolitan liberalism began to prevail in the midst of the civil rights struggles of African Americans, Hispanics, Asian Americans in the 1960s, and succeeded in actualizing its visions in the passage of the *Immigration and Nationality Act of 1965*, which abolished the system of national origin quotas for immigration and gave rise to new tides of colored immigration over decades.

With the rising tide of colored immigration after 1965, the American society has grown increasingly multi-racial and multi-ethnic, and new visions of the society have developed in the course of the struggle of people of color to overcome their historical exclusion from the American cultural identity. These visions are expressed in the movements of multiculturalism in the 1980s as spin-offs of social movements in the 1960s. In the 1990s, multicultural movements was further expanded to include feminism, gay rights, and the movement for the interests of the handicapped. The main propositions of multiculturalism as a socio-political theory entail: 1) constitutional democracy with participation of minorities in the policy making beyond a demand for equal civil rights, which calls for a proportional representation of minorities in politics; 2) politics of recognition, namely, identity politics, which puts a stress on the group identity of minorities. These propositions thus reveal the difference of multiculturalism from cosmopolitan liberalism, as multiculturalism doesn't confine itself to a co-existence of minorities as subcultures, but seeks to redefine American national identity by restructuring power relations between majority and minorities, and by deconstructing the "male-centric and white-centric" social discourse. In this sense, multiculturalists perceives what nativisits and cosmopolitan liberals essentially have in common: both of them attach importance to the centrality of European, protestant, white culture as the mainstream of the American society. The division between them, however, is the fear of the former, and confidence of the latter, concerning sturdiness of American national identity defined by mainstream culture. In this sense, cosmopolitan liberalism can be defined as "cultural pluralism" which can accommodate an "integrationist pluralism," with a co-existence of minority subcultures under the dominance of mainstream culture that is white, European and Protestant in character.

Since the 1990s, multicultural education has been at the forefront of multicultural thoughts and movement, which proposed educational reforms by incorporating minority perspectives into the design of textbooks and curriculum, embodying cultural values and historic heritage of minority groups in historical and cultural narratives, and enlarging minority representation in student and faculty recruitment. The fruits of multicultural education were manifest in a flourishing of fields in American studies, including African American studies, Hispanic, Asian American studies, Native American studies, women studies, queer studies, etc. African Americans, among other racial minorities, have moved furthest in group identity politics resulting from the special history with a common experience of enslavement, and racial segregation. Collective memory of traumatic experience facilitated a distinct black culture that embraces "Black English" as a Creole, black religion and black churches, black music, and black lifestyle. Black Power movement in the late 1960s and early 1970s was, above all, the immediate pushing force behind the establishment of black studies programs and research centers across the nation. With the Afrocentric movement of the 1990s, black studies programs developed further into African American studies in colleges and universities amid the rising tide of multiculturalism.

Overall, the fruits of multicultural movement have been best represented in the cultural ascendancy of minorities in education and academia with the development of ethnic studies, women studies, queer studies, etc. as well-established fields of American studies, alongside an increase in minority proportion in student and faculty population. Further, there's a rise in the "market-driven multiculturalism" with markets targeting ethnic minorities in selling goods ranging from daily necessities to works of art. There have been marketing campaigns running on the platform of multiculturalism that appeal to ethnic minorities, which in turn builds prominence of ethnic minorities in popular culture. On the other hand, backlashes to the multicultural movement have also found expression in campaigns for a tightened immigration policy, rollback of Affirmative Action, and a call for "moral traditionalism" with evocations of traditional protestant, patriarchal, heterosexual family values. Ideologically, critics of multiculturalism often label it "minority nationalism" as a competing vision with American nationalism, or even as "separatist pluralism" that undermines the cohesion of the American society.

Essentially, there have been two competing visions of a multi-ethnic, multicultural American society that underline the current immigration debate:

Optimism about the increasing assimilation and decline of adversary identity politics of minorities points to the positive social trends including: 1) linguistic assimilation: Surveys reveal that the position of English in the American society has grown stronger, and reported competency in English of immigrants has increased, as the trends of globalization assists linguistic assimilation based on the preeminence of English as a worldwide language. 2) Racial and ethnic boundary crossing and blurring with increasing rate of interracial marriage among the younger generations, which gave rise to 3) a racial and ethnic boundary change with the narrowing in the social distance between majority and minority groups.

Pessimists about the prospect of a multi-cultural America, nevertheless, conceptualized scenarios of the "segmented assimilation" of immigrants, with the narrowing of social distance not between majority and minorities, but between very disadvantaged segments of the new immigrant groups and the native, urban underclass. Segmented assimilation thus rarely involves upward socioeconomic mobility between the first-generation immigrant and subsequent generations. Pessimists point to the main signals of segmented assimilation including the adoption of the oppositional subculture by the second and third generation immigrant youth and inner-city ghetto culture of the underclass, which may give rise to adversary identity politics of minorities and "minority nationalism." Concerns over the dissimilation trends of immigrants, in this sense, provided justifications for immigration control and revealed the intensity of the immigration debate.

Essay Questions:

1. What's the role of partisan politics, interest group politics and electoral politics in gun control as a policy issue?
2. Discuss your perceptions of the prospect of gun control in the US, given the competing social, political forces and divided public opinion.
3. What are the rationale and underlying philosophies of opposing and supporting views of the Affirmative Action?
4. Discuss the competing claims of "liberty"(fairness) and "equality"(justice) as represented in the Affirmative Action.

Unit 10　Major Public Policy Issues as Controversies in Contemporary American Society

5. How did abortion rights evolve into a political issue in the US?
6. What are the significant social and political forces behind the pro-life movement?
7. How did nativism and cultural pluralism shape the immigration policies and legislation in different phases of American history?
8. Discuss the competing visions of a multi-ethnic, multicultural American society that underline the current immigration debate.

Unit 11　American Women

Since American colonial times, though American women, like American men, made indelible contributions to the society, they were denied as full citizens until almost one century and a half later after the founding of the nation when they were finally enfranchised. That was already eight years later after white men got the right to vote and sixty years later after black men obtained suffrage. Before winning suffrage, American women were treated as powerless "others" in the nation which purported to uphold liberty and democracy, and marginalized in economic, political, cultural and religious life of the society. However, baptized by the ideal of the Enlightenment and Republicanism and prompted by scientific development, education improvement, industrial advancement and westward movement, American women have awoken from sexual oppression and made consistent efforts in fighting for their own rights: they plunged into social reforms, launched feminist movements, walked out of the "woman's sphere", broke the glass ceiling, dismantled the maternal wall, and tried to stand shoulder to shoulder with men in the public arena. Nevertheless, American women continue to face hidden sexual discrimination of every stripe in the 21st century.

1　White Women and the Feminist Movement

American white women, like women of color, played a subordinate role at home and experienced prevalent sexism in the society. Although American white women spearheaded feminist movements, their heroic struggle did not happen overnight; instead, ever since American colonial times, various social factors as well as their own lived experiences defined and redefined their female roles, as well as shaped and reshaped their female consciousness.

1.1 The Female Helpmeet: Women in Colonial America of the 17th Century

The seventeenth-century Europe, which experienced dramatic transformation from feudalism to capitalism, offered a lot of avenues for women, including the opportunity for European women to emigrate to the open lands of the New World. No matter which region the early women pioneers settled down, either New England town or the middle or southern colonies, no matter which class they were from, no one could be exempt from relying on medieval farming and subsistence household economies to ensure the survival in the isolated settlements. Needless to say, what women encountered were arduous and ceaseless tasks in the wildness. In general, their central tasks at home included but not limited to: bearing and rearing the children (usually 6-8 kids a household), with reproductive function as women's irreplaceable value; feeding the family – food preparation, breeding the poultry, keeping the garden, cooking, processing and preserving the food, etc.; clothing the family – knitting, weaving, spinning, sewing, etc.; keeping the house – sweeping, laundering, scrubbing, etc. Apart from all of this, women also carried the essential duties to work in the field alongside men, such as tending the land, planting, cultivating, harvesting, and going out of doors to barter their surplus products to support the family. Viewed in such a context, it can be argued that hard times and survival necessity in the nearly self-sufficient agrarian society somehow blurred the sexual division of labor between men and women, presenting a sort of casual but unintended practical equality. Under such circumstances, women found themselves in an ironic situation. On the one hand, as men's working partners, they made tremendous and ineffaceable contribution to the economic development and social prosperity of preindustrial America; on the other hand, in spite of the central and important economic roles that they assumed, women lived in the largely patriarchal household and society with men as their supreme authority, taking the leadership in economic, legal, political and cultural affairs.

In colonial times, the distribution of land was mostly determined by the situation and status of the male household head, while women's rights to independently hold title to landed property were eliminated in each town and every colony. Following the European tradition and English common law, the colonial statutes and legal practice favored men's ownership and exchanges of property. Before marriage, single women, living in the male-headed and father-dominating family system, were denied equal inheritance of property with their brothers. After marriage, the control of their dowries, the privilege of acquiring lands and the liberty of exchanging property were transferred to their husbands, who were regarded as wives' superiors, with the exception of widowed family units where the widowed woman was allowed to take possession of a sizeable number of her husband's estates at her disposal. The unequal property allocation and partial legal codes led to women's dependent, submissive and even inferior status to men, which just fit the broad social context and expectation for sex role. It was assumed that, women's obedience to the patriarchal head of the family could avoid household conflicts and ensure the good cooperation between the two sexes, thereby promoting stability and order in both the family and society.

Although women were industrious and productive, they were still set apart from the center of political life in the agrarian community. Considered as apolitical beings, they were excluded from full political participation in the town meetings and the colonial assemblies, as they were barred from expressing their opinions and denied voting rights in the public sphere. For instance, they were neither granted any office in the communal administration nor admitted as judges or even reliable jurors or witnesses in the tribunals. As a matter of fact, such political deprivations made it impossible for women to effectively exercise their political wisdom and actively engage in the construction of the communal well-being, much less to safeguard and improve their social rights through making or amending colonial laws. Besides, the political alienation exacerbated the inferior and circumscribed status of women in both public and private spheres, because they were voiceless and vulnerable subjects standing aside under the patriarchal authority of the male rulers. Evidently, the deprivation of women's political rights and obligations was not so much relief and benefit as constraint and repression for the awakening of women.

Additionally, an important part of colonial life centered around the church, which through delivering the sermons, teachings and lectures, the clergymen shouldered the responsibility of sending and reinforcing values and beliefs to build a close-knit community. The church also served as an essential channel for women to learn knowledge, draw lessons and enrich their cultural and moral life, for the doors of institutions of higher education were slammed in their faces and the public school system open to a vast majority of residents hadn't been established yet. Though there existed certain degree of religious equality in such Christian theology as "there is neither Jew nor Greek, Bond nor Free, Male nor Female, for you all are one in Christ Jesus", women couldn't escape the fate of being dependent and subservient, since, according to Genesis 3:16, God told Eve that "thy desire shall be to thy husband, and he shall rule over thee". After all, she was just an "Adam's Rib". Thus, seldom could women become clergywomen at that time and consequently they had exerted little influence on the religious field. It is not unusual to see that women just read the Scripture, passively accepted its interpretation from the clergymen, and then submissively abided by the tenets. The rare bold cases were Anne Hutchinson and Mary Dyer. Motivated by the religious utopia of a rough sexual equality, both of them transgressed the theological boundary for women, challenged the authority of the patriarchal religious leaders, as well as demanded religious tolerance toward the sexes and a deserved religious place for woman. However, what awaited them were such severe punishments as ruthless banishment and torturing death.

During decades of colonial settlement, there is no denying that without women's devotion and sacrifice, it is impossible to plant a society in the frontier wildness. In comparison with their English middle and lower class counterparts, colonial women, forced by the harsh living environments, were blessed with more opportunities and freedom to exert their strengths and intellects in the self-sufficiency of a well-ordered family and the economic development of a prosperous society, which put them on relatively equal terms with men regarding their economic function. Nevertheless, other than the major role women played in the economic production, they were lowly at home and inferior in the society as obedient partners in the private sphere and "invisible" others in the public arena. Moreover, most of them were far from being aware of their unequal and disadvantaged status. Yet, the republic ideals spread before and after the founding of the New Republic in the eighteenth century gradually raised women's consciousness of liberty and equality, laying an initial foundation for their consciousness of rights.

1.2 Founding Mothers: Women in the 18th Century

The eighteenth century was undergoing sea changes in American society: the rising of commercial economy, the decline of the patriarchal household, and the founding of the New Republic. During the historical process, though women's subordinate status hadn't been altered both in and out of the house, their tasks, demands, pursuits and awareness changed with the tide of the Age of Reason and the ideal of Republicanism. During this period, American womanhood took myriads of shapes and a new femininity was fostered.

The growth of commercial capitalism brought fundamental changes in the society, which further affected women in a subtle but seminal way. The forces of the expanding commercial trade changed the traditional agricultural subsistence household economy, which had great impacts on women's economic lives. Since the vast majority of the population still resided in rural areas, the wives of the farmers became familiar with commodities and trade, and adapted themselves to the demands of the economic production and social exchange in the market. As the farmland supply had been exhausted and the original distribution of township fields no longer existed, a large number of farmers who were not able to climb the ladder to success in their hometowns decided to uproot themselves, either to swarm to the factories and shops in cities and towns, or to join in the movement to the western frontier for lands and opportunities. Among the displaced famers, a small number of them were young women, mostly single women from the lower strata whose families needed their incomes to support the whole family. As for those women, working in the urban areas not only helped them win their economic independence, but also enabled them to escape from the patriarchal surveillance and obtain a partial psychological freedom. At the same time, as for the families whose male heads like husbands and fathers had departed from rural areas, women were left alone with the economic duties at home in a variety of ways, e.g. taking care of the household manufacturing, controlling the sale of home production, maintaining the taverns, etc. All these social threads revealed the dissipation of the patriarchal family system, the vital role that women played in the commercial economy, as well as the expansion of some degree of freedom in their economic and private life. For the moment, it is not rare to see women married at a more random rather than fixed age, and bore at least two fewer children than their grandma's generation, which led to a declining family size and an increasing concern about the financial burden of the family in the commercial era.

In addition to the economic transformation, the American Revolution, even if it hadn't made any real changes in women's rights and position, still compelled women to get involved in the public events, so that their political awareness was nurtured and their ability to participate in social activities was expanded. As early as the colonial resistance against the imperial new taxes in the pre-Revolutionary period, women plunged themselves into the protests. They not only organized such groups as the Daughters of Liberty to support the boycott of British and European goods, but also took an active role in manufacturing home-made products, and urging the Americans to use domestic goods instead of those made in Britain, in the hope that the colonies could win its economic independence. During wartime, while men went to fight in the battleground, women took over the responsibilities that used to be men's duties, e.g. managing the farms, governing the home, attending to the family's business, etc. There emerged some courageous heroines like Molly Pitcher who accompanied her husband to the battlefield and went on fighting after her husband died, and Deborah Sampson who disguised herself as a man to endure canon fire and fought for freedom as a frontline soldier. Due to women's extensive participation and outstanding performance before and in the revolutionary period, women's public images were much improved, and their self-confidence and self-respect were greatly bolstered.

However, after the smoke was cleared and peace was back, though the Revolutionary ideals of liberty and democracy inspired women to reflect on their life and question their place, they were, in reality, still kept off from the political or public sphere, and the subordination of their social and political status remained untouched. Women's disenfranchisement still denied them access to the political power, making them inferior or lesser human beings. Yet, in the wake of the Revolution, the recognition of women's contributions and abilities gave an impetus to the reform in female education. The opportunities for women to attend primary schools and women's literacy rates were on the increase, and secondary schools began to accept female students who could afford it. But in most instances, education was just a privilege reserved for women from wealthy families, through which they could learn, aside from the rudimentary knowledge of reading and spelling for the purpose of serving the husband and the family, the "ornamentals", for example, drawing, embroidery, French, and even history, religion, geography, and politics.

The significant development of female education was inseparable from the need of cultivating "Republican Motherhood". Within the theme of "Republican Motherhood", educated mothers carried a crucial mission for the country – not only bringing up the republican citizens, but also shaping the values and reasoning power of their children, especially male children, for democratic citizenship in the liberating American culture. To some extent, it recognized women's virtues especially their moral superiority in instilling morality in the minds of children and cultivating their patriotic feelings. As a result, it legitimated women's demands for further education, heightened their consciousness of emotional attachments and personal feelings, and stirred up a storm in their hearts conducive to future feminist movements. It came as no surprise that the first generation of American feminists, such as Elizabeth Stanton and Lucretia Mott, were mostly born of democratic families and raised by well-educated mothers. However, it should be pointed out that the important responsibilities that Republican mothers assumed were by no means the remedy to ameliorate the virtual female impotence in politics, nor the means to elevate them to any higher position in society. On the contrary, since the appearance of seemingly important Republican Motherhood, women were confined to familial roles, which distanced them even further from the public arena.

Fortunately, the doors of the church were not closed to women. Hence outside the home they flocked to benevolent associations to assist the needy and the weak in orphan asylums, almshouses, schools, hospitals, prisons, etc. The social services around the cause of religion and charity provided women a relatively open access to social activities and broader companionship, and nurtured their organizing and communicating capabilities. The contact with the outside world gradually made them feel dissatisfied with the narrow limits of the domestic circle, and finally stirred them to launch the women's rights movement in the next half-century.

1.3　Homemakers & Moral Reformers: Creating and Expanding Woman's Sphere, 1800 – 1860

The antebellum period marked the rapid transition to industrial capitalism and momentum in westward movement. An increasing number of people either relocated themselves to urban areas, or joined the waves of heading west. Under the shifting circumstances, America started the industrializing process, with household production turning to mechanized manufacturing in steam-powered workshops or factories. Trade and commerce continued to grow, with more frequent speculative land dealings and expansive business investment. The public school system reached every state, with more female admission to primary and secondary schools and more women teachers at the elementary-school level, because it is generally believed that they were fit to be teachers. For the time being, there came the simultaneous and paradoxical emergence of the domestic ideology and feminist movement. Taken together, these historical changes meant a dramatic social mobility, rising quickly or failing easily, accompanied by an emerging urban middle class and enlarging role divisions.

    The detachment of home and workplace together with the geographic mobility drove men to work away from home and rise in the world, but kept women at home, reigning in the domestic circle. Gradually, the doctrine of "woman's sphere" was coined and promoted. This ideology did not merely refer to a metaphor indicating the enclosed and limited spatial area but a value system revealing the assigned distinctive roles and character traits to the second sex. In the "woman's sphere", women were required to be invested with "true womanhood", including such virtues as domesticity, submissiveness, piety and purity. First, women must be efficient housekeepers, diligent rears and good educators, since both God and nature dictated that home was women's appropriate station and men's refuge from competitive world. In order to secure the domesticity, a proper female education was further advocated. Through advice books, sentimental novels and fashion magazines likes *Godey's Lady's Book* and *Ladies Magazines*, the society pronounced and propagated emphatic directives and heated discussion of women's domestic duties and obligations to thousands of the female audience. Second, being submissive was in accordance with the patriarchal tradition and women's anatomy. As men were creators of history, organizers of the Industrial Revolution, initiators of the westward expansion and breadwinners of the family, there was hardly any reason for women not to feel inferior to men and be subject to men's rule. Third, piety was associated with women's moral strength and religious charity. Their qualities like benevolence, gentleness, modesty and subordination were none other than what the church prescribed. Thus, they were trusted to bear spiritual excellence and moral superiority over men who were corrupted by the materialistic world and exert their maternal influences at home and religious impacts in the society by participating in the church-related associations. Last but not least, purity referred to women's pure body and mind, which means women must be faithful to their husbands and have sexual control over themselves. After all, lustfulness and fleshliness were men's propensities.

Unit 11　American Women

　　As a rule, there were double standards for both sexes: premarital sexual behaviors and extra-marital relationships were taboos and ever-lasting shame for women, while men's infidelity and evil were understandable and pardonable, because temptations from the outside world were everywhere and it was natural for men to fell prey to them. The contrasting standards clearly showed the differentiated treatment towards men and women. All in all, the distinctive woman's sphere in no way shattered male dominance and authority in family, religion and the public world; instead, in fact, the doctrine cooped women up in a rather narrow circle and restrained their influence. However, even if impacts upon women were subtle and unobtrusive in the particular sphere, they were still stirred by their distinctive roles and domestic accomplishments to realize their strengths and importance. Meanwhile, their moral superiority and maternal qualities enable them to be worthy of "moral reformers" to engage in removing social evils through moral-related social activities or charity events, which unexpectedly expanded the woman's sphere. Within this limited and expanding area, women gradually found that they shared the same experiences and faced similar problems, which fostered benevolent sisterhood and intense identification with each other. Interestingly, both the social practice and group consciousness derived from the woman's sphere further promoted reform movements including the feminist movement at that time.

　　The various social reforms that large numbers of women entered ranged from moral reforms (i.e. the education of sexual morality to the public, the transformation of the prostitutes and the criminals), temperance movement (i.e. alerting individuals to stop drinking, and petitioning the government to pass the Prohibition law), to the antislavery movement and women's rights movement. The wives and daughters of businessmen, artisans, professionals formed associations, exercising influences directly or indirectly over their neighbors, family members and close friends. Additionally, they tactically utilized such methods as the petition campaign, lectures and reports to catch public attention and achieve political success without outraging their guardians. It was through those reform movements that they slowly widened the social boundaries of their sex.

While women were playing an active role in the growing abolitionist movement, they recognized their own fetters. The female activists intended to participate in the World's Anti-Slavery Convention in London in 1840, only to receive the refusal to seat them in an all-male meeting. At the same time, the anti-slavery crusaders like Angelina and Sarah Grimké who lectured and wrote against the evils of slavery were attacked and denounced by both church and political leaders. Hence, the enraged and disappointed female abolitionists became the first American feminists to question men's superiority in rights and status, which eventually led to early feminists to decide to fight for women's equal rights and positions in society. In 1848, led by Elizabeth Cady Stanton, Lucretia Mott, and a number of like-minded women, the first women's rights convention was held in Seneca Falls, New York. The Seneca Falls Convention issued the *Declaration of Sentiments* and passed twelve resolutions. Modeled on the *Declaration of Independence*, the Seneca Falls declaration called for the same inalienable natural rights for women including the property right, the education right and even the then controversial voting right, demanding an end to all the male privileges and unjust laws. Even if some delegates believed that the right to vote was too radical to be put in the resolutions, the convention finally voted for the inclusion of the demand. This event became a milestone in American feminism, paving the way for the influential women's suffrage movement after the Civil War.

During the decades before the American Civil War, the allocated space of women and the cult of true womanhood became firmly imprinted on the American mind. Fundamentally speaking, they were manifestations of the ongoing development of individualization in the family and society. Furthermore, they became the way to reestablish a sense of order so as to relieve the anxieties trigged by the economic, political and social transformations of the time. Even though women were confined to the walls of their homes under the ideology of domesticity, their importance and influence were on the slow increase nevertheless. This enabled women to recognize their power and go beyond their families to exert their influences on certain public issues. Despite all the difficulties, American women successfully launched the women's rights movement, which, for various reasons, lasted for more than a half century before they won their suffrage.

1.4 New Women & The Suffrage Movement: 1860 – 1920

Between the American Civil War and WWI, the heritage from last period – the enlarged influence created through the broadening of woman's sphere beyond the domestic circle, the expanded public space carved out through voluntary associations and social reforms, the liberating ideology of women's rights – passed down to the younger generation of American women. At this point, industrialization and urbanization were in full swing across the country, reshaping the nation in the direction of modernization. By 1920, 52 percent of the American population were city dwellers. Integral to the social transformation, women were exposed to new economic and political opportunities and more options for education and occupation, which were actually hard-fought gains inseparable from the persistent efforts of women's rights movement, as well as a different homemaking situation due to the progress of science and technology.

By 1890, about 70 percent of the state legislatures had stipulated that married women had the right to their inherited property and other forms of income. By the same year, women had been allowed to vote in school board elections or even some municipal elections in around 40 percent of the states. By the end of the 19th century, women in such four states as Wyoming, Utah, Colorado, Idaho were enfranchised, decades earlier than the ratification of the Nineteenth Amendment at the federal level which granted women suffrage all over the nation. The industrial power vigorously liberated productive forces, promoting the economic development and technological advancement. Under such circumstances, the whole society made higher requirements for the labor force, which broadened the opportunities for women to receive more and higher education. In the latter half of the nineteenth century, all the primary and secondary schools were open to women, and the number of college-educated women rose significantly. Moreover, the Midwestern land-grant colleges accepted women and allowed co-education, and women's college like Vassar, Smith, Wellesley, Bryn Mawrwere were founded in the late nineteenth century to admit women students. As of 1900, 80 percent of the American institutions of higher learning welcomed women. By 1910, 40 percent of college-age Americans who received college education were women, surging from 21 percent in 1870. The growing economy together with the better education for women accelerated the changes in their work. In addition to a small range of female occupations such as domestic servants, seamstress, teachers and other menial odd jobs, new jobs were provided and opened up to women, including labor-intensive and unskilled work in textile, printing, food-manufacturing and tobacco-making factories as well as white-collared work opportunities like teachers, typewriters, secretaries, clerks, librarians, telephone operators, etc. Throughout the era, women made inroads into different professional careers, and the number of the national working women in 1910 tripled the size of the group in 1870. Nonetheless, the legal and medical fields were hard for them to enter. By 1920, only 1.4 percent of the lawyers and judges as well as 5 percent of the doctors were women. Technological improvements introduced new home inventions, such as the electric washing machine, the electric sewing machine, the electric vacuum cleaner, and the gas stove. As a result of all these changes, homemakers on the one hand were in great measure emancipated from laborious and time-consuming domestic tasks. On the other hand, housewives were expected to take new obligations and meet stricter standards of homemaking, for instance, to be a scientific mother, learning and then using the scientific guidance to keep the family sound and take good care of children.

All these profound changes enabled women to either go outside the home and come into contact with the outside world or have more time and enough education to reflect on their situation and development. During the process, they found more capabilities of themselves and encountered more unequal issues in the daily life, which altogether increased their awareness of being an independent and active citizen to fight for their legitimate rights. At this particular moment, the New Woman emerged and shone brightly over the American social landscape. In general, New Women obtained an increasing power at home and strove for an essential role alongside men in the public sphere. How did all this come about? Specifically speaking, first, they were products of middle-class families that could afford higher education, offer them a secure family life and provide financial support for their career goals as well as social engagement. Second, they were beneficiaries of the Second Industrial Revolution, blessed with rare opportunities to become competent white-collar workers and well-educated college graduates. Third, they were no longer fragile and passive angels who wore long dresses with trails on the ground, constricting corsets and heavyweight girdles, and distanced from sports; instead, they put on divided skirts or sports dresses, looser corsets and lightweight girdles, did outdoor sports like biking, playing golf, tennis and badminton. Last but not least, they inherited and redefined the doctrine of true womanhood with an elevated sense of self and society as well as an enhanced awareness of gender and mission. With the ambition to uplift the nation and reform the social evils spawned by industrial capitalism, they formed and headed a myriad of female associations like women's clubs – the Women's Trade Union League, the Women's Christian Temperance Union, the alumnae association, the settlement association, the suffrage association, and established the national organizational networks to strengthen their influences. Compared with the benevolent women who were active in the charity activities and a small range of social reforms in the antebellum period, New Women were seasoned and ardent social housekeepers in the wide-ranging public affairs in the late nineteenth century.

Among all the social campaigns, the women's suffrage movement was of the most far-reaching significance, for it resulted in the full citizenship of women and their equal political rights with men. Due to the deep-rooted sexual discrimination, the lengthy and complicated legislative process, the lack of organization and fighting experience of the suffragists in early times, the movement turned out to be a hard-fought prolonged campaign. As a matter of fact, in the antebellum period, the women's rights movement fought for piecemeal and dispersed objectives such as the right to property, the guardianship of children after divorce. It was immediately after the consecutive ratification of the Fourteenth and Fifteenth Amendments which granted black male suffrage that women activists came to realize their political marginality and powerlessness. Within the suffragists, the radical faction headed by Elizabeth Stanton and Susan B. Anthony organized the National Woman Suffrage Association (NWSA), working on the federal level for a national amendment for the redress of inequality, while the moderate wing led by Lucy Stone formed the New England Woman Suffrage Association (NEWSA) in 1868 and NEWSA became the American Woman Suffrage Association (AWSA) one year later, trying to court public support and the voting rights on the state level. By the 1890s when women's social housekeeping activities began to reach an all-time peak, suffragists started to realize that without the right to casting votes, they were still sidelined in the political arena and unable to make crucial decisions together with male voters. Hence, in 1890, the two wings merged to form the National American Woman Suffrage Association (NAWSA), pooling their respective resources for the same goal of suffrage. Besides, the new association went all out to cooperate with other women's organizations so as to capitalize on their strengths and networks. Furthermore, the sophisticated and enterprising suffragists utilized the rhetoric of motherhood and the internalized doctrine of woman's sphere to emphasize woman's moral superiority, acute perceptions and special motherly power. Those outstanding qualities justified women's purifying function in the political field, guaranteed the maternal influence on the children, and maintained white supremacy over blacks and newly-arrived immigrants. During WWI, suffragists endorsed and contributed to the war, facilitating their efforts to win more support for the passage of the Nineteenth Amendment. Through women's expedient strategies, finally the Nineteenth Amendment was passed in 1920, signaling an unprecedented triumph for women.

1.5 Declining Feminism & Rising Domesticity: The 1920s – 1950s

Though women were already officially admitted to the men's world since the ratification of the Nineteenth Amendment, the rules of the political universe were still made and controlled by men. Besides, suffrage, even if it opened up avenues for women's political involvement, did not eliminate the sex-specific divisions of labor, nor did it change the subordinate roles that women had played in every aspect of daily life. The eventful and tumultuous decades from the 1920s to the 1950s found the contrasting facts between the improvements in women's economic, political and cultural status and the inadequacy in their political influence, the thrilling confrontation between feminism and domesticity, and the shift back from the public world to the private sphere.

At first glance, during the 1920s, women obtained many remarkable equal economic rights. The number of professional women was on the rapid rise. In 1920, the proportion was 11.9 percent, but ten years later, it reached 14.2 percent. At the same time, more and more women entered the legal and medical professions, and even became businesswomen, bankers, enterprisers. The situation seemed to be fairly encouraging. No wonder some historians described it as the era of women's economic liberation. Yet it obscured the inequalities in reality. First, most women still took up traditional low-paid female jobs, like domestic workers, seamstresses, secretaries, teachers, nurses, saleswomen. Second, even if women broke free of gender restrictions to work in the legal and medical professions that used to deny them, they were mostly the assistants to male lawyers or male doctors. Third, the occupation and position determined that women's wages were much lower than those of men. Fourth, the discriminatory recruitment and treatment not only happened in private enterprises and social institutions but also existed in the federal, state and local governments. In other words, gender discrimination against women was still prevalent in the society as a whole, for the progress in women's economic rights was quantitative rather than qualitative, and women largely remained lingering in the margin of the economic field.

However, considerable political victories were made after women were enfranchised. The League of Women Voters (LWV), in place of the National American Woman's Suffrage, led women to pressure the state legislatures and federal government for more legislation to protect women's rights. Their efforts were quite productive, winning women's rights protection as well as child-care and child-labor protection. Some of the most influential laws included those concerning the minimal wage for women workers, equal pay for equal work (in such states as Michigan and Montana), the federally funded health care of expectant mothers and infants (the *Sheppard-Towner Act of 1921*) and the prohibition of employing children under 14. Women social activists, on the one hand, successfully persuaded the government to set up the Women's Bureau which was responsible for securing women's wages and welfare; on the other hand, they formed the National Woman's Party and proposed an Equal Rights Amendment (ERA) to the Constitution which meant to end all the inequalities between the two sexes. At this point, a number of women even ran for office and became the heads of the municipal and state governments. These remarkable achievements displayed women's concerted efforts in female reform and enhanced adroitness in their political tactics. However, since the mid-1920s, women encountered backlashes against their projects and activities. The influence of conservatives was so sweeping that the Sheppard-Towner Bill was repealed, and the child-labor act and the minimum wage act were declared unconstitutional. The controversies surrounding the ERA further split women, incurring the scattering of a voting bloc. All these circumstances reflected the limits of women's political influence and power.

If the 1920s proved a hard time for women's fight, then the 1930s became even more unfriendly to women's movement. Faced with hard times ahead, the country as a whole focused on economic recovery, not in the mood for women's equal rights, as was shown in the dwindling size and marginal role of the National Woman's Party. Despite all the odds against feminism, the New Deal which pulled the nation from the economic crisis also benefited women and children. The *National Industrial Recovery Act of 1933*, the *Social Security Act of 1935*, and the *Fair Labor Standards Act of 1938* incorporated measures concerning maximum working hours and minimum wages as well as women and children's welfare. When these acts came into force, the employers could not reject hiring women nor reduce their wages because of their biological traits. More significantly, Aid to Dependent Children, a part of the *Social Security Act*, funded the female-headed family whose male breadwinners were dead, absent, or unable to work. It became Aid to Families with Dependent Children of 1950, setting the stage for the modern welfare system. During the process, the then First Lady Eleanor Roosevelt, together with other social reform heroines, was engrossed in promoting humane government policies, aiding the disadvantaged groups and families, and safeguarding the well-being of the nation. Even if the fundamental goal of the New Deal was to revive the failing economy rather than guarantee the gender equality, the actual protection and enhancement of women's rights could never be denied.

  WWII broke out before Americans got rid of the shadow of the Great Depression. The US geared itself for the mobilization of human resources as well as industrial and military capacities to support the war. As millions of men were dispatched to the battlefields, a tremendous shortage of manpower occurred in not only war industry but also the private sector across the nation. Under the emergency, there was a sudden change of view about female workers, and women were actually exhorted to fill job vacancies as womanpower. The previous objections and hostility to women wage earners from governments, enterprises, social media, and public opinions all changed overnight. In fact, the whole society launched a propaganda campaign to attract and spur women into the labor force. Social media platforms appealed to the patriotic behaviors and altruistic characters of women, through making war posters and writing articles in praise of women's deeds, creating wartime heroine images like Rosie the Riveter in the newspaper and Lucille Ball on the Hollywood screen, and associating the industrial production with women's domestic work and special qualities. Indeed, governments at all levels removed the bar to the hiring of women. For example, policies against the employment of married women during the Depression were reversed and prohibition against women workers in heavy industry was abolished. All of these measures brought unprecedented opportunities for women. First, war time witnessed a rapid growth of women's participation in the work force, with the portion of working women accelerating from less than 25 percent of the work force in 1940 to 35 percent in 1944. As more and more married women entered the labor market, the age of womanpower picked up its pace. Second, women were allowed to take those jobs that used to be considered inappropriate for them to do in peacetime. For instance, women were invited to work in well-paid defense factories as engine makers, shell loaders, gun assemblers, airplane workers, toolmakers, and die cutter operators. Due to the scarcity of men, women even enlisted in the navy, army, and air force corps. Without doubt, WWII was a watershed for the female labor force, which elevated their economic status, broadened their vision, as well as improved their self-confidence and self-satisfaction.

However, the wartime acceptance of female workers was a matter less of the fundamental change than of expediency. Thus, it did not end gender inequity and sexual discrimination. Women were less paid than men even if they worked in the same profession, and normally the employers would argue that that is because they worked in different job categories and men assumed harder and heavier duties. As an increasing number of women entered the labor market and joined the armed services, the unfair treatment towards women became so conspicuous that it aroused another round of argument over the ERA within the feminists. In view of the prevailing discrimination, even some women's organizations that were former opponents of the ERA like the conservative General Federation of Women's Clubs and the National Education Association came round to supporting it. But the opposing forces from labor unions and the LWV that favored protective laws were so strong that the ERA failed to win enough support in the Senate in 1950. The feminists' efforts in achieving equality were again made to no avail.

When the end of the war was around the corner, the temporary acceptance of female wage earners gave way to the endorsement of traditional sex-typing of jobs and woman's sphere. Upon the demobilization of returning veterans, women were called on to leave their jobs for the male soldiers and go back to their proper places. Holding jobs was no longer considered as women's patriotic devotion to the nation; instead, it was against the economic needs and a threat to social stability. But many women were not willing to quit jobs. According to a survey, as many as 75 percent of working women in defense plants hoped to keep holding jobs. At this point, despite the fact that a large scale of laying off women workers took place in the post-war era, a considerable number of women tried every means to secure their job opportunities or get reemployed in other ways. Thus, the postwar affluent society found such a paradoxical phenomenon: the revival of the domestic ideal and the rising number of women in the work force. The widely-promoted domestic ideology in the conservative era exhorted women to assume their traditional roles as amiable wives, conscientious mothers and tireless homemakers with feminine fulfillment, the suburban housewife being its typical example. Content with the shrunken space for personal development, many homebound women focused on home and family. Yet for those women who had already tasted the benefits of economic independence and personal freedom obtained from work, realized the importance of their income to continue their living standards and middle-class status, and felt the strength and power given by their income, there was no way of holding them back from the labor market. Just within a decade from 1950 to 1960, women's proportion of the labor force grew by 13 percent. Up till 1960, the number of female workers was twice as many as that two decades ago. By the postwar period, suburban housewives and employed women did not share common interests or issues like suffrage, so women were hardly united for any intense activism. They mostly volunteered their services for some family-related and community-associated local causes, rather than seeking to play an active and leadership role in social affairs. As it turned out, feminism again fell to a new low.

1.6 Struggling for Gender Equality: Since the 1960s

In the early 1960s, smoldering complaints about the triviality, boredom and dissatisfactions of housewifery were made by the postwar suburban housewives; meanwhile, rumblings of grievances, frustrations and discontent came from women wage earners, who suffered from the unfair treatment and sexual inequity in the labor market. It was from their respective dissatisfactory experiences that their feminist awareness was aroused, which provided a great number of female supporters and participants for the resurgence of feminism. Betty Friedan, though a suburban housewife herself, was unwilling to bear the status quo any more. More significantly, in 1963, as a social activist and a feminist leader, she wrote a onetime best-seller *The Feminine Mystique* to expose the "problem that has no name" as a social problem and criticize the hazards of the cult of domesticity, which won the wide endorsement of women readers and inspired them to reflect on their status and problems. Under the administration of president J. F. Kennedy, the social climate tended to be more liberal and reform-minded. One of Kennedy's important actions was to set up a Presidential Commission on the Status of Women responsible for women's issues. The agency made quite a few achievements, for example, establishing state commissions across the country, building a nationwide communication network, gathering evidence about sexual inequality, promoting the passage of the *Equal Pay Act of 1963*, the first federal law against gender discrimination. All of these endeavors laid the foundation for the upcoming women's movement. Last but not least, the sweeping Civil Rights Movement stimulated women activists to associate their secondary status with black people's status, learning and borrowing the fighting tactics that had been utilized in the influential movement.

In 1964, the *Civil Rights Act*, which included the prohibition of employment discrimination on the basis of race and gender, was enacted by Congress and went into effect a year later. In line with the new law, the Equal Employment Opportunities Commission (EEOC) was founded to ensure the implementation of employment equity. Yet the EEOC took it for granted that the severity of gender discrimination was less than that of racial discrimination in the work force, and paid scant attention to women's issues. At that time, women's organizations like the LWV and the American Association of University Women also ignored women's discontent and demands. The disappointing attitudes and behaviors propelled a number of women activists to form the National Organization of Women (NOW), the first explicit feminist organization in the US, to fight for their own civil rights. The constituency was comprised of ambitious, educated, sophisticated middle-class professional women, with an early focus on remedying the labor-force discrimination through legal means, for example, urging the EEOC into action, or pressing the legislature to repeal the out-of-mode protective laws. Aiming at women's full participation and equal rights in mainstream society, NOW was well organized and carefully operated with clear goals and agendas, elected leaders and officers, and set up a headquarter and local chapters. In the late 1960s, NOW's concern extended to a broad range of reforms such as education, equal pay, family reform, political power, poverty, etc.

During the second-wave women's movement of the 1960s, apart from the moderate wing NOW, a radical faction made up of younger women activists, who once had participated in the Civil Rights Movement and allied with the New Left, came to name itself as "women's liberation" group and launched its distinctive feminist campaigns since 1967. The backbones of "women's liberation", mostly from white middle-class families, were raised in a peaceful and prosperous social environment. With a college education, ardent aspirations and fearless courage, the idealistic young women got involved in various social movements, which enhanced their political competence, self-confidence and political awareness. However, discouraged and infuriated by the male chauvinism and misogyny prevalent in such civil rights organizations as the Student Nonviolent Coordinating Committee (SNCC) and the New Left organization like Students for a Democratic Society (SDS), the new feminists determined to have their own movement. Unlike NOW, "women's liberation" was a structureless and decentralized organization with disparate views on the source of their oppressions. The New Left feminists believed that the capitalist system was the culprit, so overturning capitalism on the basis of class resistance was the final solution; meanwhile, the radical feminists held that all-pervasive sexism was responsible for inequality, so ending the male-dominant institution on the basis of sex roles could straighten it out. In spite of the disagreement, both groups reached the consensus that, women's oppressions were so serious that only by radical means could they win their liberation.

Stepping into the 1970s, the women's movement gained momentum and made extraordinary achievements. By the mid-1970s, with the proliferation of feminist organizations, the feminist movement exerted significant impacts on issues like abortion, the daycare system, employment and education equity, the ERA, resulting in major shifts in attitudes and opportunities. In the moral climate for reform, there was an outburst of distinctive women's groups, representing women from different races, classes, sexuality with disparate interests, backgrounds and projects, which amounted to several thousand. The diffusing structure and the flexible operation of these groups won a wider constituency, which vigorously spurred the activism and generated more social support. Though moderate and radical feminists held different ideologies and put forward different agendas, they shared the same ultimate goal of removing sexism and faced the same animosity from conservatives. Consequently, both were inclined to take the ERA as the leading cause.

The Congressional houses passed the ERA in huge majorities in 1972 and twenty-eight states approved its ratification within one year, which signaled an initial feminist triumph. Just as the ERA activism reached its peak, the antifeminist crosscurrent erupted, launching the "Stop ERA" campaign, headed by the conservative right-wing leader Phyllis Schlafly. Finally, the ERA was defeated in 1982 with just three states short of required number for ratification. However, in spite of these roadblocks, feminists nonetheless made further progress in redressing the judicial inequity for women, which, for instance, involved married women's property rights, the passage of no-fault divorce law, alimony and guardianship after divorce. Even if the feminist agenda and crusade did not win the universal endorsement, the feminist movement did make tremendous changes in men and women's attitudes as well as female positions. Men became more tolerant and egalitarian towards female wage earners and women leaders, and women were more aware of their own rights, feelings and status. By the end of the 1970s, accompanied by a gradual upward mobility in women's social ranks, more than half of American women joined the labor force, and an increasing number of women became lawyers, doctors, engineers, judges, professors, as well as service women in the armed forces.

After decades of efforts in the elusive ideal of gender equity, in the 1980s and 1990s, feminism was reduced to a nadir. Feminist organizations could no longer launch a powerful movement across the country, but they were still an influential force with widespread consequences. Though the battle over the EAR turned into a standoff and the disputes around abortion were in a stalemate, feminists sought to take more women's issues such as the interests of women of color into consideration, and new women's groups with different goals were formed one after another to meet women's disparate demands. In response to the large proportion of women in the labor force (58 percent in 1990), some feminists gave priority to remedying sex discrimination in employment and wage. The feminist movement and other social movements in the previous decades promoted the enactment of equity laws, which paved the way for women to enter the fields traditionally dominated by men, such as managerial, technical, and professional occupations. Aside from combating the sex labeling of jobs, the wage gap between male and female workers was another big concern of feminists. All through the 1980s, the average earnings of female workers were 60 to 70 percent of their male counterparts'. Under such circumstances, women activists launched a massive "pay equity" (or "comparable worth") campaign to raise women's pay levels through law suits, legislation, collective bargaining not only at the federal level but also at the state and local levels.

Meanwhile, women made remarkable progress in political life. They did not just capitalize on assembly, petitioning, lobbying, sit-in, strike, and demonstration, but also began a steep upward climb into political parties and public offices. In doing so, women were aided by the National Women's Political Caucus and other women's fund-raising groups, which were committed to supporting female candidates for offices at all levels of government. Hence, the proportion of women representatives in the Republican convention rose from 17 percent in 1968 to 40 percent in 1980, while in the same period the proportion in the Democratic convention surged from 13 percent to 50 percent. At the same time, a record number of women ran for office and became state and local officials. In the statewide office campaign of 1985, four times as many women had participated in it as had done so in 1969. In 2001, state legislatures were 22.4 percent women compared to 18.2 percent in 1991 and 4.8 percent in 1971. In 2006, Hilary Clinton, the former First Lady, became the first female presidential candidate after she served as the Secretary of State, making a historical record in the US. Once women voters, candidates and elected officials increased, their opinions, demands and votes carried political weight in the decision-making process and caught the public attention in their efforts to realize their ideals. Obviously, they were approaching the center of the political arena.

During centuries-long heroic struggle, women grew from a totally disenfranchised and politically invisible population in the domestic sphere to a pivotal political and labor force in public life, from inactive enfranchised citizens to sophisticated political leaders and social activists, adroit in making rules and manipulating the political system. Because of women's movements, women's issues have now become national issues, and feminism has reshaped public values, family patterns, social institutions as well as government policies. Still, on women's way to full equality, aside from formidable roadblocks from the conservative forces, persistent problems such as conflict over "difference vs. equality" exemplified by abortion and the ERA disputes, inadequate child care, unequal distribution of housework, inherent sex discrimination in employment remain to be skillfully dealt with and strategically settled. Standing on the shoulders of foremothers, the young generation of the twenty-first century will, no doubt, have to work together to counter the challenges and overcome the difficulties lying ahead.

2 The American Women of Color and the Feminist Movement

According to US Census Bureau, white women accounted for 60.3 percent of American women in 2018. In other words, white women were the majority among American women. Moreover, the leaders and participants of American feminist movements were mostly middle-class white women. However, it does not mean that white women can represent all the American women, nor does it signify that women of color haven't made any contribution to American history and women's movements. Unlike white women who have been mainly exposed to sexism, women of color have been subject to both racism from the mainstream society and sexism within their ethnic groups. Besides, with distinctive racial, ethnic and religious characteristics, different skin colors, social backgrounds, historical experiences and life patterns, the awakening of American women of color vary from each other, and their attitudes towards the white feminist movement and tactics to win their rights take on distinguishing features, which have injected diversity and vitality to American women's history. Among women of color, African American women, Mexican American women, Asian American women are the major groups.

2.1 African American Women

Ever since they were forcibly taken to the American continent, enslaved African American women were treated as subhuman and chattels, enjoying no rightful freedom or basic human rights, let alone dignity and respect. After the slavery system became self-perpetuating and genealogy of slaves followed the status of slave mothers, white slave owners capitalized on the fertility and reproductive ability of slave women, making them bear as much labor and property as possible. When slave women approached the childbearing age of late teens, they would be prepared to conceive. Usually, a slave woman had 7 children on average in her lifetime. Besides, like slave men, slave women had to do backbreaking work in the fields from cotton picking to fence building under the supervision of slave overseers, or were arranged laborious tasks in house service such as cooking, washing and cleaning. On this score, slave men were not able to play a patriarchal role as white men, and slave women were by no means allowed to be as subordinate as white women. Such being the case, the status of slave led to the minimization of gender distinction and relative sexual equality between slave men and women. Furthermore, after strenuous physical labor in the daytime for slave owners, slave women still assumed crucial family roles as housekeepers and caretakers in their own families – cooking, sewing, cleaning, telling ancestor's stories to the children. Due to the vulnerability of slave family when there was forced sale of a male spouse or slave men were abused to death, slave women often became head of the family, and played an independent role even if they lost their economic independence in the larger society. In order to deal with their difficult situations, black women made use of a variety of tactics to fight against oppression. For example, since producing slaves was seen as a profitable investment, breeding had been used wisely as the leverage to preserve the family. At the same time, an autonomous black community with an extended kinship network and a black church built up by both slave men and women served as a refuge from the adverse environment and a shelter for consoling black souls. In the black church, some well-respected elderly slave women performed the worship leadership and taught traditional values, which nurtured the mind for social activism.

In the post-emancipation period, black people won some of their basic human rights and individual freedom, under which black women did not have to worry about the rapid reproduction or the forced separation from their husbands or children. As a matter of fact, immediately after the Civil War, freedmen and freedwomen tried to find the missing family members and reconstitute the broken families. Besides, the newly freed slaves viewed female domesticity as the ideal of black family life. Influenced by the cult of true womanhood of white people, in the beginning, black women tended to follow this pattern to elevate and refine the children, but harsh realities broke their dream of staying at home. First, on the basis of slave codes, the newly-made black codes required black people, women and children included, to work on former plantations, so black women were hindered from adopting a womanly role in the home. Second, from the emancipation onward, the entrenched racism prevalent in the society and an increasing political impotence of black people made it difficult for black men to find a job, while black women were always able to obtain some sort of intense, low-paid and unskilled jobs, supplementing or providing family earnings. Thus, women working outside the home were widely accepted by the black community. From the late nineteenth century to the early twentieth century, urbanization and industrialization created plenty of job opportunities in cities, which drew southern rural black women in great numbers to cities especially northern cities where living conditions were relatively better and racism was generally not as overt as that in the South. As a rule, whatever jobs they got in urban areas, the work was concentrated in domestic work and related services at the most menial levels that white women did not want to do. Due to the high mortality and unemployment rate of black men, women workers became the family head, the provider, the homemaker and the caretaker.

By the end of the nineteenth century, most black women were from low-income families, uneducated or under-educated, but thanks to the expansion of female education opportunities and the abolition of slavery, a small number of black women from middle-class families who were able to receive college education led the first-wave of the black feminist movement. As white women's clubs and the suffrage movement normally did not welcome black women, black female activists formed their own clubs. When the black clubwomen's movement gathered momentum across the nation, black women activists formed a federation of clubs – the National Association of Colored Women (NACW) in 1896. With the focus on the interests of the community and race, the NACW dealt with both gender issues like temperance, women's suffrage and employment, and child rearing and racial causes like anti-lynching and racial uplift. Ultimately, the activism of black feminist foremothers greatly enhanced black women's education and consciousness as well as largely promoted the moral standing of the black community.

Between the 1910s and 1920s, a rising number of the black population moved from the Deep South to the North or the Midwest. They, subject to discriminatory employment, customarily worked as daywork servants in service jobs or performers in the entertainment profession, while white-collar jobs like secretaries and clerks were reserved for white women. The Great Depression witnessed an unusually high unemployment rate of black women, three times more than that of white women, but at the same time, black women were more likely than white women to be excluded from the federal work relief programs and remained the bottom-level status. The wartime emergency broadened black women's options for work: twice as many as black female workers in the pre-war period got the jobs in industry, and a small proportion even joined the armed forces. Still, racial barrier hampered black women's employment in the white-collar fields. In Postwar America, despite the prevailing "feminine mystique", black women continued to work and contribute immensely to family income. In the 1950s, 60 percent of black wives were in the labor force, in comparison with 19 percent of white ones. Another prominent change for black working women was that more white-collar positions and professional jobs were gradually open to black women, which resulted in the growth of black women's income and black middle-class households. What is worth mentioning is the major role and extensive participation of black women in the Civil Rights Movement which started in 1955 and continued into the 1960s. It was the black women activist Rosa Parks' refusal to give her seat to a white passenger on a bus that triggered the movement. Meanwhile, a group of black women in the South attacked the sexual politics within the Civil Rights Movement. For example, in the SNCC, women were assigned the menial tasks like typing, leafleting, or even suffering from male-on-female sexual harassment. Black women's challenge to male chauvinism and their organizing competence inspired white women in the second-wave feminist movement.

The emergence of the second-wave women's movement did not evoke much enthusiasm from black women, because most of them viewed racial discrimination as more oppressive and serious than sexual discrimination. Hence, they gave wholehearted support to Civil Rights Movement rather than the women's movement, even if they remained to be influenced more or less by white radical feminists, paying attention to women's rights and women's role at home. Stirred by the women's movement and empowered by the black power movement in the civil rights era, a number of educated middle-class black women activists launched the second-wave black feminist movement and formed their own feminist organizations, the National

Black Feminist Organization (NBFO) in 1973 and the Combahee River Collective in 1974, setting the tone for modern black feminism. Like the feminism held by white women, black feminism carried on the emancipatory mission of gender equity. But disparity of race and class caused the differences between the two feminisms. Generally speaking, white feminism addressed issues affecting middle-class white women, usually around their individual development, e.g. abortion rights, equal employment and promotion, the ERA, etc., since survival was no longer a problem for them. By contrast, black feminism tackled such issues as were unique to working-class black women, mostly about their necessities and survival, e.g. education, housing, welfare, health care, racial segregation, etc. The modern black feminist movement nurtured a large number of well-known African American women writers, politicians and stars, for example, the Noble Prize winner Toni Morrison, the Pulitzer Prize laureate Alice Walker, the first black Congresswoman Shirley Chisholm, the first black women Secretary of State Condoleezza Rice, the famous talk-show presenter Winfrey Oprah, the Oscar Award winner Halle Berry, etc.

In recent years, black women, as always, have become an indispensable and unswerving force in the anti-racist crusade like Black Lives Matter. Undoubtedly, both the ideology and practice of black feminism have expanded the scope of women's movement, providing much room for handling the feminist disputes, all of which has made great contribution to the world's women emancipatory cause.

2.2 Mexican American Women

Like African American women, Hispanic/Latino women differ from white women in significant aspects. As Hispanic women are now the largest group among women of color, their experiences, oppressions and resistance should never be ignored. Hispanics refer to those whose ancestors mainly came from Mexico, Puerto Rico, Cuba, and other Spanish-speaking Central or South American countries, with the Mexican origin accounting for 62 percent of the Hispanic population. Since Mexican American women/Chicanas constitute the majority of Latinas, their situations, to a large degree, reflect a major part of Latinas' life.

Early Mexican Americans stuck to Mexican traditions which were filled with sexism and patriarchy. According to Mexican traditional values, males hold absolute control over females, and women ought to be submissive and faithful to men. Women are born weak, indecisive, and subject to temptations. Besides, motherhood was a glorious and respectable mission in women's lifetime. Along this line of thinking, women were expected to bear and rear as many children as possible, and make sure that their children would live as happily as possible. Therefore, following traditional gender division of labor, Chicanas were not allowed to work outside except helping in their family's fields. Before they got married, they lived under the supervision of male heads – fathers or brothers, doing housework at home or planting in the field, and their marriages were even arranged by the patriarch. After their marriage, their husbands became their guardians, watching them perform housewifery and take care of children. Fortunately, there lay a legal tradition for Mexican American women to keep their maiden names and property separate from their husbands as well as the ability to sue in the court, which protected their rights in certain degree.

In the first two decades of the twentieth century, Mexican immigration to the US reached a new height. The 1910 revolution in Mexico drove over a million Mexicans to cross the border and settle in the Southwest. They mostly moved in family groups, though some single women migrated alone. Poor and helpless, many of them, together with part of early Mexican Americans, were reduced to the cheap labor of Anglo-American employers who came to settle there at the same time. As low-paid and insecure jobs that Chicanos took were unable to raise the entire family, Chicanas faced the dilemma between role expectations of Mexican traditions and the urgent necessity of American life. Ultimately, even if Mexican American women's wages were underpaid, they went out of the home sphere, worked as domestic servants and held blue-collar jobs in garment factories or food-processing industry. When they became economically independent, their traditional roles and division of labor were mitigated. Besides, the "Americanization" program proposed by social reformers in the 1920s also split Chicanas' traditional roles at home. The program aimed to assimilating ethnic groups and newly-arrived immigrants into American belief systems. As for the first generation of Mexican immigrant women at the beginning of the twentieth century, they, on the one hand, adapted themselves to the new environment and turned to work in the labor market; on the other hand, they showed resistance to the assimilation and tried all means to maintain their traditional culture. But with regard to their children who were immersed in American culture and market economy, the young generation inevitably fell prey to Americanization, identifying American values and adopting American ways; thus, the children were often found in conflict with their mothers. Cultural barrier, generation gap, together with longtime working outside made it hard for Mexican American mothers to exert the same influence on their children as before. For that moment, though Chicanas felt somewhat a sense of loss about their motherhood, the favorable social climate to American women motivated and benefited them. With the hard-won suffrage, expanding job options, and social recognition of women's contribution and power in hand, Chicanas were no longer placed in gender subjugation and inferiority; instead, the elevated social and political status enabled them to have a big say in family matters and therefore higher family status. In face of the severe challenges of racism and assimilation from the mainstream society, Mexican American women adhered to traditional family values, strengthened the family relationship, and consolidated the association within the community. In their traditional culture, family means more than the nuclear family, covering the extended family and the extended kinship, i.e. the whole community. Giving full play to their role as emotional ties in the family, Chicanas succeeded in sustaining their traditional cultural values and building up a strong buffer against the hardships of American life. There is no doubt that, in doing so, their prestige and influence were much acknowledged.

  When the booming economy required more labor, Mexican Americans were favored by employers and allured to various menial jobs, filling the low-paid job vacancies. But when depression hit the nation, like African Americans, Mexican

Americans were the first to be fired so as to reserve limited jobs for Anglo-Americans. During the economic crisis, Chicanas usually did piecework of garment making or consumer goods at home, and their average payment was about 60 percent of that of Anglo-American women if they took the same job. What's worse, when more and more unemployed Mexican Americans were included in work relief programs, the federal government took a vigorous measure towards them by implementing a repatriation policy. Nowadays the federal repatriation policy is still carried out from time to time in the light of American economic situation and political necessity. WWII served as a watershed for Mexican American working women, for it not only provided unprecedented job possibilities, but also offered them a golden chance to have access to a broader world. While around 500,000 Mexican Americans enrolled in the armed forces, Chicanas found work in war plants like the aircraft industry, manufacturing industry, service industry, light industry and even some white-collar professions like the clerical job. By the end of the 1940s, one out of four Mexican American young women worked, six percent more than that of their mothers' generation. Yet the large number of working women and the new scope of employment can never conceal the fact that most of the jobs that Chicanas held were low-level, underpaid, labor-intensive and insecure ones; thus, in fact, they still lived at the bottom rung of the vocational and social ladder. After WWII, the postwar domestic ideal and the image of suburban housewife enjoyed ample acceptance among Chicanas, because the widely-promoted feminine mystique in many aspects fit the traditional role expectation and cultural traditions of Mexican Americans. Nonetheless, the economic and social limits reduced the domestic ideology to a fantasy for them.

  The African Americans' struggle for civil rights inspired Mexican Americans to start their own civil rights movement – the Chicano movement. From the 1960s to the 1970s, the Mexican American civil rights activists led Chicanos to fight against systemic racism, combat cultural assimilation, improve education and workers' rights, and obtain community empowerment. Chicanas, who put community liberation in the first place, devoted themselves whole-heartedly to this movement. In their mind, even if racism and sexism were intertwined, racism remained a greater evil than sexism. Besides, they placed emphasis on the survival and development of family and community, with a conviction that they shouldered the responsibility of revitalizing their culture and keeping ethnic solidarity. In this connection, they had less in common with the mainstream feminists, who held that marriage was bondage for women and the traditional family pattern was the source of sexism. Moreover, they had different concerns and demands from the mainstream feminists. Thus, it was easier for Chicana activists to be engrossed in the Chicano nationalist movement with their brothers and sisters rather than build up sisterhood with Anglo-American feminists in the women's movement. Although Mexican American women had been active in the male-dominated Chicano movement, they encountered sexism and misogyny within their ethnic group, and their leadership roles in the community were downplayed or even ignored. Dissatisfied with exclusion from both the nationalist movement and the mainstream feminist movement, in 1973 and 1974, Mexican American feminists formed their own organizations – the Comisión Femenil Mexicana Nacional (CFMN, or National Mexican Women's Commission) and the Mexican American Women's National Association (MANA), organized consciousness-raising workshops and held women conferences, addressing the issues that directly affected Chicanas. In order to socially, politically and economically empower Mexican American women, Chicana feminist organizations gave priorities to women's health, female education, career development, community involvement, domestic violence and gender equity. Yet whatever feminist activities Mexican American feminists arrange, they invariably put family and community in heart, carrying the mission of cultural preservation and community empowerment.

2.3 Asian American Women

The term "Asian Americans" refers to a diverse group consisting of people whose ancestry originates from more than fifty countries of East Asia, South Asia, or Southeast Asia such as China, Japan, Korea, Vietnam, India, Thailand, Singapore, and the Philippines. In 2018, Asian American women comprised 6.1 percent of the American female population. Within the pan-ethnic heterogeneous group of Asian Americans, Chinese Americans were early Asian Immigrants to the US and are still among the largest Asian ethnic groups in the US. In general, described as "model minority", Asian Americans are hard-working and well-educated. Due to the big differences in languages, religions, historical experiences, socio-economic backgrounds and cultural rituals among Asian Americans, it is impossible to introduce each ethnic group of Asian American women. For this matter, Chinese American women who have enjoyed lengthy historical record of living in the US will be given detailed depiction so as to present part of Asian American women's life, work and activism.

Though Filipinos were the first recorded Asian Americans as early as the sixteenth century, the first large-scale Asian immigration to the US started with the arrival of 300 Chinese men and the establishment of the Chinese American community in California in the mid-19th century. During the Gold Rush, the early Chinese immigrants, pushed by scarce land, scanty opportunity and miserable life back in China and allured by the golden opportunity and better life in America, travelled to the American West as the Chinese coolies who worked in the gold mines, built the transcontinental railroad, and tended farmlands. Even if family was of crucial importance to the Chinese, most of Chinese laborers did not migrate in family groups except those wealthy Chinese businessmen, because they only hoped to stay for several years and intended to go back to China after they made some money. Under such circumstances, there were imbalanced sex ratios in the Chinese community, since 90 percent of the Chinese immigrants between 1849 and 1882 were male, and they mostly came alone. In order to tighten the control of the Chinese immigrants, the US government put a series of anti-Chinese ordinances and legislation into effect, including the *Foreigner Miner's Tax* (1850), the *Cubic Air Ordinance* (1870), the *Sidewalk Ordinance* (1870), the Page Law (1875), the *Chinese Exclusion Act* (1882), the *Anti-Miscegenation Law* (1906). The stringent discriminatory laws not only barred the wives and children of Chinese Americans from entering the US but also prohibited them from marrying non-Chinese. Apart from that, as very few Chinese immigrant women lived in the Chinese community, Chinese men felt it hard to start their family, live a normal family life and continue the family line, which adversely affected the growth of the Chinese population in the US and even created a special "bachelor society". From 1860 to 1890, Chinese males outnumbered Chinese females from 12:1 to 27:1. Besides, some employers took occasion to hold down the wages of Chinese men by offering the excuse that Chinese male immigrants did not have families to raise.

Actually, before WWII, even if there were just a small number of Chinese women, racism remained virulent. For this reason, the second Chinese female immigrant generation and their daughters, who adopted American ways and got better education, hardly found work equivalent to their education. It was even worse during the Great Depression when job possibilities were so limited. Chinese American women were excluded from such white-collar occupations, because secretarial, teaching, and social work were open to white women. Thus, they held mainly such bottom-level jobs as elevator operators, store basements workers, piece workers, and domestic labor. The hardships of life and work faced by Chinese Americans remained unchanged until WWII when the US and China became allies. After that, the US repealed the *Chinese Exclusion Act* and welcomed Chinese women to immigrate and reunite with their husbands and families in the US through the *War Brides Act* (1945) and the *Immigration and Nationality Act* (1965). Under the favorable social climate, the Chinese American families and community were revitalized and stabilized with steady increase in population. Meanwhile, the lack of labor force in the US in WWII made Chinese American female's entry into white-collar fields possible and reasonable. It was during wartime that Chinese American women finally found suitable jobs matching their education, and their incomes accordingly improved which contributed to the family prosperity.

As for Asian American women, specific racial and ethnic concerns of Asian

Americans as well as Asiatic traditional values of female obedience and "family first" hindered them from actively participating in the white middle-class women's movement. Like black women and Latinas, even if Asian American women came to realize women's rights and sexual oppressions, they still put racial, class, health problems as their major concerns, but those issues were far from being the foci of the mainstream feminist movement. Since the 1960s, inspired by the Civil Rights Movement, the Black Power and the Asian American movement, and disappointed by the pervasive male chauvinism and misogyny in those movements, Asian American women built their own coalition to strive for their own rights and social justice. Owing to ethnic diversity and cultural differences among Asian Americans, between the 1960s and 1970s, Asian American feminists either established women's organizations of a specific Asian ethnicity such as the Organization of Chinese American Women and the Filipino American Women Network, or the women's groups of all the Asian ethnicities like the Organization of Pan Asian American Women and National Network of Asian and Pacific Women. In 1969, Asian American feminists created their own newspaper *Gidra* to make their voice heard and publicize Asian feminism. In 1971, the Vancouver Indochinese Women's Conference was held and the Asian Women's Center was formed to address the issues concerning the large Asian American community. Consequently, Asian American women were able to not only struggle for women's rights of their own ethnic group, but also effect bigger social changes through Asian sisterhood and collective efforts. The Asian feminist activism was dormant from the late 1970s to the 1980s. Since the 1990s, Asian American feminism has come to revival. The new Asian American feminists, based on the achievements of their foremothers, are committed to building a multiracial and transnational network with other women of color since they shared common issues of racism, colonialism and imperialism. In 2018, a group of intellectuals and social activists in New York City organized the Asian American Feminist Collective (AAFC) to promote community building and political education. So far, AAFC has collaborated with black feminists to advance collective liberation. Undoubtedly, the feminist consciousness and activism of Asian American women have been cultivated and enlarged to maximize their political participation in the larger society and advance the cause of gender equality in the world.

> **Essay Questions:**
>
> 1. In the awakening of American women, what are the shaping factors for the improvement of women's rights and social status?
> 2. How do you define and interpret true womanhood in American cultural context?
> 3. There was a simultaneous emergence of domestic ideology and feminism between 1800 and 1860 in American history. Discuss the seemingly paradoxical phenomenon.
> 4. Do you think there was and is still a "woman's sphere" for American women? If so, what did it refer to in the past and what does it mean at present? If not, what roles did and do American women assume?
> 5. Examine one ethnic group among American women of color to illustrate different tactics in their struggle for women's rights from those utilized by white women, and analyze the reasons for the differences.

Unit 12　The American Family and Community

1　The American Family

  Family is the cell of society, which tremendously facilitates social development. It is also the major means of human reproduction and cultural continuity. As time passes by, American family values and patterns evolve. Generally speaking, before the 1960s, such traditional family values as "the sense of responsibility" and "the sense of satisfaction" prevailed. Meanwhile, the mainstream family pattern was the traditional family pattern, which was characterized by heterosexual marriage and separate spheres of men and women. From the 1960s onwards, the traditional family structure faded. With the rise of the second-wave women's movement and the countercultural movement, American family values have started to lay emphasis on each member's freedom and satisfaction, as well as equality and mutual respect among family members. Meanwhile, family patterns have become increasingly diverse. In a number of different shapes and sizes, diverse families include but not limited to blended families, single parent families, families with foster parents, families with gay or lesbian parents, etc. In the changing circumstances, family conflicts and social problems turn out to be more prominent than ever.

1.1　The Evolution of American Family Values and Patterns

  The evolution of American family values goes hand in hand with the evolvement of American family patterns. The changing social milieu fosters new family values which influence the transformation of family patterns. Meanwhile, the changed family pattern affects and alters existing family values. Their interaction profoundly revolutionizes the American family.

American family values do not come from nowhere. First, they are associated with the American way of life and personal values. Combining individualism with existentialism, most Americans believe that the meaning of life lies in not only the expression and improvement of oneself, but also the cooperation and coordination with others in the society. Their life philosophy, in turn, has greatly affected their family values. It is evidenced by the fact that Americans tend to take their families as the stages to show themselves and the bases to perfect themselves. Either the free life that they pursue or domestic problems that they face fully reveals the American individualistic values. Second, they go hand in hand with the ever-changing family law and marriage law. Based on the Christian cultural ideology, American marriage law in earlier times hardly approved of divorce. It is up till the post-WWII era, especially in the 1960s and 1970s, that the legislation of marriage and family tended to favor individual freedom. Since then, the requirements for divorce have been loosened. Presently, all states allow some form of divorce on no-fault grounds. Besides, the line between legitimate and illegitimate children is blurred. Furthermore, state courts no longer interfere in unwed cohabitation. Finally, the advancement of science and technology enables people to modify their established ideas about family. Due to the invention of modern transportation means, people with different nationalities can travel long distances to meet each other and live together. The breakthroughs in reproductive technology make vitro fertilization, homologous insemination, heterologous insemination, embryo transfer and asexual reproduction possible in daily life. This in large measure transforms contemporary American family values.

Specifically speaking, the changing family values can be divided into three aspects, i.e. the notion of equality, love and marriage, and reproduction. In terms of the notion of gender equality, it, to a large extent, reshapes family values. For a very long time, it had been a patriarchal society where men were rulers and dominators and women were followers and subordinates. In fact, gender inequality was even more noticeable at home than in the society. The unequal status between men and women defined the different gender roles in the family, with men as decision makers and women caretakers in the "woman's sphere". Surprisingly, the limited woman's sphere foregrounded women's moral excellence and maternal influence, which enabled them to go outside their home and participate in various social reforms. The women's movements in the 19th and 20th century challenged men's superiority in status and rights as well as unjust laws. At the same time, they struggled for equal rights and fair treatment for women. Owing to the big influences of the women's movements, the ideal of gender equality not only prevails in the society but also pervades the family. A number of laws have been passed and implemented to ensure equal rights between men and women, e.g. the minimum wage act, the family violence prevention and services act, the no-fault divorce law, etc. Consequently, the conjugal relationship and the relations between siblings have been altered. Though women are still more likely to be primary caretakers and homemakers, men nowadays spend more time on domestic responsibilities like taking care of the children and doing housework. Even if there still exist unpleasant fighting and quarrelling between siblings, they tend to enjoy more equal relationship, irrespective of their age and gender. In addition, the equal notion is so pervasive in the family that the parent-child relationship has been deeply influenced and thereby changed. In the patriarchal family, parental authority was exercised over children, so corporal punishment and scolding were common phenomena. But in the contemporary American family, children are granted more respect and freedom, and their opinions are given more attention to by their parents. Thus, they have a better chance of developing the habit of independent thinking. Even though children may sometimes do wrong, they will still receive tolerance and encouragement from parents or elder siblings. In everyday life, parents and children frequently say "thank you" to each other. Findings show that, socialized in such a harmonious family, children are more self-disciplined and gain more self-autonomy. Besides, it is more probable that they will establish an equal family relationship when they grow up and start their own families. Therefore, an awareness of an equal family relationship can be reinforced from generation to generation.

Another evolving family value is around love and marriage. In the 17th and 18th centuries, marriage was primarily a functional partnership rather than a romantic relationship. Family traditions, loyalty and solidarity were high above personal affections and choice. Free love was a luxury for everyone. Instead, responsibility was advocated and emphasized in the marriage relationship. In the 19th century and the first half of the 20th century, the westward movement, industrialization, immigration and urbanization profoundly transformed views of love and marriage. Different from their ancestors, Americans bore higher expectation for marriage, hoping to establish a compassionate relationship with their partners. Marriage built upon friendship, love and attractiveness instead of the practical needs of life or bearing and rearing children. The sense of satisfaction was given priority. In order to ensure compassionate marriage, early and unrestricted dating were allowed so that people were more likely to find their soul mates. Beginning in the 1960s, a number of social movements, especially the women's movement and the countercultural movement, questioned the mainstream moral conducts and norms of behavior. Feminists and countercultural activists held radical views on love and marriage. Based on self-realization and women's emancipation, they called for breaking the restrictions of monogamy and heterosexuality. Under the influence of radical views, Americans began to separate love from marriage and attach more importance to love and physical sensations.

Thus, there emerge novel phenomena in the society. First, delayed marriage is widely prevalent for both sexes. For instance, the average marriage age of Americans climbed from 22.8 for men and 20.3 for women in 1960 to 26.1 and 23.9 respectively in 1990. Second, there is an increasing number of unwed couples who cohabitate. At the same time, not all couples get married are heterosexual; with the gradual legitimization of same-sex marriage, the number of the same-sex couples is growing rapidly. Third, the divorce rate is surging. Statistics show that, in the 1980s, the divorce rate of first marriages reached 50 percent, doubling that in the 1960s. There are a number of reasons that result in divorce. To begin with, since the 20th century, a growing number of women have had more access to education or even higher education. Equipped with education, they can find good jobs and obtain financial security, which embolden them to end unsatisfactory marriages as they are economically independent. Before the 20th century, most women had to rely on marriage to support themselves. Moreover, along with the sweeping feminist movement in the 1960s, one's awareness of protecting rights has been greatly heightened. Women who used to be wronged are no longer willing to bear it. Furthermore, influenced by social movements in the 1960s and 1970s, public opinions become more tolerant about divorce. Divorcees do not have to face as much blame and pressure from the public as their predecessors. Finally, one's emotional satisfaction has become an essential part of marriage, which is recognized by new divorce laws and individual persons. If marriage fails to satisfy the emotional needs of either of the partners, there will be enough reason for their marriage to fall apart. In recent two decades, older couples aged 50 and above have joined the divorce trend to seek independence and satisfaction. The divorce rate for the higher age group has already doubled. In face of surging divorce, the American government, social organizations and religious groups take actions to tackle the problem. Some call for repealing the no-fault divorce laws, some suggest that there should be more marriage counseling to help resolve conflicts and improve relationship, and others advise young people to finish college education and earn stable incomes before they get married.

It should be noted that, nowadays young people can make decisions on their love and marriage, free from the intervention of their families. A case in point is that, in recent years, interracial marriage has become more frequent than in the past. As early as 1667, the colonial law stipulated that mulattoes were taken as illegitimate children. At the end of the 18th century, interracial marriage between whites and blacks were banned. Even if some states allowed interracial marriage after the Civil War, the deep-rooted racism prevented it from happening in the real life. Up until the end of WWII, there were still over 30 states that forbade intermarriage. The Civil Rights Movement and the women's movement in the 1960s invariably used the intermarriage issue as a means to win freedom and achieve equality. The decision of *Loving v. Virginia* (1967) made by the US Supreme Court eliminated the legal barrier for interracial marriage and acknowledged its legitimacy. Spurred by this, the number of interracial marriages quadrupled within just two decades from 1970 to 1990, although 33 percent of whites remained to oppose intermarriage between whites and blacks in 1990.

Actually, compared with previous views of love and marriage, the contemporary notion of love and marriage tends to not only emphasize obligations and responsibilities, but also stress the sense of freedom and individual fulfilment. Apart from that, physical and mental care are equally important for American couples at present. If the couple meet the problem in the marriage, they will normally try new ways to solve it, rather than make do in a dead marriage.

Last is the perception of reproduction. In the traditional society, reproduction served as the main purpose of marriage. Moreover, it was commonly held that the more children, the more happiness. Furthermore, religion played an important role in influencing one's view of reproduction. Equating abortion with infanticide, the Christian doctrine forbade birth control and abortion. In the agrarian society, life for early European settlers in the North American centered around family and each family had at least five to six children. At that time, the major responsibility of parents was to raise children, and when parents got old, they relied on their children to take care of them. The size of family shrank in the age of industrialization and urbanization. In modern nuclear families, there were fewer children. In addition to bringing up children, parents were devoted to developing children's personalities and potentials.

Since the 1950s, the US birth rate has continued to decline dramatically. In 1950, it was 24.268 per thousand people. In 1980, it reduced to 14.986. In 2020, it further dropped to 11.990. How has the sharp decline come about? First, the upbringing costs keep growing, making it unaffordable for average families to raise many children. As a matter of fact, under recent economic circumstances, the real family income has been falling, and the living standards and education expenses have been rising. Hence, a large number of American families are unable to sustain a big family. Second, due to the enhanced female awareness of independence and autonomy, a great many women choose to have fewer or even no children. Affected by the women's movement, they hope to enjoy personal fulfilment in their careers. They think that bearing and rearing children are time and energy consuming. Different from early Americans who viewed children as blessings of the family, they see children as burdens that may prevent them from pursuing their own dreams. Therefore, some of them stay single and don't expect to have children in their life. Third, beginning in the 1980s, Double Incomes, No Kids (DINK) became popular among the young generation. Partly for personal enjoyment, partly for their careers, partly for worrying about the permanence of marriage, partly for shouldering parental responsibilities, the young couple are not willing to become parents. Fourth, with the introduction of pensions and social security, the American elders no longer have to depend on their children to take care of them. This, to a certain extent, reduces the need for them to raise children when they are young.

American family patterns have undergone substantial changes since colonial America. In colonial times, most American families took the form of nuclear family, with an average number of six people in a household. As for the newly arrived European settlers, it was impossible for them to have the extended family immigrate with them. Customarily, they came alone or at most settled with their nuclear families. Besides, as for slaves who were forcibly taken from Africa to America, it was even less possible for them to come in family units. In order to promote economic development, the colonial government encouraged people to get married and start a family by levying heavy taxes on single persons. Moreover, in some states, singles were even blamed for being selfish, irresponsible and pleasure-seeking. Hence, they were required to live with certain families that would guide single people's behaviors.

In pre-industrial America, families were largely patriarchal households, with the eldest men serving as the head and authority of the family. Early American families generally took on production and education functions. In the self-sufficient agrarian society, all families relied heavily on farming, with both men and women working alongside in the field. Central domestic tasks included building the house, making furniture, raising children, feeding the family and keeping the house. The subsistence household economies ensured the survival of the family. In addition, families served the purpose of educating children. Even if a number of schools had been set up, parents still shouldered the major responsibility of teaching. Children learned a rudimentary knowledge of religion, domestic and survival skills from their parents. As a rule, led by the patriarchal head, each family gathered for prayer and psalm readings.

Following English Common Law and the European cultural traditions, legal statutes and practice in early America placed women and children under the authority of male heads. Women and children were viewed as no more than the property of their husbands and fathers. Married women were not allowed to keep her own property, and all of their former belongings were transferred to their husbands after marriage. The family property was at husbands' disposal until they died. Moreover, considered as "Adam's Rib," women were inferior to men. In the southern colonies, white middle-class women exerted certain influences, because black slaves were under their supervision and control. Thus, their social status was higher than white women in New England. Laws not only favored men's rights, but also made it hard for women to get divorced. Even if on most occasions divorce was requested by women, seldom was it approved. Between 1639 and 1692, only 25 couples dissolved their marriages in Massachusetts.

By the same token, children were subservient to their fathers, obtaining fathers' permission and obeying their orders. For instance, during the courtship, the young man had to get the permission of his lover's father if he wanted to date his lover. If the couple decided to get married, their marriage needed to be first approved by both families. Men usually got married around 24 years old, and women 22 years old. When they were about to enter marriage life, a notice of the marriage was put up to inform the public. When the wedding ceremony was held, a respectable person was invited as the witness. Young men and women generally had more freedom in American than those in the Old World. If they were not satisfied with the dating person that their fathers selected for them, they were allowed not to date with this person. For those who were in a loving relationship, they were even allowed to travel together. In some remote areas, due to the insufficient number of officials and clergymen, young people had fewer restrictions on getting married. They could get married before they went through formalities of marriage registration and held wedding ceremonies.

Two categories of marriage were strictly banned. One was the marriage between two people who were closely related, and the other was interracial marriage. New England and middle colonies forbade intermarriage between whites and blacks, while the southern colonies prohibited intermarriage between any races. In regard to sexual norms, there lay double standards for men and women. Premarital sex and extra-marital affairs were ever-lasting disgrace for women. But if men had done similar things, those behaviors could be tolerated and they could be forgiven in a short time. Sometimes wives would be blamed for their husbands' infidelity. In the eyes of the public, the fact that wives hadn't done well enough that consequently led to the adultery of their husbands. Usually men in the South enjoyed a higher sexual freedom than those in New England. Puritan Americans in New England colonies generally took sex as an original sin and practiced sexual restraint. But in the South, with the existence of large numbers of women slaves who were under the dominance of white masters, it was easier for white men to have an affair. Actually, double standards not only worked for gender, but also applied to race. For example, white men could have relationships with black women at their will, but black men were to be tortured to death if they stayed close to white women.

Beginning in the 19th century, commercialization, westward expansion, industrialization and urbanization challenged the patriarchal family system. The expanding commercial capitalism dismantled the traditional subsistence household economy in the agrarian society. While an increasing number of Americans were joining in the westward movement, their reliance on kinship and land were diluting. Everyone, men and women alike, had to start anew with painstaking efforts in the new and harsh environment. In other words, they were placed at the same starting point and exposed to the same opportunities. This led to the emphasis of individualism and a more equal relationship in the family. For instance, in the past, property inheritance in colonial America borrowed the system of primogeniture from English Common Law. But in the 19th century, property was distributed in accordance with the will made by the testator. Children had relatively equal access to family property, irrespective of gender and birth order. Besides, while moving west and developing the unexplored area, pioneering Americans tended not to cling to real estate. Instead, they accumulated wealth in a flexible way, including selling real estate for investment in current assets or long-term investment. Furthermore, the rapid growth of industrialization gave an impetus to urbanization, profoundly changing the family pattern. Males heads like fathers and husbands left rural sites and swarmed to factories and shops in urban areas. At the same time, women began to take charge of home production and household affairs. Some women, especially single women, even worked in the factory, which not only brought them economic independence but also distanced them from patriarchal surveillance.

  Compared with families in colonial times, American families in this period had greater mobility and flexibility, with a declining family size and estrangement from kinsmen. In many aspects, the family relationship for the time being based more on what family members could do for each other, rather than loyalty and responsibility. In 1790, the average number of people per household was 5.7. It dropped to 3.67 in 1960 and went on reducing to 3.29 in 1980. Once children came of age, they would move out of their parents' house and live independently. Consequently, parents' control over children has been weakening from the mid-19th century onwards, though family backgrounds still played an important role in influencing children's future development. Industrialization also created job and educational opportunities for women. In order to maintain middle-class living standards, a growing number of women worked outside. Women's movements in the 19th and 20th centuries raised women's consciousness of rights, which helped them counter gender discrimination and win equal rights. This in great measure changed their view of marriage. Young men and women expected companion love in their relationship. They felt free to make their own decisions on marriage. More often than not, they would break the barriers of race, class, religion and nationality to pursue love. Interestingly, in the industrial age, with the help of automobiles, Americans had more activities with their colleagues and friends outside the family, while the time spent with their family became less. For instance, they preferred meeting friends in the church to staying at home and praying with their family. In addition, such household appliances as TVs, stereos, radios and computers did not bring the family together. Instead, these appliances are more likely to isolate family members from each other and reduced their communication, for each family member could have one's own TV, computer and stereo and use those appliances on their own.

Since the 1960s, spurred by social movements in the 1960s and 1970s, American family structures have taken on the features of diversity and flexibility. Nowadays there no longer exists the American family. Instead, diverse families have become the new norm. In general, diverse families include families with a dad and a mom, single parent families, adoptive families, blended families, and two-dad and two-mon families. Moreover, the male breadwinner and female housekeeper pattern have faded. If the family has two parents, both of them are more likely to be working. Furthermore, with rising rate of divorce and separation, the number of two-parent families has been reducing. Taken together, responding to the ever-changing social and individual needs, diverse families stress personal freedom and equality, and the respect for disparate lifestyles, whether traditional or non-traditional.

The waning of traditional family values and the fading of the traditional family fueled unease in conservative Americans. Conservatives believed that all these changes incurred a crisis in the American family, which posed a big threat to social stability. But liberal Americans held different views. They claimed that all forms of discrimination and government inaction resulted in the plight of disadvantaged groups, which gave rise to family disintegration and social instability. Central to the dispute between conservative and liberals was whether the traditional family pattern should be restored or not. In other words, should diverse family structures be allowed? In the heat of their controversy, the White House Conference on the Family was held in the early 1980s to address the contentious issue. Conservatives ardently supported the hierarchical order and the whole interest of the family. Because of different family roles and responsibilities, the hierarchical order arose naturally. Though the hierarchical order would inevitably lead to unequal relationship among family members, it would bring stability and promote harmony at home. From their perspective, unequal family status just indicated different family roles. Besides, moral education which provided clear moral standards and defended traditional family values was of great significance to each family. By contrast, liberals were steadfast in their belief in equality and individual rights. They claimed that special attention should be paid to personal willingness as well as individual happiness and fulfilment. Hence, rights and obligations of family members ought to be equal. At the same time, mutual respect, tolerance and care were equally important in the family. Their dispute continued into the new century, and pertained to a series of social issues like day-care center, same-sex marriage, abortion and single parent families.

Viewed from the evolvement of American family values and patterns, major changes have taken place in the following aspects. First, the authoritative patriarchal family system and the extended family structure have diminished, while the family system with equal partnership and the nuclear family have risen. On the one hand, industrialization and commercialization help to devastate the primogeniture, which supports the patriarchal structure and defends the interests of the eldest son in the family. In modern American families, children enjoy the equal right to inherit the family property. In addition, Americans tend to treat real estate as a commodity, which can be used to enhance wealth. On the other hand, during the process of industrialization, the compassionate conjugal relationship and equal family relations have played a dominant role in holding the family together, taking the place of patriarchy. Both free love and rising divorce reflect this social trend. Second, family functions are on the decrease. In earlier times, American families were comprehensive social institutions which encompassed multiple functions, e.g. production, reproduction, education, entertainment, socialization, etc. But presently, a lot of previous family responsibilities are assumed by various specific social institutions, and thereby families are left with limited functions. Third, the status of women and children are on the increase. Waves of feminist movements have challenged bias and discrimination against women, raised the consciousness of female independence, and struggled for equal rights and status for women. Meanwhile, with social development and technological advances, women are no longer cooped up in the home sphere. Instead, they enter different professions, obtain economic independence, and win equal political rights with men. This, to a large extent, enhances women' status both in the public and private spheres. Furthermore, in response to the heightened demand for marriage and family legislation, the legislature at all levels strengthens the legislation concerning women and children. For instance, the no-fault divorce law makes it easier for women to end the unhappy marriage (e.g. spousal abuse and adultery) and start a new life rather than endure it. Child protection laws prohibit child labor, child marriage and child prostitution. Domestic violence laws are introduced to eliminate the violence or abuse against women and children. With individual rights protected by laws and regulations, not only the conjugal relationship but also the parent-child relationship are more equal than in the past. In contemporary times, children can decide on their marriage, career and education, with parents' advice as reference. Fourth, in comparison with their status in previous times, the elderly experience declining status. Along with the weakening of the patriarchy system and improved status of women and children in the family, the elderly now undergo the relative decline in family status. Such being the case, generation gaps are enlarging and the aging problem are even more acute than ever.

In spite of the above-mentioned dramatic transformations, American families continue to play an essential role in the society, irreplaceable by any social institution. Besides, from ancient times to the present, one's start and development have been affected by their family backgrounds. Even if the traditional family pattern has disintegrated, marriage and kinship are still important family elements. Given the importance of the family, it is imperative to fully address the crisis facing American families. So far, two complementary solutions have been proposed. One is to increase one's sense of responsibility and redress moral decline via enhancing moral education and self-discipline. The other is to eliminate gender discrimination, remove deep-rooted stereotypes and bias, and rectify social injustice. Only when individual morality is improved and social conflicts are ameliorated can family issues be better resolved.

1.2 Single Parent Families in America

Single parent families, or one-parent families, are households constituted by a single parent, either a father or mother, and at least one minor child. As a rule, they are primarily female-headed families. For instance, in the 1990s, births to single mothers accounted for more than 1/3 of all the children. By 2019, as many as 86 percent of single parent families were headed by women. When the second feminist movement gained momentum in the 1970s, the number of single parent families doubled. From the 1970s to the 2000s, the female-headed households increased by 7 million, and the male-headed families grew by 1.5 million. In 2017, about 1/4 of American households were single parent families. More often than not, single parents have to face such problems as economic difficulties, inability to balance work and life and lack of social activities. Moreover, single parent families have distinctive racial features. About one half of African American children spend most of their childhood in one-parent families. The rapid growth and increasing prevalence of single parent families make the phenomenon a severe and thorny social issue.

There are a variety of reasons for the emergence of large numbers of single parent families. They include, but not limited to, divorce, separation, death of the other parent, abandonment, single-person birth or adoption. In the past, the majority of single parent families were caused by divorce or death of the spouse. But since the latter half of 20th century, most of single parents have been unwed young women who are undereducated and unskilled. A great number of them have grown up in single parent families. As single mothers barely have any income, it is hard for them to raise the family singlehandedly. At present, of all the families below the poverty line, approximately 60 percent are single parent families consisting of divorced women and their children. Undoubtedly, the feminization of poverty has become a widespread and serious social issue. Apart from the rise of female-headed families and the surging number of divorced and separated women, the sex revolution is another important reason for the feminization of poverty. On the one hand, the sex revolution liberates people from rigid restraints on body and mind. On the other hand, it loosens the moral control on one's sexual behaviors. Negatively impacted by the sex revolution, the number of unwed mothers has been increasing dramatically, especially teenage mothers. Most of the unwed mothers are unfinanced, living an impoverished life with their children. They invariably have no choice but to turn to government aid for help. For example, in 1987, the number of women recipients who benefited from the Aid to Families with Dependent Children (AFDC) program was six times larger than that in 1995. Among all women recipients, single mothers made up more than half. In addition, generational poverty is another characteristic of single parent families. As for children who grow up in one-parent families, later in their life, they have a higher rate of unwed birth and school dropout, along with a lower rate of entering university and finding jobs.

It should be noted that the feminization of poverty is a severe problem in the African American community. First, there is a high proportion of black female-headed families, and the number of such families is increasing quickly. In 1950, 8 percent of black families were headed by women. Four decades later, it reached 57 percent. Second, black women are more likely to become unwed teenage mothers. In the early 1980s, the proportion of illegitimate children in black children was 55 percent, compared with 15 percent in 1940. About 85 percent of these out-of-wed children were born to black teenager mothers. Third, black single parent families headed by women suffer the highest poverty rate in the US. In the early 1990s, more than 60 percent of children in black female-headed families lived in poverty, in contrast to 40 percent in white female-headed families. Besides, the high poverty rate is more likely to breed single parent families. Actually, it is commonly believed that apart from crime and drugs, the surging number of black female-headed families pose a threat to the stability and development of the black community. It has galvanized the attention of government agencies and non-governmental organizations.

  Why have black female-headed families grown so quickly and significantly? Scholars have put forward two important reasons. The first is the enlarging gender gap among black people resulting from entrenched racial discrimination. Due to the second feminist movement and Civil Rights Movement, more black women than black men receive higher education. In the 1980s, black women accounted for 3/5 of black college students. Climbing up the educational ladder, black women have a better chance of holding respectable jobs with higher income than black men. Not surprisingly, of all professional jobs obtained by black people, black women get about 70 percent. Meanwhile, since the 1960s, the economic restructuring and deindustrialization have incurred the joblessness of black men who are usually unskilled and undereducated. The employment rate of black men dropped from 74 percent in 1960 to 55 percent in the 1980s. In this situation, for one thing, stress and anxiety caused by rising unemployment give rise to divorce and separation in black families. For another, unemployed black men lose their economic independence and financial means, let alone start their own families. In other words, black women may feel that the options of finding black men with stable jobs or incomes are dwindling. Furthermore, situated at the bottom of the society, the black men are subject to accidents, diseases, incarceration and even death. For instance, according to the statistics released by the National Association for the Advancement of Colored People (NAACP) in 2017, black people accounted for 43 percent of all the prisoners, 6 times more than the proportion of white prisoners. Besides, black men are 2.5 times more likely to be shot to death by the police than white men. Therefore, in terms of educational, vocational and financial circumstances, the number of eligible black men for black women are declining.

  The second is associated with social ethos in the mainstream society and family values in the black community. Adversely affected by the trend of sex revolution and moral decline in the larger society, black men and women take few responsibilities for their sexual behaviors. Moreover, motherhood is highly valued and glorified in black culture. In West Africa, black mothers enjoyed high status and much respect, while sterile women were treated coldly and even marginalized. Beginning from slavery times, it was not rare to see black female-headed families in the society. Black men were prone to be sold or abused to death by slave owners. Nurtured in this culture, unwed black women tend to keep and raise the child on their own when they get pregnant, whatever economic situation they face.

Most black female-headed families live in poverty-stricken areas with a high crime rate. Needless to say, the substandard living conditions and dangerous living environment negatively affect black children, both their characters and development. Witnessing the poverty and break-up of the family in the childhood, black girls who are brought up by single black mothers are more likely to continue the same path as their mothers, while black boys who grow up in such conditions are more prone to misdemeanor and even crime. As for black single mothers, they are labelled as "bad mother" or "welfare mother," because they can hardly find jobs and have to rely on social support. These disfigured images have become stereotypes of black women, which turn out to be barriers for eliminating gender discrimination. It is worth mentioning that characteristics used to be solely of black people, like rising divorce, a high proportion of female-headed families, and a growing number of illegitimate children, have become more pronounced in the mainstream society.

Overall, American families have become increasingly diversified since the latter half of the 20th century, with the evolution of American family values over time. The recent decades find divorce, remarriage, same-sex marriage and interracial marriage on the increase. Meanwhile, the number of single-parent families, out-of-wedlock births and single-person households keeps rising. Presently, it is imperative to solve such serious social problems as the feminization of poverty, juvenile crime, domestic violence spawned by the changes in American families.

Unit 12 The American Family and Community

2 The American Community

America is one of the first countries that have carried out community building and management. For one thing, as a basic local unit to exercise self-determination and self-governance, the community bonds individuals together and enhances mutual help. For another, as a social unit, the community plays a crucial role in facilitating economic growth and improving social services in the US. The major functions of the American community are as follows. First, it is a self-governing institution, with its own administration – the community board. All the inhabitants participate in the community affairs, according to "one person, one vote" and the principle of majority rule. Second, each community maintains facilities to support the life of local residents. These facilities include schools, churches, recreational facilities like parks, green space, theatres, museums, cinemas and libraries, business facilities like department stores and super markets, etc. All of these facilities improve the living environment and enrich the inhabitants' life. Third, every community not only has a unique physical landscape, but also features a distinctive cultural landscape. Local residents have created distinguishing folk culture, ethnic culture, gender culture, voting culture, business culture, club culture, green culture, etc. The diverse and distinctive community cultures foster a sense of belonging in American communities, which is conducive to community solidarity. Fourth, as community members vary in values and personal interests from each other, the community serves as an important channel to seek common ground and resolve conflicts. Thus, the interaction between community members has become a vital part of community life.

2.1 The Community Self-Governance Tradition

From the end of the 19th century onwards, a number of philanthropic organizations were set up to aid the poor in the US. At the same time, the settlement house movement was launched to help the poor immigrants and low-income families in the impoverished communities. Around WWI, the concept of "community" was introduced to the US, after American sociologist Frank Farrington proposed "community development" in his book *Making the Small Town a Better Place to Live and A Better Place in Which to Do Business* (1915). Since then, community work has been put on the right track. The War on Poverty program initiated by president Lyndon B. Johnson in the 1960s created community action agencies to eliminate poverty. Through government funding and community self-help efforts, community development and improvement were advanced. Beginning in the 1980s, community work shifted the attention to people with special needs, e.g. the elderly, people with physical or mental impairment, single parents, etc. In response to these needs, some community development companies were established to address the employment problem and improve substandard living conditions in the slum. Another milestone in community development was reached during the Clinton administration. Since 1993, the American government has made consistent efforts to revitalize underserved communities. The vigorous measures included bringing private enterprises, creating a community development financial network, designating Enterprise Communities and Empowerment Zones across the nation. So far, American communities have been well developed with multiple functions. In fact, the brilliant achievements in community development are inseparable from the profound community culture in the US, especially the tradition of self-governance.

The community self-governance tradition can be traced back to colonial times. In 1620, 102 passengers boarded the Mayflower boat, including puritans, poor farmers and craftsmen, set sail for the colony of Virginia in America. They hoped to enjoy religious freedom and search for a better life. However, because of a storm, the boat deviated from the original course, and these immigrants were forced to land in New England. In order to prevent everyone from wantonly utilizing their liberty and build an orderly society, they signed a contract named the *Mayflower Compact* before landing. In this document, they agreed to form "a civil Body Politick" "for the general Good of the Colony." In other words, for the sake of the survival and well-being of the whole community, the signers were willing to give up some personal rights and obey

Unit 12　The American Family and Community

the law and order of the new colony.

　　Significantly, the compact contained many embryonic forms of American democratic ideals, which were passed down from generation to generation. The essence of these ideals is self-governance, which is reflected throughout the compact. According to the compact, the formation of the civil body politick is out of the signers' own will, rather than be forced by the authority. This is in line with the freedom of contract in civil society. Since the civil body politick takes responsibility for enacting laws and regulations, it indicates that the group abides by laws. While making laws and regulations, the civil body politick takes the common good of the new colony into account. In addition, the legislation should not only accommodate local needs but also maintain justice. These stipulations show the public, feasible and universal nature of laws and policies in civil society. Furthermore, the signers promise to fully obey laws, which reveals the self-consciousness of the rule of law and civic awareness. Upon immigrants setting foot in New England, they established the Plymouth Colony in accordance with the *Mayflower Compact*. When they formed their community, they transplanted the idea of English towns and villages to the new colony. According to the English tradition of local autonomy, free from outside intervention, each area was a self-sufficient community that dealt with its own affairs and made its own decisions. The tradition is largely based on the belief that, only when one participated in community affairs could one's sense of responsibility for one's community be kept. It was the sense of responsibility and the sense of belonging that triggered people's motivation to improve community governance. With local autonomy in mind, early English settlers built churches, schools, cottages, roads and bridges. The community was consolidated by pious religious beliefs. Neighbors offered mutual help when someone was in need. Later on, local governments and churches got involved in aiding the needy. Ever since then, self-governance has become the main thread of American social development.

　　If it is believed that self-governance was budding in the *Mayflower Compact*, the New England township can be taken as the prototype of the self-governing polity.

The township is a complete and orderly governing entity, with a population of 3000 in its jurisdiction. The power of township originates from the people, and direct democracy is exercised. As a rule, local residents directly elect selectmen and grant them administrative power to take charge of local affairs. The selectmen have to work under the rules and principles set by local residents. Hence, if the selectmen hope to change the established rules or start a new project, they must ask township residents for permission. While they are dealing with major issues pertaining to vital interests of local residents, such as taxation, appropriation, constructing roads and setting up schools, they will hold town meetings and invite local residents with voting rights to attend. In colonial America, not every one of the inhabitants had the right to vote. Only the adult male with property ownership and church membership could have access to voting right. In the town meetings, the participants listen to selectmen's reports, and then they discuss and vote on those issues. On the basis of the voting result, the selectmen make the final decision. This procedure applies to both local affairs and out-of-town issues that involve local interests. Through town meetings, local residents can select local officials other than selectmen, who will be paid according to their workload. Moreover, the township organization fully protects people's electoral freedom. If local people are not satisfied with certain officials, they can vote for other suitable people during the reelection next year.

Generally speaking, the township organization takes on two distinctive features. One is that local residents have a high sense of belonging to the township. As the township is built and developed upon the principle of self-governess, local people tend to identify personal interests with the advancement of the township. Since their destinies are closely linked, township inhabitants are more likely to play an active in putting forward suggestions and new ideas, exercising their rights and performing their obligations. The other is the mode of power-sharing in the township. In order to prevent the concentration of power, as many local residents as possible are encouraged to engage in public affairs and assigned different positions. In addition, town meetings are frequently organized, so that the public can be informed of important township matters, and then have a discussion and make a decision. According to Alex de Tocqueville, by the mid-17th century, the self-governing township had completely come into being. In many aspects, the New England Township can be considered as the earliest form of the American self-governing community.

Apart from the *Mayflower Compact* and the New England township, westward expansion is a milestone for developing the spirit of self-governance. Customarily, for each self-organized group that was about to move westward, the group members signed an agreement similar to the *Mayflower Compact* when they discussed the westward route. The agreement was actually the bylaw of the group, which specified persons in charge at different levels and their responsibilities, as well as the procedure of revising the bylaw. In most instances, it required 2/3 majority vote to get the bylaw revised. Needless to say, it was necessary for those pioneers to make bylaws before they set out. Because they were going to settle in unexplored areas of the country, where laws did not exist. Such being the case, they had to make concerted efforts to protect themselves. By abiding by the bylaw and fulfilling their obligations, they were able to enjoy the rights set by the bylaws. For example, they could get help from other members when their wagons were stuck in the mire or they were under the attack of American Indians.

It is worth mentioning that, when group members made decisions, they followed the principles of "one person, one vote" and "a majority decides." In other words, everyone's vote was worthy of equal attention, irrespective of their social status. In the organization, one's individual status was irrelevant to his/her family backgrounds or education attainment. Instead, their ability and morality counted. Besides, obeying majority vote was a traditional and feasible means to settle issues. Americans generally held that, there must have been various groups and individuals with different interests in an organization or community, and those interests inevitably came into conflict with each other. When that happened, Americans reached the consensus that they would act on the will of the majority. At present, the two principles have been widely accepted and fully observed. Another legacy left by the westward movement is a new perception of individualism. Though individualism has long been held dear in the US, the trailblazers' experiences made Americans realize that only through a powerful and effective organization could their rights and interests be secured. The respect for individualism does not mean that they do not obey the community rules. In fact, they are willing to conform to laws and disciplines made by themselves or the representatives elected by them. The agreements and laws that they comply with convey the message: one's freedom can be achieved on the condition that it does not offend the interests of the community and other community members.

2.2 The Community Service

As the community is more directly related to Americans' daily life, community agencies and organizations are real implementors of social programs. American community service plays a crucial role in enhancing social prosperity and stability. Besides, it fully displays the long community tradition of self-governance.

Community agencies and organizations assume the responsibility of a wide range of social service. There are reasons accounting for this phenomenon. First, while the federal, state and local governments are distributing social relief, the community takes charge of bringing the aid to the needy. In other words, the community is the major implementor and coordinator of social welfare programs at all levels. Usually there could be some misfortunate people who are in dire need of help, but for various reasons, they are exempt from the government's aid. At this particular moment, the community can play a complementary role in providing timely help and considerate service. Second, the community has a better understanding of the real needs of local residents, who are in great need and who qualify for public assistance. American residents have a great geographical mobility, and thereby it is easier for the community to acquire first-hand information. Third, as neighborhood residents have various needs, the community offers a broad range of social service in accordance with these needs. For example, community development, housing assistance, community safety, culture, education and environment, public facilities maintenance, helping newly-arrived immigrants integrate into society, service for the elderly, etc. Therefore, a great variety of community agencies and organizations are founded to implement numerous service programs. Among those services, volunteer service, community library service and community college service are most influential programs.

Volunteer service has long been the distinctive feature of American community culture, which is in line with its cultural tradition of communitarianism. As voluntary activities have been deeply rooted in the grassroots, the community has undoubtedly become the main territory for volunteer service. Since the childhood of Americans, they have been taught either by their families or schools that they ought to serve others and give back to society. More significantly, the *National and Community Service Trust Act* was signed into effect in 1993 to encourage volunteerism in American society. The law awards outstanding young volunteers with scholarships for higher education or vocational training. Besides, as a rule, primary and secondary schools list community service as one of the measurements for evaluating students' performance. Meanwhile, during the admission, American colleges and universities prefer to take students' volunteer experiences into account. A number of famous companies also value the history of applicant's community service while recruiting employees. Hence, American students are willing to take part in the community service when they receive primary and secondary education. Apart from these motivations, some Americans are dedicated to volunteer work to fulfil Christians' responsibilities, some to realize one's personal worth and social aspirations, and others to build more social connections or accumulate work experience.

Generally speaking, volunteers come from all walks of life. There are children, adults and even the elderly, both the rich and the poor, as well as working and unemployed people. Actually, there is a blurred line between the volunteers and recipients who get volunteer help. In certain periods, they serve as volunteers. But in other times, their roles are changed to recipients. According to the statistics, half of American adults take part in at least one volunteer activity each week. Each year, there are as many as 60 million Americans involving in volunteering. Usually, people with higher education attainment and income are more likely to lend a hand in volunteer work. Voluntary service at the community level almost covers every aspect of community life, such as helping the elderly, the disabled, the orphaned children and the poor, improve the environment, education, security and public health. It fully meets the basic needs of local inhabitants, protecting the disadvantaged groups in particular.

At present, the US has the world's largest number of volunteer organizations. As non-profit organizations, they normally receive financial support from government funds, private donations, corporate funds, charitable foundations, etc. On the one hand, these organizations reduce the management costs in the community, and enhance the quality of life in the neighborhood. On the other hand, they have direct or indirect impacts on the government policies, so as to improve the relationship between governments and citizens. So far, these organizations, together with governments and corporations, have laid the groundwork for American civil society. In order to guarantee their operation and development, strict rules and regulations have been set. Before one engages in voluntary service, he/she has to receive certain training, getting to know the dos and don'ts. For instance, volunteers should make work plans and act upon these plans. Moreover, they should have a high sense of responsibility. Once they cannot fulfil their work, they have to notify the organizers as soon as possible and take remedial measures. Furthermore, by no means are they allowed to take the volunteering opportunities to obtain personal interests. While volunteer work becomes widespread in the US, the National Volunteer Day and the National Volunteer Week have been established to further promote volunteer service and honor those who have made great contributions to volunteer work. In the new era, the spread of the internet greatly expands the range and transforms the means of organizing voluntary service. In the past, volunteers mostly received support from people in local and nearby places. But nowadays with the help of the internet, they are able to gain support from across the world. In addition, participants who are far away from each other can transmit information, exchange opinions and coordinate actions quickly and conveniently online.

In addition to volunteer service, the community library offers a variety of service to neighborhood residents. It is commonly recognized as the cultural center in each community. As community libraries spread across the nation, almost all Americans benefit from them. The rich book collection in these libraries completely satisfies local needs for reading and learning. More than 90 percent of community libraries have access to internet, and over 70 percent of these libraries provide online borrowing service. It is easy to apply for a library card. First, fill in an application form with your basic information. After that, show any of the certificates that can prove your identity. Finally, present a letter with a mailing address that can prove your current address, e.g. the utility billing letter. Within a few minutes, you can have your library card. With the card in hand, you are able to read books, newspapers and magazine, as well as borrow books, sound recordings and videotapes.

However, the function of the modern community library is not limited to providing borrowing service. Instead, it performs multiple social service functions. The first is enhancing the educational level and employability of local residents. The library oftentimes invites authors, poets, playwrights and literature professors, who live in the surrounding neighborhoods to the reading salons. In so doing, the educated readers can have direct communication with professionals, so that they can acquire a deeper understanding of certain works. As for readers with basic literacy, the librarians will recommend the simplified edition of literary classics to improve their literary accomplishments. In order to help newly-arrived immigrants in the community, the library organizes a series of activities on employment guidance. For instance, free English classes are offered to immigrants from non-English speaking countries to help them break language barriers. Successful persons are invited to share with the community newcomers how they start from scratch. Career experts are invited to teach the immigrants who are fresh off the boat how to seek job information, write CVs and prepare for the interview.

The second is providing comprehensive service to the elderly and young adults.

The Senior Citizen Corner has been set up in the library, where the aged can read books with large letters. The library offers free mailing service to the elderly and the disabled readers. Additionally, with a nice environment and a short distance from old readers' homes, the library is a convenient place for the elderly to meet their friends and acquaintances. Apart from the specific corner for senior citizens, the library also makes room for the Young Adult Service Corner, stacked with books fit for the reading in this age group. With vivid language and exquisite illustrations, these books arouse young readers great interest. Moreover, after class, children can search for information to finish their homework such as duty report, book report and research project. Furthermore, free lectures on various subjects such as literature, art, drama, music, history, astrology, environmental protection and communication skills are delivered to enrich the children's knowledge.

  The third is taking the role of community information center. On the one hand, the readers can get a lot of information about community life from the information bulletin board and the Community Information Service. The information includes the introduction to community non-profit organizations, the wide range of service provided by community educational, housing, health care and environmental protection institutions, as well as the latest information concerning voluntary, cultural and recreational activities and job opportunities. Normally, the information bulletin board is set up at the entrance of the library or put on the website of the library. On the other hand, the pamphlets which show mass transit routes and the contact information of community services are available to readers for free. Moreover, Green Books made by local governments have listed the contact information of certain government sectors, including their websites, addresses, telephone numbers and e-mail addresses. For any questions, local residents feel free to make inquiries.

  Last but not least, because of the convenient location and spacious room, the community library is often the first choice for holding community public hearing and organizing cultural activities. It is worth mentioning that people who give free lectures in the library are not only librarians, but also volunteers and local residents. Directly meeting the spiritual needs of local inhabitants, the community library reflects the virtues of mutual help, active engagement and altruism.

2.3 Slums and the Gentrification Project

Even if America is one of the most developed countries in the world, poverty still plagues the powerful nation. In the highly urbanized country, most of Americans live in urban areas. Therefore, urban poverty is a serious social problem. In fact, a significant number of Americans now live in the slum.

2.3.1 The Slum Problem in the US

According the US Census Bureau, from 1990 to 2019, the poverty rate kept at above 10 percent, with the peak of 15 percent in certain years. The US poverty line refers to the minimum income level that accommodates the basic living of people. In other words, it is set in accordance with the needs of social development. Specifically speaking, it is made in line with such indicators as the consumption structure, the rate of inflation and the price level. Customarily, it is three times more than the household expenditure on food. Usually, those whose annual incomes are less than the poverty line are viewed as the poor. Due to inflation and changes in the price and income levels, the federal poverty level has increased steadily. In 1980, the poverty line for a household of four people was an annual income of 8414 dollars. Three decades later, it reached an income of 22,314 dollars per year. In 2020, it grew to 26200 dollars.

The poor population takes on distinctive features, affected by such factors as the family structure, gender, race and age. First, the majority of poor families are single parent families, especially single parent families headed by women. The poverty rate of female-headed families are almost six times higher than two-parent families. Next, the poverty rate of racial minorities is the highest among all racial groups. Black people and Hispanics have long had the highest rates of poverty in the US. For instance, in 2019, 18.8 percent of African Americans and 15.7 percent of Hispanics were below the poverty line, compared with 7.3 percent of the whites. Finally, in terms of age, children and the elderly account for almost half of the poor in America. In fact, most of poor children are from female-headed families and ethnic minority families. Owing to the high poverty rates of African Americans and Hispanics, the children from these families are much more likely to fall into poverty than from white families. As for the retired people, they mostly rely on pensions. But for those who used to be the long-term unemployed before retirement, they have no pensions to receive. Under such circumstance, it is more probable for them to live under the poverty line.

It should be noted that not all poor people are stuck in long-term poverty. As a matter of fact, due to economic recession or accidents, many people are reduced to poverty for just several months. Besides, in comparison with people in underdeveloped countries, American poor people generally live a comfortable life. Over half of American poor families have their own houses. 2/3 of them own at least one car. Almost each poor family has at least one TV set. More than 3/4 of them have at least one air-conditioner. At present, the poor receive the earned income tax credit, food stamps, housing and rental subsidizes, as well as medical assistance from the government. With support of social welfare, the poor can reduce much expenditure on daily necessities so as to live a respectable life.

Slums refer to areas with bad living conditions that are inhabited by poor people. To certain extent, they are the products of urbanization. Since the late 19th century, urban slums have emerged as common phenomena in the US. At the end of the 19th century, the rapid development of industrialization led to fast growth of urbanization, giving rise to the unprecedented concentration of the population and economic production. With the development of industrialization by leaps and bounds, the urban economic structure and cultural activities kept improving. For one thing, the dynamic urban economic activities created a large number of job opportunities. For another, such urban public places as theatres, parks, clubs and pubs provided recreational service, which helped people fully relax and enjoy themselves. The two important city functions allured people from rural areas and foreign countries to swarm into city. As the industry in the northeastern and midwestern regions of the US was more

Unit 12 The American Family and Community

developed and job opportunities there were more bountiful, these regions become top destinations of migration and immigration. In large cities like New York, Boston, Philadelphia and Chicago, more than 2/3 of the residents were immigrants. The newly-arrived immigrants were more likely to settle down in the community, which consisted of people of the same ethnic group.

With an increasing number of the rural and immigrant population pouring into cities, the city failed to provide adequate housing to the newcomers. As for those who were not able to purchase houses, they had no choice but to pack into the substandard housing close to downtown areas. The real estate developers changed dilapidated apartment buildings into tenements, whose rooms were further divided into smaller ones. In so doing, at least three people lived in the room that used to hold just one person, and over eight people crowded into the apartment that used to hold four people. By letting them out, the developers made huge profits. But poor people suffered the substandard living. The rooms were not only small but also dark with bad ventilation. Few tenement houses had cooling and heating equipment, sewers, or fire exits. Oftentimes several families had to share a toilet. Outside, smelly animal wastes and garbage accumulated in city muddy streets. The bad living conditions caused health and sanitation problems. Contagious diseases like smallpox, tuberculosis and cholera spread quickly through the neighborhood. As poor people concentrated in this area, social crimes such as theft, robbery, drug trafficking, kidnapping, and even murder frequently took place. Over time, the residential areas of the poor became the infamous slums. And the slums expanded along with the growth of the city. Beginning in the 20th century, especially after WWII, the white middle-class families and commercial industry moved to suburban areas, leaving the underclass in the inner city. Hence slums have turned into ghettos, isolated from the mainstream society.

Gradually, the residents in the slums are stratified into two groups. Not willing to endure long-term poverty, some of them improve their living conditions and obtain better opportunities through their hard work and ceaseless efforts. With improved financial situations, they normally move their families to the suburbs, which boast nice environments. Others who don't have strong aspirations or lack the skills of employability are locked in poverty. They have no place to go but to live in the slums permanently. Due to few resources and bad living conditions, it is easier for the residents in the slums to fall into generational poverty. As the immigrants account for a high proportion of slum residents, they are often blamed for facilitating the shaping of the slum. Actually, the problem of slums is not a unique American phenomenon. Instead, it appears in all nations. As for some newly-arrived poor immigrants, they do rely on social aid for a while. But later on, most of them choose to find a job and earn their own livelihoods. Additionally, the crime rate of immigrants is lower than that of native-born Americans.

What are the roots causes of American slums? One is the laissez-faire economic policy held by the government. Facing the deteriorating conditions of residential areas, the government remains inactive. It is until the city development and city environment are in terrible shape that the government eventually put forward the zoning policy. The new policy intends to show businessmen which area has a high risk of investment and which one has high returns. Under the policy, it is impossible for the slums to get any investment or development. Thus, the business becomes more languished and housing more crumbling in the slum. In other words, the improper measure speeds up the decaying of the slum. The other is the American market economy. The economic development inevitably attracts the inflow of manpower. Though the newcomers make great contributions to economic growth, their arrival also puts much stress on housing, public transportation, social security and environment, and gives birth to a series of social problems. If the government does not take action or implement proper policies, slums are bound to go hand in hand with economic prosperity in the city. Sadly, slums have received much condemnation and little care from the public. In addition, the government does not give enough attention or assistance to slums, so the problem of slums is far from being resolved. However, it should be remembered that slums offer a bit of place to the friendless and helpless labor force, who largely promotes social advancement. Without the existence of slums, it would be impossible for the US to achieve economic prosperity.

In order to address the problem of slums, the government launched the urban renewal movement from the 1950s to the 1970s. Specific programs were carried out in two phases. In the first phase, the rundown houses in the slums were dismantled, and housing and business development were strengthened. In the second phase, the focus was put on the comprehensive management of urban housing, commercial facilities and cultural environments. But it was proved to be a failed move. Local governments played a major role in urban renewal, with the emphasis on reviving the economy of slums. They hoped to provide more job opportunities, improve residents' living conditions and increase city revenues through economic improvement. However, this line of thinking did not eliminate slums, it just forced residents in one slum to be relocated to another neighborhood, which later on became a new slum. Undoubtedly, it increased both financial and psychological burdens for the former residents in the slum. At the same time, it gave birth to more racial violence and conflicts, worsening the situation in the slum.

2.3.2 The Gentrification Movement

When the urban renewal movement ended, the gentrification movement started to be prevalent in large American cities. Gentrification was coined by British sociologist Ruth Glass when she described the changes of inner-city neighborhoods in London. Nowadays the term generally means the process of renovating a rundown neighborhood in central cities through the inflow of the middle class. It often improves the physical landscape and business environment in the district. Meanwhile, it increases the property price and living expenses, which changes local racial composition. As for the residents who move in the gentrified street, most of them are middle-class white young people, who are managers, professionals and clerks. They enjoy high economic status than the original residents. Some are singles, some are conjugal families, and others are homosexuals. So far, gentrification has experienced uneven development. It develops substantially in former industrial centers of the northeastern and midwestern regions. In addition, it becomes widespread in national or regions hubs like New York, Boston, Chicago, Atlanta, Los Angeles, San Francisco and Seattle. Furthermore, the gentrified district is located in the blighted area close to the Central Business District, where white-collars concentrate. Normally, the gentrified district is full of unique architecture and rich culture.

Gentrification started with the unique renovation of homes by some artists and those who lived an alternative life in a deteriorating area. With the neighborhood invested with a high culture character, affluent people or middle-class residents are attracted to settle down in this district. After that, because of extensive media reports and improved community environment, a lot of financial capital flows into this area for further development. Along with gentrification comes the forced relocation of original residents. The ultimate outcome of gentrification is that former residents are partially or totally replaced by newcomers. The fundamental reason is the appreciation in real estate in the gentrified area. On the one hand, the rapid growth in property price largely increases the property tax. Such being the case, homeowners with little income are so overwhelmed by the high tax that they have to sell their houses. On the other hand, the surging property price gives rise to the rapid increase in rent, which is beyond the affordability of most of the low-income tenants. In this case, they had no choice but to move out of the neighborhood. It should be pointed out that, when the gentrified district has been much developed, not only former low-income residents but also the middle class who move in at the early stage of gentrification have to be uprooted from the district.

Why does the gentrification movement happen in the United States? There are several reasons for the phenomenon. First and foremost, the changes in the economic function of cities during post-industrialization and globalization prompt the gentrification movement. After WWII, the US changed from the industrial society to the post-industrial society, with an increasing proportion of the service sector. During the process, the function of the city changed from industrial production to management and services, such as finance, banking, consulting, accounting, advertising, communications, software development and network technology. Hence cities have become the service and decision-making centers. At the same time, under globalization, large cities have turned into headquarters of global economy. As the management and operation of corporations are complicated, the management, professionals and administrators are required to work together and make quick decisions. In order to save commuting time, white-collars who work for financial and service industries in the Center Business District usually choose to live close to their companies. Thus, the blighted area close to the Center Business District becomes their first choice. When they move in, they renovate former dilapidated houses and improve the neighborhood.

Second, the transformed city planning idea spurs the movement. The urban renewal movement expanded the Central Business District, and sped up the process of post-industrialization. In spite of the achievements, it also incurred severe social problems. With the dismantling of a lot of slum housing and small businesses, a huge number of the poor became homeless and lost their jobs. Meanwhile, it destroyed previous social networks in the community, and did great harm to lots of precious historical sites. Drawing upon the lessons from urban renewal, the gentrification movement lays emphasis on small-scale maintenance and renovation projects. The so-called "gentrifiers" or the middle class who move to the rundown neighborhood of inner cities protect historic sites, repair houses and rebuild the district. It is a significant shift in urban planning and development.

Third, the decay of central cities and the accompanying rent gap theory stimulate the movement. During the suburbanization in the post-WWII era, a great number of the white middle class moved to the suburbs. Their relocation crippled the tax base of central cities. Meanwhile, the concentration of the low-income class and ethnic groups in central cities inevitably increased their burden of social welfare. It engendered the financial crisis, the spreading of slums and intense racial conflicts. But supported by the theory of the rent gap, gentrification seemed to offer a possible solution to the problem. Put forward by Neil Smith in 1979, the rent gap stressed the disparity between the current value of a property and its potentially achievable value. The disparity aroused the interest of some developers who were able to identify the difference and capitalize on certain renovation projects. Their investment resulted in an increase in rent and brought huge profits to them.

Finally, the gentrification movement is in line with the changing family structure, life styles and social values. The 1970s and 1980s started to witness tremendous changes in American families, e.g. delayed marriage and childbearing, single parenthood, smaller family size, etc. Different from their parents, the new generation wishes to enjoy their lives and pursue their careers in urban areas. By contrast, suburban life is dull and meaningless for them. It should be noted that, the first gentrifiers were middle-class Americans who led an alternative life, such as avant-garde artists, singles and DINKs. In comparison with the majority of the middle-class, they paid more attention to cultural taste and experience instead of material consumption. With good education and decent work, the early gentrifiers held that cities especially old ones featured profound culture, and city life was colorful and dynamic. In the cities, one could not only have access to classical cultures like ancient buildings and historic sites, but also experience popular cultures like pop music, Hollywood movies, entertainment and leisure. Therefore, gentrification provides an opportunity for them to express and enjoy themselves.

Presently, the gentrification movement is still in controversy. As for proponents, one of the most positive effects is that the blighted neighborhood has been revitalized. With gentrifiers' pioneering efforts, the dilapidated slum housing is renovated, and the community environment is improved. On the one hand, the changing situation allures the developers to invest in this area, which largely increases local property value. On the other hand, the nice living environment also attracts affluent people to move in and settle down. These new circumstances lead to social stability and a sharp decrease in crime. Moreover, along with the development of gentrification and business comes a large increase in the employment rate. Furthermore, the revival of deteriorating neighborhoods and the arrival of gentrifiers supply the Central Business District with high-quality employees. Consequently, this helps to promote the prosperity of the Central Business District, and reverses the decline of central cities.

Nevertheless, the opponents believed that, gentrification caused a further decline in non-gentrified neighborhoods. While the gentrified districts and suburban areas are attracting an increasing number of the middle-class and more investment, the living standards and environment of non-gentrified areas are deteriorating. Eventually, these areas become new slums. Besides, the original residents in gentrified areas are forcibly relocated to other places, suffering economic and psychological blows. But the reality is, if gentrification does not happen, local residents still have to move away sooner or later. Because when crumpling slum housing fails to receive timely maintenance, it can no longer hold people anymore. Such being the case, it is imperative for the government or the community to assist low-income residents in finding a suitable place to live through legislation and regulation.

Essay questions:

1. From colonial America to the present, American family values and patterns experience tremendous changes. Trace the evolvement of American family values and patterns, and examine the continuities and changes in the historical course. Further, analyze the major challenges to contemporary American families.

2. Since the 1960s, the traditional American family has faded and American family structures have become more diverse. The number of single-parent families has increased dramatically, black female-headed families in particular. At the same time, feminization of poverty has become a prominent phenomenon. Examine the social impacts of single-parent families, and discuss the causes of the feminization of poverty.

3. The American community is the grassroots social unit for American citizens to practice self-governess. Since earlier times, it has played an irreplaceable role in providing social aid and service. First, trace the historical development of the profound tradition of self-governess held by the American community. Next, list a number of major social service activities organized by the community. Finally, analyze the motivations and philosophy

of American community service.

4. The problem of poverty inflicts on underdeveloped, developing and developed countries. Explore the distinctive features and the root causes of poverty in the US.

5. In the US, the problem of poverty is not an accidental or isolated phenomenon. Instead, it is a serious social problem that cannot be underestimated. Examine the relationship between the slums and American political system, and analyze why the American slums can never be eradicated.

Unit 13 American Environmental Issues and Protection

In the process of accumulating wealth growth and promoting social development throughout centuries, the US has been facing serious challenges such as the depletion of natural resources and the deterioration of the ecological environment, which called the attention of governments at all levels to environmental issues, triggered the awakening of the environmental awareness among the public, and galvanized Americans into environmental movements across the nation. In many ways, environmental issues help Americans reflect on not only the relationship between humankind and nature, but also the role of the human race in the ecological system as well as the unscientific mode of production and the wasteful lifestyle of human beings in the world. Aiming at solving environmental issues, American environmental thoughts and environmental movements are dedicated to protecting both the natural and built environment into consideration. In general, American environmental protection mirrors the characteristics and dynamic changes of American perception of nature as well as the relationship between the human race and nature.

1 The Origin of American Environmental Issues

Environmental issues expose the disharmonious relationship between man and nature, and reveal the imbalanced social relationship among human beings. American environmental issues started to arise when European settlers set foot on the American continent. In order to survive, the early settlers cleared forest ranges, dug wells, changed the course of rivers, plowed the field, built roads and houses, transformed the landscape and altered the physical environment. Imbued with a sense of unrealistic optimism and unlimited expansion, they were exploiting the promised land in the New World. At that time, the myth of abundance about inexhaustible natural resources in the North American continent was prevalent, dominating Americans' perception of nature. Moreover, the protestant legacy greatly influenced the relationship between man and nature. According to *Genesis* 1:26 and *Genesis* 1: 28, God told human beings to subdue and rule over every living thing on earth. It means that humankind was granted the power of dominion and control over nature, which led to over-exploitation. With these values in mind, in the name of civilization conquering barbarism, European colonists, while bringing huge ecological disasters to Native Americans, enormously changed the ecological system of North America. For example, on the one hand, they were destroying native animal and plant species; on the other hand, they were introducing animals and plants of the Old World to the New World, so as to create an ecological system familiar to them. However, their activities were at the cost of the biodiversity of colonial America.

After the founding of the nation, a series of land policies like the Ordinance of 1784, the Land Ordinance of 1785 and the Northwest Ordinance of 1787 were implemented to encourage Americans to cut down trees, extend the frontiers, explode the mountains, and slaughter the animals, which intensified the confrontation between man and nature, and caused a huge waste of natural resources and environmental degradation. Moreover, on the basis of demands for technological change and engineering improvements, new technologies were created to support both industrial manufacturing and westward expansion. Furthermore, after 1815, American became a capitalist society driven by market economy, reinforcing the idea of nature as commodities for utilization and consummation. While the development of the West and the industrialization of the East sped up the process of modernization in America, Americans witnessed devastating environmental tragedies and left hard lessons behind the unprecedented economic growth and social progress.

Unit 13　American Environmental Issues and Protection

There was reckless and wasteful use of natural resources during westward expansion, which exerted irreversible negative impacts on the earth. First, large tracts of forest were wiped out and pristine areas of wildness disappeared. During American colonial times, nearly half the land was covered with as many as 1,281,250 square miles of forest, which was like a blanket stretching along the Appalachian Mountains, the Great Lakes region, the Rocky Mountains and the Mountainous area on the West Coast. As forest was taken as a hurdle for farming, 460,000 square miles of forest were cleared from the mid-17th century to the mid-19th century under axe and saw, with the majority of forest in the east vanishing. From the mid-19th century to the beginning of the 20th century, another 800,000 square miles of forest, especially those in the mid-west and west regions, were removed, because after the Civil War, the rapid development of railroad construction, mining, house-building in cities and towns increased the market demands for timber. By the 1920s, the total forest area dwindled to merely 470 million acres, with 138 million acres of the primeval forest, and the northeastern and mid-western United States lost approximately 96 percent of the primeval forest. What's worse, when farmers tried to turn forest to farmland in the mid-west, they came to find that the soil where forest grew was so sandy that it was not suitable for agricultural production, so they went on moving to the far west, leaving a sterile land behind.

Second, wildlife faced extinction due to the dramatic loss of wildlife habitat and the continuing slaughter of wildlife. For instance, beavers and seals were at one time frequently seen in North America, but because of fur trade, they were subject to inhuman hunting and slaughter. Around 40 million seals lost their lives between 1800 and 1915. By the end of the 19th century, it was hard to find beavers and seals in their natural habitat like the Great Lakes region. Apart from beavers and seals, buffalos and pigeons did not escape the calamity during the westward movement either. Buffalos, which once spread across the Great Plains, shrank from 60 million when Christopher Columbus discovered the New World in 1492 to almost none at the end of 19th century. As it is generally believed that buffalos crossing the Great Plains in droves would prevent trains from running safely, so the railway bureau hired hunters to kill buffalos. A western cowboy nick-named "Buffalo Bill" shot 4,000 buffalos to death in merely one and a half years, and for his hunting feats, he was hailed as a buffalo hunting hero. After the buffalo hide and bones were used to make leather and fertilizers, the killing became even more rampant. Likewise, countless pigeons in colonial times reduced to 2 billion at the beginning of the 19th century, and almost died out at the end of the 19th century.

Third and worst of all, serious land abuses brought forth troublesome environmental issues. In the 19th century, American farmers and planters customarily made the most of land productivity, but paid little attention to water and soil conservation. Once soils lost fertility, they migrated to the west in search of rich land. In most instances, abusing land happened in tobacco or cotton plantations in the south, for tobacco depleted land fertility quickly. It was usually two or three years after tobacco was cultivated in the field that land became barren. Facing this situation, most planters deserted the barren land and went further west to find new land. By the 1870s, tens of thousands of people came to the Great Plains, yet the changeable weather conditions and intertwined grassroots in the soil forced them to leave just one decade later. Up till the beginning of the 20th century, about two thirds of the farmers in the Great Plains relocated to other areas. Due to long-time over-exploitation and little conservation, a sweeping sand storm, the most destructive environmental disaster in the west, hit five states west of Kansas and formed the dust bowl in the 1930s. An average of 408 tons of topsoil per acre were swept away, and a total of 850 million tons of topsoil were blown away in the affected area, which resulted in serious soil erosion and huge water loss.

Aside from westward expansion, industrialization left resource development to enterprises, giving rise to resource waste and environmental pollution. As an important part of industrial development, the rapid growth of mining incurred salient environmental issues, with hydraulic mining in the 19th century as a case in point. Washed away by water hoses, the topsoil and gravel, together with the effluent, flew

Unit 13 American Environmental Issues and Protection

to rivers and streams, finally causing water pollution and becoming sediment in the bottom. In Central Valley, California, the sediment accumulated as high as 100 feet. In the gold mines, a large amount of gold could be found from slag after hydraulic mining. Meanwhile, the booming industrial cities like Chicago and Minneapolis were heavily polluted by soot, litter and other waste. For example, as the center of processing and manufacturing, Chicago directly poured waste into Mississippi River and negatively affected downstream water. Minneapolis discarded hundreds of millions of cubic feet of sawdust as well as hundreds of tons of waste into rivers. The growth of industrial cities allured peasants and immigrants to look for jobs in large urban cities and become city dwellers. The turn of the 20th century found urbanization on a large scale. The surge of the urban population brought about a number of social and environmental issues. As people poured into cities so fast that housing could not meet the increasing demand of accommodation, several newly-arrived families rented small and dark rooms in an apartment building with substandard living conditions, such as sharing a water tap and a toilet. Without the sewage system and garbage disposal system, the tenement building was a completely crowded and dirty slum. In city streets, garbage and animal manure were everywhere. Human waste could not be handled by the sewers and accumulated in each household. Diseases like tuberculosis and typhoid spread quickly across the urban area. The city soon became a place swarming with living, sanitation and health problems.

After WWII, the US economy gained great momentum, and entered an age of the affluent society, with a noticeable increase in the middle-class families and a large growth in real income. The endorsement of over-consumption by governments and enterprises, together with the introduction and prevalence of the credit card, propelled consumerism and stimulated Americans' desire for goods. Such consumption patterns as the installment plan, mortgage, car loan and student loan were popular among the young generation. Under such circumstances, the exploitation of natural resources was aggravated, and house refuse and production waste were generated, which damaged the urban environment. In general, in the first two decades of the postwar era, environmental issues in American society centered around the automobile exhaust, disposal of house waste, and photochemical smog, which impacted a large scope of the society with a higher degree of pollution. One of the world's best-known public hazardous events is the decade-long Los Angeles photochemical smog episode. Lasting from the 1940s to the 1950s, a series of photochemical smog incidents took place in the city of Los Angeles, where a vast increase in automobiles led to a surge in fuel consumption and exhaust emission. A large number of hydrocarbons in a UV effect formed photochemical reaction – a blue-brown smog, which invited a devastating environmental disaster. The haze with a bleach smell was indeed detrimental to the health of local people, irritating the eyes, respiratory system and skin, and causing headache, cough, sore throat, lung failure, heart attack and even death.

  If air pollution was a big environmental concern in the 1940s and 1950s, the fear of chemical and nuclear pollution prevailed in the 1960s and 1970s. The wide use of such chemical products as plastic products, pesticides, fertilizers, food additives, detergents and solvents brought about new chemical pollution. Nuclear plants, though providing electricity at a low price, led to radiation pollution. The life-threatening environmental issues caught the high attention of the government and the public. Beginning in the 1960s, environmental organizations were set up, environmental movements swept across the nation, and a number of environmental laws were passed and put into effect. However, America's retreat from the Kyoto Protocol in 2001 and its withdrawal from the Paris Agreement in 2018 cast a shadow over worldwide crusades against greenhouse gas emission and climate change. So far, both the natural environment protection and the urban environmental management have become major environmental issues. Nowadays, the hydrosphere, atmosphere, pedosphere, lithosphere and biosphere in the ecological system are all under preservation and protection, and at the same time, environmental issues like air pollution, water pollution, noise pollution, garbage pollution are vigorously tackled.

  It should be noted that environmental issues, essentially speaking, result from an aggressive sense of anthropocentricism. A humble sense of anthropocentricism once helped the human race deepen their understanding of the world and create splendid civilization. But science and technology, together with economic prosperity, make people arrogant and conceited with insatiable desires. At present, guided by anthropocentricism, the human kind ignores common characteristics between man and nature, exaggerates human beings' abilities to understand and change nature, preaches dominion and control over nature by use of reason and scientific knowledge. In other words, nature is taken as the means to the end. Thus, the solution to American environmental issues should not be separate from readjusting anthropocentrism and putting forward new environmentalist thoughts.

2 The Evolution of American Environmentalist Thoughts

Since the birth of the nation, America has experienced modernization including industrialization, urbanization, scientific advancement and social prosperity, and at the same time swallowed the bitter pill of a decreased quality of life and environmental degradation. American environmentalist thoughts are in fact the product of American society, which change with the times. In other words, the ever-changing American environmentalist thoughts are motivated by the changing environment and updated knowledge of the environment. Besides, environmental awareness developed by the elite and the public, politicians and ordinary people, ultimately contributes to the formation of American environmentalist thoughts, and American environmentalist thoughts further heighten the public sense of environmental protection and promote American environmental activism.

2.1 The Birth of American Environmentalist Thoughts

In the late 18th century, the American continent, in Europeans' eyes, was the New World full of opportunities and hopes, as was portrayed in *Letters from an American Farmer* (1782) by French-American author J. Hector St. John de Crèvecœur. Many English and French philosophers also took America as the ideal place to realize their dreams, for they believed that the US hadn't been corrupted by greed and idleness yet. In Americans' view, compared with developed European countries with long history and profound culture, due to its short history, lack of cultural traditions, backward economy, the young country could take pride in only one thing – the beauty of nature or the wildness. What Americans hadn't been aware was that the abundance of wildness and natural resources created a land of plenty, which helped to shape distinctive conceptions of the society and environment. During this particular period, the mechanical conception of nature, which held that the relationship between man and nature was confrontational, coexisted with the ecological view that endorsed a harmonious relation between the two.

Thomas Jefferson (1743 – 1862), third president of the United States, thought that industry and commerce in Europe not only incurred poverty and corruption, but also invited social instability. Therefore, he believed that, in order to prevent those problems from occurring in the US, America should build an agrarian society, and America's exceptional geographical and natural conditions would make that happen. "The Jeffersonian Idyll" designed a nation consisting of small independent self-sufficient farmers, where great importance would be attached to human resources rather than natural resources, because, in the US, land was abundant but labor was scarce, while in Europe, it was just the opposite. Undoubtedly, in the blueprint laid out by Jefferson, land was the means to secure one's survival as well as pursue freedom and happiness, which emphasized man's control and rule over nature. Thus, land should be distributed to individuals, and yeoman ought to be made the master of land. In doing so, on can create a better life on his own land, so as to make the whole society stable and the nation's ethos simple and unsophisticated. In the Jeffersonian era, America became a real agrarian society, where 90 percent of the total population were farmers; besides, in keeping with the economic structure and demographic composition characterized by a predominantly agricultural nature, American society and American governments at all levels were simple and plain.

Evidently, Jefferson's vision of an agrarian society, in many ways, reflected the

Unit 13　American Environmental Issues and Protection

Arcadian ideal and physiocracy in the European cultural tradition. And their thoughts, to a great extent, affected American land and economic policies in the 19th century, which allured a large number of European immigrants to continuously move to the US. When the newly-come immigrants found no more fertile land in the east, they began to cross the Appalachian Mountains and journeyed westward. At this moment, they needed to conquer wildness, wildlife and Native Americans on their way to the west. Different from American Indians who believed in animism and treated land as their mother, the white settlers capitalized on land, regarding it as a form of property and capital. With this in mind, the frontiersmen cleared up forest, reclaimed land, and got the maximum of land. But after land lost its fertility, they deserted the sterile land and searched for new land, leaving eroded soil, denuded slopes, and litter behind. At the same time, Jefferson's ideals of an idyllic life and a beautiful natural environment also laid the foundation for shaping early environmentalist thoughts, because their efforts in building an agrarian nation, to a certain extent, slowed down the destruction and erosion of the pastoral life and vast areas of wildness caused by industrialization and capital expansion.

　　If Thomas Jefferson stood for the government stance, Ralph Waldo Emerson (1803 – 1882) and Henry David Thoreau (1817 – 1862) represented voices of a number of social elites who expanded their vision from agriculture to nature. Ralph Waldo Emerson, one of the founders of American literature and mind, spearheaded the transcendentalist movement in New England in the mid-19th century. Drawing on European romanticism which idealized nature, the philosophy of transcendentalism, expressed in Emerson's essay "Nature" (1837), held that nature's spirit was the Supreme Being, so nature could be used for regeneration and spiritual guidance. As a young and independent nation, in Emerson's view, American should shake off the shackles of European cultural traditions and religious thought, and form its own culture and thought. Hence, the key to American intellectual independent was to understand nature from a new perspective. Here, nature was more philosophically defined as a power to evoke people's emotion so as to purify and uplift their spirit, rather than a practical material to bring a large amount of wealth to capitalists. Emerson encouraged everyone to use their eyes, body and heart to experience nature and feel divinity. Viewed in such a light, the divine, man and nature were inseparable and integrated.

Emerson espoused the idea that the universe consisted of nature and the soul. Nature referred to the material world and physical form of the soul. The soul, independent of consciousness, was eternal and absolute in the universe. The mythic power was named by Emerson as "the over-soul", equal to the omnipotent and the deity. As part of nature, the humankind was part of the physical form of the over-soul, and everyone bore an inner power of communicating with the over-soul. Thus, nature was the agent between the over-soul and human-beings. If one loved nature, his internal sense was closely bound up with his external sense. For instance, when one was appreciating the beauty of nature, there occurred a swell of emotion like joy, sadness, excitement in one's heart. For the time being, the over-soul in nature and one's mind echoed and mingled with each other. However, if one's unsophisticated mind was corrupted by desires for wealth, power and fame, he would lose the ability to communicate with nature and the over-soul. Emerson thought that, with the nation engaged in industrialization and commercialization, the physical value of nature had been overstated, so people were more likely to be at a loss to realize the fundamental significance of existence. For this matter, it is better for men to keep a distance from the hustle and bustle, enjoy the solitude, and open their hearts to nature.

Overall, Emerson started the trend of rethinking nature, inspiring many people to look to nature for spiritual power. Nature extolled and respected by Emerson was divine and ever-lasting, with purifying and reviving strength as well as inexhaustible resources. Therefore, Emerson, like most of his contemporaries, had a mixed feeling toward nature: on the one hand, worshiping nature and on the other hand, supporting the invasion of nature by industry and technology. Undeniably, Emerson's meditation on nature was still anthropocentric, placing human as his central concern. Emerson's experiment with transcendentalism concentrated on constructing thought, and it was

Unit 13 American Environmental Issues and Protection

his student Henry David Thoreau who put transcendental ideas into real practice and formed a deeper understanding of nature.

Having read Emerson's "Nature" and having maintained close contact with Emerson, Thoreau was not unfamiliar with transcendentalism. Moreover, he realized the importance of the unity of practice and knowledge, i.e. enriching the understanding of nature through direct contact with nature. In Thoreau's lifetime, apart from writing and making a living, he spent most of his time on strolling around and observing nature. He was quite a hit in town when he left his hometown to live at Walden Pond on the Independence Day of 1845, a small lake that was 3.4 kilometers away from the town center. He cut off pine trees in the bank and built a little wooden cabin facing the lake; besides, he grew corn, beans and potatoes around the cabin. He lived a self-sustained and secluded life by the lake for two years plus two months and two days. One side of the lake was close to the railroad, and the other side was a paralleled road. In short, the place was not an inaccessible area, but still far enough to separate from the bustling society. Then, Thoreau started to explore the meaning of life by living a simple life. Though Thoreau lived in a time of industrialization and secularization, when dominion over nature and exploitation of nature were accepted by most Americans, he thought that strong desires for materials and material comforts disturbed the peaceful mind and incurred the spiritual barrenness of the society. So his experiences were designed to prove that with basic necessities, one could live well and maintain a healthy life. In Thoreau's daily life, he neither ate meat nor drank coffee or liquor. There was only a handful of furniture in his cabin: a bed, a desk, a table, three chairs, a frying pan, a saucepan, a kettle, three plates, two sets of knife and fork, a cup and a kerosene lamp. He found that, it only took him around six weeks a year to work in order to earn his living, and then he could enjoy the rest of the year and do what he felt like doing, such as going for a stroll in the woods, observing nature, reading, pondering and writing, etc. His living experiences at Walden Pond enabled him to establish intimate relationship with nature, treating the squirrel, the raven and the marmot as his family. He realized that, this lifestyle was not only beneficial to man's spiritual advancement, but also conducive to the balance and tranquility of nature. At last, Thoreau put his experiences, thoughts and feelings of the living experiment in his masterpiece *Walden*, which has been published in over 200 versions and different languages.

After Thoreau left the Walden Pond, he began a transcendental way of life: understanding the self through studying nature. He kept contact with nature, immersing in and integrating himself with nature. Each day, he observed and perceived nature through touching and smelling the natural world. Even in the cold weather, he would wear a coat and sit on the rock or stump overgrown with moss, listening to the sound of by-passing sparrows, tasting roots, leaves, acorns, and breathing the smell of the earth. It occurred to him that, there lay a rich collection of living beings on the earth, which was composed of varied natural relations, and anything in the collection, including animals, plants, even stone and sand, was a form of life. He called this collection as "a love community," a wonderland for all the living beings. In the community, nature provided aesthetic joy and health to human-beings, and showed sympathy to those who were sad and in miserable situations. More significantly, nature was able to cure man's moral evils. So, if one had frequent contact with nature, his morality could be enhanced and vices reduced. In full communion with nature, it enabled Thoreau to show respect to everything around him, which conflicted with man's dominion over nature in the doctrines of Protestantism and humanism that put men above animals and other living beings in nature. Because of this, he did not go to church, and couldn't tolerate the arrogance that humanists showed to nature. What's worth mentioning is that, while pursuing integration with nature, Thoreau was also in pursuit of a life that transcended nature, i.e. a self-liberating and self-displaying life without natural bondage. His saying "in wildness is the preservation of the world" manifested an ideal status – a balance between the wild and the civilized, a world imbued with both a cultural ethos and a natural smell. In general, Thoreau unconsciously took the eco-centric stance, and what he advocated and practiced, though not widely understood and accepted in his days, has been fully borrowed and applied as well as further developed in modern environmentalist thoughts and activism.

Taken together, there are two groups of environmentalist thoughts in this period, with one embraced by government officials and the other advocated by social elites. Both groups start from individualism, but they have distinct differences. Jefferson emphasized control over nature and utilization of land, which took nature as a material provider. By contrast, Emerson and Thoreau attached importance to man's integration with nature, which to a large extent, put man in a proper position and reduced tension between man and nature. According to Emerson's and Thoreau's ideal, the omnipotent power suffused nature and nature was brimming with vitality and divinity, which inspired people to renew their understanding of nature and respect nature. Nevertheless, the majority of Americans were too intoxicated with the benefits from conquering nature to realize the severity of environmental issues, and the views of Emerson and Thoreau did not immediately affect American public policies until the end of the 19th century.

2.2 The Environmental Awakening

In the antebellum period, the industrial output of the US was less than half that of the UK, but after the Civil War, America soon became the top industrial nation in the world. Indisputably, America's tremendous development rested on its abundant natural resources. However, capitalists' predatory exploitation of nature, together with Americans' indifference to natural resources, gave rise to massive waste and severe damage. For example, in the era of the territorial expansion and economic advancement, large areas of forest vanished, wildlife was on the verge of extinction, and the ecological environment in the west, subject to large-scale agricultural, husbandry, mining development, deteriorated. Besides, the Civil War brought back unity and stability to the nation, but at the same time, it did great damage to the natural world, which prompted people to realize that their huge impacts on nature had causative connection with the occurrence of modern environmentalist thoughts.

Afterwards, under the guidance of laissez-faire economic development pattern, individual Americans accumulated wealth in an unrestricted way. For instance, frontiersmen wantonly developed the Great Plains, and companies monopolized and operated exclusively for profit, which invited class polarization and wealth disparity between the rich and the poor. Meanwhile, industrialization, urbanization and immigration incurred heaps of garbage, the spread of disease, and environmental deterioration, which posed a threat to man's life, health and quality of livelihood. The increasingly serious environmental and social problems spurred the public to, on the one hand, be aware that their attitudes and government policies toward nature should be adjusted, and on the other hand, reflect on the laissez-faire capitalism and use progressive and pragmatic perspectives to tackle problems. Crowned as a secular third Great Awakening, progressivism emphasized equality, by showing concern for disadvantaged groups and opposing the law of the jungle. Moreover, it aimed to restrict the private economic power by utilizing the national public power, marking the transition from classical liberalism to modern liberalism. Pragmatism, the everlasting dominant philosophy in American society, believed that truth was as always in the making, and advocated taking flexible measures in accordance with circumstances. "Resource conservation" and "wildness preservation," two leading schools of environmentalist thoughts, arose out of the particular historical background.

Echoing the Fair Deal policies, president Theodore Roosevelt (1858 – 1919) and the 4th chief of the Division of Forestry Gifford Pinchot (1865 – 1946) promoted the concept of "conservation" at the White House Conference on Conservation in 1908. It brought water, forests, rangelands that used to be developed separately under the government's regulation. Through the wise and efficient use of natural resources, conservation served for "the greatest good of the greatest number for the longest time." Because of this, conservation was also defined as utilitarian thought that utilized natural resources to enhance one's happiness. Actually, as early as the 18th century, naturalists had noticed a wonderful balance and order in nature and the practical utility of nature to human beings, laying the ground for the idea of conservation in the 20th century.

Unit 13 American Environmental Issues and Protection

In 1902, the first chief of the Division of Forestry Bernard Fernow (1851 – 1923) came up with a utilitarian policy of faire-marcher (a French term), meaning "to make it work," which served as the basis of conservation. As advocates for conservation and architects of the conservation movement, Roosevelt and Pinchot took conservation as an important measure to secure the public interest and social morality, and branded it with nationalism and pragmatism. After president Roosevelt spiritedly made a speech on conservation at the 1908 conference, the American government started the conservation movement to replant trees, reseed rangelands, construct dams, preserve forests and watershed across the country, which soon became a national crusade. During this period, the US Forest Service and the National Conservation Commission were set up to present findings for resource management. Meanwhile, the National Conference on Conservation and the North American Conservation Conference were held to promote the conservation movement, with 100 million acres of land reclaimed and 118 forest reserves established. The national forest reserves expanded from 46 million acres to 150 billion acres across the nation. But the achievements could not hide the fact that conservation built upon the protection of the national economic system rather than "nature's economy," which treated all the living beings on the earth as an integrated whole. Therefore, nature was taken as "other" which provided resources and materials. With this guiding principle in mind, such animals as cattle and deer were viewed as being useful to man and thus needed to be protected. By contrast, such ferocious beasts as wolves and mountain lions were considered to be useless varmints and therefore should be exterminated. The progressive approach made conservation activists optimistic that meticulous management carried out by the government would automatically result in rational planning and development of resources. Yet the reality proved that, driven by utilitarianism and pragmatism, the government, like individuals and private enterprises, could become a destructive power that brought discords to nature, and at the same time, technologies did not necessarily bring efficiency and order to nature.

Apart from the conservation movement started by prominent government officials, there arose the preservation movement to preserve wilderness supported by social elites. According to John Muir, one of the earliest advocates for preservation and an influential figure in the preservation movement, wild nature, like mountains, lakes, meadows, valleys and deserts, should be set aside for aesthetic appreciation and recreational benefits. Thus, preservation was also called "aesthetic preservation," i.e. the protection of nature beyond utility. Like conservationists, preservationists stood on the shoulders of previous naturalists and social activists. Moreover, it drew inspiration from romantic and transcendentalist artwork. In 1832, George Catlin, a famous explorer in the American west and painter of landscape, conceived an idea of preserving natural landscape through creating national parks. The transcendentalist Henry David Thoreau suggested in 1859 that every town should set aside 500 to 1000 acres of parks or pristine forest areas for intellectual nourishment and entertainment. In the 1860s, Frederick Law Olmsted added the appreciation of natural beauty to the right of "the pursuit of happiness" in the *Declaration of Independence*, and supported the government to take charge of wildness for common use. As an outstanding landscape architect, Olmsted stressed the importance of getting in touch with nature, which served as therapy for one's tired body and disturbed mind. In view of this, he designed Central Park in New York City, which made it possible for the rich and the poor to have easy access to at least man-made landscape similar to natural landscape. In historian Frederick Jackson Turner's eyes, wilderness was closely related to the formation of American individualism, national character and democratic system. In the public mind, nature was associated with vigor, toughness, and even the supreme power of God, which was exemplified by Muir's view of mountains as God's cathedrals. Hence, one could reaffirm and reassert his/her strength and identity, as well as acquire and regain moral and intellectual forces through getting out into the wilderness. Influenced by natural theology, Muir was adamant that all the living beings should be viewed as equal and the human race belonged to the natural community created by God. One of his well-known sayings was that there was the hope of the world in the wilderness made by God. He believed that only when man returned to the wilderness could he restore his nature. From the 1870s onward, he wrote articles, set up the environmental club and popularized the preservationists' ideas to arouse the public awareness of environmental protection, and called for the government's involvement in founding national parks and forest reserves.

As a matter of fact, beginning in the 1890s, wilderness was no longer synonymous with savagery, danger, evil; instead, it became the fortress for American democracy, a spiritual source and pure land. There emerged the craze for wilderness. For instance, outdoor activities including hiking, horse-riding, fishing, camping, canoeing, and skiing attracted an increasing number of Americans, and related outdoor groups such as the Appalachian Mountain Club (1876), the Boone and Crockett Club (1887), the Campfire Club of America (1897) were organized. Parents encouraged their children join the Scouts, so as to cultivate children's independent and tough characters by means of exposure to the wilderness. Books and pamphlets, which celebrated the value and virtues of wilderness and displayed picturesque landscape, were popular among the general public. What's worth mentioning was that, by setting up their own clubs such as the General Federation of Women's Clubs (1890) and the Garden Club of America (1913), women expressed their concern over lost wilderness and vanishing wildlife, and heroically took up the cause of protecting nature. Thanks to the unfailing efforts of Muir, women's organizations, naturalists, foresters, sportsmen, artists, and other preservation activists, the first national park Yellow Stone National Park was created in 1872 and Yosemite (1890), Sequoia (1890), General Grant (1890), Mt. Rainier (1899) were established within the following three decades. During the administration of president Roosevelt, 53 wildlife reserves and 16 national forest reserves were founded.

As two important camps of environmentalist thoughts between the late 19th century and the 1920s, conservation and preservation bear similarities and differences, leaving enduring legacy in American history. First, branded as progressivism, both conservation and preservation stressed that everyone had equal right to use natural resources and appreciate the scenic beauty of wilderness. Furthermore, they emphasized the government's involvement in and regulation of environmental issues through legal means. It signified a start in utilizing social justice to dilute the negative impacts of "rugged individualism" advocated by classic liberalism. Second, conservation and preservation contained an undertone of pragmatism. Based on the actual needs of American society for the time being, conservation focused on improving material benefits for production and living, while preservation, on the basis of long-term development, laid stress on mental benefits of purifying the mind and uplifting the spirit. Third, the stance of conservationists was both in conflict and complementary with that of preservationists. Conservationists, while exploiting water and forests for economic growth and public good, also made efforts in preserving nature. For example, the US Forest Service, once led by Pinchot, introduced laws and regulations concerning wilderness preservation in the 1930s. Meanwhile, in their propaganda, preservationists argued that, since wilderness provided abundant recreational and scenic resources, mental benefits of wilderness would ultimately lead to and even multiply material benefits. This assertion made it easier for the public to accept the ethic of preservation and then support the preservation movement. Fourth, conservation and preservation modified the public perception of individual rights and responsibilities, and created the environmental management state, paving the way for modern liberalism. Last but not least, both resource conservation and wilderness preservation deeply influenced powerful government leaders like president Theodore Roosevelt and modern environmental policies and activism. Starting from the administration of president Roosevelt, the American government redressed the laissez-faire policies imposed on utilization of natural resources, implemented a wise and efficient use of water and forest resources, and preserved wilderness and recreational areas. In fact, "the scientific use of resources" advocated by Pinchot affected the formation of the concept of "sustainable development" in modern environmental policy-making and the conservative faction of modern environmentalism, while Muir's preservation ethic nurtured the thought of the radical wing of modern environmentalism.

2.3 The Advancement of American Environmentalist Thoughts

Along with the economic growth by leaps and bounds in the 1920s, America became the richest country in the world. With a noticeable increase in salary and a decrease in working time, ordinary Americans obtained time and money to purchase a large number of consumer goods, ranging from radios, watches, lighters, vacuum cleaners to washing machines, etc. Laissez-faire, which was once checked in the progressive era, regained the upper hand. There arose a modern lifestyle based on such secular values as materialism, hedonism and consumerism. Nevertheless, social crisis hid beneath economic prosperity. In 1929, the stock market crash triggered a severe economic recession. During the Great Depression, factories were closed and workers were laid off. To make matters worse, upon the implementation of the New Deal, the largest sand storm in history swept across the Great Plains and went on hitting the east coast in 1934. Farmlands and cities were clouded with a thick coat of dust and dirt. Quickly after the sand storm, a long spell of destructive drought in the Great Plains caused a sharp drop in harvest. From 1935 onwards, the nation known as "the bread basket of the world" had no choice but to import agricultural products from other countries. Families in the drought-stricken "dust bowl" of the Midwest fled in succession to California, the nearby place with pleasant weather and lucrative agriculture. Facing the drastic economic decline and the worst natural disasters, Americans couldn't help searching for the causes of as well as the solutions to those problems. They came to realize that those natural disasters they suffered were the results of reckless human activities. In other words, unrestrained individualism and heroism of frontiersmen were responsible for the disasters. Recognizing the real culprits, Americans began to take a more collective attitude, including maintaining the integrity and wholeness of the ecological system. With such changes in perception, America entered the era of modern liberalism, with the government's comprehensive involvement and limited intervention in economy. Besides, governments took the responsibilities for the public welfare. In this particular period, based on organism and holism, the ecological study gave a comprehensive examination of the relationship between humans and nonhuman nature. All of these circumstances exerted huge impacts on environmental policy-making and reshaped environmentalist thoughts. In many aspects, environmentalist thoughts at the time was the continuation and development of conservation and preservation in the first two decades of the 20th century.

One of the most influential environmentalist thoughts is "New Deal conservation" championed by president Franklin D. Roosevelt, which is in line with "conservation" advocated by Theodore Roosevelt. Like the former conservation policies, New Deal conservation gives priority to the utilitarian ethic and scientific use of natural resources, but it has distinguishing features from earlier conservation. Marked with the spirit of the New Deal, New Deal conservation integrated conservation with social welfare. First, under the guidance of New Deal conservation, the federal government went all out to implement wise management of natural resources which were essential to social advancement and well-being, such as public works programs, forest management, large-scale irrigation projects, soil conservation, etc. Among all the welfare state programs, the Civilian Conservation Corps (CCC) operating from 1933 throughout 1942 stood out most conspicuously. As a federal work-relief program, CCC provided vocational training for unemployed young men to plant trees, construct roads, build dams and parks in the back country, which not only brought social security by benefitting jobless people, but also promoted the conservation of natural resources and the preservation of national parks in the particular period. Aside from CCC, large dam-building projects sponsored by the government also represented remarkable conservation achievements in the New Deal era. The Tennessee Valley Authority (TVA) on the Tennessee River (1933) and Hoover Dam on the Colorado River (1935) exemplified man's strength and wisdom to make full use of hydroelectric power for flood control, easy irrigation, and social welfare. Furthermore, influenced by the rise of ecology, New Deal conservation underscored the stability and balance of the biotic community including soil, grasses, wildlife and their habitats, revealing a trace of ecological holism. Comparatively speaking, conservation under the administration of Theodore Roosevelt paid attention to forests, water resources, and rangelands, but lacked systematic and comprehensive planning. Finally, New Deal conservation emphasized immediate actions and actual effects. Serious sand storms forced the federal government to send the Great Plains Committee to investigate environmental issues of the Great Plains. The committee found out that, in order to obtain speculative profits, people destroyed the ecosystem of the Great Plains by plundering cultivation. In accordance with the report presented by the Great Plains Committee, a series of laws were passed to regulate farmers' activities and preserve soil. The *Taylor Grazing Act* (1934) was made to control the grazing time and limit the number of animals in the Great Plains. One year later, the *Soil Conservation Act* (1935) was passed to create soil conservation districts and shelter forests. Both acts helped prevent soil erosion and promoted the soil to restore its fertility. By the end of 1941, a total of 75 soil conservation districts were established across the nation, and a belt of billions of shelter forests stretched from the state of Texas to the US-Canadian border. The *Pittman-Robertson Wildlife Restoration Act* (1937) intended to advance the restoration of wildlife and its habitat for multiple purposes of economic growth, scientific research and recreational use. Along with the act came changing attitudes towards wildlife resources, especially the predators used to be taken as varmints. The indispensable role of each species in the ecosystem had been rediscovered and reassessed by ecologists, conservationists and preservationists. Nonetheless, due to the utilitarian and pragmatic basis of conservation and the anthropocentric belief, one could be easily swayed by the present benefits and immediate comfort. For instance, while initiating soil conservation districts, farmers still as usual regarded nature as servants of social progress, so they carried out the policies that benefited them immediately like soil preservation, instead of maintaining ecological equilibrium of the Great Plains from the perspective of its long-term development. At that time, the destruction of resources was ascribed to technology rather than the social and economic system, and conservation organizations were mostly clubs set up by wealthy men, in short of mass participation and a broad social base.

Regarding the flaws of New Deal conservation, ecologist Aldo Leopold explicitly pointed out the source of the environmental problem and its ultimate solution. He believed that the majority of what the utilitarian conservation protected was not of economic value, so the way to solve the problem was to discard putting human interest first and defining things according to their economic value. Since childhood, Leopold loved outdoor activities, observing birds in particular. When he grew up, Leopold studied at the Forest School of Yale University, served in the Forest Service of the Southwestern United States after graduation. As one of Gifford Pinchot's followers, he once firmly believed in the utilitarian conservation ethic, dividing resources into two categories – useful and useless, and even participated in the extermination of predators like wolves, mountain lions and coyotes supported by the federal government. When working as a forester, he was well aware that soil erosion could not be simply attributed to the changing climate; instead, the unwise use of land or abusing land was the most significant reason. In addition, in the 1930s, the popularization of ecology in the US brought home to Leopard a holistic and comprehensive perspective to perceive the ecosystem, and the visit to Germany to learn the management of forestry and wildlife left a deep impression on him, which helped him to establish the first university curriculum on wildlife management at the University of Wisconsin. In order to experience the whole process of ecosystem restoration, he bought a deserted farm in a suburban area and lived there for thirteen years. In the past, this place was inhabited by Native Americans who led a pastoral life on it. But later on, because of the over-exploitation of white settlers, it became a sandy land named "sandy county". For the sake of helping nature recover, Leopold planted thousands of pine trees and shrubs. In doing so, he acquired a new understanding of man and nature. It was Leopold's study, work and living experiences in his early years that taught him lessons, discarded the utilitarian conservation ethic, and turned to propose a new ethic – the Land Ethic.

In Leopold's land ethic, the role of the human race changed from conqueror to plain member of the land community, which was composed of soils, waters, plants, animals and human-beings, and members of the community were equal and interdependent. He asserted that only love, respect and admiration for the community as well as high regard for the land's philosophical value could lead to the integrity, stability and beauty of the land community. According to his ethic, the individual rights and obligations to other members were stressed, including respect for other members and the community, which implied the restrictions and constraints for man's behaviors. Leopold went on to put forward the principle of the land ethic: when a thing was conducive to the preservation of the integrity, stability and beauty of the land community, it was right; when it was the other way round, it was wrong. On the basis of this idea, he further pointed out that human kind should shoulder the responsibility of the land ethic, so as to alleviate the decentralization of the government functions and the utilitarian guiding thought. Leopold put his experiences in the sand county and his land ethics in *A Sand County Almanac,* which was crowned as the Bible for the modern American conservation movement.

In many aspects, the land ethic, full of rich philosophical and ecological significance, reflected the collective ethos of the New Deal era. It draws inspiration from various philosophers and ecologists. For instance, the idea expressed by Peter D. Ouspensky that all the living things in the universe have lives and feelings, the opinion held by Alfred North Whitehead that all the living and nonliving things were integrated and interdependent with each other, the humanistic concern of reverence for life extolled by Albert Schweitzer, and the concept of the food chain, niche, energy flow, biotic community, etc. All of these insights contribute to the formation of the land ethic. The most significant part of the land ethic lies in its deconstruction of the anthropocentric conservation ethic, the expansion of the ethical application range, as well as the construction of ecocentrism that integrated natural science and social science, scientific spirit and ethics. History has shown that the forward-looking perspective and profound meaning of the land ethic have greatly broadened the vision of the concept of community and the interest of the subject, spurring the arrival of the environmental era. It should be noted that, while ecology tended to be similar to mechanism and reductionism relying on quantitative analysis, the land ethic, on the foundation of ecology, was also getting narrower. In addition, although Leopold criticized the conservation ethic again and again, he himself more often than not understood the land ethic from the instrumental angle. The paradox occurred, partly because he thought that, the discourse, if made from the instrumental perspective, would be easier for the public to accept, and partly because his assertions hardly escaped being influenced by pragmatism. To put it simply, the land ethic, to a certain degree, was in essence a means of wealth expansion and accumulation.

Overall, both the New Deal conservation and the land ethic came into being when the US slumped from its prime time to the nadir. Imbued with the enterprising and pragmatic spirit of American traditions, they advocate increasing government functions and the collective mentality, as well as taking the holistic perspective of ecology. Apart from the similarities that they share, there lie distinctive differences between the two. The New Deal conservation lays emphasis on the economic value and equality within the human-beings community. As the further development of conservation, apart from productivity and benefits, the New Deal conservation is also dedicated to the improvement of social welfare and well-being. By contrast, the land ethic lays stress on the philosophical and ethical values as well as equality within the biotic community. As a huge advancement of preservation, the land ethic signifies the transformation from anthropocentrism to ecocentrism. Serving as the link between past and future environmentalist thoughts, the New Deal conservation and the land ethic not only promoted the environmental consciousness-raising of the public and the further development of environmental movements, but also pushed forward the historical change from respecting individual freedom to upholding equality and justice.

2.4 The Vigorous Growth

After WWII, America enjoyed unprecedented prosperity, stepping into an affluent society. American industrial output accounted for one-half of the world's industrial output and its gross domestic product per capita increased by 106 percent within just three decades, far ahead of other developed countries. By the mid-1950s, American's actual disposable income was already twice that in the prime time of the 1920s. Besides, American agriculture was fully mechanized by the 1960s and electrified by the 1970s. Those improvements, together with widespread use of fertilizers and pesticides, the agricultural productivity and output experienced significant growth, which made America an agricultural power. Meanwhile, the third technological revolution promoted the invention and application of new energy, new materials, space technology and the computer. From the 1950s onwards, large numbers of nuclear plants were put into production, and lots of light and durable synthetic products such as synthetic fiber, synthetic detergent, synthetic building materials came into areas of production and life. In 1969, the Apollo Moon Landing showed enormous human power.

The post-war era also witnessed the modernization of the lifestyle, which was characterized by electrification, convenience, efficiency and comfortableness. Such household appliances as the TV, the telephone, the refrigerator, the air-conditioner, the hair dryer as well as the automobile found their way into every American family. As large as 80 percent of all the families owned one TV set, and 13% of the families purchased more than two TV sets. Each day, Americans spent four to five hours watching TV. Television largely enriched American life, and played an important role in sending environment-related news and information. The invention and popularity of the credit card assisted in consumerism. To some extent, Americans took consumption quantity as the measurement of their happiness, and treated consumption as the symbol of social status. In most instances, American's consuming behavior was influenced by morbid views such as keeping up with the Joneses, and wasteful spending. During the latter half of the 20th century, there was a noticeable increase in the size of middle-class families and education attainment, with 60 percent of the total population belonging to the middle class, and 50 percent of youth between 18 to 21 attending colleges or universities by the end of the 1960s. Politically speaking, modern liberalism, in full swing for three decades since the New Deal era, reached its peak during the administration of president Lyndon Johnson, and liberalism had become the dominant or even the single intellectual tradition at that time. Under modern liberalism, the government fully intervened and administered social affairs, trying to meet the demands of different interest groups.

The prosperous life, technological change, growing education attainment, together with enhanced social security drove people to make a higher demand for quality of life. Accordingly, public concern displayed a shift in focus from leisure and recreation in the 1950s, pollution and pesticides in the 1960s, to human health and energy in the 1970s. For instance, in the post-war years, a surging number of middle-class families moved to suburban areas with better environments. By 1970, there were approximately 80 million Americans living in suburbs, while 65 million Americans lived in urban areas. Meanwhile, American citizens longed to return to the wildness and have more contact with nature. The craze for wilderness once occurred in the 1920s reemerged in this period, and a variety of outdoor activities like mountain-climbing, skiing, hiking, camping and fishing enjoyed popularity again. The gradual reduction in yearly work hours made it possible for people to spend more leisure time on travelling, recreation and entertainment. In this social milieu, Americans' memory of the dust bowl was diluted, and they began to be intoxicated with progress and abundance for the moment. A large number of Americans held that they had created an environment of their own rather than depend on the natural environment, overflowing with arrogant anthropocentrism. The publication of Rachel Carson's *Silent Spring* in 1962 brought the abuse and health effects of pesticides to public attention and enlarged the environmental consciousness of the nation. Afterwards, environmentalism, arising out of this historical period, became the dominant environmentalist thoughts, and environmental activism exploded.

Based on ecocentrism and guided by ecology, environmentalism viewed the environmental problem and man's position in the environment by adopting the stance of the ecological system as a whole. It has inherited the efficiency-oriented,

Unit 13 American Environmental Issues and Protection

technology-driven conservation and recreation-oriented wilderness preservation, recognized the importance and profundity of Leopold's land ethics and put it into full application. Moreover, it absorbed the essence of a variety of thoughts fostered by the Civil Rights Movement, the feminist movement, the counterculture movement, the New Left movement and the anti-Vietnam war crusade. First, in environmentalists' minds, the Civil Rights Movement advocated the elimination of racial discrimination and the establishment of an egalitarian society, which indicated that each subject of right, both the mainstream and disadvantaged groups included, should be able to enjoy the same healthy environment. Striving for the right to the environment and fighting against poverty became the link between environmental activism and the Civil Rights Movement. Second, environmentalism also drew much inspiration from feminism, and they intermingled with each other to form eco-feminism. According to eco-feminism, an analogy was made between women and nature in terms of their ability to procreate and cultural connections between them, so the social oppression of women was in parallel with man's exploitation and pollution of nature. In line with this logic, the feminist movement and the environmental movement shared the same goal of fighting against a mechanistic and hierarchical worldview as well as liberating both women and nature. Third, hippies in the countercultural movement believed that, society at this point was reduced to a morbid one that kept to technological rationality and spawned insatiable desires. However, technological progress and industrial development preached by mainstream society engendered the degradation of the ecological environment and the alienation of the mass. Therefore, they called for ending the American way of life, getting closer to nature, as well as respecting and preserving the natural environment. Fourth, the New Leftists, to a certain extent, contributed to environmentalism. They sharply criticized the American lifestyle and modern technology, which brought social conformity and materialism and eroded the mind and environment. In addition, they argued that the rule over nature inevitably led to control over the human. Furthermore, their strong opposition to involvement in the Vietnam war and the nuclear arms race was in accordance with environmentalists' standpoint. Last but not least, the anti-Vietnam war movement opposed the use of such weapons of mass destruction as nuclear weapons and biochemical weapons, with a disgust for violence, war and technocracy, because those destructive behaviors would not only cause significant casualties, but also incur long-term irreversible damage on the battlefields and even the global natural environment. In this connection, the environmental movement and the anti-Vietnam war movement went hand in hand.

Greatly influenced by environmentalism, the US finally entered the environmental decade – the 1970s. The public's perception of environment experienced transformation, the government enlarged its involvement in environmental management and environmental activities gained momentum across the nation and around the world. Specifically speaking, the environmental awareness and participation of the American people increased considerably. The denotation of "environment" expanded from wilderness and physical resources before WWII to all the external factors such as air quality, water quality, noise, working and living environment that affected human health in the post-war years. Moreover, with the improvement of living conditions and development of medical and health care services, the physical conditions of the public were enhanced, which spurred the expansion of the view of health and connected health with environment. Furthermore, the value of environment was fully recognized and widely accepted, especially nature's aesthetic and scenic value, so that more and more people were willing to support and join environmental organization and activities. The members of the five big environmental organizations (the Izaak Walton League, the National Wildlife Federation, the National Audubon Society, the Wilderness Society, the Sierra Club) increased by 177 percent within nine years, including a number of well-known scientists and intellectuals, whose involvement made environmental crusades more effective and professional. Meanwhile, new organizations were founded, such as the Environmental Defense Fund (1967), the International Fund for Animal Welfare (1967), Friends of the Earth (1969), the Nature Preserves Commission (1970), Greenpeace (1971), etc. In daily life, Americans recycled waste, reduced the use of disposable items, and picked up

Unit 13 American Environmental Issues and Protection

litter in their community. On April 22, 1970, American citizens from all walks of life, from little children to the elderly, took part in marches, rallies and debates to call for environmental protection, and after that, April 22 was set up as Earth Day. Each year, the theme of Earth Day would be determined in accordance with the environmental situation and urgent environmental issues, so as to help environmental activities become more focused. With the enhancement of environmental awareness, ecology-related terms, pamphlets and books enjoyed popularity, the reports and documentaries presented by journals, newspapers, radios and TV programs were on the increase, and environmental protection was written into textbooks of colleges as well as primary and secondary schools.

Equally significant, in the era of environmental regulation, large numbers of new environmental laws were passed and implemented, a number of new environmental agencies were established, and environmental disputes were challenged and resolved. Through the passage of environmental legislation that set high standards for environmental protection, such as the *Clean Air Act* (1963), the *Wilderness Act* (1964), the *Water Quality Control Act* (1965), the *Wild and Scenic Rivers Act* (1968), the *National Environmental Policy Act* (1969), the *Environmental Pesticide Control Act* (1972), the *Endangered Species Act* (1973), the *Safe Drinking Water Act* (1974), the *Resources Conservation and Recovery Act* (1976), the *Toxic Substances Control Act* (1976) and the *Clean Water Act* (1977), the US government mounted great efforts to regulate human behaviors and activities. In order to vigorously enforce environmental laws, several agencies under the executive branch were created, e.g. the Environmental Protection Agency (1970), the Nuclear Regulatory Commission (1974), and the Water Resources Council (1979), etc. As a rule, these agencies would administer the regulation of water and air quality, harmful substances, and waste disposal. Environmental litigation developed by nonprofit organizations like the Environmental Defense Fund (1967) and the National Resources Defense Council (1970) brought lawsuits to courts at all levels. Rulings of the Judiciary promoted environmental protection for preservation and conservation purposes, and curtailed serious environmental pollution. By taking a comprehensive environmental response and an integrated management approach, the US, with the long-term use of resources and quality of life in mind, reinforced and expanded its role as an environmental management state, working towards establishing a harmonious relationship between man and nature.

All these improvements, from the public's awareness and participation to laws, regulations and court cases, from marches and researches to international cooperation, revealed that environmentalism under modern liberalism made breakthrough in theoretic understanding, popular support, and the extent of influence. Consequently, the influential environmentalist thoughts not only transformed the public's environmental perception and awareness, but also injected vitality to liberalism to move further left. It should not be ignored that, like the plural cultural elements in modern liberalism that were hard to be unified, the myriad of values included in environmentalist thoughts may be in conflict with each other. For instance, the guidance of government policies may not meet the environmental demands of the grassroots, and either government management or environmental activities could hardly escape from being more or less tainted with anthropocentrism and utilitarianism. What's worth particular attention is that, though environmentalism was the dominant environmentalist thoughts, counter-environmentalism, on the basis of mechanical approach and technological reason, won support among businessmen especially chemical entrepreneurs, a group of politicians and low-class people. When the publication of *Silent Spring* caused a stir in the chemical industry, the majority of the chemical enterprises either kept silent about or passively resisted against pollution treatment as well as the prevention and control of occupational diseases. Contrasting views on whether to build the dam in certain national park among government officials, and rounds of debate over nuclear pollution in the presidential election, showed the obstinateness and might of counter-environmental force. Besides, as for people from low class, survival was the first necessity, so they gave priority to the improvement of material well-being rather than the enhancement of quality of life.

2.5 The Rich Diversity

The end of the 1970s found stagflation and soaring unemployment rate in American society, with the decrease in actual family income and living standards. Challenged by social movements in the turbulent 1960s, the traditional values and beliefs were questioned and even shattered, while new values and beliefs hadn't taken root in the heart of Americans, which resulted in value vacuum in their minds. New technologies like biological genetic engineering, optical fiber communication technology, space technology, and internet technology boosted Americans' optimism towards future, but most of them were rather dissatisfied with the increase in taxation, the expansion of welfare, the addition of government agencies, and the new social injustice caused by meeting the demands of different social groups unlimitedly. In this social context, accompanied with the administration of president Ronald Reagan, conservative forces began to dominate America. Since then, the neoconservatives who upheld classic liberalism have won the political discourse and readjusted the extent of liberty and equality, marking the arrival of contemporary liberalism. Both president Reagan and president Bush who believed in neo-conservatism, and president Clinton who implemented a centrist liberalism, pushed American society back to its liberal tradition to varying degrees, and searched for the middle ground between liberty and equality in the political spectrum. Responding to this, environmental conservatism and contemporary environmentalism arose out of these social changes.

Giving full play to the ethic of conservation – the wise and efficient use of natural resources, environmental conservatism aimed to maximize the profits of enterprises and turn around the economy, permeated with strong utilitarian purposes and pragmatic ends. The Reagan administration invited commercial and industrial representatives to take part in setting environmental regulations, allowed the vigorous development of mining industry, oil industry and forestry which caused damage to environment, and even hampered the expansion of national parks with the proposal that 80 million acres of federal land be handed over to private developers by the end of 2000. What's worse, in line with small government and reduction in expenditure advocated by conservatism, environmental conservatism permitted enterprises to perform self-regulation, reduced the government's intervention in company's environmental protection, and dramatically cut the financial budget on the Environmental Protection Agency and occupational safety and health programs. According to the price of dollar in 2004, the federal expenditure on environmental protection and resource conservation amounted to 26.22 billion dollars in 1980, but in 1988, it dropped to 21.98 billion dollars. Worst of all, at this point, anti-environmental conservatives pervaded the environment-related administration, such as the Department of the Interior, the Environmental Protection Agency, the Forest Service, the National Park Service, which exerted direct and enormous influences on government's environmental policies. For instance, James Watt, appointed by president Reagan as Secretary of the Department of the Interior, belonged to the Christian right wing of the Republican conservatives. He argued for the strict interpretation of the *Bible* and the binary opposition between man and nature. He went so far as to claim that his responsibility was to follow the *Bible* and occupy the land. Government's deregulation and reduction in financial support fueled the growth of anti-environmental forces. Such anti-environmental movements as the wise use movement, the county supremacy movement, and the property-rights movement intended to expand private land ownership on the public land, which exerted great influences on environmental legislation. They not only resisted environmental policies on forest, land and wetland, but also, in the name of protecting property rights and job opportunities, urged the government to modify or even repeal those policies through lobbying and litigation. These movements won large support from oil, mining, timbre, electricity corporations as well as ranchers and farmers, building up roadblocks for the environmental cause. At the same time, taking advantage of this situation, large corporations reduced their input into pollution abatement devices and technologies, over-exploited and abused natural resources, displaced toxic wastes onto the neighborhoods of minority ethnic groups and lower classes, or even exported wastes and garbage to the Third World. The strong attack from environmental conservatism triggered the counterattack from

Unit 13 American Environmental Issues and Protection

environmental forces.

Confronting environmental conservatism, contemporary environmentalism fought back. Contemporary environmentalism was mainly comprised of mainstream environmentalism, environmental justice thought, and radical environmentalism. Mainstream environmentalism, advocated by mainstream environmental organizations, asserted that environmental protection should be advanced within the political and economic system of capitalism by means of lobbying, propaganda, education and litigation. Normally, with a mild form of struggle, it had great influence and won wide support, becoming the major force in the environmental cause. Relatively speaking, environmental justice thought and radical environmentalism had fewer followers and were practiced in a limited area, but both of them added vigor and inspiration to mainstream environmentalism.

Continuing to hold the ecological ethic of preserving nature and protecting the earth, mainstream environmentalism reinforced the education and guidance of the public's environmental awareness. In addition, facing the mighty anti-environmental forces, in order to survive and develop, mainstream environmentalism proposed to adopt the pragmatic tactics to achieve the ends by avoiding the confrontation with anti-environmental forces as well as cooperating and negotiating with the government and enterprises. For instance, leaders of mainstream environmental organizations ran for office and served as government officials, and then, through lobbying and litigation, they pressured the government to implement favorable environmental policies. When the government cut expenditure on environmental protection, mainstream environmental organizations courted sponsor from large enterprises for their operation, such as enlarging the membership and securing the organization of environmental activities. Meanwhile, these organizations promoted the concept of "green production" in enterprises, which were encouraged to take environmental-friendly manufacturing processes to achieve profitability. Once enterprises realized the importance and benefits of environmental production, they would use this philosophy to catch the attention of consumers, which would, in turn, imperceptibly influence the eco-consciousness of the public. Therefore, it is safe to say that mainstream environmentalism was in the middle of environmentalism and environmental conservatism. Nonetheless, it should be noted that as mainstream thought, mainstream environmentalism was inextricably linked with the government and enterprises, which would inevitably reduce its depth, criticalness and instructiveness. In most instances, mainstream environmentalism stood for the environmental interests of the white middle class, ignoring the environmental demands of disadvantaged groups and the environment of the inner-city neighborhoods which were inhabited by the ethnic groups and low-income class. Hence, even if mainstream environmentalism was widely spread across the nation, its focus was restrained and narrowed by its stance and perspective.

Regarding the flaws of mainstream environmentalism, environmental justice thought was formed to represent the environmental demands and interests of the ethnic groups and low-income class. It grew out of the environmental justice movement beginning in the late 1970s. "Environmental justice" laid stress on "the fair treatment and meaningful involvement" of all the American citizens in spite of their race, skin color, national origin, or income while environment-related policies were enforced. The word "justice" in "environmental justice" referred to equality and freedom which guaranteed that everyone enjoyed environmental interests. Specifically speaking, it can be understood in three different dimensions. First, strongly opposing environmental racism, environmental justice thought held that it was because of the political impotence of disadvantaged groups that they lacked the discourse in the environmental decision-making process and then became the victims of environmental issues. For this matter, environmental justice thought was the extension of civil rights thought in the environmental field in the post-civil rights era. Second, multiculturalism provided the theoretical and practical inspiration to environmental justice thought. Rising in the 1970s, on behalf of oppressed people like African Americans, women, the poor and the disable, multiculturalism strove for equal status and treatment in terms of political, economic and cultural rights. This standpoint and ideology greatly prompted environmental justice thought to break free of the limits of white elites, and fight for the equal environmental rights for marginalized groups. Third, environmental justice thought drew on John Rowls' theory of distributive justice, which asserted that equal opportunities during competition and equal basic right to liberty should be secured for everyone. This theory, to a large extent, offered vigorous theoretic support to the idea of sharing environmental responsibilities and enjoying equal environmental interests. Undoubtedly, compared with mainstream environmentalism which stood in the middle of the political spectrum, environmental justice thought moved toward equality in the scales of liberalism.

In real life, it is not unusual to see those who were poor and politically powerless subject to the hazards of environmental degradation, and exposed to toxic air, water and annoying noise, because neighborhoods and work sites of the underclass were more likely to become toxic waste dumps. Thus, they were more often than not haunted by a variety of health problems such as cancer, fetal malformation, miscarriage, and respiratory problems. The unequal relationship between two people incurred a series of social, political and human rights problems, leading to environmental racism and class oppression. In fact, what environmental issues revealed was not only the disharmony between man and nature, but also unbalanced human relations. Unlike mainstream environmentalism, environmental justice thought did not prefer to cooperate with the government and enterprises; instead, it adhered to an uncompromising stance. Owing to this, environmental justice thought made up for the flaws of mainstream environmentalism, and expanded the scope of subject that enjoyed environmental interests as well as the connotation of justice. The emergence of environmental justice thought and the environmental justice movement compelled mainstream environmental organizations to take into serious consideration the legitimate rights of the disadvantaged groups, and reinforce the cooperation with environmental justice organizations. Meanwhile, it pressured the government to redress the unfair political and economic system, and called upon enterprises to take on environmental responsibilities and disposed of wastes and pollutants properly. In this connection, environmental justice thought promoted the environmental cause and social changes in the US. But it should be admitted that, since environmental justice thought hasn't won a place in the mainstream discourse, its influence remains to be improved in the future. Though environmental justice thought began to spread across the world, it bears more complexities and uncertainties due to the changing subject of environmental interests as well as more complicated and broader social contexts.

Aside from environmental justice thought, radical environmentalism is another emerging environmental force. Breaking away from mainstream environmentalism and targeting at its shortcomings, radical environmentalism is dedicated to bringing changes in the environmental cause through radical means and sticking to the principle. Basically speaking, radical environmentalism intends to transform the deep values, ethics, and political views of human beings by use of eco-centric egalitarianism and self-realization in deep ecology. It consists of three major parts. The first part is the process philosophy of Alfred North Whitehead, which emphasized the connection and interdependence of all parts. The second part is Heidegger's thought in his later years, including the criticism against anthropocentrism and technology, the advocacy of restraining human desires, and the poetic dwelling on the earth, etc. Borrowing modern psychological research findings, the third part has three aspects – desire/hobby (id), reason/judgment (ego) and morality/evaluation (superego), corresponding to three attitudes towards nature – exploitation of resources, protection of resources, and the environmental ethics, so as to realize the Self. The Capitalized "Self" differentiates from "self" in that "Self" stresses a bigger entirety when the isolated "self" is well integrated with others and nature. It is not difficult to see that, radical environmentalism recognizes the equal values of man and other living beings, while oriented towards the social system and values that have sparked the ecological crisis. Equally significant, radical environmentalism learned civil disobedience from Henry David Thoreau, fighting against anti-environmental forces via noncooperation, resistance and eco-sabotage, so as to alert the public and catch their attention. For instance, at one time, radical environmentalists safeguarded nature's rights by exploding the dam and liberating the river, whose radical actions helped the public to know their moral standing. As a matter of fact, it is another big step toward equality that liberalism has made in the environmental field, with the expansion of the subject of rights from the human race to the entire biosphere. However, its radical stance and attitude could not avoid being associated with "violence" or "terrorism" in American society which admires gradual change and mild reform.

In short, when conservatism staged a comeback and began to be dominant, environmental conservatism has become extremely conservative and powerful, while contemporary environmentalism has grown more diversified with more profundity. These environmental ideologies display man's novel exploration of values, ethics and political views in pursuit of the balance between liberty and equality, and reveal the diversified development of liberalism in the environmental field. At the same time, they have been integrating with American traditions and the essence of previous environmentalist thoughts, paving the way for liberalism to move steadily in the years to come.

2.6 Social Implications

Throughout American history, different environmental ideologies mirror man's reflections on the relationship between man and nature, and reveal the status quo of liberalism in a particular period, with either a radical or conservative tendency. Moreover, they help to strike a balance between liberty and equality, and readdress the imbalanced relationship between man and the ecosystem. Though there lies the conflicts and confrontation between individualism and holism, anthropocentrism and ecocentrism within various schools of environmentalist thoughts, common characteristics can be summarized as follows.

First, pragmatism can be located in American environmentalist thoughts. As the unique belief and philosophy of the American nation, pragmatism serves as one of the guiding principles for the shaping of environmentalist thoughts. While liberalism changes from classical liberalism which advocates the laissez-faire mode to modern liberalism which emphasizes the governmental intervention and management, to contemporary liberalism which keeps the relative balance between individual freedom and social equality, these changes were reflected in environmentalist thoughts in different historical stages. Although the purposes and aims of different environmental ideas seem to vary from each other, all of them take specific environmental issues into consideration on the basis of either short-term or long-term development of American society, and learn from each other's strengths so as to integrate these strengths with themselves. While these ideas were put into practice, various tactics and strategies were adopted flexibly in the process in order to win a favorable situation.

Second, accompanied with the transformation of environmentalist thoughts' stance from individualism to holism, from anthropocentrism to ecocentrism, the denotations of "environment" and "community" are enlarging. "Environment" nowadays covers not only nature or wilderness, but also the urban environment and even the social environment. Meanwhile, "community" expands from the human community to a larger community with human-beings and the biosphere included. All environmental ideas affirm a commitment to the protection of individual freedom and respect for an equal community, differentiating from each other in the definition of the free subject and the range of the community.

Third, the social foundation and the scope of participation enjoy a gradual expansion. At first, only social elites and government officials noticed the burgeoning environmental issues and took actions. Later on, the rise of the ecological crisis and the spread of the ecological knowledge triggered the environmental awareness across the nation, which spurred people from all walks of life to get involved in environmental activities. Even if they may have different demands and propose different environmental solutions, their efforts jointly promote the environmental cause in America. Their strong environmental awareness, rich experience in struggle and immediate actions towards environmental issues are worth learning from.

At present, theoretically, American environmentalist thoughts are working towards reconciliation between man and nature as well as between people, and devoted to strengthening the global communication and international cooperation. So far, American environmentalist thoughts have helped to advance the environmental cause and construct an ecological society across the world. Nevertheless, US's withdrawal from the Kyoto Protocol in 2001 and the Paris Agreement in 2017 cast a shadow over the future of the American environmental standpoint and its environmental cause.

Essay Questions:

1. In American history, alongside westward expansion, industrialization and urbanization, there had occurred many ecological disasters. Explore the root causes of these disasters.
2. Brisk modernization, on the one hand, promoted social advancement and economic prosperity; on the other hand, incurred environmental pollution and destruction of wilderness. Examine the ways that American society has tackled environmental issues spawned by modernization.
3. In terms of environmental regulation, the US evolved from a laissez-faire state to an environmental management state through the enactment and enforcement of vigorous environmental laws. Examine the changing process as well as the driving forces behind it.
4. Historically, American environmentalist thoughts have gone through five phases. Examine the historical and social context for the development of American environmentalist thoughts.

Unit 14 American Popular Culture

Modern American popular culture began with the baby boomer generation and "buying power." As baby boomers came of age with their disposable incomes – that influence led to the pop culture revolution. It began during the 1950s with rock n' roll, TV, Dick Clark and the hula hoop, transistor radios, into the 1960s and beyond. The term "pop culture" became mainstream during the 1980s. Before this, we used "popular" to describe things such as top song playlists, or "pop" as in art or "best" or "top" selling, as in books.

The term "popular culture" was coined in the 19th century or earlier. Traditionally, popular culture was associated with poor education and with the lower classes, as opposed to the "official culture" and higher education of the upper classes. The stress in the distinction from "official culture" became more pronounced towards the end of the 19th century, a usage that became established between two world wars. From the end of World War II, following major cultural and social changes brought by mass media innovations, the meaning of popular culture began to overlap with those of mass culture, media culture, image culture, consumer culture, and culture for mass consumption. The most common pop-culture categories are: film, music, sports, fashion, among other categories.

1 Film

The cinema of the United States has had a large effect on the film industry in general since the early 20th century. The dominant style of American cinema is the classical Hollywood cinema, which developed from 1913 to 1969 and is still typical of most films made there to this day. While Frenchmen Auguste and Louis Lumière are generally credited with the birth of modern cinema, American cinema soon came to be a dominant force in the emerging industry. It produces the largest number of films of any single-language national cinema, with more than 700 English-language films released on average every year. Hollywood has also been considered a transnational cinema. It produced multiple language versions of some titles, often in Spanish or French. Contemporary Hollywood often outsources production to Canada, Australia, and New Zealand.

Hollywood is considered to be the oldest film industry, in the sense of being the place where the earliest film studios and production companies emerged. It is also the birthplace of various genres of cinema – among them comedy, drama, action, musical, romance, horror, science fiction, and war epic – and has set the example for other national film industries.

In 1878, Eadweard Muybridge demonstrated the power of photography to capture motion. In 1894, the world's first commercial motion-picture exhibition was given in New York City, using Thomas Edison's kinetoscope. In the following decades, production of silent film greatly expanded, studios formed and migrated to California, and films and the stories they told became much longer. The United States produced the world's first sync-sound musical film, *The Jazz Singer*, in 1927, and was at the forefront of sound-film development in the following decades. Since the early 20th century, the US film industry has largely been based in and around the thirty-mile zone in Hollywood, Los Angeles, California. Director D.W. Griffith was central to the development of a film grammar. Orson Welles's *Citizen Kane* (1941) is frequently cited in critics' polls as the greatest film of all time.

The major film studios of Hollywood are the primary source of the most commercially successful and most ticket-selling movies in the world. Moreover, many of Hollywood's highest-grossing movies have generated more box-office revenue and ticket sales outside the United States than films made elsewhere. Today, American film studios collectively generate several hundred movies every year, making the United

States one of the most prolific producers of films in the world and a leading pioneer in motion picture engineering and technology.

1.1 The Rise of Hollywood

In early 1910, director D. W. Griffith was sent by the Biograph Company to the West Coast with his acting troupe, consisting of actors Blanche Sweet, Lillian Gish, Mary Pickford, Lionel Barrymore and others. They started filming on a vacant lot near Georgia Street in downtown Los Angeles. While there, the company decided to explore new territories, traveling several miles north to Hollywood, a little village that was friendly and enjoyed the movie company filming there. Griffith then filmed the first movie ever shot in Hollywood, In *Old California*, a biograph melodrama about California in the 19th century, when it belonged to Mexico. Griffith stayed there for months and made several films before returning to New York. Also in 1910, Selig Polyscope of Chicago established the first industry film studio in the Los Angeles area. After hearing about Griffith's success in Hollywood, in 1913, many movie-makers headed west to avoid the fees imposed by Thomas Edison, who owned patents on the movie-making process. Nestor Studios of Bayonne, New Jersey, built the first studio in the Hollywood neighborhood in 1911. Nestor Studios, owned by David and William Horsley, later merged with Universal Studios; and William Horsley's other company, Hollywood Film Laboratory, is now the oldest existing company in Hollywood, now called the Hollywood Digital Laboratory. California's more hospitable and cost-effective climate led to the eventual shift of virtually all filmmaking to the West Coast by the 1930s. At the time, Thomas Edison owned almost all the patents relevant to motion picture production and movie producers on the East Coast acting independently of Edison's Motion Picture Patents Company were often sued or enjoined by Edison and his agents while movie makers working on the West Coast could work independently of Edison's control.

In Los Angeles, the studios and Hollywood grew. Before World War I, films were made in several American cities, but filmmakers tended to gravitate towards southern

California as the industry developed. They were attracted by the warm climate and reliable sunlight, which made it possible to film their films outdoors year-round and by the varied scenery that was available. War damage contributed to the decline of the then-dominant European film industry, in favor of the United States, where infrastructure was still intact. The stronger early public health response to the 1918 flu epidemic by Los Angeles compared to other American cities reduced the number of cases there and resulted in a faster recovery, contributing to the increasing dominance of Hollywood over New York City. During the pandemic, public health officials temporarily closed movie theaters in some jurisdictions, large studios suspended production for weeks at a time, and some actors came down with the flu. This caused major financial losses and severe difficulties for small studios, but the industry as a whole more than recovered during the Roaring Twenties.

There are several starting points for cinema (particularly American cinema), but it was Griffith's controversial 1915 epic *The Birth of a Nation* that pioneered the worldwide filming vocabulary that still dominates film to this day.

In the early 20th century, when the medium was new, many Jewish immigrants found employment in the US film industry. They were able to make their mark in a brand-new business: the exhibition of short films in storefront theaters called nickelodeons, after their admission price of a nickel (five cents). Within a few years, ambitious men like Samuel Goldwyn, William Fox, Carl Laemmle, Adolph Zukor, Louis B. Mayer, and the Warner Brothers (Harry, Albert, Samuel, and Jack) had switched to the production side of the business. Soon they were the heads of a new kind of enterprise: the movie studio. (The US had at least two female directors, producers and studio heads in these early years: Lois Weber and French-born Alice Guy-Blaché.) They also set the stage for the industry's internationalism; the industry is often accused of Amero-centric provincialism.

Other moviemakers arrived from Europe after World War I: directors like Ernst Lubitsch, Alfred Hitchcock, Fritz Lang and Jean Renoir; and actors like Rudolph Valentino, Marlene Dietrich, Ronald Colman, and Charles Boyer. They joined a homegrown supply of actors – lured west from the New York City stage after the introduction of sound films – to form one of the 20th century's most remarkable growth industries. At motion pictures' height of popularity in the mid-1940s, the studios were cranking out a total of about 400 movies a year, seen by an audience of 90 million Americans per week.

The Hollywood Sign in the Hollywood Hills has become a landmark representing the Southern California film industry. Sound also became widely used in Hollywood in the late 1920s. After *The Jazz Singer*, the first film with synchronized voices was successfully released as a Vitaphone talkie in 1927, Hollywood film companies would respond to Warner Bros. and begin to use Vitaphone sound – which Warner Bros. owned until 1928 – in future films. By May 1928, Electrical Research Product Incorporated (ERPI), a subsidiary of the Western Electric company, gained a monopoly over film sound distribution.

A side effect of the "talkies" was that many actors who had made their careers in silent films suddenly found themselves out of work, as they often had bad voices or could not remember their lines. Meanwhile, in 1922, US politician Will H. Hays left politics and formed the movie studio boss organization known as the Motion Picture Producers and Distributors of America (MPPDA). The organization became the Motion Picture Association of America after Hays retired in 1945. In the early times of talkies, American studios found that their sound productions were rejected in foreign-language markets and even among speakers of other dialects of English. The synchronization technology was still too primitive for dubbing. One of the solutions was creating parallel foreign-language versions of Hollywood films.

Also, foreign unemployed actors, playwrights, and winners of photogenia contests were chosen and brought to Hollywood, where they shot parallel versions of the English-language films. These parallel versions had a lower budget, were shot at night and were directed by second-line American directors who did not speak the foreign language. The productions, however, were not very successful in their intended markets, due to the lower budgets, inexperienced theater actors and the mix of foreign accents, etc. In spite of this, some productions like the Spanish version of *Dracula* compare favorably with the original. By the mid-1930s, synchronization had advanced enough for dubbing to become usual.

1.1.1 Classical Hollywood Cinema and the Golden Age of Hollywood (1913–1969)

Classical Hollywood cinema, or the Golden Age of Hollywood, is defined as a technical and narrative style characteristic of American cinema from 1913 to 1969, during which thousands of movies were issued from the Hollywood studios. The classical style began to emerge in 1913, was accelerated in 1917 after the US entered World War I, and finally solidified when the film *The Jazz Singer* was released in 1927, ending the Silent Film era and increasing box-office profits for film industry by introducing sound to feature films.

Most Hollywood pictures adhered closely to a formula – Western, Slapstick Comedy, Musical, Animated Cartoon, Biographical Film (biographical picture) – and the same creative teams often worked on films made by the same studio. For example, Cedric Gibbons and Herbert Stothart always worked on MGM films, Alfred Newman worked at 20th Century Fox for twenty years, Cecil B. De Mille's films were almost all made at Paramount, and director Henry King's films were mostly made for 20th Century Fox.

At the same time, one could usually guess which studio made which film, largely because of the actors who appeared in it; MGM, for example, claimed it had contracted "more stars than there are in heaven." Each studio had its own style and characteristic touches which made it possible to know this – a trait that rarely exist today. For example, *To Have and Have Not* (1944) is famous not only for the first pairing of actors Humphrey Bogart (1899–1957) and Lauren Bacall (1924–2014), but because it was written by two future winners of the Nobel Prize in Literature: Ernest Hemingway (1899–1961), the author of the novel on which the script was nominally based, and William Faulkner (1897–1962), who worked on the screen adaptation.

After *The Jazz Singer* was released in 1927, Warner Bros. gained huge success and were able to acquire their own string of movie theaters, after purchasing Stanley Theaters and First National Productions in 1928. MGM (Metro-Goldwyn-Mayer) had also owned the Loews theaters since forming in 1924, and the Fox Film Corporation owned the Fox Theatre as well. RKO (a 1928 merger between Keith-Orpheum Theaters and the Radio Corporation of America) also responded to the Western Electric/ERPI monopoly over sound in films, and developed their own method, known as Photophone, to put sound in films.

Paramount, who already acquired Balaban and Katz in 1926, would answer to the success of Warner Bros. and RKO, and buy a number of theaters in the late 1920s as well, and would hold a monopoly on theaters in Detroit, Michigan. By the 1930s, almost all of the first-run metropolitan theaters in the United States were owned by the Big Five studios – MGM, Paramount Pictures, RKO, Warner Bros., and 20th Century Fox.

1.1.2　The Studio System

Movie-making was still a business, however, and motion picture companies made money by operating under the studio system. The major studios kept thousands of people on salary – actors, producers, directors, writers, stunt men, crafts persons, and technicians. They owned or leased Movie Ranches in rural Southern California for location shooting of westerns and other large-scale genre films, and the major studios owned hundreds of theaters in cities and towns across the nation in 1920 film theaters that showed their films and that were always in need of fresh material.

In 1930, MPPDA president Will Hays created the Hays (Production) Code, which followed censorship guidelines and went into effect after government threats of censorship expanded by 1930. However, the code was never enforced until 1934, after the Catholic watchdog organization The Legion of Decency – appalled by some of the provocative films and lurid advertising of the era later classified Pre-Code Hollywood– threatened a boycott of motion pictures if it did not go into effect. The films that did not obtain a seal of approval from the Production Code Administration had to pay a $25,000 fine and could not profit in the theaters, as the MPPDA controlled every theater in the country through the Big Five studios.

Throughout the 1930s, as well as most of the golden age, MGM dominated the film screen and had the top stars in Hollywood, and they were also credited for creating the Hollywood star system altogether.

Another great achievement of US cinema during this era came through Walt Disney's animation company. In 1937, Disney created the most successful film of its time, *Snow White and the Seven Dwarfs*. This distinction was promptly topped in 1939 when Selznick International created what is still, when adjusted for inflation, the most successful film of all time in *Gone with the Wind*.

The apogee of the studio system may have been the year 1939, which saw the release of such classics as *The Wizard of Oz, Gone with the Wind, Stagecoach, Mr. Smith Goes to Washington, Wuthering Heights, Only Angels Have Wings, Ninotchka* and *Midnight*. Among the other films from the Golden Age period that are now considered to be classics: *Casablanca, It's a Wonderful Life, It Happened One Night*, the original *King Kong, Mutiny on the Bounty, Top Hat, City Lights, Red River, The Lady from Shanghai, Rear Window, On the Waterfront, Rebel Without a Cause, Some Like It Hot*, and *The Manchurian Candidate*.

The studio system and the Golden Age of Hollywood succumbed to two forces that developed in the late 1940s: a federal antitrust action that separated the production of films from their exhibition; and the advent of television.

In 1938, Walt Disney's *Snow White and the Seven Dwarfs* was released during a run of lackluster films from the major studios, and quickly became the highest grossing film released to that point. Embarrassingly for the studios, it was an independently produced animated film that did not feature any studio-employed stars. This stoked already widespread frustration at the practice of block-booking, in which studios would only sell an entire year's schedule of films at a time to theaters and use the lock-in to cover for releases of mediocre quality.

Assistant Attorney General Thurman Arnold – a noted "trust buster" of the Roosevelt administration – took this opportunity to initiate proceedings against the eight largest Hollywood studios in July 1938 for violations of the *Sherman Antitrust Act*. The federal suit resulted in five of the eight studios (the "Big Five": Warner Bros., MGM, Fox, RKO and Paramount) reaching a compromise with Arnold in October 1940 and signing a consent decree agreeing to, within three years: eliminating the block-booking of short film subjects, in an arrangement known as "one shot," or "full force" block-booking; eliminating the block-booking of any more than five features in their theaters; no longer engaging in blind buying (or the buying of films by theater districts without seeing films beforehand) and instead having trade-showing, in which all 31 theater districts in the US would see films every two weeks before showing movies in theater; setting up an administration board in each theater district to enforce these requirements.

The "Little Three" (Universal Studios, United Artists, and Columbia Pictures), who did not own any theaters, refused to participate in the consent decree. A number of independent film producers were also unhappy with the compromise and formed a union known as the Society of Independent Motion Picture Producers and sued Paramount for the monopoly they still had over the Detroit Theaters – as Paramount was also gaining dominance through actors like Bob Hope, Paulette Goddard, Veronica Lake, Betty Hutton, crooner Bing Crosby, Alan Ladd, and longtime actor for studio Gary Cooper too – by 1942. The Big Five studios did not meet the requirements of the Consent of Decree during WWII, without major consequence, but after the war ended they joined Paramount as defendants in the Hollywood antitrust case, as did the Little Three studios.

The Supreme Court eventually ruled that the major studios ownership of theaters and film distribution was a violation of the *Sherman Antitrust Act*. As a result, the studios began to release actors and technical staff from their contracts with the studios. This changed the paradigm of film making by the major Hollywood studios, as each could have an entirely different cast and creative team.

The decision resulted in the gradual loss of the characteristics which made Metro-Goldwyn-Mayer, Paramount Pictures, Universal Studios, Columbia Pictures, RKO Pictures, and 20th Century Fox films immediately identifiable. Certain movie people, such as Cecil B. DeMille, either remained contract artists until the end of their careers or used the same creative teams on their films so that a DeMille film still looked like one whether it was made in 1932 or 1956.

1.1.3　New Hollywood and Post-classical Cinema (the 1960s–1980s)

Post-classical cinema is the changing methods of storytelling in the New Hollywood. It has been argued that new approaches to drama and characterization played upon audience expectations acquired in the classical period: chronology may be scrambled, storylines may feature "twist endings", and lines between the antagonist and protagonist may be blurred.

The New Hollywood is the emergence of a new generation of film school-trained directors who had absorbed the techniques developed in Europe in the 1960s as a result of the French New Wave after the American Revolution; the 1967 film *Bonnie and Clyde* marked the beginning of American cinema rebounding as well, as a new generation of films would afterwards gain success at the box offices as well. Filmmakers like Francis Ford Coppola, Steven Spielberg, George Lucas, Brian De Palma, Stanley Kubrick, Martin Scorsese, Roman Polanski, and William Friedkin came to produce fare that paid homage to the history of film and developed upon existing genres and techniques.

In the 1970s, the films of New Hollywood filmmakers were often both critically acclaimed and commercially successful. While the early New Hollywood films like *Bonnie and Clyde* and *Easy Rider* had been relatively low-budget affairs with amoral heroes and increased sexuality and violence, the enormous success enjoyed by Friedkin with *The Exorcist*, Spielberg with *Jaws*, Coppola with *The Godfather* and *Apocalypse Now*, Scorsese with *Taxi Driver*, Kubrick with *2001: A Space Odyssey*, Polanski with *Chinatown*, and Lucas with *American Graffiti* and *Star Wars*, respectively helped to give rise to the modern "blockbuster," and induced studios to focus ever more heavily on trying to produce enormous hits.

The increasing indulgence of these young directors did not help. Often, they'd go overschedule, and overbudget, thus bankrupting themselves or the studio. The three most famous examples of this are Coppola's *Apocalypse Now* and *One from the Heart* and particularly Michael Cimino's *Heaven's Gate*, which single-handedly bankrupted United Artists. However, *Apocalypse Now* eventually made its money back and gained widespread recognition as a masterpiece, winning the Palme d'Or at Cannes.

1.2 The Rise of the Home Video Market (the 1980s – 1990s)

The 1980s and 1990s saw another significant development. The full acceptance of home video by studios opened a vast new business to exploit. Films which may have performed poorly in their theatrical run were now able to find success in the video market. It also saw the first generation of filmmakers with access to videotapes emerge. Directors such as Quentin Tarantino and Paul Thomas Anderson had been able to view thousands of films and produced films with vast numbers of references and connections to previous works. Tarantino has had a number of collaborations with director Robert Rodriguez. Rodriguez directed the 1992 action film *El Mariachi*, which was a commercial success after grossing $2 million against a budget of $7,000.

This, along with the explosion of independent film and ever-decreasing costs for filmmaking, changed the landscape of American movie-making once again and led a renaissance of filmmaking among Hollywood's lower and middle-classes – those without access to studio financial resources. With the rise of the DVD in the 21st century, DVDs have quickly become even more profitable to studios and have led to an explosion of packaging extra scenes, extended versions, and commentary tracks with the films.

In the US, the PG-13 rating was introduced in 1984 to accommodate films that straddled the line between PG and R, which was mainly due to the controversies surrounding the violent content of the PG films *Indiana Jones and the Temple of Doom* and *Gremlins* (both 1984).

1988's *Die Hard* established what would become a common formula for many 90s action films, featuring a lone everyman against a colorful terrorist character, who's usually holding hostages, in an isolated setting.

1.3 Contemporary Cinema

In the early 21st century, the theatrical market place has been dominated by the superhero genre, with the Marvel Cinematic Universe and The Dark Knight Trilogy being two of the most successful film series of all time.

The COVID-19 pandemic has had a substantial impact on the film industry, mirroring its impacts across all arts sectors. Across the world and to varying degrees, cinemas and movie theaters have been closed, festivals have been cancelled or postponed, and film releases have been moved to future dates or delayed indefinitely. As cinemas and movie theaters closed, the global box office dropped by billions of dollars, streaming became more popular, and the stock of film exhibitors dropped dramatically.

The 2019 film *Frozen II* was originally planned to be released on Disney+ on June 26, 2020, before it was moved up to March 15. Disney CEO Bob Chapek explained that this was because of the film's "powerful themes of perseverance and the importance of family, messages that are incredibly relevant." On March 16, 2020, Universal announced that *The Invisible Man*, *The Hunt*, and *Emma* – all films in theaters at the time – would be available through Premium video on demand as early as March 20 at a suggested price of US $19.99 each. After suffering poor box office since its release at the start of March, Onward was made available to purchase digitally on March 21, and was added to Disney+ on April 3. Paramount announced on March 20, *Sonic the Hedgehog* is also planning to have an early release to video on demand, on March 31. On March 16, Warner Bros. announced that *Birds of Prey* would be released early to video on demand on March 24. On April 3, Disney announced that *Artemis Fowl*, a film adaptation of the 2001 book of the same name, would move straight to Disney+ on June 12, skipping a theatrical release entirely.

Trolls World Tour was released directly to video-on-demand rental upon its release on April 10, with limited theatrical screenings in the US via drive-in cinemas. NBCUniversal CEO Jeff Shell told *The Wall Street Journal* on April 28 that the film had reached $100 million in revenue, and stated that the company had not ruled out performing releases "in both formats" as cinemas reopen. The US National Association of Theatre Owners, have highly discouraged film distributors from engaging in this practice, in defense of the cinema industry. On April 28, in response to Shell's comments, US chain AMC Theatres announced that it would cease the screening of Universal Pictures films effective immediately, and threatened similar actions against any other exhibitor who "unilaterally abandons current windowing practices absent good faith negotiations between us." On July 28, the two companies announced an agreement allowing Universal the option to release a film to premium video on demand after a minimum of 17 days in its theaters, with AMC receiving a cut of revenue. On September 23, Disney postponed *Black Widow* to May 7, 2021, *Death on the Nile* to December 18, 2020, and *West Side Story* to December 10, 2021. As a result, *Eternals* was also delayed to November 5, 2021 in order to maintain the MCU continuity. Warner Bros. Pictures announced in December 2020 that it would simultaneously release its slate of 2021 films both as theatrical releases and available for streaming on HBO Max for a period of one month.

2 Music

The music of the United States reflects the country's pluri-ethnic population through a diverse array of styles. It is a mixture of music influenced by the music of the United Kingdom, West Africa, Ireland, Latin America, and mainland Europe, among other places. The country's most internationally renowned genres are jazz, blues, country, bluegrass, rock, rock and roll, R&B, pop, hip-hop, soul, funk, gospel, folk music, etc. American music is heard around the world. Since the beginning of the 20th century, some forms of American popular music have gained a near global audience.

2.1 Folk Music

Folk music in the US is varied across the country's numerous ethnic groups. The Native American tribes each play their own varieties of folk music, most of it spiritual in nature. African American music includes blues and gospel, descendants of West African music brought to the Americas by slaves and mixed with Western European music. During the colonial era, English, French and Spanish styles and instruments were brought to the Americas. By the early 20th century, the United States had become a major center for folk music from around the world, including polka, Ukrainian and Polish fiddling, Ashkenazi, Klezmer, and several kinds of Latin music.

The Native Americans played the first folk music in what is now the United States, using a wide variety of styles and techniques. Some commonalities are near universal among Native American traditional music, however, especially the lack of harmony and polyphony, and the use of vocables and descending melodic figures. Traditional instrumentations use the flute and many kinds of percussion instruments, like drums, rattles, and shakers. Since European and African contact was established, Native American folk music has grown in new directions, into fusions with disparate styles like European folk dances and Tejano music. Modern Native American music may be best known for pow wows, pan-tribal gatherings at which traditionally styled dances and music are performed.

The thirteen colonies of the original United States were all former English possessions, and Anglo culture became a major foundation for American folk and popular music. Many American folk songs are identical to British songs in arrangements, but with new lyrics, often as parodies of the original material. American-Anglo songs are also characterized as having fewer pentatonic tunes, less prominent accompaniment (but with heavier use of drones) and more melodies in major. Anglo-American traditional music also includes a variety of broadside ballads, humorous stories and tall tales, and disaster songs regarding mining, shipwrecks, and murder. Legendary heroes like Joe Magarac, John Henry, and Jesse James are part of many songs. Folk dances of British origin include the square dance, descended from the quadrille, combined with the American innovation of a caller instructing the dancers. The religious communal society known as the Shakers emigrated from England during the 18th century and developed their own folk dance style. Their early songs can be dated back to British folk song models. Other religious societies established their own unique musical cultures early in American history, such as the music of the Amish, the Harmony Society, and the Ephrata Cloister in Pennsylvania.

The ancestors of today's African American population were brought to the United States as slaves, working primarily in the plantations of the South. They were from hundreds of tribes across West Africa, and they brought with them certain traits of West African music including call and response vocals and complexly rhythmic music, as well as syncopated beats and shifting accents. The African musical focus on rhythmic singing and dancing was brought to the New World, where it became part of a distinct folk culture that helped Africans "retain continuity with their past through music". The first slaves in the United States sang work songs, field hollers and, following Christianization, hymns. In the 19th century, a great awakening of religious fervor gripped people across the country, especially in the South. Protestant hymns written mostly by New England preachers became a feature of camp meetings held among devout Christians across the South. When blacks began singing adapted versions of these hymns, they were called Negro spirituals. It was from these roots, of spiritual songs, work songs, and field hollers, that blues, jazz, and gospel developed.

Spirituals were primarily expressions of religious faith, sung by slaves on southern plantations. In the mid to late 19th century, spirituals spread out of the US South. In 1871 Fisk University became home to the Fisk Jubilee Singers, a pioneering group that popularized spirituals across the country. In imitation of this group, gospel quartets arose, followed by increasing diversification with the early 20th-century rise of jackleg and singing preachers, from whence came the popular style of gospel music.

Blues is a combination of African work songs, field hollers, and shouts. It developed in the rural South in the first decade of the 20th century. The most important characteristics of the blues is its use of the blue scale, with a flatted or indeterminate third, as well as the typically lamenting lyrics; though both of these elements had existed in African American folk music prior to the 20th century, the codified form of modern blues (such as with the AAB structure) did not exist until the early 20th century.

In addition, many American immigrant communities have kept alive the folk traditions of their homeland, often producing distinctively American styles of foreign music. Some nationalities have produced local scenes in regions of the country where they have clustered, like Cape Verdean music in New England, Armenian music in California, and Italian and Ukrainian music in New York City.

Spain and subsequently Mexico controlled much of what is now the western United States until the Mexican–American War, including the entire state of Texas. After Texas joined the United States, the native Tejanos living in the state began culturally developing separately from their neighbors to the south, and remained culturally distinct from other Texans. Central to the evolution of early Tejano music was the blend of traditional Mexican forms such as mariachi and the corrido, and Continental European styles introduced by German and Czech settlers in the late 19th century. In particular, the accordion was adopted by Tejano folk musicians around the start of the 20th century, and it became a popular instrument for amateur musicians in Texas and northern Mexico.

2.2 Classical Music

Classical music was brought to the United States with some of the first colonists. European classical music is rooted in the traditions of European art, ecclesiastical and concert music. The central norms of this tradition developed between 1550 and 1825, centering on what is known as the common practice period. Many American classical composers attempted to work entirely within European models until late in the 19th century. When Antonín Dvořák, a prominent Czech composer, visited the United States from 1892 to 1895, he iterated the idea that American classical music needed its own models instead of imitating European composers; he helped to inspire subsequent composers to make a distinctly American style of classical music. By the beginning of the 20th century, many American composers were incorporating disparate elements into their work, ranging from jazz and blues to Native American music.

During the colonial era, there were two distinct fields of what is now considered classical music. One was associated with amateur composers and pedagogues, whose style was originally drawn from simple hymns and gained sophistication over time. The other colonial tradition was that of the mid-Atlantic cities like Philadelphia and Baltimore, which produced a number of prominent composers who worked almost entirely within the European model; these composers were mostly English in origin, and worked specifically in the style of prominent English composers of the day.

Classical music was brought to the United States during the colonial era. Many American composers of this period worked exclusively with European models, while others, such as William Billings, Supply Belcher, and Justin Morgan, also known as the First New England School, developed a style almost entirely independent of European models. Of these composers, Billings is the most well-remembered; he was also influential "as the founder of the American church choir, as the first musician to use a pitch pipe, and as the first to introduce a violoncello into church service." Many of these composers were amateur singers who developed new forms of sacred music suitable for performance by amateurs, and often using harmonic methods which would have been considered bizarre by contemporary European standards. These composers' styles were untouched by "the influence of their sophisticated European contemporaries," using modal or pentatonic scales or melodies and eschewing the European rules of harmony.

2.3 Popular Music

The United States has produced many popular musicians and composers in the modern world. Beginning with the birth of recorded music, American performers have continued to lead the field of popular music, which out of "all the contributions made by Americans to world culture... has been taken to heart by the entire world."

Unit 14 American Popular Culture

Most histories of popular music start with American ragtime or Tin Pan Alley; others, however, trace popular music to the Renaissance and through broadsheets, ballads, and other popular traditions. Other authors typically look at popular sheet music, tracing American popular music to spirituals, minstrel shows, vaudeville, and the patriotic songs of the Civil War.

The patriotic lay songs of the American Revolution constituted the first kind of mainstream popular music. These included "The Liberty Tree" by Thomas Paine. Cheaply printed as broadsheets, early patriotic songs spread across the colonies and were performed at home and at public meetings. Fife songs were especially celebrated, and were performed on fields of battle during the American Revolution. The longest lasting of these fife songs is "Yankee Doodle," still well known today. The melody dates back to 1755 and was sung by both American and British troops. Patriotic songs were based mostly on English melodies, with new lyrics added to denounce British colonialism; others, however, used tunes from Ireland, Scotland or elsewhere, or did not utilize a familiar melody. The song "Hail, Columbia" was a major work that remained an unofficial national anthem until the adoption of "The Star-Spangled Banner," Much of this early American music still survives in Sacred Harp. Although relatively unknown outside of Shaker Communities, "Simple Gifts" was written in 1848 by Elder Joseph Brackett and the tune has since become internationally famous.

During the Civil War, when soldiers from across the country commingled, the multifarious strands of American music began to cross-fertilize each other, a process that was aided by the burgeoning railroad industry and other technological developments that made travel and communication easier. Army units included individuals from across the country, and they rapidly traded tunes, instruments and techniques. The war was an impetus for the creation of distinctly American songs that became and remained wildly popular. The most popular songs of the Civil War era included "Dixie," written by Daniel Decatur Emmett. The song, originally titled "Dixie's Land," was made for the closing of a minstrel show; it spread to New Orleans first, where it was published and became "one of the great song successes of the pre-Civil War period." In addition to popular patriotic songs, the Civil War era also produced a great body of brass band pieces.

Following the Civil War, minstrel shows became the first distinctively American form of music expression. The minstrel show was an indigenous form of American entertainment consisting of comic skits, variety acts, dancing, and music, usually performed by white people in blackface. Minstrel shows used African American elements in musical performances, but only in simplified ways; storylines in the shows depicted blacks as natural-born slaves and fools, before eventually becoming associated with abolitionism. The minstrel show was invented by Daniel Decatur Emmett and the Virginia Minstrels. Minstrel shows produced the first well-remembered popular songwriters in American music history: Thomas D. Rice, Daniel Decatur Emmett, and, most famously, Stephen Foster. After minstrel shows' popularity faded, coon songs, a similar phenomenon, became popular.

The composer John Philip Sousa is closely associated with the most popular trend in American popular music just before the start of the 20th century. Formerly the bandmaster of the United States Marine Band, Sousa wrote military marches like "The Stars and Stripes Forever" that reflected his "nostalgia for [his] home and country," giving the melody a "stirring virile character."

In the early 20th century, American musical theater was a major source for popular songs, many of which influenced blues, jazz, country, and other extant styles of popular music. The center of development for this style was in New York City, where the Broadway theatres became among the most renowned venues in the city. Theatrical composers and lyricists like the brothers George and Ira Gershwin created a uniquely American theatrical style that used American vernacular speech and music. Musicals featured popular songs and fast-paced plots that often revolved around love and romance.

2.3.1 Blues and Gospel

The blues is a genre of African American folk music that is the basis for much of modern American popular music. Blues can be seen as part of a continuum of musical styles like country, jazz, ragtime, and gospel; though each genre evolved into distinct forms, their origins were often indistinct. Early forms of the blues evolved in and around the Mississippi Delta in the late 19th and early 20th centuries. The earliest blues music was primarily call and response vocal music, without harmony or accompaniment and without any formal musical structure. Slaves and their descendants created the blues by adapting the field shouts and hollers, turning them into passionate solo songs. When mixed with the Christian spiritual songs of African American churches and revival meetings, blues became the basis of gospel music. Modern gospel began in African American churches in the 1920s, in the form of worshipers proclaiming their faith in an improvised, often musical manner (testifying). Composers like Thomas A. Dorsey composed gospel works that used elements of blues and jazz in traditional hymns and spiritual songs.

Ragtime was originally a piano style, featuring syncopated rhythms and chromaticisms. It is primarily a form of dance music utilizing the walking bass, and is generally composed in sonata form. Ragtime is a refined and evolved form of the African American cakewalk dance, mixed with styles ranging from European marches and popular songs to jigs and other dances played by large African American bands in northern cities during the end of the 19th century. The most famous ragtime performer and composer was Scott Joplin, known for works such as "Maple Leaf Rag".

Blues became a part of American popular music in the 1920s, when classic female blues singers like Bessie Smith grew popular. At the same time, record companies launched the field of race music, which was mostly blues targeted at African American audiences. The most famous of these acts went on to inspire much of the later popular development of the blues and blues-derived genres, including the legendary delta blues musician Robert Johnson and Piedmont blues musician Blind Willie McTell. By the end of the 1940s, however, pure blues was only a minor part of popular music, having been subsumed by offshoots like rhythm & blues and the nascent rock and roll style. Some styles of electric, piano-driven blues, like boogie-woogie, retained a large audience. A bluesy style of gospel also became popular in mainstream America in the 1950s, led by singer Mahalia Jackson. The blues genre experienced major revivals in the 1950s with Chicago blues musicians such as Muddy Waters and Little Walter, as well as in the 1960s in the British Invasion and American folk music revival when country blues musicians like Mississippi John Hurt and Reverend Gary Davis were rediscovered. The seminal blues musicians of these periods had tremendous influence on rock musicians such as Chuck Berry in the 1950s, as well as on the British blues and blues rock scenes of the 1960s and 1970s, including Eric Clapton in Britain and Johnny Winter in Texas.

2.3.2 Jazz

Jazz is a kind of music characterized by swung and blue notes, call and response vocals, polyrhythms and improvisation. Though originally a kind of dance music, jazz has been a major part of popular music, and has also become a major element of Western classical music. Jazz has roots in West African cultural and musical expression, and in African American music traditions including blues and ragtime, as well as European military band music. Early jazz was closely related to ragtime, with which it could be distinguished by the use of more intricate rhythmic improvisation. The earliest jazz bands adopted much of the vocabulary of the blues, including bent and blue notes and instrumental "growls" and smears otherwise not used on European instruments. Jazz's roots come from the city of New Orleans, Louisiana, populated by Cajuns and black Creoles, who combined the French-Canadian culture of the Cajuns with their own styles of music in the 19th century. Large Creole bands that played for funerals and parades became a major basis for early jazz, which spread from New Orleans to Chicago and other northern urban centers.

Though jazz had long since achieved some limited popularity, it was Louis Armstrong who became one of the first popular stars and a major force in the development of jazz, along with his friend pianist Earl Hines. Armstrong, Hines, and their colleagues were improvisers, capable of creating numerous variations on a single melody. Armstrong also popularized scat singing, an improvisational vocal technique in which nonsensical syllables (vocables) are sung. Armstrong and Hines were influential in the rise of a kind of pop big band jazz called swing. Swing is characterized by a strong rhythm section, usually consisting of double bass and drums, medium to fast tempo, and rhythmic devices like the swung note, which is common to most jazz. Swing is primarily a fusion of 1930s jazz fused with elements of the blues and Tin Pan Alley. Swing used bigger bands than other kinds of jazz, leading to bandleaders tightly arranging the material which discouraged improvisation, previously an integral part of jazz. Swing became a major part of African American dance, and came to be accompanied by a popular dance called the swing dance.

Jazz influenced many performers of all the major styles of later popular music, though jazz itself never again became such a major part of American popular music as during the swing era. The later 20th-century American jazz scene did, however, produce some popular crossover stars, such as Miles Davis. In the middle of the 20th century, jazz evolved into a variety of subgenres, beginning with bebop. Bebop is a form of jazz characterized by fast tempos, improvisation based on harmonic structure rather than melody, and use of the flatted fifth. Bebop was developed in the early and mid-1940s, later evolving into styles like hard bop and free jazz. Innovators of the style included Charlie Parker and Dizzy Gillespie, who arose from small jazz clubs in New York City.

2.3.3 Country Music

Country music is primarily a fusion of African American blues and spirituals with Appalachian folk music, adapted for pop audiences and popularized beginning in the 1920s. The origins of country are in rural Southern folk music, which was primarily Irish and British, with African and continental European musics. Anglo-Celtic tunes, dance music, and balladry were the earliest predecessors of modern country, then known as hillbilly music. Early hillbilly also borrowed elements of the blues and drew upon more aspects of 19th-century pop songs as hillbilly music evolved into a commercial genre eventually known as country and western and then simply country. The earliest country instrumentation revolved around the European-derived fiddle and the African-derived banjo, with the guitar later added. String instruments like the ukulele and steel guitar became commonplace due to the popularity of Hawaiian musical groups in the early 20th century.

The roots of commercial country music are generally traced to 1927, when music talent scout Ralph Peer recorded Jimmie Rodgers and The Carter Family. Popular success was very limited, though a small demand spurred some commercial recording. After World War II, there was increased interest in specialty styles like country music, producing a few major pop stars. The most influential country musician of the era was Hank Williams, a bluesy country singer from Alabama. He remains renowned as one of country music's greatest songwriters and performers, viewed as a "folk poet" with a "honky-tonk swagger" and "working-class sympathies". Throughout the decade the roughness of honky-tonk gradually eroded as the Nashville sound grew more pop-oriented. Producers like Chet Atkins created the Nashville sound by stripping the hillbilly elements of the instrumentation and using smooth instrumentation and advanced production techniques. Eventually, most records from Nashville were in this style, which began to incorporate strings and vocal choirs.

By the early part of the 1960s, however, the Nashville sound had become perceived as too watered-down by many more traditionalist performers and fans, resulting in a number of local scenes like the Bakersfield sound. A few performers retained popularity, however, such as the long-standing cultural icon Johnny Cash. The Bakersfield sound began in the mid to late 1950s when performers like Wynn Stewart and Buck Owens began using elements of Western swing and rock, such as the breakbeat, in their music. In the 1960s performers like Merle Haggard popularized the sound. In the early 1970s, Haggard was also part of outlaw country, alongside singer-songwriters such as Willie Nelson and Waylon Jennings. Outlaw country was rock-oriented and lyrically focused on the criminal antics of the performers, in contrast to the clean-cut country singers of the Nashville sound. By the middle of the 1980s, the country music charts were dominated by pop singers, alongside a nascent revival of honky-tonk-style country with the rise of performers like Dwight Yoakam. The 1980s also saw the development of alternative country performers like Uncle Tupelo, who were opposed to the more pop-oriented style of mainstream country. At the beginning of the 2000s, rock-oriented country acts remained among the best-selling performers in the United States, especially Garth Brooks.

2.3.4 Soul, R&B and Pop

R&B, an abbreviation for rhythm and blues, is a style that arose in the 1930s and 1940s. Early R&B consisted of large rhythm units "smashing away behind screaming blues singers (who) had to shout to be heard above the clanging and strumming of the various electrified instruments and the churning rhythm sections". R&B was not extensively recorded and promoted because record companies felt that it was not suited for most audiences, especially middle-class whites, because of the suggestive lyrics and driving rhythms. Bandleaders like Louis Jordan innovated the sound of early R&B, using a band with a small horn section and prominent rhythm instrumentation. By the end of the 1940s, he had had several hits, and helped pave the way for contemporaries like Wynonie Harris and John Lee Hooker. Many of the most popular R&B songs were not performed in the rollicking style of Jordan and his contemporaries; instead they were performed by white musicians like Pat Boone in a more palatable mainstream style, which turned into pop hits. By the end of the 1950s, however, there was a wave of popular black blues rock and country-influenced R&B performers like Chuck Berry gaining unprecedented fame among white listeners.

Motown Records became highly successful during the early and mid-1960s for producing music of black American roots that defied racial segregation in the music industry and consumer market. Music journalist Jerry Wexler (who coined the phrase "rhythm and blues") once said of Motown: "[They] did something that you would have to say on paper is impossible. They took black music and beamed it directly to the white American teenager." Berry Gordy founded Motown in 1959 in Detroit,

Michigan. It was one of few R&B record labels that sought to transcend the R&B market (which was definitively black in the American mindset) and specialize in crossover music. The company emerged as the leading producer (or "assembly line," a reference to its motor-town origins) of black popular music by the early 1960s and marketed its products as "The Motown Sound" or "The Sound of Young America" – which combined elements of soul, funk, disco and R&B. Notable Motown acts include the Four Tops, the Temptations, the Supremes, Smokey Robinson, Stevie Wonder, and the Jackson 5. Visual representation was central to Motown's rise; they placed greater emphasis on visual media than other record labels. Many people's first exposure to Motown was by television and film. Motown artists' image of successful black Americans who held themselves with grace and aplomb broadcast a distinct form of middle-class blackness to audiences, which was particularly appealing to whites.

Soul music is a combination of rhythm and blues and gospel which began in the late 1950s in the United States. It is characterized by its use of gospel-music devices, with a greater emphasis on vocalists and the use of secular themes. The 1950s recordings of Ray Charles, Sam Cooke, and James Brown are commonly considered the beginnings of soul. Charles' *Modern Sounds* (1962) records featured a fusion of soul and country music, country soul, and crossed racial barriers in music at the time. One of Cooke's most well-known song "A Change Is Gonna Come" (1964) became accepted as a classic and an anthem of the American Civil Rights Movement during the 1960s. According to AllMusic, James Brown was critical, through "the gospel-impassioned fury of his vocals and the complex polyrhythms of his beats," in "two revolutions in black American music. He was one of the figures most responsible for turning R&B into soul and he was, most would agree, the figure most responsible for turning soul music into the funk of the late '60s and early '70s."

Pure soul was popularized by Otis Redding and the other artists of Stax Records in Memphis, Tennessee. By the late 1960s, Atlantic recording artist Aretha Franklin had emerged as the most popular female soul star in the country. Also by this time, soul had splintered into several genres, influenced by psychedelic rock and other styles. The social and political ferment of the 1960s inspired artists like Marvin Gaye and Curtis Mayfield to release albums with hard-hitting social commentary, while another variety became more dance-oriented music, evolving into funk. Despite his previous affinity with politically and socially-charged lyrical themes, Gaye helped popularize sexual and romance-themed music and funk, while his 70s recordings, including *Let's Get It On* (1973) and *I Want You* (1976) helped develop the quiet storm sound and format. One of the most influential albums ever recorded, *Sly & the Family Stone's There's a Riot Goin' On* (1971) has been considered among the first and best examples of the matured version of funk music, after prototypical instances of the sound in the group's earlier work. Artists such as Gil Scott-Heron and the Last Poets practiced an eclectic blend of poetry, jazz-funk, and soul, featuring critical, political and social commentary with afrocentric sentiment. Scott-Heron's Proto-rap work, including *The Revolution Will Not Be Televised* (1971) and *Winter in America* (1974), has had a considerable impact on later hip-hop artists, while his unique sound with Brian Jackson influenced neo-soul artists.

During the mid-1970s, highly slick and commercial bands such as Philly soul group The O'Jays and blue-eyed soul group Hall & Oates achieved mainstream success. By the end of the 1970s, most music genres, including soul, had been disco-influenced. With the introduction of influences from electro music and funk in the late 1970s and early 1980s, soul music became less raw and more slickly produced, resulting in a genre of music that was once again called R&B, usually distinguished from the earlier rhythm and blues by identifying it as contemporary R&B.

The first contemporary R&B stars arose in the 1980s, with the dance-pop star Michael Jackson, funk-influenced singer Prince, and a wave of female vocalists like Tina Turner and Whitney Houston. Michael Jackson and Prince have been described as the most influential figures in contemporary R&B and popular music because of their eclectic use of elements from a variety of genres. Prince was largely responsible for creating the Minneapolis sound: "a blend of horns, guitars, and electronic synthesizers supported by a steady, bouncing rhythm." Jackson's work focused on smooth balladry or disco-influenced dance music; as an artist, he "pulled dance music out of the disco doldrums with his 1979 adult solo debut, *Off the Wall*, merged R&B with rock on *Thriller*, and introduced stylized steps such as the robot and moonwalk over the course of his career." Jackson is often recognized as the "King of Pop" for his achievements.

By 1983, the concept of popular music crossover became inextricably associated with Michael Jackson. *Thriller* saw unprecedented success, selling over 10 million copies in the United States alone. By 1984, the album captured over 140 gold and platinum awards and was recognized by the Guinness Book of World Records as the best-selling record of all-time, a title it still holds today. MTV's broadcast of "Billie Jean" was the first for any black artist, thereby breaking the "color barrier" of pop music on the small screen. *Thriller* remains the only music video recognized by the National Film Registry.

Janet Jackson collaborated with former Prince associates Jimmy Jam and Terry Lewis on her third studio album *Control* (1986); the album's second single "Nast" has been described as the origin of the new jack swing sound, a genre innovated by Teddy Riley. Riley's work on Keith Sweat's *Make It Last Forever* (1987), Guy's *Guy* (1988), and Bobby Brown's *Don't Be Cruel* (1998) made new jack swing a staple of contemporary R&B into the mid-1990s. New jack swing was a style and trend of vocal music, often featuring rapped verses and drum machines. The crossover appeal of early contemporary R&B artists in mainstream popular music, including works by Prince, Michael and Janet Jackson, Whitney Houston, Tina Turner, Anita Baker, and The Pointer Sisters became a turning point for black artists in the industry, as their success "was perhaps the first hint that the greater cosmopolitanism of a world market might produce some changes in the complexion of popular music."

The use of melisma, a gospel tradition adapted by vocalists Whitney Houston and Mariah Carey would become a cornerstone of contemporary R&B singers beginning in the late 1980s and throughout the 1990s. Hip-hop came to influence contemporary R&B later in the 1980s, first through new jack-swing and then in a related series of subgenres called hip-hop soul and neo-soul. Hip-hop soul and neo-soul developed later, in the 1990s. Typified by the work of Mary J. Blige and R. Kelly, the former is a mixture of contemporary R&B with hip-hop beats, while the images and themes of gangsta rap may be present. The latter is a more experimental, edgier, and generally less mainstream combination of 1960s and 1970s-style soul vocals with some hip-hop influence, and has earned some mainstream recognition through the work of D'Angelo, Erykah Badu, Alicia Keys, and Lauryn Hill. D'Angelo's critically acclaimed album *Voodoo* (2000) has been recognized by music writers as a masterpiece and the cornerstone of the neo-soul genre.

2.3.5 Rock, Metal, and Punk

Rock and roll developed out of country, blues, and R&B. Rock's exact origins and early influences have been hotly debated, and are the subjects of much scholarship. Though squarely in the blues tradition, rock took elements from Afro-Caribbean and Latin musical techniques. Rock was an urban style, formed in the areas where diverse populations resulted in the mixtures of African American, Latin and European genres ranging from the blues and country to polka and zydeco. Rock and roll first entered popular music through a style called rockabilly, which fused the nascent sound with elements of country music. Black-performed rock and roll had previously had limited mainstream success, but it was the white performer Elvis Presley who first appealed to mainstream audiences with a black style of music, becoming one of the best-selling musicians in history, and brought rock and roll to audiences across the world.

The 1960s saw several important changes in popular music, especially rock. Many of these changes took place through the British Invasion where bands such as The Beatles, The Who, and The Rolling Stones, became immensely popular and had a profound effect on American culture and music. These changes included the move from professionally composed songs to the singer-songwriter, and the understanding of popular music as an art, rather than a form of commerce or pure entertainment. These changes led to the rise of musical movements connected to political goals, such as the American Civil Rights Movement and the opposition to the Vietnam War. Rock was at the forefront of this change.

In the early 1960s, rock spawned several subgenres, beginning with surf. Surf was an instrumental guitar genre characterized by a distorted sound, associated with the Southern California surfing youth culture. Inspired by the lyrical focus of surf, The Beach Boys began recording in 1961 with an elaborate, pop-friendly, and harmonic sound. As their fame grew, The Beach Boys' songwriter Brian Wilson experimented with new studio techniques and became associated with the counterculture. The counterculture was a movement that embraced political activism, and was closely connected to the hippie subculture. The hippies were associated with folk rock, country rock, and psychedelic rock. Folk and country rock were associated with the rise of politicized folk music, led by Pete Seeger and others, especially in the Greenwich Village music scene in New York. Folk rock entered the mainstream in the middle of the 1960s, when the singer-songwriter Bob Dylan began his career. *AllMusic* editor Stephen Thomas Erlewine attributes The Beatles' shift toward introspective songwriting in the mid-1960s to Bob Dylan's influence at the time. He was followed by a number of country-rock bands and soft, folky singer-songwriters. Psychedelic rock was a hard-driving kind of guitar-based rock, closely associated with the city of San Francisco. Though Jefferson Airplane was the only local band to have a major national hit, the Grateful Dead, a country and bluegrass-flavored jam band, became an iconic part of the psychedelic counterculture, associated with hippies, LSD and other symbols of that era. Some say that the Grateful Dead was truly the most American patriotic rock band to have ever existed; forming and molding a culture that defines Americans today.

Following the turbulent political, social and musical changes of the 1960s and early 1970s, rock music diversified. What was formerly a discrete genre known as rock and roll evolved into a catchall category called simply rock music, which came to include diverse styles developed in the US like punk rock. During the 1970s most of these styles were evolving in the underground music scene, while mainstream audiences began the decade with a wave of singer-songwriters who drew on the deeply emotional and personal lyrics of 1960s folk rock. The same period saw the rise of bombastic arena rock bands, bluesy Southern rock groups and mellow soft rock stars. Beginning in the later 1970s, the rock singer and songwriter Bruce Springsteen became a major star, with anthemic songs and dense, inscrutable lyrics that celebrated the poor and working class.

Punk was a form of rebellious rock that began in the 1970s, and was loud, aggressive, and often very simple. Punk began as a reaction against the popular music of the period, especially disco and arena rock. American bands in the field included, most famously, The Ramones and Talking Heads, the latter playing a more avant-garde style that was closely associated with punk before evolving into mainstream new wave. Other major acts include Blondie, Patti Smith, and Television. In the 1980s some punk fans and bands became disillusioned with the growing popularity of the style, resulting in an even more aggressive style called hardcore punk. Hardcore was a form of sparse punk, consisting of short, fast, intense songs that spoke to disaffected youth, with such influential bands as Bad Religion, Bad Brains, Black Flag, Dead Kennedys, and Minor Threat. Hardcore began in metropolises like Washington, D.C., though most major American cities had their own local scenes in the 1980s.

Hardcore, punk, and garage rock were the roots of alternative rock, a diverse grouping of rock subgenres that were explicitly opposed to mainstream music, and that arose from the punk and post-punk styles. In the United States, many cities developed local alternative rock scenes, including Minneapolis and Seattle. Seattle's local scene produced grunge music, a dark and brooding style inspired by hardcore, psychedelia, and alternative rock. With the addition of a more melodic element to the sound of bands like Nirvana, Pearl Jam, Soundgarden, and Alice in Chains, grunge became wildly popular across the United States in 1991. Three years later, bands like Green Day, The Offspring, Rancid, Bad Religion, and NOFX hit the mainstream (with their respective then-new albums *Dookie*, *Smash*, *Let's Go*, *Stranger than Fiction* and *Punk in Drublic*) and brought the California punk scene exposure worldwide.

Metallica was one of the most influential bands in heavy metal, as they bridged the gap between commercial and critical success for the genre. The band became the best-selling rock act of the 1990s.

Heavy metal is characterized by aggressive, driving rhythms, amplified and distorted guitars, grandiose lyrics, and virtuosic instrumentation. Heavy metal's origins lie in the hard rock bands who took blues and rock and created a heavy sound built on guitar and drums. The first major American bands came in the early 1970s, like Blue Öyster Cult, KISS, and Aerosmith. Heavy metal remained, however, a largely underground phenomenon. During the 1980s the first major pop-metal style arose and dominated the charts for several years was kicked off by the metal act Quiet Riot and dominated by bands such as Mötley Crüe and Ratt; this was glam metal, a hard rock and pop fusion with a raucous spirit and a glam-influenced visual aesthetic. Some of these bands, like Bon Jovi, became international stars. The band Guns N' Roses rose to fame near the end of the decade with an image that was a reaction against the glam metal aesthetic.

By the mid-1980s heavy metal had branched in so many different directions that fans, record companies, and fanzines created numerous subgenres. The United States was especially known for one of these subgenres, thrash metal, which was innovated by bands like Metallica, Megadeth, Slayer, and Anthrax, with Metallica being the most commercially successful. The United States was known as one of the birthplaces of death metal during the mid to late 1980s. The Florida scene was the most well-known, featuring bands like Death, Cannibal Corpse, Morbid Angel, Deicide, and many others. There are now countless death metal and deathgrind bands across the country.

2.3.6 Hip-hop

Hip-hop is a cultural movement, of which music is a part. Hip-hop music for the most part is itself composed of two parts: rapping, the delivery of swift, highly rhythmic and lyrical vocals; and DJing and/or producing, the production of instrumentation through sampling, instrumentation, turntablism, or beatboxing, the production of musical sounds through vocalized tones. Hip-hop arose in the early

Unit 14　American Popular Culture

1970s in the Bronx, New York City. Jamaican immigrant DJ Kool Herc is widely regarded as the progenitor of hip-hop; he brought with him from Jamaica the practice of toasting over the rhythms of popular songs. Emcees originally arose to introduce the soul, funk, and R&B songs that the DJs played, and to keep the crowd excited and dancing; over time, the DJs began isolating the percussion break of songs (when the rhythm climaxes), producing a repeated beat that the emcees rapped over.

Unlike Motown which predicated its mainstream success on the class appeal of its acts that rendered racial identity irrelevant, hip-hop of the 1980s, particularly hip-hop that crossed over to rock-and-roll, was predicated on its (implicit but emphatic) primary identification with black identity. By the beginning of the 1980s, there were popular hip-hop songs, and the celebrities of the scene, like LL Cool J, gained mainstream renown. Other performers experimented with politicized lyrics and social awareness, or fused hip-hop with jazz, heavy metal, techno, funk and soul. New styles appeared in the latter part of the 1980s, like alternative hip-hop and the closely related jazz rap fusion, pioneered by rappers like De La Soul.

Gangsta rap is a kind of hip-hop, most importantly characterized by a lyrical focus on macho sexuality, physicality, and a dangerous criminal image. Though the origins of gangsta rap can be traced back to the mid-1980s style of Philadelphia's Schoolly D and the West Coast's Ice-T, the style broadened and came to apply to many different regions in the country, to rappers from New York, such as Notorious B.I.G. and influential hip-hop group Wu-Tang Clan, and rappers on the West Coast, such as Too Short and N.W.A. A distinctive West Coast rap scene spawned the early 1990s G-funk sound, which paired gangsta rap lyrics with a thick and hazy sound, often from 1970s funk samples; the best-known proponents were the rappers 2Pac, Dr. Dre, Ice Cube, and Snoop Dogg. Gangsta rap continued to exert a major presence in American popular music through the end of the 1990s and early into the 21st century.

The dominance of gangsta rap in mainstream hip-hop was supplanted in the late-2000s, largely due to the mainstream success of hip-hop artists such as Kanye West. The outcome of a highly publicized sales competition between the simultaneous release of his and gangsta rapper 50 Cent's third studio albums, *Graduation* and *Curtis* respectively, has since been accredited to the decline. The competition resulted in record-breaking sales performances by both albums and West outsold 50 Cent, selling nearly a million copies of *Graduation* in the first week alone. Industry observers remark that West's victory over 50 Cent proved that rap music did not have to conform to gangsta-rap conventions in order to be commercially successful. West effectively paved the way for a new wave of hip-hop artists, including Drake, Kendrick Lamar and J. Cole, who did not follow the hardcore-gangster mold and became platinum-selling artists.

The American music industry is dominated by large companies that produce, market, and distribute certain kinds of music. Generally, these companies do not produce, or produce in only very limited quantities, recordings in styles that do not appeal to very large audiences. Smaller companies often fill in the void, offering a wide variety of recordings in styles ranging from polka to salsa. Many small music industries are built around a core fanbase that may be based largely in one region, such as Tejano or Hawaiian music, or they may be widely dispersed, such as the audience for Jewish klezmer.

Among the Hispanic American musicians who were pioneers in the early stages of rock and roll were Ritchie Valens, who scored several hits, most notably "La Bamba" and Herman Santiago wrote the lyrics to the iconic rock and roll song "Why Do Fools Fall in Love." "Feliz Navidad"(1970) by José Feliciano is another famous Latin song. Demi Lovato rose to prominence in 2008 when she starred in the Disney Channel television film *Camp Rock* and signed a recording contract with Hollywood Records.

The single largest niche industry is based on Latin music. Latin music has long influenced American popular music, and was an especially crucial part of the development of jazz. Modern pop Latin styles include a wide array of genres imported from across Latin America, including Colombian cumbia, Puerto Rican reggaeton, and Mexican corrido. Latin popular music in the United States began with a wave of dance bands in the 1930s and 1950s. The most popular styles included the conga, rumba, and mambo. In the 1950s Perez Prado made the cha-cha-cha famous, and the rise of Afro-Cuban jazz opened many ears to the harmonic, melodic, and rhythmic possibilities of Latin music. The most famous American form of Latin music, however, is salsa. Salsa incorporates many styles and variations; the term can be used to describe most forms of popular Cuban-derived genres. Most specifically, however, salsa refers to a particular style that was developed by mid-1970s groups of New York City-area Cuban and Puerto Rican immigrants, and stylistic descendants like 1980s salsa romantica.

Latin American music has long influenced American popular music, jazz, rhythm and blues, and even country music. This includes music from Spanish, Portuguese, and (sometimes) French-speaking countries and territories of Latin America. Today, the American record industry defines Latin music as any type of release with lyrics mostly in Spanish. Mainstream artists and producers tend to feature more on songs from Latin artists and it's also become more likely that English language songs crossover to Spanish radio and vice versa.

The United States played a significant role in the development of electronic dance music, specifically house and techno, which originated in Chicago and Detroit, respectively. Today Latin American music has become a term for music performed by Latinos regardless of whether it has a Latin element or not.

Essay Questions:

1. What is the historical context of the rise of modern American pop culture?
2. The classical Hollywood cinema is deemed as the dominant style of American film. Discuss the impact of Golden Age of Hollywood on American film industry.
3. What are the defining features of African American folk music?
4. What are the different phases of historical development of classical music in the United States?
5. Discuss the defining features of the popular music styles in the United States and their implications for the American pop culture.

Unit 15　American Sports Culture

Sports constitutes an integral part of American leisure. American football is the most popular spectator sport to watch in the United States, followed by baseball, basketball, ice hockey and soccer, which make up the "5 major sports." Indoor soccer, indoor American football, rugby, tennis, golf, auto racing, softball, field lacrosse, box lacrosse, handball, volleyball, cricket, Australian rules football, field hockey, and water polo are also played in the country. Based on Olympic Games, World Championships, and other major competitions in respective sports, the United States is one of the most successful nations in baseball, basketball, athletics, swimming, lacrosse, beach volleyball, figure skating, tennis, golf, boxing, diving, shooting, rowing and snowboarding, and is all time one of the top 5 most successful nations in ice hockey, wrestling, gymnastics, volleyball, speed skating, alpine skiing, bobsleigh, equestrian, sailing, cycling, weightlifting and archery, among others. This makes the United States one of the most successful Olympic sports nations in the world.

1　Popular Team Sports

The most popular team sports in the United States are American football, baseball, basketball, ice hockey, and soccer. All five of these team sports are popular with fans, are widely watched on television and played by millions of Americans, have a fully professional league, enjoy varsity status at many Division I colleges, and are played in high schools throughout the country.

Unit 15　American Sports Culture

1.1　American Football

Football has the most participants of any sport at both high school and college levels, the vast majority of its participants being male. The NFL (National Football League) is the preeminent professional football league in the United States, and the world. The NFL has 32 franchises divided into two conferences. After a 16-game regular season, each conference sends seven teams to the NFL Playoffs, which eventually culminate in the league's championship game, the Super Bowl. Nationwide, the NFL obtains the highest television ratings among major sports. Watching NFL games on television on Sunday afternoons has become a common routine for many Americans during the football season. Super Bowl Sunday is the biggest annual sporting event held in the United States. The Super Bowl itself is always among the highest-rated programs of all-time in the Nielsen ratings. The NFL has the highest average attendance (67,591) of any professional sports league in the world and has the highest revenue out of any single professional sports league.

Millions watch college football throughout the fall months, and some communities, particularly in rural areas, place great emphasis on their local high school football teams. The popularity of college and high school football in areas such as the Southern United States (Southeastern Conference) and the Great Plains (Big 12 Conference and Big Ten Conference) stems largely from the fact that these areas historically generally did not possess markets large enough for a professional team. Nonetheless, college football has a rich history in the United States, predating the NFL by decades, and fans and alumni are generally very passionate about their teams.

During football season in the fall, fans have the opportunity to watch high school games on Fridays and Saturdays, college football on Saturdays, and NFL games on Sundays, the usual playing day of the professional teams. However, some colleges play games on Tuesday and Wednesday nights, while the NFL offers weekly games on Monday (since 1970) and Thursday (since 2006). In 2013, one could find a nationally televised professional or college game on television any night between Labor Day and Thanksgiving weekend.

Indoor football or arena football, a form of football played in indoor arenas, has several professional and semi-professional leagues. The Arena Football League was active from 1987 to 2008 and folded in 2009, but several teams from the AFL and its former minor league, af2, relaunched the league in 2010. The AFL folded again in 2019. Most extant indoor leagues date to the mid-2000s and are regional in nature.

Dedicated women's football is seldom seen. A few amateur and semi-professional leagues exist, of varying degrees of stability and competition. Football is unique among scholastic sports in the US in that no women's division exists for the sport; women who wish to play football in high school or college must compete directly with men.

1.2 Baseball

Baseball and a variant, softball, are popular participatory sports in the US. Baseball was the first professional sport in the USA. The highest level of baseball in the US and the world is the Major League Baseball. The World Series of Major League Baseball is the culmination of the sport's postseason each October. It is played between the winner of each of the two leagues, the American League and the National League, and the winner is determined through a best-of-seven playoff.

The New York Yankees are noted for having won more titles than any other US major professional sports franchise. The Yankees' chief rivals, the Boston Red Sox, also enjoy a huge following in Boston and throughout New England. The Philadelphia Phillies of the National League are the oldest continuous, one-name, one-city franchise in all of professional American sports, and enjoy a fanbase renowned for their rabid support of their team throughout Philadelphia and the Delaware Valley, and have famously been dubbed as the "Meanest Fans in America." Midwest baseball has also grown exponentially with teams like the Chicago Cubs, St. Louis Cardinals, and Cincinnati Reds. Particularly with Chicago sports fans who avidly follow the Chicago Cubs and the Chicago White Sox despite the comparative lack of success for the teams, with Chicago Cub fans being known throughout the country as one of the best baseball fans in the country, most notably for their passionate loyalty to the team despite their not having won a championship from 1908 to 2016 (108 years) which stands as the longest championship drought in US sports history. The sport has also taken hold of fans on the West Coast, most notably the rivalry between the San Francisco Giants and The Los Angeles Dodgers. Historically, the leagues were much more competitive, and cities such as Boston, Philadelphia and St. Louis had rival teams in both leagues up until the 1950s.

Notable American baseball players in history include Babe Ruth (714 career home runs), Ty Cobb, Honus Wagner, Ted Williams, Lou Gehrig, Joe DiMaggio, Mickey Mantle, Stan Musial, Willie Mays, Yogi Berra, Hank Aaron, Mike Schmidt, Nolan Ryan, Roger Clemens, Derek Jeter and Jackie Robinson, who was instrumental in dissolving the color line and allowing African-Americans into the major leagues.

An extensive minor league baseball system covers most mid-sized cities in the United States. Minor league baseball teams are organized in a six-tier hierarchy, in which the highest teams are in major cities that do not have a major league team but often have a major team in another sport, and each level occupies progressively smaller cities. The lowest levels of professional baseball serve primarily as development systems for the sport's most inexperienced prospects, with the absolute bottom, the rookie leagues, occupying the major league squads' spring training complexes.

Some limited independent professional baseball exists, the most prominent being the Atlantic League, which occupies mostly suburban locales that are not eligible for high level minor league teams of their own because they are too close to other major or minor league teams.

Outside the minor leagues are collegiate summer baseball leagues, which occupy towns even smaller than those at the lower end of minor league baseball and typically cannot support professional sports. Summer baseball is an amateur exercise and uses players that choose not to play for payment in order to remain eligible to play college baseball for their respective universities in the spring. At the absolute lowest end of the organized baseball system is senior amateur baseball (also known as Town Team Baseball), which typically plays its games only on weekends and uses rosters composed of local residents.

1.3 Basketball

Of those Americans citing their favorite sport, basketball is ranked second (counting amateur levels) behind football. However, in regards to revenue the NBA is ranked third in popularity. More Americans play basketball than any other team sport, according to the National Sporting Goods Association, with over 26 million Americans playing basketball. Basketball was invented in 1891 by Canadian physical education teacher James Naismith in Springfield, Massachusetts.

The National Basketball Association (NBA) is the world's premier professional basketball league and one of the major professional sports leagues of North America. It contains 30 teams (29 teams in the US and 1 in Canada) that play an 82-game season from October to June. After the regular season, eight teams from each conference compete in the playoffs for the Larry O'Brien Championship Trophy.

Since the 1992 Summer Olympics, NBA players have represented the United States in international competition and won numerous important tournaments. The Dream Team was the unofficial nickname of the United States men's basketball team that won the gold medal at the 1992 Olympics.

Basketball at both the college and high school levels is popular throughout the country. Every March, a 68-team, six-round, single-elimination tournament (commonly called March Madness) determines the national champions of the NCAA Division I men's college basketball.

Most US states also crown state champions among their high schools. Many high school basketball teams have intense local followings, especially in the Midwest and Upper South. Indiana has 10 of the 12 largest high school gyms in the United States, and is famous for its basketball passion, known as Hoosier Hysteria.

Notable NBA players in history include Wilt Chamberlain (4 times MVP), Bill

Russell (5 times MVP), Bob Pettit (11 times all NBA team), Bob Cousy (12 times all NBA team), Jerry West (12 times all NBA team), Julius Erving (won MVP awards in both the ABA and NBA), Kareem Abdul-Jabbar (6 times MVP), Magic Johnson (3 times MVP), Larry Bird (3 times MVP), Michael Jordan (6 times finals MVP), John Stockton (#1 in career assists and steals), Karl Malone (14 times all NBA team), Kobe Bryant (NBA's third all-time leading scorer), Tim Duncan (15 times NBA all-star), Shaquille O'Neal (3 times finals MVP) and Jason Kidd (#2 in career assists and steals).

Notable players in the NBA today include James Harden, LeBron James (4 MVP awards), Stephen Curry (2 times MVP), Dwyane Wade (10 times all-star), and Kevin Durant (MVP, 4 NBA scoring titles). Ever since the 1990s, an increasing number of players born outside the United States have signed with NBA teams, sparking league interest in different parts of the world.

Professional basketball is most followed in cities where there are no other sports teams in the four major professional leagues, such as in the case of the Oklahoma City Thunder, the Sacramento Kings, the San Antonio Spurs, the Memphis Grizzlies, or the Portland Trail Blazers. New York City has also had a long historical connection with college and professional basketball, and many basketball legends initially developed their reputations playing in the many playgrounds throughout the city. Madison Square Garden, the home arena of the New York Knicks, is often referred to as the "Mecca of basketball."

Minor league basketball, both official and unofficial, has an extensive presence, given the sport's relative lack of expense to operate a professional team. The NBA has an official minor league, known since 2017 as the NBA G League under a naming rights agreement with Gatorade. The most prominent independent league is BIG3, a three-on-three league featuring former NBA stars that launched in 2017. Several other pro basketball leagues exist but are notorious for their instability and low budget operations.

The WNBA is the premier women's basketball league in the United States as well as the most stable and sustained women's professional sports league in the nation. Several of the 12 teams are owned by NBA teams. The women's national team has won eight Olympic gold medals and 10 FIBA World Cups. Historically, women's basketball in the United States followed a six-woman-per-team format in which three players on each team stayed on the same side of the court throughout the game. The six-person variant was abolished for college play in 1971, and over the course of the 1970s and 1980s was steadily abolished at the high school level, with the last states still sanctioning it switching girls over to the men's five-on-five code in the mid-1990s.

1.4 Ice Hockey

Ice hockey, usually referred to in the US simply as "hockey," is another popular sport in the United States. In the US the game is most popular in regions of the country with a cold winter climate, namely the northeast and the upper Midwest. However, since the 1990s, hockey has become increasingly popular in the Sun Belt due in large part to the expansion of the National Hockey League to the southern US, coupled with the mass relocation of many residents from northern cities with strong hockey support to these Sun Belt locations.

The NHL is the major professional hockey league in North America, with 24 US-based teams and 7 Canadian-based teams competing for the Stanley Cup. While NHL stars are still not as readily familiar to the general American public as are stars of the NFL, MLB, and the NBA, average attendance for NHL games in the US has surpassed average NBA attendance in recent seasons, buoyed in part by the NHL Winter Classic being played in large outdoor stadiums.

Minor league professional hockey leagues in the US include the American Hockey League and the ECHL. Additionally, nine US-based teams compete in the three member leagues of the Canadian Hockey League, a "junior" league for players aged sixteen to twenty. College hockey has a regional following in the northeastern and upper midwestern United States. It is increasingly being used to develop players for the NHL and other professional leagues (the US has junior leagues, the United States Hockey League and North American Hockey League, but they are more restricted to protect junior players' college eligibility). The Frozen Four is college hockey's national championship. The US now has more youth hockey players than all other countries, excluding Canada, combined. USA Hockey is the official governing body for amateur hockey in the United States. The United States Hockey Hall of Fame is located in Eveleth, Minnesota.

Internationally, the United States is counted among the Big Six, the group of nations that have historically dominated international ice hockey competition. (The others include Canada, Finland, Sweden, the Czech Republic, and Russia.) One of the nation's greatest ever sporting moments was the "Miracle on Ice", which came during the 1980 Winter Olympics when the US hockey team beat the Soviet Union 4–3 in the first game of the medal round before going on to beat Finland to claim the gold medal.

Historically, the vast majority of NHL players had come from Canada, with a small number of Americans. As late as 1969–70, Canadian players made up 95 percent of the league. During the 1970s and 1980s, European players entered the league, and many players from the former Soviet bloc flocked to the NHL beginning in the 1990s. Today, slightly less than half of NHL players are Canadian, more than 30% are Americans, and virtually all of the remainder are European-trained.

Notable NHL players in history include Wayne Gretzky (leading all-time point scorer and 9 times MVP), Mario Lemieux (3 times MVP), Guy Lafleur (2 times MVP), Gordie Howe (6 times MVP), Nicklas Lidström (7 times NHL's top defenseman), Bobby Hull (3 times MVP and 7 times leading goal scorer), Eddie Shore (4 times MVP), Howie Morenz (3 times MVP), Maurice "Rocket" Richard (5 times leading goal scorer), Jean Beliveau (2 times MVP), Bobby Clarke (3 times MVP), and Bobby Orr (8 times NHL's best defenseman). Famous NHL players today include Sidney Crosby and Alexander Ovechkin.

The National Women's Hockey League, founded in 2015, is the first women's ice hockey league in the country to pay its players and features five teams in the northeast and upper midwest, plus one Canadian team. Three of the five US-based teams (the Buffalo Beauts, Minnesota Whitecaps and Metropolitan Riveters) are either owned or operated by, or affiliated with, their metro area's NHL franchise (the Buffalo Sabres, Minnesota Wild and New Jersey Devils, respectively). At the international level, the United States women's national ice hockey team is one of the two predominant international women's teams in the world, alongside its longtime rival Team Canada.

1.5 Soccer

Soccer has been increasing in popularity in the United States in recent years. Soccer is played by over 13 million people in the US, making it the third-most played sport in the US, more widely played than ice hockey and football. Most NCAA Division I colleges field both a men's and women's varsity soccer team, and those that field only one team almost invariably field a women's team.

The United States men's national team and women's national team, as well as a number of national youth teams, represent the United States in international soccer competitions and are governed by the United States Soccer Federation (US Soccer). The US women's team holds the record for most Women's World Cup championships, and is the only team that has never finished worse than third place in a World Cup. The US women beat the Netherlands 2–0 in the 2019 FIFA Women's World Cup final to claim their second consecutive Women's World Cup title, and fourth overall.

Carlos Bocanegra with the United States men's national soccer team in 2010 Major League Soccer is the premier soccer league in the United States. As of its 2021 season, MLS has 27 clubs (24 from the US and 3 from Canada). The league plans to expand to 30 in 2023. The 34-game schedule runs from mid-March to late October, with the playoffs and championship in November. Soccer-specific stadiums continue to be built for MLS teams around the country, both because football stadiums are considered to have excessive capacity, and because teams profit from operating their stadiums. With an average attendance of over 21,000 per game, MLS has the third-highest average attendance of any sports league in the US after the National Football League (NFL) and Major League Baseball (MLB), and is the ninth-highest attended professional soccer league worldwide. Other professional men's soccer leagues in the US include the current second division, the USL Championship (USLC) and the third-level USL League One (USL1), which launched in 2019 under the auspices of the USLC's operator, the United Soccer League. Another competition, the second North American Soccer League, had been the second-level league until being demoted in 2018 due to instability, and soon effectively folded. The USL organization now has a formal relationship with MLS, and a number of its teams (both in the Championship and League One) are either owned by or affiliated with MLS sides.

Younger generations of Americans have strong fan appreciation for the sport, due to factors such as the US hosting of the 1994 FIFA World Cup and the formation of Major League Soccer, as well as increased US television coverage of soccer competitions. Many immigrants living in the United States continue to follow soccer as their favorite team sport. United States will host the 2026 FIFA World Cup, sharing with Canada and Mexico.

Women's professional soccer in the United States has not seen sustained success. Following the demise of two professional leagues in the early 21st century, the Women's United Soccer Association (1999 – 2001) and Women's Professional Soccer (2009 – 2011), US Soccer established a new National Women's Soccer League (NWSL) in 2013. The NWSL has now survived longer than both of its two professional predecessors combined. Of its current 10 teams, six share ownership with professional men's clubs – three are wholly owned by Major League Soccer (MLS) team owners, two are wholly owned by USL sides (one each in the USLC and USL1), and another is primarily owned by a French Ligue 1 side. However, at the lower levels of the salary scale, the NWSL is effectively semi-professional.

Many notable international soccer players played in the US in the original North American Soccer League, usually at the end of their playing careers – including

Pelé, Eusébio, George Best, Franz Beckenbauer, and Johan Cruyff – or in MLS – including Roberto Donadoni, Lothar Matthäus, David Beckham, Thierry Henry, Kaká, David Villa, Wayne Rooney, and Zlatan Ibrahimović. The best American soccer players enter the US Soccer Hall of Fame.

2 Other Popular Sports

2.1 Golf

Golf is played in the United States by about 24 million people. The sport's national governing body, the United States Golf Association (USGA), is jointly responsible with the R&A for setting and administering the rules of golf. The USGA conducts four national championships open to professionals: the US Open, US Women's Open, US Senior Open, and the US Senior Women's Open, with the last of these holding its first edition in 2018. The PGA of America organizes the PGA Championship, Senior PGA Championship and Women's PGA Championship. Three legs of the Grand Slam of Golf are based in the United States: the PGA Championship, US Open and The Masters.

The PGA Tour is the main professional golf tour in the United States, and the LPGA Tour is the main women's professional tour. Also of note is PGA Tour Champions, where players 50 and older compete. Golf is aired on several television networks, such as Golf Channel, NBC, ESPN, CBS and Fox.

Notable American male golfers include Walter Hagen (11 majors), Ben Hogan, Jack Nicklaus (record 18 major wins), Arnold Palmer, and Tiger Woods (15 major wins). Notable female golfers include Patty Berg (record 15 major wins), Mickey Wright (13 majors), Louise Suggs and Babe Zaharias. (Jack Nicklaus is widely regarded as the greatest golfer of all time, winning a total of 18 career major championships.)

2.2 Tennis

Tennis is played in the United States in all five categories (Men's and Ladies'

Singles; Men's, Ladies' and Mixed Doubles); however, the most popular are the singles. The pinnacle of the sport in the country is the US Open played in late August at the USTA Billie Jean King National Tennis Center in New York. The Indian Wells Masters, Miami Open and Cincinnati Masters are part of the ATP Tour Masters.

The United States has had considerable success in tennis for many years, with players such as Don Budge, Billie Jean King (12 major singles titles), Chris Evert (18 major singles titles), Jimmy Connors (8 major singles titles), John McEnroe (7 major singles titles), Andre Agassi (8 major singles titles) and Pete Sampras (14 major singles titles), and Ricardo Alonso González (14 major singles titles) dominating their sport in the past. More recently, the Williams sisters, Venus Williams (7 major singles titles) and Serena Williams (23 major singles titles), have been a dominant force in the women's game, and the twin brothers Bob and Mike Bryan have claimed almost all significant career records for men's doubles teams.

2.3 Track and Field

USA Track & Field is the governing body for track and field in the United States. It organizes the annual USA Outdoor Track and Field Championships and USA Indoor Track and Field Championships. The Diamond League currently features one round in the United States, the Prefontaine Classic; the series formerly included the Adidas Grand Prix as well. Three of the World Marathon Majors are held in the United States: the Boston Marathon, Chicago Marathon and New York City Marathon. The Freihofer's Run for Women is also an IAAF Road Race Label Event. Amateur organizations such as the National Collegiate Athletic Association and Amateur Athletic Union sanction cross-country running in fall, indoor track and field in winter, and outdoor track and field in spring.

Florence Griffith Joyner is considered the fastest woman of all time; the world records she set in 1988 for both the 100 m and 200 m still stand. Jesse Owens was a notable US track athlete who achieved international fame at the 1936 Summer Olympics in Berlin, Germany, by winning four gold medals: 100 meters, long jump,

200 meters, and 4 × 100-meter relay. He was the most successful athlete at the Games and, as a black man, was credited with "single-handedly crushing Hitler's myth of Aryan supremacy," although he "wasn't invited to the White House to shake hands with the President, either."

Americans have frequently set world standards in various disciplines of track and field for both male and female athletes. Tyson Gay and Michael Johnson hold various sprint records for male athletes, while Florence Griffith Joyner set various world sprint records for female athletes. Mary Slaney set many world records for middle-distance disciplines.

A turning point occurred in the US track in the running boom of the 1970s. After a series of American successes in various distances from marathoners Frank Shorter and Bill Rodgers as well as middle-distance runners Dave Wottle and Steve Prefontaine, running as an American pastime began to take shape. The US won in the 1976 Olympic men's decathlon, achieved by then-Bruce Jenner, which made Jenner a national celebrity. (Many decades later, he transitioned to a woman and changed his first name to Caitlyn.) High school track in the United States became a unique foundation for creating the United States middle-distance running talent pool, and from 1972 to 1981 an average of 13 high school boys in the United States would run under 4'10" in the mile per year. During this time, several national high school records in the United States were set and remained largely unbroken until the 2000s. The number of high school boys running the mile under 4'10" per year dropped abruptly from 1982, and female participation in many distance events was forbidden by athletic authorities until the 1980s. However, a renaissance in high school track developed when Jack Daniels, a former Olympian, published a training manual called "Daniels' Running Formula," which became the most widely used distance training protocol among American coaches along with Arthur Lydiard's high-mileage regimen. Carl Lewis is credited with "normalizing" the practice of having a lengthy track career as opposed to retiring once reaching the age when it is less realistic of gaining a personal best result. The United States is home to school-sponsored track and field, a tradition in which most schools from middle school through college feature a track and field team. Owing to the number of American athletes who satisfy Olympic norm standards, the US holds national trials to select the best of its top-tier athletes for Olympic competitions.

2.4 Boxing

Boxing is an iconic sport in the US and is the focus of the most successful sporting movies both critically and commercially with Oscar-winning films like *Rocky*, *Raging Bull* and *The Fighter*. As with many sports, it has allowed black athletes to break through to become major figures of US culture, with Joe Louis, Mike Tyson and Muhammad Ali famous on the world stage.

Boxing in the United States became the center of professional boxing in the early 20th century. The National Boxing Association was founded in 1921 and began to sanction title fights. Joe Louis was an American professional boxer who competed from 1934 to 1951. He reigned as the world heavyweight champion from 1937 to 1949, and is considered to be one of the greatest heavyweight boxers of all time. In 2005, Louis was ranked as the best heavyweight of all time by the International Boxing Research Organization, and was ranked number one on *The Ring* magazine's list of the "100 greatest punchers of all time." Louis had the longest single reign as champion of any heavyweight boxer in history. Louis is widely regarded as the first person of African-American descent to achieve the status of a nationwide hero within the United States, and was also a focal point of anti-Nazi sentiment leading up to and during World War II. He was instrumental in integrating the game of golf, breaking the sport's color barrier in America by appearing under a sponsor's exemption in a PGA event in 1952.

In the 1960s and 1970s, Muhammad Ali became an iconic figure, transformed the role and image of the African American athlete in America through his embrace of racial pride, and transcended the sport by refusing to serve in the Vietnam War. In the 1980s Mike Tyson emerged as a serious contender. Nicknamed "Iron Mike," Tyson won the heavyweight unification series to become the world heavyweight champion at the age of 20 and the first undisputed champion in a decade. Tyson soon became the most widely known boxer since Ali due to an aura of unrestrained ferocity, such as that exuded by Jack Dempsey or Sonny Liston. His career culminated in Evander Holyfield vs. Mike Tyson II where he famously bit off a piece of Holyfield's ear.

Since the late 1990s boxing has declined in popularity for a myriad of factors such as more sports entertainment options and combat alternatives such as MMA's UFC amongst a younger demographic; lack of mainstream coverage in newspapers and access to major television networks.; also the lack of a US heavyweight world champion.

It was hoped in 2015 that the Floyd Mayweather Jr. vs. Manny Pacquiao fight would re-invigorate interest in the sport in the United States but because the fight was disappointing it was perceived as doing further harm to the image of the sport in the United States.

2.5 Swimming and Water Sports

Swimming is a major competitive sport at the high school and college levels, but receives little mainstream media attention outside of the Olympics. Surfing in the United States and watersports are popular in the US in coastal areas. California and Hawaii are the most popular locations for surfing. The Association of Surfing Professionals was founded in 1983.

Five separate national governing bodies (NGBs) make up USAS: USA Swimming, USA Diving, United States Synchronized Swimming, USA Water Polo, and US Masters Swimming. Of the five, only US Masters Swimming (USMS) is not a member of the United States Olympic Committee (USMS's main aim is adult swimming, exclusive of Olympic swimming which is the domain of USA Swimming).

3 Professional and Amateur Sports

3.1 Professional Sports

For the most part, unlike sports in Europe and other parts of the world, there is no system of promotion and relegation in American professional sports. Major sports leagues operate as associations of franchises. The same 30–32 teams play in the league each year unless they move to another city or the league chooses to expand with new franchises.

All American sports leagues use the same type of schedule. After the regular season, the 10–16 teams with the best records enter a playoff tournament leading to a championship series or game. American sports, except for soccer, have no equivalent to the cup competitions that run concurrently with leagues in European sports. Even in the case of soccer, the cup competition, the Lamar Hunt US Open Cup, draws considerably less attention than the regular season. Also, the only top-level US professional teams that play teams from other organizations in meaningful games are those in MLS. Since the 2012 season, all US-based MLS teams have automatically qualified for the US Open Cup, in which they compete against teams from lower-level US leagues. In addition, three or four US-based MLS teams (depending on the results of the US Open Cup) qualify to play clubs from countries outside the US and Canada in the CONCACAF Champions League. NBA teams have played European teams in preseason exhibitions on a semi-regular basis, and recent MLS All-Star Games have pitted top players from the league against major European soccer teams, such as members of the Premier League.

International competition is not as important in American sports as it is in the sporting culture of most other countries, although Olympic ice hockey and basketball tournaments do generate attention. The first international baseball tournament with top-level players, the World Baseball Classic, also generated some positive reviews after its inaugural tournament in 2006.

The major professional sports leagues operate drafts once a year, in which each league's teams selected eligible prospects. Eligibility differs from league to league.

Baseball and ice hockey operate minor league systems for players who have finished their education but are not ready or good enough for the major leagues. The NBA also has a development league for players who are not ready to play at the top level.

3.2 Amateur Sports

The Amateur Athletic Union claims to have over 670,000 participants and over 100,000 volunteers. The AAU has existed since 1888, and has been influential in amateur sports for that same time span.

In the 1970s, the AAU received growing criticism. Many claimed that its regulatory framework was outdated. Women were banned from participating in certain competitions and some runners were locked out. There were also problems with sporting goods that did not meet the standards of the AAU. During this time, the *Amateur Sports Act of 1978* organized the United States Olympic Committee and saw the re-establishment of state-supported independent associations for Olympic sports, referred to as national governing bodies. As a result, the AAU lost its influence and importance in international sports, and focused on the support and promotion of predominantly youthful athletes, as well as on the organization of national sports events.

4 Government Regulation

No American government agency is charged with overseeing sports. However, the president's Council on Physical Fitness and Sports advises the president through the Secretary of Health and Human Services about physical activity, fitness, and sports, and recommends programs to promote regular physical activity for the health of all Americans. The US Congress has chartered the United States Olympic Committee to govern American participation in the Olympic Movement and promote Olympic sports. Congress has also involved itself in several aspects of sports, notably gender equity in college athletics, illegal drugs in pro sports, sports broadcasting and the application of antitrust law to sports leagues.

Unit 15 American Sports Culture

Individual states may also have athletic commissions, which primarily govern individual sports such as boxing, kickboxing and mixed martial arts. Notable state athletic commissions are the Nevada Athletic Commission, California State Athletic Commission, New York State Athletic Commission and New Jersey State Athletic Control Board. Although these commissions only have jurisdiction over their own states, the Full Faith and Credit Clause of the US Constitution is often interpreted as forcing all other states to recognize any state athletic commission's rulings regarding an athlete's fitness for participating in a sport.

5 Sports Media

Sports have been a major part of American broadcasting since the early days of radio. Today, television networks and radio networks pay millions (sometimes billions) of dollars for the rights to broadcast sporting events. Contracts between leagues and broadcasters stipulate how often games must be interrupted for commercials. Because of all of the advertisements, broadcasting contracts are very lucrative and account for the biggest chunk of major professional teams' revenues. Broadcasters also covet the television contracts for the major sports leagues (especially in the case of the NFL) in order to amplify their ability to promote their programming to the audience, especially young and middle-aged adult males.

The advent of cable and satellite television has greatly expanded sports offerings on American TV. ESPN, the first all-sports cable network in the US, went on the air in 1979. It has been followed by several sister networks and competitors. Some sports television networks are national, such as CBS Sports Network, Fox Sports 1 and NBC Sports Network, whereas others are regional, such as NBC Sports Regional Networks, Fox Sports Networks and Spectrum Sports. General entertainment channels like TBS, TNT, and USA Network also air sports events. Some sports leagues have their own sports networks, such as NFL Network, MLB Network, NBA TV, NHL Network, Big Ten Network, Pac-12 Network and SEC Network. Some sports teams run their own television networks as well.

Essay Questions:

1. Name a few major sports leagues in the United States. How are these sports leagues formed and what functions do they have?

2. Discuss the mechanism of mass media in promoting American sports industry.

3. Explore the linkage between sports and business in the US as well as the commercial and social impact of American sports.

4. Joe Louis and Muhammad Ali, as popular boxing stars, have often been looked upon by many Americans as cultural icons. Discuss the influences these sports stars may have on the American sports and popular culture.

5. Discuss the role sports plays in American family and society in general and the way it shapes American national characters.